203 ROLLING MILL ROAD
OLD HICKORY, TN 37138
October 17, 2008

Memo to interested readers.

My Novel, "But for the Grace of God", is a published work. Should you be interested in obtaining a copy for your personal library, please call me at (615) 847-4976 and I will sell you a copy for $21.00. That price is a $3.95 discount off the list price of $24.95. I live in the Brandywine Sudivision and will be pleased to deliver your book to any local Nashville address.

BUT FOR THE GRACE OF GOD

JAPANESE INVASIONS CARRIED OUT BY THE U.S.S. ZEILIN IN WORLD WAR II

THE KAMIKAZE ATTACK

By Melvin E. Hacker

Cover Design and Page Layout by Bart Dawson

ISBN 0-7414-4816-5

Published by:

INFINITY
PUBLISHING.COM

1094 New DeHaven Street, Suite 100
West Conshohocken, PA 19428-2713
Info@buybooksontheweb.com
www.buybooksontheweb.com
Toll-free (877) BUY BOOK
Local Phone (610) 941-9999
Fax (610) 941-9959

Printed in the United States of America

Printed on Recycled Paper

Published September 2008

PROFILE VIEW OF U.S.S. ZEILIN

U.S.S. Zeilin shown at anchor in San Francisco Bay in 1945.

MAP OF PACIFIC OCEAN LOCATIONS WHERE THE U.S.S. ZEILIN ENGAGED JAPANESE MILITARY FORCES— MAP IS NOT TO SCALE.

TABLE OF CONTENTS

Thomas A. Hoffman,
Chief Bos'n Mate. U.S.S. Zeilin
who is presently the president of
the U.S.S. Zeilin Association.

Martin Luther Mathis,
Signalman United States Navy,
who died on 21 July 2007.
Photo circa 1943.

DEDICATION

It is to the memory of my deceased Gunner's Mate friend,
Calvin Honeycut, that I dedicate this story.
His young 19-year-old life, like so many others in WWII,
was cut short on that fateful day 62 years ago
with his human potential never to be realized,
but such are the fortunes of war.

ACKNOWLEDGMENTS

In the process of distilling the essence of my story on these pages, I chose to solicit assistance from several former shipmates who served on the U.S.S. Zeilin; namely, Messers. Luther Mathis (of Cookeville, TN recently deceased), Thomas A. Hoffman (of Yucaipa, CA), and Mr. Richard N. Schell (of Hershey, PA), and Mr. Richard L. Nihlean of (Bartlett, IL). Luther very kindly agreed to review my draft manuscript and it is to him that I owe a profound debt of gratitude for keeping me honest with respect to the dates of certain events as well as reporting on the accuracy of other aspects of U.S. Navy wartime life. On the other hand, I owe Tom Hoffman a similar debt of gratitude for providing me the information that I needed with respect to Captain Fitzpatrick's KAMIKAZE 'After Action Report'. Dick N. Schell provided the U.S.S. Zeilin photographs, attributed to him, while other Zeilin photos were obtained from official U.S. Navy Historical archives and are so marked. Official U.S. National Archives also provided several photos of the Aleutian Islands Campaign. Dick Nihlean provided the record of Transport Division 23 convoy composition for the Kamikaze incident described in Chapters #3 and #4 and illustrated on page 528. In addition, I would be remiss if I did not mention the very meaningful editorial assistance that I received from my wife and sweetheart Charo Carrero-Hacker, as well as my daughter Susan Marie Salzman. Suzy was particulatly helpful in enhancing the Japanese flavor seen in Chapter three.

I am also indebted to Mr. Bart Dawson for his untiring efforts in the design of the covers for my book and his masterful treatment of the photographs and drawings present in my text. Bart demonstrated a complete mastery of the art of making things happen with computers. Absent the able assistance of all of the individuals mentioned above, the quality of my story would have suffered greatly. I am pleased to express my appreciation to them all.

AUTHOR'S NOTES

After contemplating the writing of this story for over 60 years, I elected, in November of 2004, to begin writing a description of the WWII event that occurred on 13 December 1945, when a Japanese Kamikaze Fighter/Bomber crashed into the U.S.S. Zeilin (APA-3) off the coast of Luzon in the Philippine Islands, killing seven crewmen, and injuring many more. At that time, I was serving on the U.S.S. Zeilin as a RADARman 2nd Class and was only a witness to the aftermath of the crash itself for the reason that our RADAR Shack, my General Quarters Duty Station, was a windowless room of solid steel walls, for darkness was necessary to facilitate the interpretation of images displayed on our RADAR System Cathode Ray Tubes.

The Japanese sneak attack on Pearl Harbor was a real event, happening as it did on 7 December 1941. The descriptions of my life leading up to the war, my entry into the U.S. Navy, as well as some of the voyages themselves are essentially autobiographical in nature. However, the chapters that describe the life and death of my close friend, Gunner's Mate Calvin Honeycut, and that of the young Japanese Kamikaze pilot, Yaeko Yamagucci, are entirely fictional, as are their names. I have taken the liberty of using my parents' and siblings' real names as well as my own. The other names appearing in the text are fictional and are not intended to represent real persons, living or dead. Nevertheless, I availed myself of historical reference material, identified in the bibliography, attempting, to the greatest extent possible, to provide historically correct dates and places in the Pacific Ocean where the various military actions took place. In those instances, particularly where the Aleutian Islands operations are concerned, I have listed the names of individuals that are identified in the relevant historical records such as the American Admirals and Army and Marine officers, as well as the Japanese officer who conceived the concept of the Kamikaze Corps. In planning this novel, I felt that the fictional elements were quite necessary to flesh out my personal recollections with fictional accounts of certain events that could not be verified by interviewing individuals long since deceased. Above all, the reader should understand that my story is not intended to be an in-depth, documentary level dissertation covering the U.S.S. Zeilin's South and North Pacific journeys and all of its ports-of-call during WWII. Regarding the Zeilin's ports-of-call, the reader is encouraged to examine Appendix, #4A through 4G, to see the work of Mr. Luther Mathis who personally visited the Navy Department in Washington D.C., following WWII and personally inspected the Zeilin's daily log and created the data listed in Appendix #4A through #4G.

In Appendix #1 of this volume, the reader will find a verbatim copy of the After Action Report that was written by Captain Thomas B. Fitzpatrick following the Kamikaze attack on his ship, on Saturday, 13 January 1945. The aspect of this report that I personally found to be most interesting, when I read it for the first time in June of 2005, was the listing of the dead and wounded. Although this event occurred about 62 years ago, I have a clear recollection of attending only one burial-at-sea ceremony, and that session involved only three crewmen. I cannot explain how it was that I could have missed the other burial details that handled the other four deceased crewmen. Nor did I realize that there were men blown over the side of the U.S.S. Zeilin, but never recovered. It is possible that, at the time, such information was treated on a confidential 'need-to-know' basis and a general dissemination of every detail of the results of the attack was not made to the crew at large. Should you have any questions or comments on my story, I can be reached via e-mail at: flyermel@aol.com.

"BUT FOR THE GRACE OF GOD"
Written by Melvin Eugene Hacker;
November 2004 to November 2007

BIBLIOGRAPHY

1. ** "Attack Transport"
The U.S.S. Zeilin in World WarII - an oral history
by Robert E. Witter. Copyright 2001 by Robert E. Witter

2. ** "The American People's Encyclopedia"
Volumes -- 1,2,9,10,11,12,13,14,15, 16, 17, 18, 19, 20.
Copyright in the United States of America by Spenser Press, Inc., 1948 thru 1957.

3. ** "Japan - A Modern History"
Author: James L. McClain
Copyright 2002, W. W. Norton & Co. Inc.

4. ** "WORLD WAR II: A COMPLETE PHOTOGRAPHIC HISTORY"
Edited by Hal Buell
Copyright 2002, Black Dog & Leventhal Publishers, Inc.

5. ** " The Navy"
Published by the Naval Historical Foundation
Copyright 2,000, Naval Historical Foundation.

6. ** "The Illustrated Directory of Fighters (Aircraft)" by Mike Spic: Copyright by Salamander Books 2002.

7. ** "Kamikaze" - Japan's Suicide Samurai" by Raymond Lamont-Brown - Copyright 1997

8. ** "Bloody Tarawa" The Second Marine Division, November 20-23, 1943, text copyright 1998 by Eric Hammel & John E. Lane - Published by Zenith Press.

9. ** "Tarawa" The story of a battle. Copyright 1944, 1954 by Robert Sherrod.

10. ** "Shattered Sword" The untold story of the Battle of Midway. Copyright by Jonathan Parshall and Anthony Tully 2005.

11. ** Blue Jacket Manual, Eleventh Edition, United States Naval Institute, Annapolis, Maryland, 1943

PROLOGUE

GROWING UP IN ONTARIO, CALIFORNIA

1300, Saturday
15 June 1935
814 East "E" Street
Ontario, California

In early June of 1935, my parents acted on the long-contemplated decision to move 'back to the farm' and hopefully overcome the lingering hardships of the 'Great Depression' then plaguing the entire United States. Both parents had been born into farm families; Mom in Tellico Plains, Tennessee, and Daddy in a cotton sharecropper family in Buffalo Gap, Texas. Having purchased one and one-half acres (three half-acre lots @ $300 each) in a newly developed agricultural subdivision southwest of Ontario, California, my parents sold their small one-bedroom cottage at 814 East 'E' Street and commenced their relocation. Lacking sufficient funds to hire a professional moving company to transport the family's possessions, Daddy, ever the resourceful man that he was, proceeded to construct a two-wheel utility trailer with which to haul all of the family's household furnishings to the new address. The flatbed, stake-body trailer that he designed was built around the serviceable front axle removed from a wrecked 1928 Nash automobile that Daddy modified by the addition of several heavy-duty, rear axle leaf springs scavenged from yet another derelict vehicle resting in the same auto wrecking yard. The trailer tongue was fabricated from the two halves of a 1926 Ford Model 'T' automobile frame. The tongue elements were straight and, when bolted together, comprised an extremely sturdy box tongue for the trailer. When finally completed over a period of four weeks, the stake body trailer was capable of hauling 2,000 pounds of cargo when loaded, and the suspension spring leaves were deflected to an approximately horizontal position. This load capacity was verified by means of a test load of sand and gravel which was weighed on the calibrated Fairbanks Morse Commercial Scales of the Holiday Rock and Gravel Company in Upland, California. Absent any welding equipment, Daddy erected his trailer by using 'U' bolt clamps and long threaded rods with which to secure the axle and leaf spring undercarriage to the wooden frame of the trailer.

On this day, the last of a great many loads of furniture, kitchen utensils, bedding, and other household possessions had been tied down by means of a sturdy rope, and the family climbed into Daddy's green, 1931, six-cylinder, Chevrolet four-door sedan for the final four-mile trip to 459 West Elm Street where our future home would be built. Pending completion of the 'home place', the five of us (father; Percy Eugene Hacker; mother, Della Leonard Hacker; sister, Marilee Ruth Hacker; brother, Harold Ray Hacker and myself; Melvin Eugene Hacker (then 10 years old) would live temporarily in the 20-foot by 30-foot garage that my father, with the help of several uncles, had built on the vacant but level easternmost lot of his property.

It would be a period of rustic living for several years since there was no water heater and no indoor plumbing. An outdoor privy, erected at the south end of the property adjacent to the cow barn, would serve the family for many years to come. A cast iron, wood-burning stove was acquired for the cooking of meals. Hot water for baths and clothes washing was heated in large galvanized laundry tubs over an open wood fire outdoors. Within a year or two, natural gas came to the subdivision and Daddy improved the garage by building on a ten-foot by twenty-foot room addition on the south end of the main structure. When the addition was complete, Daddy installed a gas water heater as well as enameled stationary tubs to facilitate clothes washing and bathing needs. Being a General Electric employee, as he was, permitted him to purchase a new GE Wringer Washing Machine for Mom at a reduced employee purchase price from Sam Wickersham, the authorized GE Dealer in Ontario. These improvements eliminated the need to heat water over an open wood fire in the back yard. Nevertheless, baths were still taken in a large galvanized tub placed conveniently in the new garage addition. At the same time, a movable curtain, installed in the room addition, provided a modicum of privacy for bathers. It would be several more years before the family could enjoy the luxury of bathing in a modern, ceramic-tiled bathtub in the bathroom of the 'home place'.

It was during the implementation of these improvements that Daddy purchased a new 'Roper' brand gas range and oven for my mother. This upgrade allowed my parents to discard the cast iron wood-burning stove that had served for cooking purposes for several years. Not long before our move, Daddy had purchased a 9-cubic foot GE, Monitor Top Electric Refrigerator from Sam Wickersham, and became the object of considerable ridicule by my Uncle Faye Fenwick (the husband of mom's sister Lois) who, for whatever reason, could not appreciate the need one might have for what he perceived to be a gigantic refrigerator at 9 cubic feet in size. Daddy did not shrink from the verbal abuse and merely explained that "When he wanted cold watermelon, he wanted cold watermelon", and a smaller refrigerator was just too restrictive. The GE Refrigerator replaced an elderly icebox of 50-pound ice capacity. A brass nameplate on the oak icebox door identified it as a 'Snow Flake' brand. With the purchase of the GE Refrigerator, the iceman no longer called at the Hacker Residence, and the daily chore of emptying the water collected from the melting ice also went away. The controversy surrounding the new refrigerator seems almost laughable today in the face of residential refrigerators commonly sized in the range of 26 to 30-cubic feet or larger.

0700 Saturday
11 June 1938
459 West Elm Street
Ontario, California

The years passed slowly by as the two-wheel trailer was pressed into service again and again to transport building materials with which to construct our new home. My parents were loath to borrow construction money from a bank, and elected instead to build their home from payday to payday on a cash-and-carry basis. Today would see yet another 60-mile round trip made to Los Angeles because the construction lumber was less expensive there. Daddy would make the trip to the Owens Park Lumber Company every Saturday and return with 2,000 pounds of needed two-by-fours, two-by- sixes, plywood, and other forms of lumber to frame the house. He also purchased all of the cement employed in his home construction at the same lumber yard. Prior to commencing the framing, Daddy rented two mules and a Fresno Blade from a neighbor, Mr. Stoner, and spent three weekends excavating an area that eventually would be beneath what would become the south end of the house in preparation for a cellar in which to place Mom's canned fruits and vegetables. In the process of excavating the eight-foot-deep hole in the ground, a huge pile of dirt was created. Upon its sloping sides, my brother and I laid one-inch pine boards to create a runway on which we could coast down in our red 'Radio Flyer' wagon. Our 'Hacker

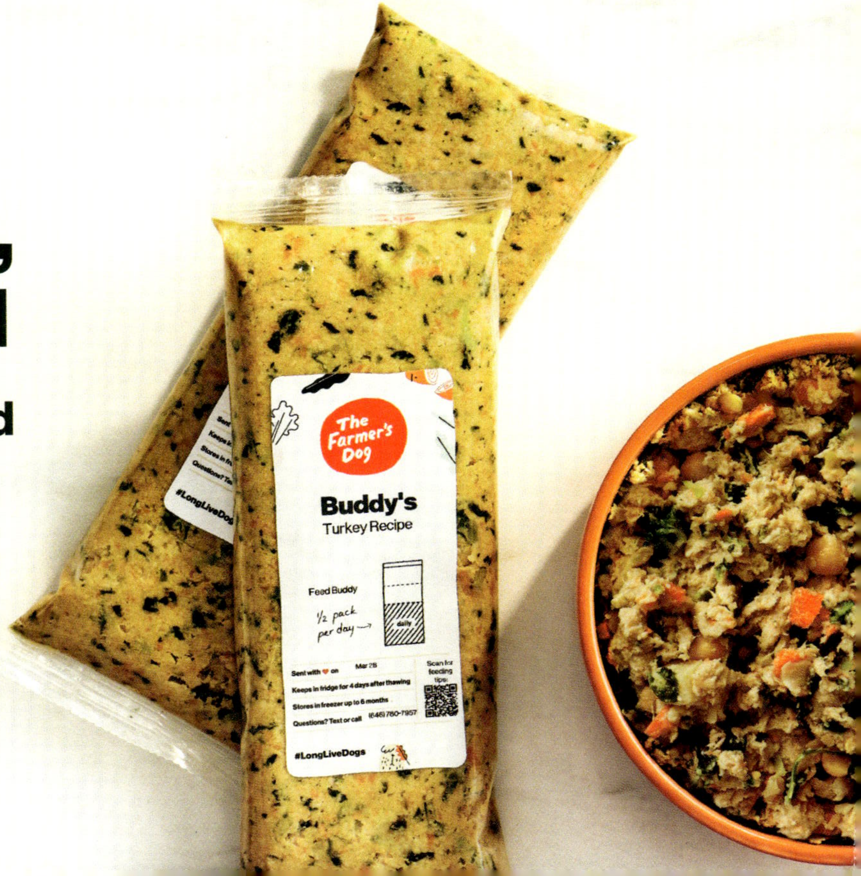

Hill' lasted for several months until the cellar concrete walls were poured, and then it disappeared as the earth was used to back-fill the space between the concrete wall and the surface of our backyard where grass was planted. In the meantime, my brother and our neighborhood boyfriends and I enjoyed many an hour of fun coasting down our crude ramp. Since the cellar room ran the entire width of the house, it was large enough to provide not only the needed food storage area, but also space for a spare double bed with which to provide additional sleeping capacity for use when expected or unexpected guests arrived. In those prewar days, the extended family of Grandpa Hacker comprised eleven children with husbands and wives and grandchildren; so aunts, uncles and cousins were plentiful and were constantly making their way to Ontario to visit my father and his family. With the excavation complete, the trailer was taken to an unimproved storm drain on the county line separating Los Angeles and San Bernardino Counties, where the site contained the correct mixture of free sand and gravel with which to mix with cement to create concrete. The site was actually a storm drain that carried runoff water from San Antonio Canyon and 10,000-foot Mt. Baldy a few miles to the north. Using an electrically-driven concrete mixer, borrowed from Daddy's neighbor, Mr. Steinow, the walls of the cellar and the footings for the 'home place' were poured over a period of two months. After the framing was well along, cement, sand and gravel supplies were brought in to construct a concrete driveway exceeding 150 feet in length and about 20 feet wide, extending from the two principal garage doors, passing along the east side of the house to an apron at the termination of the lot boundary at its Elm Street property line. The task of laying the driveway was broken up into a series of individual slabs, essentially sized such that a 15-foot section could be poured and finished in a single day. The driveway was completed on weekends over a period of three months and, as one might imagine, represented an extremely labor-intensive effort on the part of my Daddy, myself and my brother, Harold. By the time that project was finished, we were all experts in the art of mixing, installing and finishing concrete of any description.

By this time in 1938, Daddy had hired Uncle Kenneth Smith (Mom's youngest brother) to install the cedar shingle roof on the house and it was finished. With the roof complete, the house was partially framed with all windows and exterior doors in place and the exterior novelty redwood siding was being installed. The house would soon be closed to the weather. Temporary one-inch pine floorboards were laid on the bare floor joists and we could walk from one unfinished room to the next as the work continued on the interior framing. However, the family was still sleeping in the garage and taking their meals there as well. Interior work continued apace as button board for plastering was installed on all of the interior walls following installation of all of the electrical wiring conduits, sanitary plumbing as well as water supply pipes. Work in progress also included installation of all of the kitchen, bedroom and bathroom cabinets. Mr. Wilbur Rowlands, a lifelong friend of my father, and a journeyman carpenter, was hired to build all of the kitchen and bathroom cabinets as well as the bedroom wardrobe closets. Another contractor was called in to install the kitchen and bathroom ceramic tile as well as to apply the finish plaster coat to all of the interior walls. In August of 1938, my youngest brother, Marvin, was born. A year later, he became a casualty of the new home as he was learning to walk. Upon losing his balance one day, Marvin accidentally slipped between two of the loose, shifting, temporary floorboards and fell to the concrete floor of the basement cellar below. Rushing him to the San Antonio Community Hospital, Marvin was found to have escaped with a slight fracture of his collarbone among other minor cuts and bruises. Needless to say, installation of the permanent floor of the home was given the highest priority following that incident.

Recalling that incident reminds me of yet another event involving baby Marvin. In those prewar days, Daddy maintained three hives of honey bees. He was well equipped to safely handle them, what with his protective hat with its screenwire mesh shield, smoker and beeswax frames on which the bees would deposit their clover honey harvests. The hives were placed on the back lot not far from the cow barn, pigpens and chicken coops. Before Marvin was able to walk very well, he was placed in his 'walker' for a few hours each day. The removable metal floor pan of the walker would be laid aside so that Marvin could propel himself about the yard by pushing his feet against the earth, grass, concrete or whatever was beneath the walker at any given moment. Anyhow, on this particular day, Mom and Daddy were attending to chores around the cow barn and Marvin had propelled his walker to that area, moving always in reverse, for he could not get enough leverage from his tiny legs to travel in a forward direction. For whatever reason, Marvin ended up pushing his walker to the vicinity of one of the three bee hives and indeed jammed the walker directly in front of one of the busy hives which, of course, greatly disturbed the bees flying in and out as they were, with their loads of honey. Since Marvin could only move his walker in reverse, he was trapped, and the bees began to attack him, and he let out a mighty 'war whoop'. Daddy ran immediately to the walker and quickly took Marvin to a place of safety and then treated his bee stings. Fortunately there was no lasting detrimental effect from the bee stings.

During the early years on the farm, Daddy frequently took the family to Corona, California, (17 miles southeast of Ontario) to visit Uncle Tom and Aunt Irma Hacker, one of Daddy's many brothers, as well as his father, William Alexander Hacker. Uncle Tom and Aunt Irma had two children; son Clifford and daughter, Catherine Lou. Around 1936, with Uncle Tom's approval, Daddy began building a small cottage on my uncle's property in which Grandpa Hacker would live. Grandpa was born on March 7, 1873 in New Madrid, Missouri. When Daddy made a trip to Corona to work on Grandpa's house, we children and my mother always accompanied him. To make way for the house, several mature eucalyptus trees were cut down. As we children were playing in the yard one Sunday afternoon, my brother Harold noticed a squirrel sitting on a felled tree laying horizontally on the ground not far from the house then under construction. Just as the squirrel began to leave the space where he had been sitting, my brother quickly reached over and grabbed the fuzzy tail that was disappearing beyond the other side of the tree trunk. Without decreasing his stride, the squirrel continued on around the tree trunk, reached up and 'nipped' Harold's right wrist. Harold let out a yelp and immediately let the tail go. Fortunately, the nip did not draw blood, but the experience taught us all to have a greater respect for animals in their natural domain. Clifford and Catherine Lou were observing the event and thought that the squirrel episode was quite hilarious. Harold, for his part, did not share their amusement. In later years, the small cottage was uprooted and moved into downtown Corona so that Grandpa could walk to the grocery store or other places since he did not drive. Grandpa Hacker was alone at this time with Grandma Hacker having succumbed to a diphtheria epidemic in 1921, at the same time as the demise of their youngest daughter, Lily Hacker. They are both buried in a cemetery in Corona, California. It has been a lifelong regret that I was not born soon enough to have met my Paternal Grandmother.

Throughout the period of the late 1930's and early 1940's, my father raised vegetables on the unimproved acre lot on the west side of his property. He raised corn, green beans, sweet potatoes, tomatoes, peanuts, bell peppers, black-eyed peas, carrots and other vegetables. He also raised strawberries, boysenberries and blackberries. Associated with the purchase of the property were owner shares in the South Side Mutual Water Company from which water to irrigate the crops was obtained from a pump house situated about a mile away on Fern Avenue, adjacent to DeAnza Park. The fluctuating demand for water among the various local farmers meant that occasionally water was only available in the wee hours of the morning. It was not unusual for Daddy, me and brother Harold to be walking around in ankle deep mud at 3:00 a.m. during the growing season. Everyone carried flashlights with which to signal over the three-hundred-odd feet length of the acre lot to identify the crop rows that should be cut off while the irrigation was in progress, and water had flowed to the end of a row. This routine, of course, took place in the days before 'walkie-talkie' radios or cell phones had been invented. What a boon to the irrigation process they would have been!

When it came time to harvest the peanut crop, the individual plants were turned over by hand by means of a shovel so that the mature peanuts faced the sun. Several days later, when the nuts had dried out sufficiently, we children were tasked to separate the nuts from the wilted vines. At times, everyone would be involved, including Daddy and Mom. On occasion, even our friends would help with the harvest. When we lived on "E" Street, Harold and I had a boyfriend named Joseph Faulkner. Joe had four sisters, Nelly, Iris, Marjory and Cecil. I recall a time when Nelly pedaled her bicycle the four miles to our Elm Street home to help us with the peanut harvest. For my part, I considered the task an extreme drudgery and was always elated when the last of the peanut crop was harvested and picking peanuts off the vines had come to an end!

When Mom and Daddy laid out their property, they

planned for and implemented the planting of several varieties of fruit and nut trees. A minimum of two each of almond, walnut, apricot, orange, lemon, avocado, cling and freestone peach trees were planted. In addition, Thompson Seedless and Concord Grape Vines were also planted. The mature trees and vines yielded more than adequate supplies of fruit, nuts and grapes to supply the family's needs. In making their selections, my parents attempted to obtain varieties of trees whose fruit or nuts matured at different times to provide an extended harvest period for the family. Of course, a large patch of 'Big Boy' tomatoes was always under cultivation in the summer time.

During the early years on the farm, my parents kept a Jersey cow, and Daddy raised over 150 rabbits for meat and sold their pelts to a glove-manufacturing company in Los Angeles. Jointly sharing expenses with Aunt Lois Fenwick (Mom's sister) and Uncle Faye, my parents also raised pigs, and the day that the meat was harvested brought quite a celebration and most enjoyable feast. When the ham, pork chops, pork roasts and bacon was fully prepared and wrapped, a trip would be made to the icehouse across the railroad tracks from the GE factory where Daddy rented a frozen food locker. (This was at a time preceding the invention of 'home freezers'). We children typically went barefoot in those days. I can clearly recall how cold the floor of the icehouse cold storage locker room felt, and the strange sensation of my bare feet adhering to the frozen floor as I followed Daddy to his locker. In that well-below zero degrees F. environment, our exhaled breath became quite visible. The icehouse was always a favorite place of mine and my brothers, especially when workers were busy filling the ice bunkers of refrigerator cars being loaded with citrus shipments for the New York market. The huge blocks of ice would be run through a scoring machine to facilitate their insertion into the railroad refrigerator car bunkers. My brother and I happily seized the resulting snow and enjoyed this cold delicacy on the hot summer days of our youth.

The mention of rabbits in the preceding paragraph reminds me of my Uncle Alton Hacker. In addition to being a Nazarene preacher, he was also an accomplished gunsmith. Periodically he would visit my parents, and late in the evening everyone would climb into Uncle Alton's Essex touring sedan and he would drive the family to Upland, California, where, several miles north of town in a remote, unimproved section of San Bernardino County land, he and Daddy would prepare to hunt wild jack rabbits among the sagebrush and manzanita bushes. Taking over the driving duties from Uncle Alton, my mother would drive slowly along meandering trails among the sagebrush and cactus after sundown, with the headlights on, while Uncle Alton and Daddy rode the front fenders and took turns shooting the rabbits with their 12-gauge shotguns as the rabbits scampered along in the headlight beams. After an hour or so, enough rabbits were available for a meal, so we returned home where Mom cooked them. I have to admit that I enjoyed the flavor of the domestic rabbits much more than I did the wild variety.

With insufficient land available on which to raise his own alfalfa hay to feed his Jersey cow, Daddy would purchase baled alfalfa hay from a farmer near the small town of Chino, California, located about seven miles southwest of our home. Using his two-wheel utility trailer, Daddy would make occasional trips to purchase the needed alfalfa hay. On one Sunday afternoon run, after having made his purchase and loaded the hay with the assistance of the seller, Daddy was driving north along Euclid Avenue adjacent to the Army Air Force Training Academy at CalAero just east of Chino. Loads of hay were invariably top-heavy and Daddy improvised a means of stabilizing the load of hay by attaching short lengths of link chain extending from the trailer bedframe on each side of the trailer and secured in two places around the single axle. Well, on this particular day, a link in one of the stabilizer chains parted and neatly pitched the entire load of hay off into the adjacent ditch at the side of the road. Although it was a disaster as far as Daddy was concerned, we children were hard pressed to smother our laughter over what seemed to us a laughable and comic event. Daddy stopped the car, jockeyed the trailer and car off to the side of the road, and then proceeded to reload the bales of hay. Of course, we children could only add moral support since we were too small to aid in lifting the heavy bales of hay onto the trailer bed. It took Daddy about an hour to reload the hay, and with the repaired chain doubly secured in place, we made the rest of the journey home unimpeded. My brother and I enjoyed the interlude as we spent the time watching the many military Stearman Training biplanes take off and land at the nearby training academy. The novice pilots flew 24 hours a day in those prewar days and the drone of the Stearman Engines rarely left the skies above Ontario and surrounding cities. The CalAero Flight Academy operated from September 14, 1940, until October 16, 1944. During those years more than 10,000 pilots graduated from the Chino facility with graduation ceremonies occurring every six weeks.

After the war was over, CalAero became a collecting site for the thousands of surplus military aircraft that survived WWII on U.S. soil. Some of the planes were sold off by the government, but those that did not find their way into private hands became fodder for an aluminum smelter that was set up on the airport property. Usable engines and other parts were salvaged, but the fuselages and wings were melted down. One day in 1946 some friends and I drove to the site to look at the row after row of now derelict aircraft. Wing tip to wing tip with Cessna Bamboo bombers were P-51's, P47's, P-38's, Bell P-39's, P-40's, Bell Air Cobras, B-

24 Liberator Bombers, B-17 Bombers, B-29 Bombers B-25 Bombers, A-26 Bombers, and any WWII military plane that you can think of was there. We climbed out of our car and crawled beneath a barbed wire fence and walked along a line of B-24 Bombers sitting ever so forlornly nose high, on their haunches, because their engines had already been removed. We climbed up into one of the nose high cockpits and were flying the plane on an imaginary bomb run over Germany when a security guard came along and spoiled our fun by chasing us away.

I would be remiss if I did not mention the fact that my father and mother profited little, if any, from their farming efforts, apart from having a plentiful supply of food for their own family's table. Times were hard in the 1930's and money was scarce, and it is my impression that my parents ended up giving away most of their excess produce to friends who could not afford to pay them for the fresh vegetables. Our Jersey cow, however, produced much more milk than our family could consume. My mother used some of the surplus to make delicious vanilla pudding, but there was still a surplus of milk. For this reason, my parents allowed each of their three elder children to sell the surplus milk to Grandma and Grandpa Bishop (Mom's mother and stepfather) and to Uncle Bill and Aunt Lucille Mathis (Lucille was Mom's youngest sister.) These relatives lived on Locust Street, the next street south of Elm Street. Thus, every third day it would be my turn to deliver the milk and collect 25 cents from each of the two families. In essence, this enterprise was our allowance for we were not given any other money by Daddy or Mom.

Following our move to the farm, my parents purchased a 20- gallon ceramic crock, bottles, metal bottle caps as well as a capper machine, and began making homemade root beer using 'Hires Extract'. Employing the recipe on the 'Hires Extract' bottle label, lots of sugar and the proper amount of yeast and fresh water, liquid root beer was prepared and bottled. Of course, when initially mixed in the crock, the solution was not palatable. It must first cure for a prescribed period of time during which the yeast accomplishes its magic and a few weeks later the root beer is ready to drink. When this enterprise began, the Hacker Family quickly became one of the most popular families along our block of Elm Street, at least insofar as our neighborhood boy and girlfriends were concerned. That crock still exists today in the possession of my sister, Ida Mae, along with the manually-operated capping machine.

Making homemade root beer was a popular endeavor in the 1930's. Soft drinks were expensive and money was scarce. My Aunt Lois and Uncle Faye Fenwick made quantities of root beer for their own purposes, and their daughter, Marietta, and her school friends enjoyed the product of her parents' labors. It turned out that Uncle Faye made a batch along the way, placed it in his basement and then forgot about it. Aunt Lois went into their basement one day and just as she was departing to return upstairs, one of the quart-size root beer bottles exploded with a resounding 'boom' accompanied by the 'tinkle' of breaking glass and a geyser of flat root beer flooding the basement concrete floor. Upon his return from his job at the General Electric plant that day, Aunt Lois issued an ultimatum, "get that root beer out of my basement!" Uncle Faye dutifully complied, gingerly carrying the crate of over-pressurized bottles to the side of his garage and there carefully removing the cap of each bottle. There were no more explosions, but as each bottle cap was removed, a geyser of stale root beer erupted and ran down the weathered garage siding. Of course, by that time the root beer was spoiled and not fit to drink anyway.

1200, Tuesday
1 July 1941
459 West Elm Street
Ontario, California

This was the day that the family had been patiently waiting for over the preceding six years. It was the day to celebrate completion of the 'home place' and enjoy the special meal that Mom prepared with all the trimmings. Enjoying the use of her new kitchen and modern gas range, Mom fixed sugar-cured ham, mashed potatoes and gravy, green beans laced with bacon, a large green salad, together with plenty of hot biscuits and apple pie and homemade vanilla ice cream for dessert. The ice cream came from Daddy's 'White Mountain Triple Motion ice cream freezer'. We children took turns turning the crank and feeding ice and salt into the freezer.

All of the raw materials for the meal came from Mom and Daddy's property and labors save for the flour, sugar and apples. None of the family left the table hungry that special day. Household furnishings were still being acquired and moved into the various rooms of the new house, and those items that were deemed usable from the garage were relocated to the new house and, at last, the garage was vacated to be used to protect Daddy's automobiles. By that time he had traded his 1931 Chevrolet for a used 1933 Plymouth 4-door sedan. Over the years, I always thought that this circumstance was quite unusual due to the fact that my father was, first last and always, a General Motors Man. I can only assume that the Plymouth became available at a very attractive price?

Indoor plumbing was now functional and no one regretted abandoning the now useless privy. The home had nice front and rear porches constructed of concrete as well as three bedrooms (four counting the spare basement bedroom), living room, dining room, kitchen and a single bathroom. Stairsteps were provided for access to an upstairs room that would be completed sometime in the future.

When we moved to West Elm Street in 1935, I had just finished the 4th grade at Lincoln Grammar School located down the alley, a block east of our 'E' Street home. I was happy to leave Lincoln School to get away from a redheaded school grounds bully who tormented me and the other kids who were smaller than he was. The closest school to our West Elm Street home was South Euclid Grammar School (five blocks away) where I attended the 5th and 6th grades. During the warm pre-vacation days in the fifth grade most boys flew balsa wood gliders during recess and lunch times. Our teacher, Miss Anderson, made it quite clear that playing with gliders during class time was absolutely forbidden under the pain of immediate destruction of the offending glider. The desk in front of me was unoccupied, so after the lunch recess, I carefully placed my glider on the desktop, but before I could warn off the student seated ahead of the vacant desk, he had turned around and picked up my glider. Miss Anderson noticed the event and quickly walked over and took the glider in her hand crushing it completely as she deposited the broken balsa wood fragments in her wastebasket. Of course, my childish spirit was crushed beyond belief. The loss of my glider so impacted my mentality that I refused to participate in class exercises the rest of the afternoon, and at the mid-afternoon recess time I merely walked home and left school behind. Later that day, Miss Anderson sent my good friend, Earl Higgins, to my home to encourage me to return to class. He owned a brand new Schwin knee-action bicycle, and we rode double as he and I returned to class. By that time, Miss Anderson had learned of the fact that the glider that she destroyed did not belong to the culprit who had broken her rule, and as a peace offering, gave tangerines to the entire class, and I found tangerines in my desk when

I took my place again in her classroom. Nothing more was said about that incident, that day or ever.

I left the South Euclid Grammar School in 1938 and rode the school bus to attend the Vina F. Danks Junior High School in the 7th and 8th grades. To my chagrin, on the very first day attending the new school, guess who met the school bus? If you guessed the redheaded bully you were correct! Only by this time he had taken up smoking and showed off at curbside (no one was allowed to smoke on the school grounds) by taking a large amount of smoke into his lungs and then blowing the smoke through a white handkerchief. That act left an ugly dark yellow stain on the white cloth and has been a lifelong reminder to me as the best reason in the world not to smoke. Three years down the road from Lincoln School, I and my friends had grown up enough so that the bully could no longer safely torment us in school. We were big enough by then to retaliate if the redheaded bully gave us any grief.

In those days, junior high school had a fine library, and during a visit one day I found a book that was devoted to the life of Thomas Alva Edison. It was a "How to do it yourself" book for boys that contained examples of electrical experiments that could be easily duplicated with very little expense involved. It is because of that book that Mr. Edison became my boyhood idol. To this day, I have regretted the fact that Mr. Edison died before I ever had an opportunity to meet him. He was a prolific inventor and made important contributions to improving the quality of life in these United States; not the least of which was his invention of the electric light bulb used throughout our country and others. Beyond that, he made important contributions to Motion Picture Photography and even the telephone, for it was his invention of the carbon granule transmitter that significantly improved the sensitivity and clarity of Bell's primitive telephones.

I checked the book out of the library and literally devoured its contents overnight. Simple electric motors and telegraph sounders and primary batteries were described in great detail. After I had read the book, I described its contents to my neighbor boyfriend, Howard Jones. We both became enamored with the possibility of running a copper wire telephone line from his bedroom to mine so that we could converse after we went to bed each evening. Applying the directions contained in the book, Howard and I installed a 400-foot long length of copper wire between our two bedrooms. It was necessary to cross over the intervening property of a neighbor who raised chickens, but he readily consented to give us 'air rights' over his chicken coops. We found two dynamic radio loudspeakers in a local junk shop (requiring a 25-cent investment) and terminated these devices on the wire and found that we could hear each other quite clearly with no amplification or batteries being necessary. We used the same technique that Alexander Graham Bell used in signaling when conversation was desired. Taking a small length of dowel, we would carefully rap on the speaker voice coil to attract each other's attention. The audible thump of the dowel striking the speaker voice coil worked just fine and the beauty of the system lay in the fact that no batteries were required. In essence, the communication system was 'sound powered'. The movement of the diaphragm generated a minute current that was quite audible on the far end and we enjoyed the privacy of our conversations for several years before WWII intervened. In retrospect, there is no doubt in my mind that, as a postwar adult, that earlier telephone influence played a key part in my choice of a vocation after I left the employ of the General Electric Company. Added to that is the fact that some of the telephone circuits on board the two Navy ships on which I served contained many 'sound powered' telephones. Of course, the Navy telephones were much more robust as one would expect from commercially manufactured telephone sets.

From junior high school, I moved on to Chaffey Union High School in September of 1940, again attending the 9th, 10th, 11th and 12th grades by riding the school bus. However, by the time I graduated to the eleventh grade I had earned enough money to purchase a used 1936 Ford automobile. At age 16, I earned my driver's license and no longer rode the bus to school. The independence that the Ford gave to me was most appreciated.

Upon entering high school, I signed up for an aeronautical engineering curriculum because of my lifelong interest in airplanes. Little did I realize then that I would never get close to designing an airplane, what with WWII about to intervene and change my life forever.

That fact notwithstanding, I devoted considerable time in my high school years to perfecting a folded-paper glider design. Although I also flew the small balsa wood gliders (the gliders cost one penny in those days), it was in the paper glider designs that I perceived a significant technical challenge. Of course, I had seen folded glider designs created by classmates but they were mostly of a sharp, more-or-less needle-nose design with inadequate wing areas to support the long thin fuselages that resulted in very inferior flying characteristics. Those glider designs were hardly worth the effort to launch them, for their flight times were so exceedingly short as to be absolutely uninteresting. In fact, those designs exhibited no soaring ability whatsoever.

In my analysis of glider requirements, I decided that the folded design necessarily required a reasonable nose weight to stabilize the flying characteristics, as well as an adequate wing area to provide reasonable support for the fuselage, wing and elevator. In the end, my design exhibited a good balance between wing area and nose weight. The nose weight was obtained by placing multiple folds on the centerline of the paper fuselage. I elected to provide a tapered wing design that also included wing tips that were folded up in a vertical plane to prevent the air flowing over the top surface of the wing from spilling off the wing laterally and adversely affecting glider stability as well as flight longevity. Of course, I folded many, many sample paper gliders in experimenting with the various configurations in search of that 'ideal' shape.

Before lunchtime one day in the summer of 1942, I folded yet another trial example of my paper glider and took it with me to the front lawn of Chaffey High School. After eating my sandwich and banana I smoothed out and aligned the wings of my glider and launched the plane straight up into the air. It reached a height of perhaps 16 feet, rolled into a horizontal attitude and began to slowly circle in the warm thermals that were traveling upward from the sun-bathed bermuda grass lawn of the school yard. The glider continued to circle and eventually landed about 20 feet from where I had launched it. I walked over and picked up the glider and was checking its wing alignment when someone tapped me on my right shoulder. Turning around, I came face-to-face with Mr. Roy Vic, my fifth period physics teacher. He asked to hold the glider and I, of course, immediately handed it over. He inquired as to my reasons for giving the glider the geometry that he observed, and I merely explained that I felt that any paper glider needed the largest wing area possible, consistent with a reasonable weight in its nose to assure that, in flight, the nose stayed in front and would not destabilize its smooth flying characteristics. Mr. Vic seemed to appreciate all that I explained and next asked if I would permit him to fly the plane. Of course, I was flattered to think that a teacher would interest himself in the work of a lowly student. I was only too willing to have my teacher, who had demonstrated an interest in my work, fly the plane. Mr. Vic was a tall, strapping man and threw the plane straight up into the air, as I had done, but the difference was that with his long, strong arm, the glider reached an initial height of about 20 feet whereupon it rolled into a horizontal attitude and began its lazy clockwise circling return to earth. It was an extremely stable flyer and stayed aloft for a considerable length of time aided, in part, by the lift provided by the summer thermals emanating from the warm, green school yard lawn. I explained to Mr. Vic that one of the secrets of the excellent flying performance of my glider was the one-half inch folded wing-tip barriers that captured the wind flowing over the wing's upper surface and prevented it from merely departing the wing laterally and losing the lift that would otherwise be provided by the surface winds being restricted to the wing. Mr. Vic retrieved the glider and asked if he could fly it again. Naturally, I told him to do so as he made the plane perform much better than I possibly could with my shorter arm. At the end of several flights, Mr. Vic commended me on the design of the glider and then went on his way back to his afternoon physics classes. It is interesting for me to observe today the refinement of present day jet aircraft wherein the designers are employing the same principles as I discovered over 64 years ago. Some of the Boeing 737 Jet Wings utilize wing tip barriers for the same purpose as in my glider design, but today, the appendages are called 'wing lets'. Performing exactly the same function as my folded paper wing tips, today's wing lets prevent air flowing over the top surface of the jet aircraft wing from spilling off laterally and thereby improves the efficiency of the wing's aileron performance.

In retrospect, it was certainly ironic that the last trailer load moved from our old house in 1935 included the skeleton of a full size, tandem cockpit, airplane fuselage and wing that my brother and I had built with the aid of a neighbor boy by the name of Hugh Sanders. Hugh's father owned a cabinet shop and he graciously supplied scrap plywood material for the wing ribs, and cut them out for us on his huge bandsaw, and he also made us a propeller from a length of 4" by 4" pine material. At the time of our move, the fuselage was complete save for it being covered with its oilcloth skin. The rudder was in place and my brother and I would sit and play for hours in the cockpit and, using our feet on the rudder pedals, move the rudder left and right as we flew on our imaginary flights into the blue sky above. Hugh told us to take the fuselage and wing to our new home since he believed it unlikely that he would ever get around to finishing the project. It also appeared that his older brother, David Sanders, had no interest in continuing the project either. As it turned out, the airplane skeleton was placed at the rear of Dad's property near the cow barn and soon had weeds and alfalfa sprouts growing up through the wing ribs and fuselage longerons. One fine day, Daddy staked Bossy out on a long rope and the Jersey cow proceeded to make kindling wood out of the wing as she walked about grazing on the green grass and alfalfa hay. The cow's sharp hooves brought an ignominious end to our grand childhood dream. At that point, Harold and I admitted defeat and abandoned the idea of trying to build our own airplane. Many years later, I was to learn, with no small amount of surprise, from cousin Clifford Hacker about how he had bragged to all of his classmates in a Corona, California grammar school about the fact that he had two cousins in Ontario who were actually building their own airplane. What price notoriety!

In 1938, there was a daily 15-minute children's radio program in the evening that was sponsored by one of the major breakfast food companies (with the passage of 69 years, I am unable to recall the name of the cereal product). The name of the program was 'Elmer Goes Hollywood.' The storyline revolved around a group of young children of 'Our Gang Comedy' ages who were running around their neighborhood having wonderful adventures making their own motion pictures. The intent of the advertisement, of course, was that children listening to the program would prevail upon their parents to purchase the breakfast cereal, and the incentive then was for the children listening in to send in their cereal box top and 25 cents and receive their director's certificate in the 'IMPS', the 'International Motion Picture Society'. I sent in my 25 cents, a colorful box top, and still have that director's certificate that I received framed and on display in my den.

That magical radio program so fired my childhood imagination with movie-making visions that nothing would do but what I obtain my own motion picture camera. One day in 1938, following classes at the Vina F. Danks Junior High School on 'J' Street, I decided to walk home instead of riding the bus and happened to pass through Ontario on Euclid Avenue (the main north-south street running through the center of town) where I noticed in a pawn shop display window a small 8-mm Univex movie camera. It was as if an irresistible magnetic attraction pulled me into that store. I walked in and spoke with a salesman and asked to see the camera. He immediately brought it out of the display window and let me hold it in my hands; what a magical thrill the feel of that tiny camera was and listening to the whir of its miniature spring-driven motor was even more thrilling. I learned that the camera was manufactured by the Universal Motion Picture Camera Company of New York City. The camera had a price tag on it of $5.00. Of course, I was an unemployed, 13-year old junior high school student and I did not have $5.00, so I asked if I could give the salesman the 25 cents that I happened to have in my pocket from one of the previous day's milk deliveries and pay the camera off a little at a time. He replied, "yes" and promptly brought out a printed cardboard contract and entered my name and address and also noted the date and amount of my 25-cent down-payment. That event became my first experience with deficit financing, and I also have that 68-year old contract framed and on display in my den. From the proceeds of my weekly milk sales, I eventually paid off the camera and then began to learn all that I could about making motion pictures. I read every book that I could find on motion picture production and quickly realized that there was much to be learned about lens settings, use of filters, editing and a myriad of related aspects of making motion pictures.

Acquiring the needed funds to purchase movie film posed a major and continuing problem, with my only income comprised of milk sales every third day of the week, but I managed somehow. I enlisted the aid of my sister and brother along with all the neighborhood boyfriends in the enterprise and we had fun making movies, just like 'Elmer' and his friends did. We even formed the Cardinal Motion Picture Company and sold shares to teachers and classmates for ten cents per share. Grandpa Bishop (peepaw) worked with me and provided advice on how to set up our book of accounts. Of course, the income from the sale of shares went toward purchasing needed movie film. The one completed epic that we made is still in my 27,000 feet motion picture film library titled 'The Cow Barn Murder Mystery'. It was made in mid-1939 on a 25-foot reel of single width 8 mm film (about two and one half minutes of screen time). Sadly, many of those friends appearing in the film have long since passed away including David Swain, Floyd Swain, Donald Swain, Bert Swain and Joseph Faulkner. Howard Jones is still living today in Victorville, California, married to Ellen, his high school sweetheart. My brother Harold played the part of the villain and is still living today in Hesperia, California. My sister, Marilee, did not take a part in the film and is living today in Ontario, California. Of course, Ida Mae and Marvin came along later so they missed the beginnings of my motion picture endeavors. Nevertheless, they show up frequently in the many Hacker Family Home Movies that I made over a period of 69 years. Needless to say, the Cardinal Motion Picture Company never made a profit that could be shared with its stockholders. In those childhood days, there was simply no way that we could show our films and charge viewers to see them.

During my Navy career in 1943, I noticed a Swiss-made Bolex movie camera in a camera shop in San Francisco and decided that, after the war, I would purchase one. It was a beautiful, finely finished machine and, best of all, it could hold 100 feet of double 8-mm film which, when processed by Eastman Kodak Company, came back from Kodak as 200 projection feet of film (about 15 minutes of screen time.) The camera was equipped with many sophisticated features such as 'back wind' that permitted film to be double exposed to lay titles over images, such as at Christmas time. After shooting our illuminated tree, I backed up the film to lay on a title of 'Christmas at the Hackers', for whatever year was appropriate. Also, the camera had an electric motor drive option which would permit exposing an entire 100-foot reel of film at one time if such became necessary. The camera was equipped with a three-lens turret which simplified shooting scenes either close-up with telephoto lenses or with a wide angle lens if needed. In 1946, I located such a camera in Boston, Massachusetts, and bought it by mail order, sight unseen. The camera turned out to be in mint condition and I enjoyed using it until my children all grew up and moved away from home and I no longer had any subjects to photograph. In later years, I passed the camera on to my youngest daughter for her use in photographing her own children. With her children now grown, the camera has returned to my collection of about 75 movie cameras of many different types and sizes that include both 16-mm and 8-mm versions.

Throughout his lifetime, my father's philosophy seemed to be one of frugal independence. My mother told me that this view of his was the result of our Scottish Heritage. It also could be attributed, I suspect, to the fact that he was never a wealthy man. He was hard working, as well as industrious to a fault. He advised me on any number of occasions that he felt capable of performing most any task if he could first be allowed to observe another person perform the same work. He proved this on more than one occasion. For example, during my lifetime I never knew him to take one of his ailing motor cars to a professional garage mechanic for the correction of some minor malfunction. He was quite capable of getting out his own mechanic's tools and, isolating the problem, then purchase any needed replacement parts and install them on his engine.

The 1928 Chevrolet automobile that he purchased for $10 from a GE coworker and then gave to me is a case in point. The automobile was totally reliable and I never hesitated to drive it anywhere in Southern California. One weekend in 1941, together with my high school boyfriend Riley Harris, I drove the Chevy to Los Angeles where we would take Lucille (my high school sweetheart) and her sister Lisa on a double date. We made the 35-mile drive to Long Beach from Los Angeles where we enjoyed the carnival rides in its beachfront 'Fun Zone', and everything was fine until it came time to return to Los Angeles. As I turned a street corner near the Long Beach roller coaster ride, there was an audible 'pop' accompanied by a roaring four-cylinder engine that had ceased applying power to the rear wheels. I was to learn later that 1926 through 1928 Chevrolets had the bad habit of occasionally breaking their rear axles for no apparent reason. Lucille's father drove to Long Beach and towed us back to his home on West 34th Street in Los Angeles where Riley and I spent the night. The next morning, with curiosity getting the better of me, I decided to start the Chevy's engine and test out the driveline. With the engine idling and the transmission in reverse, I slowly released the clutch and, lo and behold, the car moved in reverse. Shifting to low gear, I performed the same test and the car moved forward. A broken axle should not have mended itself, but I was not about to argue with success. Riley and I hurriedly hit the road to Ontario and made the trip home with no further problem. In fact, the car seemed to recover and run trouble free thereafter. A year or so later, however, it was necessary to perform an engine overhaul which included grinding the valves, taking up the crankshaft main bearings along with the four connecting rod bearings, and installing new piston rings and a new crankcase oil pan gasket. At this point, I expect that I should plead 'like father, like son', for all the knowledge that I needed to attempt the engine overhaul was obtained while following my Daddy around and looking over his shoulder as he worked on his engines over the years. This was especially true of the knowledge needed to work on the various bearings. Learning the use of the bearing scrapers, feeler gauges and bluing dye to find high spots in the bearings that needed to be reduced came both from watching my Daddy, as well as him allowing me to practice on his engines as well. Once such an overhaul job is completed, the engine is so tight that the starter cannot turn the crankshaft over when it is time to start the engine. The usual treatment for this problem is to tow the car on the highway with another vehicle while placing the transmission in high gear and slowly letting out the clutch; normally, the engine will turn over and start without any trouble. However, in my case, when I gingerly let the clutch out, the broken rear axle reared its ugly head again and slipped such that the engine could not be started. So, we towed my car back home, jacked up the right rear wheel and Daddy proceeded to demonstrate how to replace a broken axle. The Chevy design was a good one from the point of view of safety. This characteristic came from the fact that even in the face of a broken axle, the wheel bearing was captured beneath a cover plate that prevented the wheel from departing the automobile and possibly causing a serious accident. After removing the bearing cover and setting the rear wheel aside, I could look into the differential housing and see the uneven end of the broken axle. Daddy fashioned a noose from a piece of hay bailing wire and slipped it into the opening over the axle remnant and easily pulled the broken end out of the differential gear box. We then made a trip to one of the local auto wrecking yards where I purchased a used axle, complete with bearing and cover plate in place, took it home, installed it, and then towed the car on the highway again and the engine started with no difficulty. Although my Daddy and I had a fair amount of time tied up in our labors to get the Chevy back on the highway again, we did not have to rely on the talents of an expensive General Motors mechanic. I believe that my father's training as the son of a sharecropper father had everything to do with the development of his mechanical repair expertise and innate engine analytical ability. As his oldest son, I inherited Daddy's collection of Sears Craftsman socket tools and box-end wrenches and have put them to good use over the years since he died in 1956.

Toward the end of WWII, Lucille Smith, my high school sweetheart, informed me that she had found another love interest and that she had decided that she would not marry me. As it turned out, she advised me face to face, so, at least, I could console myself with the fact that I did not receive a 'Dear John' letter from her while far away at sea, for by then I was part of the RADAR gang on board the Troop Transport U.S.S. Zeilin (APA-3). Later on, I met a young lady by the name of Shirley Maxine Chapman at our local skating rink in Pomona, California, during one of my Navy leaves of absence and we dated during the balance of WWII. In November 1946, we were married by a Justice of the Peace in Yuma, Arizona. We raised three children (Susan

Marie Salzman 1947 today living in Penfield, New York), (Christine Yvonne Hacker 1949 today living in Nashville, Tennessee) and (Royce Eugene Hacker 1953, today living in Alta Loma, California). Royce plies the trade that I enjoyed for 50 years, that of a telephone man. He works out of the Ontario, California, Central Office of the Verizon Telephone Company specializing in fiber optic communications.

The following chapters describe my Navy career, with fictional chapters included covering the life of a dear friend who died in the crash of a Japanese Kamikaze airplane into our ship in January of 1945. Also included is a fictional account of the life and death of the Kamikaze pilot. While portions of this book are autobiographical in nature such as the description of the events leading up to my joining the Navy, as well as most of the descriptions of the WWII invasion cruises of the U.S.S. Zeilin, the text as a whole is best viewed as a work of fiction. The book is most certainly not intended to be a documentary treatise on the cruises of the U.S.S. Zeilin over the years covered by my story.

Melvin E. Hacker
November, 2007
Nashville, Tennessee

CHAPTER ONE

MELVIN GOES TO WAR

1400 Sunday
7 December 1941
Back Yard of 459 West Elm Street
Ontario, California

It was a sunny blue-sky day in Ontario, California, and the vintage monitor top Philco Radio was providing more and more details about the Japanese raid and destruction of America's Pearl Harbor Military Base and U.S. Navy ships while the Percy Hacker Family gathered around to listen in the back yard of their home. Coincidentally, it was the 15th birthday of second son, Harold, although no celebration was in progress. It was just another Sunday and Daddy had busied himself painting the wood frames of several screens for the windows of the 'home place'. All of the family members were present; sons Melvin, Harold and Marvin together with daughters Marilee, and year old Ida Mae as well as mother Della who was relaxing in a lawn chair nearby. "Buster", the nondescript family dog, was sunning himself on our picnic table until Ida Mae began tickling his nose. 'Buster' showed his indignation by quickly moving to his favorite hiding place in the hayloft of Daddy's cow barn. There was little discussion of the Pearl Harbor attack. The family was content to merely listen to the coverage provided by the Network radio announcer.

The news reports were originating in Hollywood, California, from Station KNX, a CBS affiliate, and the instantly famous 'Day of Infamy' speech articulated by

President Franklin Delano Roosevelt had been recorded and played back numerous times that afternoon.

THE COMPLETE TEXT OF THAT SPEECH IS:

"DECEMBER 7, 1941, A DATE WHICH WILL LIVE IN INFAMY.... NO MATTER HOW LONG IT MAY TAKE US TO OVERCOME THIS PREMEDITATED INVASION, THE AMERICAN PEOPLE IN THEIR RIGHTEOUS MIGHT, WILL WIN THROUGH TO ABSOLUTE VICTORY."

At long last, the United States had joined World War II that had been raging in Europe since September of 1939. The formality of confirming the declaration of war by the United States merely awaited the convening of a joint session of the Senate and House of Representatives the following day and the recording of the affirmative votes of the senators and congressmen.

Monday's issue of the Daily Report, Ontario's only local newspaper, carried substantial text and photographic coverage of the death and destruction visited by Japan upon the United States Navy, Air Force, and other military and civilian populations. It was clear from the newspaper accounts that the U.S. Pacific Fleet had been decimated with the loss of eight battleships as well as several cruisers, destroyers, oil tankers and many other 'ships of the line', let alone the destruction of hundreds of aircraft and maintenance hanger facilities. Fortunately, the Navy's major aircraft carriers were at sea and escaped the destruction intended for them by the Japanese strike. Aside from the extreme loss of the U.S. Navy's ships and sailors, there were the attendant deaths of hundreds of Navy, Army, Marine and civilian inhabitants of Pearl Harbor.

As a sixteen-year-old high school student at the time, I

did not fully comprehend the ultimate effect of the Japanese raid upon my own life, or that of my family for that matter. Named in part after my father, whose full name is Percy Eugene Hacker, my parents gave me his middle name, thus, Melvin Eugene Hacker. I was born on March 30, 1925, at the San Antonio Community Hospital located in Upland, California. This facility was located approximately three miles north of our residence in the town of Ontario. As it turned out, all of my mother's children were born in that hospital. Brother, Harold Ray was born on December 7, 1926; brother, Marvin Dean, was born on August 28, 1938; sister, Marilee Ruth, was born on August 10, 1928, while sister, Ida Mae, was born on January 13, 1941.

In 1941, I was a junior attending the Chaffey Union High School located in Ontario, California. As students, our teachers insisted upon our being attentive to world events and the war in Europe was an active current event topic. In addition to reading current events reports in our school library documents, the local Daily Report Newspaper provided up-to-date coverage of major European and South Pacific battles. Although, at the time, the battles seemed quite remote and essentially meaningless to my own and my friends' lives. However, this was to change all too soon when in 1942 some of my older classmates were caught up in the army draft and soon became casualties in the Philippines where the Japanese were attacking the island of Corregidor at the entrance to Manila Bay. I clearly recall the horror of the news of my close friend, Ralph Emmons, dying in a skirmish line near Mariveles on the Bataan Peninsula. The Japanese conquered Bataan on May 6, 1942, where they captured 11,000 Americans and 30,000 Filipinos. That event, perhaps more than any other, made me realize that, eventually, I was destined to become a participant in the war along with my brother, Harold. It turned out that Ralph had been drafted into the army when he became 18.

That realization together with the knowledge that I gained from viewing photographs of soldiers of the U.S. Army in Europe and elsewhere helped me make up my mind. The thought of living in foxholes to escape enemy bullets and scrambling for food or living on 'K' rations did not give me a comfortable feeling. For that reason, I began to analyze the wartime service opportunities that might exist for senior high school students. Of course, I was too young to have any chance of obtaining a deferment for purposes of attending an officer candidate school, nor was a similar deferment available to permit me to attend college. Thus, my search for a potential military home seemed limited to either the Marines or the Navy. Realistically, I never spent any time researching either the Coast Guard or the Marines as potential candidates for military service. During this period of my developing awareness of military careers, months passed by and I moved from my junior to senior year in high school.

By that time, the high school student ranks were being thinned by the draft as well as by enlistments in the various military services. In the fall of 1942, I began my senior year studies. Commencing in September of 1942 these studies would lead me to my eighteenth birthday on March 30, 1943 and possible graduation. (I say possible, for there was always the possibility that the draft would take me prior to my June 1943 graduation). Therefore, it seemed to me that time was running out and that I would necessarily have to take some concerted action to avoid the draft which I was resolved to do with my abhorrence of military life in the Army.

As an aside, I want to mention that I obtained my automobile driver's license while in high school. My first automobile was a 1928 Chevrolet Cabriolet cloth-top coupe that my father purchased from a co-worker at the General Electric small appliance factory in Ontario for $10. It was a 1928 Chevrolet four-cylinder rumble seat coupe that provided many pleasurable trips to Long Beach, Laguna Beach and other beach cities as well as transportation to Los Angeles to skating rinks and movie theaters. In the early 1940's, high school boys favored Ford vehicles and there were many coupes and sedans in the Chaffey High School parking lots. In my own case, I eventually purchased a 1936 Ford V-8 four-door humpback trunk sedan for $325 in 1942. With the scarcity of automobiles immediately following Japan's surrender, I sold the Ford in 1946 for $650 and later purchased a used 1940 Buick, super model, eight-cylinder four-door sedan. It had an attractive two-tone blue and cream paint job and with its straight eight-cylinder engine, it had power to burn. The little 1928 Chevrolet saw duty throughout the war years as my father's means of transportation to the GE factory on Main Street in Ontario, California. The factory was located between the Transcontinental Southern Pacific and Union Pacific railroad tracks, and was Ontario's principal source of employment in both prewar and postwar years. Not long after war was declared, GE became a government supplier of mechanics socket tools and timers for the fuses of aircraft bombs among other military-related products. My father was hired by the General Electric company in 1924, and worked there continuously for 32 years until his untimely death in 1956 at the age of 56.

It is also appropriate to mention at this point that I had a very close high school friend by the name of Lee Smith. In my high school association with Lee, I met one of his sisters by the name of Lucille, and we fell in love. We corresponded continuously during the early part of WWII and Lucille and I mutually agreed that, at war's end, we would be married. However, in 1945 Lucille lived across the street from a University of Southern California branch in Los Angeles, California, and along the way she met a gentleman assigned to the Navy V-12 Officer Candidate program at UCLA and their relationship resulted in her marrying him in 1946. Subsequently, I met a young lady by the name of Shirley

Maxine Chapman and we eloped to Yuma, Arizona, on November 9, 1946, where we were married by a Justice of the Peace.

1300 Monday
1 February 1943
Navy Recruiter's Office
Ontario, California

From my year-long study of possibilities, I decided that the U.S. Navy represented the best opportunity for me insofar as military service choices were concerned. In the U.S. Navy, one would have a dry and reasonably comfortable place to sleep at the end of each day and be fed three meals a day. (In actuality, the meal situation became two meals a day while I was assigned to a troop transport, and we had over 1,000 troops on board.) The two ships to which I was eventually assigned (U.S.S. Zeilin APA-3 and U.S.S. Warren APA-53) hauled Army, Marine and even Canadian troops to all of the major invasions undertaken by the United States in the North and South Pacific regions. At the same time, I realized that, depending upon the assignment I received, there could still be hazardous duty involved, but I willingly overlooked that remote possibility. So it was that I drove my Ford to the navy recruiter's office to sign on the dotted line. Unfortunately for me, I was underage at 17 and the officer in charge advised me that my parents would have to sign the enlistment papers before I could become a sailor in the U.S. Navy. Although I left his office greatly disappointed, I nevertheless felt that my mother and father would likely approve of my desire to enter the Navy.

1400 Monday
22 March 1943
Ontario, California

With seven weeks having passed since I first spoke with the Navy recruiting officer, and with my 18th birthday fast approaching, I realized that immediate action was necessary on my part. When my father returned home from his employment at the General Electric small appliance factory that Monday evening, I sought him out and asked to speak with him and my mother about the prospect of my enlisting in the U.S. Navy. Luckily for me, neither parent expressed any significant objection to my interest in avoiding the draft and did not disagree with my rationale. Although they disliked the prospect of my possible assignment to some type of hazardous duty, they nevertheless agreed to sign the necessary under age enlistment forms to permit me to join the U.S. Navy. It was after my conversation with Daddy and Mom that I felt a sense of relief and could devote my time to spending my few remaining civilian days with my sweetheart, Lucille. We concentrated on roller skating sessions, viewing many motion pictures and, of course, keeping the waitresses at Price's Drive-in busy with our food orders. It was a pleasant time as we reinforced our love for each other.

1200 Thursday
25 March 1943
Euclid Avenue
City Hall, Ontario, California

Accompanied by my parents, I drove to the U.S. Navy recruiting office, then located in the Ontario City Hall, and the officer-in-charge, Lt. (jg) G.W. Buster prepared the necessary forms which were duly signed, and I became a sailor in the U. S. Navy. I was directed to report in to the Navy Boot Camp located in San Diego, California, on a March date that is now so dim that I do not recall what it was. Nevertheless, I showed up at the appointed time and became a member of the 119th Recruit Company formed in the year of 1943; 43-119 being the official designation of my company. As a new recruit, I received the necessary medical immunization shots and many hours of training in marching, attention to commands, knot tying, and rifle target shooting, how to abandon a sinking vessel and indoctrination in the myriad aspects of Navy history and Navy duties in general. The San Diego boot camp was a large and extremely busy place at that time. Thousands of new recruits were being processed and transferred to staff the many existing as well as new ships being pressed into service to support the United States' war effort.

0800 Monday
29 March 1943
Navy Boot Camp
San Diego, California

Not all Navy training was given on the boot camp grounds themselves. In the case of abandon ship drills, the two platoons of each company were marched north for several miles on local San Diego streets to Mission Beach, California, where there existed a large recreation complex that included an enclosed olympic-size swimming pool. There, under the watchful eyes of several chief petty officers and our company commander, all recruits were required to put on kapok life jackets, climb a twenty-foot high diving platform and launch themselves into flight toward the 12-foot deep water below. Launching preparations were accomplished by first taking several deep breaths and, holding the last one, as you stepped off the platform. The recruit companies from the entire boot camp were run through the complex continuously and this concentrated duty schedule meant that all of the kapok life- jackets were completely and seemingly permanently waterlogged and represented the proverbial 'millstone around your neck'. Upon hitting the water, one found himself immediately dragged helplessly to the bottom of the pool which meant that, to survive, it was necessary to shed the life jacket and swim mightily to the surface of the pool and gulp in a lung-full of life-sustaining fresh air. It was, as always, just one of a series of hectic boot camp learning experiences. It only required one jump to teach an individual how to cope with the waterlogged kapok life jackets and their inability to float.

On a given day, it was required that recruits practice multiple launchings during a period of about four hours. During this time, recruits were also required to demonstrate their proficiency in swimming as well as lifesaving procedures. This latter effort included following instructions in handling swimmers in distress and safely pulling them from the water's surface at the edge of the pool. A midday break period of one hour was scheduled during which time food was provided and the time not needed to eat was available for rest. The abandon-ship exercises were carried out during one day of each of the first three weeks of boot camp training for Company 43-119.

During my first few weeks in boot camp, Lucille's parents moved their family to Los Angeles from Ontario where Mr. Smith had accepted a position as a welder with the Kaiser Ship Yards in San Pedro, California. At that time, assembly line manufacture of Kaiser liberty ships was running at a high production rate in support of the war effort. Both Lisa (Lucille's sister) and Lucille elected to remain in Ontario to finish their high school studies. Their brother, Lee, had already graduated in 1942 and was soon to leave to join the Navy V-12 Officer Candidate program at DePauw University in Greencastle, Indiana. Upon his graduation, Lee became the skipper of a mine sweeper for the remainder of WWII.

As it turned out, Lucille was invited to make her home with my parents and rode the bus to Chaffey Union High School each day together with my sister, Marilee. On weekends, Lucille and Marilee teamed up to work in the tomato harvesting victory gardens south of Ontario and ended up having their photographs appear in the Daily Report Newspaper along with the other high school girls who participated in the harvesting activities.

Arriving in my mail on Tuesday, 6 April 1943, was a note from my mother advising that the family was planning to drive to San Diego the next Friday evening and was bringing Lucille with them. What a delightful and totally unexpected surprise! I had not seen Lucille since I arrived at the Navy Boot Camp so I was especially anxious to see her and give her a loving kiss. Friday could not get here too soon to suit me.

1800 Friday
9 April 1943
San Diego, California
Navy Boot Camp

With the duty day finished, I waited impatiently at the boot camp main gate for the arrival of my parents, brother, Marvin, and sister, Ida Mae and, of course, sweetheart Lucille. About 1830, Daddy parked my 1936 Ford at the main gate and I ran to the car for a short liberty of perhaps seven hours. Having shown my liberty pass to the duty shore patrol petty officer, I climbed into the back seat with Marvin, Ida Mae and Lucille; space became a little cramped with four bodies seated in the narrow Ford rear seat, so Lucille ended up sitting on my lap. What a treat for me to inhale the fragrance of Lucille's delightful perfume and feel her lithe body close to mine. Daddy drove to a nearby restaurant where we exited the car and went inside for a meal. In the process, I was able to hug everyone, and nicest of all, give Lucille a lingering hug and kiss. Thus it was that I had a mini-date with Lucille accompanied by most of my family. I say most, because brother, Harold, was away on a Boy Scout trip. Later in the war, he would join the Navy and eventually be stationed at Clark Field in the Philippines where he performed sheet metal repair work on damaged aircraft, and sister, Marilee, was with her new soldier-husband, Eugene Van, in Texas. But who was complaining! Certainly not me! After all, it was wartime and everyone had to make sacrifices.

We lingered over dessert after the meal and I learned about the week's events in Ontario as well as Lucille's progress in her studies. She was an excellent student and always earned good grades. I had to be back on base by 2100, so Daddy drove the family back to the boot camp main gate where I stepped out after kissing Lucille good-bye and hugging her tight. It was a brief but wonderfully pleasant interlude, and I did not envy the family's two-hour return trip drive to Ontario. Passing through the main gate, I left my liberty pass with the duty shore patrol petty officer and hurried to my barracks where I brushed my teeth and fell into my bunk, hoping to dream of sweet Lucille. It had been a busy day marching on the Boot Camp Grinder and the barracks was full of tired sailors, many of them snoring softly.

1400 Friday
16 April 1943
San Diego, California
Navy Boot Camp

At the end of our third week of boot camp training, the company commander favored each of his new recruits with a weekend liberty pass from 1400 Friday afternoon to 0600

Monday morning. Although, in theory, recruits were not authorized to travel more than 50 miles from San Diego, my hometown of Ontario proved to be an irresistible target merely 120 miles distant, and I promptly joined many of my boot camp comrades walking along the main highway leading north out of San Diego to Los Angeles hoping to find some kind soul who would give me a ride home, or at least take me part way in that direction. As it turned out, I made it home that day through the kindness of two thoughtful and generous individuals.

The first was a gentleman who was traveling home to La Habra, California, from a business trip to San Diego. It was after sundown when we reached Brea, California, his turnoff point, and I exited his automobile amid profuse thanks for taking me at least three-quarters of the way home. He dropped me off on the main highway leading east toward Ontario, and I began to walk along the sidewalk fronting a number of commercial businesses that were still open for evening customers. Within just a few minutes, a car stopped ahead of me and the occupants waved vigorously with their arms for me to hurry and catch up with their vehicle. I ran as fast as I could hoping that they were going as far as Ontario. Upon entering the automobile which, as I recall, was a rather elderly 4-door Pontiac sedan, I introduced myself and learned that the lady driver and her daughter were on their way home to La Habra just north of Brea. After driving for a few miles, the lady inquired as to my destination. I told her that my home was in Ontario, and about that time we arrived at the turnoff road for La Habra. I knew the territory quite well because my Uncle Alton Hacker and his wife and family of four children lived there and my family visited them quite frequently over the years. Instead of turning as I had fully expected her to do, the lady continued east on the road toward Ontario. I made a remark about her missing her turnoff and she merely replied, "Well, sailor, tonight we are going home via Ontario", and that is exactly what she did. She drove me all the way to my home at 459 West Elm Street in Ontario, and then refused to allow me to pay her for the transportation or even accept any money to replace the fuel she had used. Gasoline rationing was in effect by then and I noticed that she had an 'A' gasoline ration sticker on her windshield. Notwithstanding my protests, she absolutely refused to accept any money, turned her car around and retraced her path to La Habra about 30 miles away. On that day, I became absolutely convinced that there were such things as angels after all and that I had met two of them that April day in 1943.

2300 Friday
16 April 1943
Home in Ontario, California

By the time I arrived home, it was almost 2300 and there were no lights visible in the house. I elected to knock on the back door, since I knew that it was closest to my parents' bedroom. In just a couple of minutes, Daddy came to the door and turned on the kitchen lights and unlocked the back door for me to enter. "Melvin, what a wonderful surprise to see and hold you", said Daddy, grabbing me about the neck and hugging me tight. Curious about the voices that she heard in the kitchen, Mom walked in and I gave her a bear hug and apologized for waking the family. Next, brother Marvin walked into the kitchen rubbing his sleepy eyes followed shortly by sister Ida Mae, and hugs were given all around, again. Mom made some hot chocolate and we enjoyed catching up on family happenings around the kitchen table. An hour later we were 'talked out' and went to bed. I had carried spare nightclothes with me and it was a wonderful treat to get to sleep in my very own civilian bed that night. My bedroom window opened upon a large night blooming jasmine bush in the front yard and the sweet, heady fragrance in the night air told me that I really was HOME AGAIN! I was not surprised to find Lucille among the missing, for Mom had called to tell me that Lucille's mother had picked her up after school and taken her to Los Angeles for the weekend. This was my first night away from boot camp since I had enlisted, and to be sleeping in my own bed was truly a delightful and most special treat. The fragrance of the jasmine bush permeated the bedroom and I relaxed in total comfort in my soft bed. Amid the continuous melody of nocturnal crickets, I fell asleep dreaming of Lucille.

0800 Saturday
17 April 1943
Home in Ontario

Being at home, I elected to sleep a couple of hours later than the usual Navy reveille time on Saturday morning. Nevertheless, the fragrance reaching my nostrils from Mom cooking breakfast of bacon and eggs got my attention so I hurried to shower and dress for the day. When I reached the kitchen, the table was set and Daddy and little brother and sister were already seated while Mom was busy at her range finishing her cooking. "Good morning all", I said. "Good-morning, Melvin" came back to me as a chorus from everyone there. Mom finished at the range and pulled a warm tray of cornbread biscuits from her oven and placed them on the table. The tantalizing aroma of the warm cornbread brought back long forgotten memories to me of the time when my family had moved to 459 West Elm Street and we were living temporarily in our 20-foot by 30-foot automobile garage until the 'home place' could be built. In those earlier times, mom cooked on a cast iron wood burning stove mounted on four bricks in the southeast corner of the garage and the oven heat was far from uniform. A six-inch diameter sheet metal chimney pipe extended several feet above the stove to a ninety-degree elbow near the ceiling from which a length of six-inch stove pipe extended horizontally through the wall of the garage gable to carry the smoke outdoors. Pans of cornbread invariably would come out of the oven with an inordinately thick area adjacent to the extremely hot firebox at the side of the oven. Such was the result of an inability to control the uniformity of heat within the oven itself. Even with its deformed surface, the cornbread was always crispy and quite delicious when treated with fresh cow butter and clover blossom honey from Daddy's bee hives, and washed down with lots of ice-cold milk. When I reminded Mom and Dad of that earlier time, they both smiled appreciatively. On the way to my seat, I gave Mom another hug as she sat down and I took the chair beside her. Neither brother, Harold, nor sister, Marilee, were at home so it was just the five of us for breakfast.

"Daddy, how is my Ford behaving these days?", I asked. "Oh, the Ford is running fine and we drive it often enough to keep the battery charged up and the gasoline from growing stale", Daddy replied. "Although the Navy frowns on its sailors in boot camp having their own automobiles nearby, I plan to drive the Ford back to San Diego on Sunday evening. I have spoken to quite a number of my boot camp friends who have their personal automobiles parked on side streets near the boot camp main gate and they have never had any difficulty with either the Navy personnel or the neighbors who live nearby. I plan to bring the Ford back to Ontario after I receive my permanent duty assignment, which should be some time in June", I explained.

"Melvin, what are your plans for today?", inquired Mom. "Actually, I have not made any plans, but had thought about possibly driving to Los Angeles and taking Lucille out on a date. If Howard Jones and Ellen Reed are available, I plan to ask them to go along", I concluded. "Well, let me give you this house key so if you return late, you can just come in and go to bed", said Mom. Pocketing the key, I replied, "Many thanks, Mom, and now if you will excuse me, I will go call Howard and find out what he and Ellen are up to today".

During my high school days, I possessed a full head of blonde hair, and inherited the name of 'Whitey' from the high school crowd that I ran around with. And this 'handle' carried over to my neighborhood friends as well. Having finished my breakfast, I then left the kitchen table, walked to the telephone hanging on the wall in the hallway and waited for the operator to say, "number please". (Dial telephones were not to appear in Ontario until 1947). I gave the operator Howard's number. Soon thereafter I heard Mrs. Jones answer my call and Howard happened to be nearby and came on the line almost immediately. "Hello, Howard. This is Whitey. Are you busy today?", I asked. "No, there is nothing special going on that I am aware of", replied Howard. "Well, I am thinking about driving to Los Angeles and taking Lucille out on a date, and wondered if you and Ellen would like to tag along?", I offered. "Give me time to check with Ellen and I will get right back to you", said Howard. We hung up the telephones and I fully expected to wait an hour or so for Howard's call. However, within ten minutes, the telephone rang and Howard told me that he and Ellen would like to make the trip. Howard lived only three houses east of our house on Elm Street so I said, "Howard, as soon as I can get the Ford started, I will stop over and pick you up, and then we can go get Ellen". "I'll be waiting for you out front", replied Howard.

Daddy was still in the kitchen enjoying a second cup of coffee as I entered. "Melvin, do you need any money?" asked Daddy. "No thank you, Daddy, but I very much appreciate your kind offer. I have been saving all of my Navy pay and have plenty of money for this weekend. Are the keys to the Ford handy?", I asked. "Yes, just look in that corner cabinet and you will find them in a green drinking glass", replied Daddy. Opening the cabinet door, I retrieved the keys and moved toward the back door. "It turns out that Howard and Ellen are going with me to Los Angeles, but no telling what time it will be when we return, so please don't wait up for me". "Very well, Son, but please drive carefully", cautioned Daddy. Walking out the back door and down the porch steps, I could not help but notice that it was a pleasantly warm, blue-sky day. A great day to spend with my sweetheart, I thought to myself.

My 1936 Ford was parked in the garage, so after opening the two hinged garage doors, I entered and climbed into the driver's seat. I had owned the automobile for about two years and had spent additional money on customizing it to suit my tastes. One of the first changes that I made was to remove the floor mounted, foot-operated starter switch and replaced it with a 'more modern' pushbutton starter control switch on the dashboard. This modification necessitated a major revamping of the electrical wiring feeding the starter, including removal of the original 'foot-operated' starter switch and replacing its function with a high current solenoid with which to feed electrical energy to the very current-hungry starter motor itself.

In addition to the starter modification, I had also removed the metal dashboard and taken it out to a chrome plating company in Pomona, California, for chrome plating. At the same time, I removed a segment of the steering wheel such that it ended up with the appearance of the control yoke one might find in an airplane cockpit. (This adaptation was consistent with my lifelong interest in airplanes.)

I also added two auxiliary fog lights on the front bumper as well as twin 'Unity' spotlights on each end of the dashboard. The strong beams of the spotlights were something to behold in the dead of night while attempting to read an obscure street sign or house number.

During the war years, Daddy traded at a Texaco service station located on the corner of Euclid Avenue and California Boulevard. In early 1944, Mr. Peterson, the proprietor, asked Daddy if he could purchase one of my spotlights because someone had stolen the one that he had installed on his 1940 Buick Special coupe. Of course, Daddy had to graciously decline his friend's request so the Buick went spotlight-less for the remainder of WWII. Unity spotlights, like so many other civilian products, were a scarce commodity during the war years. And all of the changes that I made in the Ford were accompanied by the installation of red leather upholstery on the seats, headliner and the entire interior of the automobile. With these improvements made, I hired an auto body paint shop to recess the license plate in the rear wall of the spacious trunk. This modification included the installation of two six-volt lamps with which to illuminate the license plate window as well as the installation of two red teardrop, 1938 Ford, stoplights on each side of the license plate and wiring them into the stoplight switch circuit.

My Ford was the 'Plain Jane' model and not the deluxe version that the Ford Motor Car Company also offered in 1936. Because of this fact, it came from the factory equipped with only a single taillight on the driver side rear fender. The resulting lack of symmetry bothered my sensibilities so I scouted around at a local auto wrecking yard until I found another 1936 taillight to add to the passenger side rear fender. Although the task required a certain amount of drilling mounting holes in the fender sheet metal, as well as the extension of the stoplight wiring, I was greatly pleased with the effect of the taillight symmetry once the job was finished. Indeed, I was very pleased by the combined effect of all of my changes and modifications. You would not be in error if you observed the fact that my 1936 Ford turned out to be a one-of-a-kind automobile. My customization also included the addition of teardrop rear fender skirts and the installation of a set of the popular chrome plated 'flicker' wheel hubcaps.

Inserting the ignition key and turning it on, I pressed the starter button and the V-8 engine sprang to life. Allowing the engine to warm up for a couple of minutes, I pushed in the clutch, shifted into reverse and backed slowly out of the garage. Stopping long enough to get out and close the garage doors, I climbed back into the car and backed out of the driveway to Elm Street and turned right (east) toward Howard's house. As I looked ahead across the three lots separating the Hacker and Jones properties, I could see Howard already standing by the side of the unpaved dirt road in front of his house. Although Ontario zoning requirements specified the paving of all roads in developing subdivisions, the paving of Elm Street was delayed because of a protest by the Armstrong Nurseries who owned the property bordering the north side of Elm Street that extended west of my father's property for a distance of about 2,000 feet all the way to San Antonio Avenue. The nursery's political clout was great enough to delay the paving of Elm Street until well after WWII had ended. In those days, the nursery operated a propagating plant on about 400 acres of land across the street from Mom and Daddy's home. Today the nursery no longer exists and wall-to-wall residential housing has taken its place.

As I slowed to a stop next to Howard, he opened the front passenger door and climbed in. "Hi, Whitey, many thanks for inviting Ellen and me to join you and Lucille", said Howard. "It is my pleasure, and besides there is a method in my madness since I will now have someone to talk to on the way to and from LA", I joked. "In case you don't remember, Ellen lives on 'J' street so let's just head over to Euclid Avenue and turn north", directed Howard. In those days, Elm Street had not yet been cut through to Euclid Avenue. (The extension of Elm Street to Euclid Avenue was a long-needed postwar improvement for the neighborhood.) So, at Fern Avenue, I turned left for three blocks and then turned right on Dessau Street that ran along the northern boundary of DeAnza Park, a popular playground and picnic area that we enjoyed throughout our childhood and adult years. Then, at Euclid Avenue, I turned left heading north toward the center of Ontario's Business District two miles away. Within ten minutes we were crossing the transcontinental Union Pacific and Southern Pacific Railroad tracks and then were stopped by the 'Red' traffic signal at 'A' Street. On the southeast corner of Euclid Avenue and 'A' Street stood the Ford Lunch Restaurant. This popular landmark was in business long before WWII and continued for many years after the war.

In 1943, the traffic signals standing on the four corners of Euclid Avenue and 'A' Street were vintage appliances. (Today, they would qualify as antiques). Comprised of a rectangular cast iron box about 24 inches high capped by a fancy sculptured finial, the signals had a very distinctive appearance. Protruding from the side of the rectangular box was a red or green metal blade, depending upon whether traffic was allowed to proceed or brought to a stop. The design also included red and green lenses mounted on the sides of the box that were illuminated to match the color of the extended signal blade. The green 'Go' blade soon rotated into view and I continued driving north on Euclid Avenue through the center of town passing the Forum, California and Granada Movie Theaters along the way. At 'B' Street we passed the Bank of America with its distinctive four-sided clock exhibiting four faces mounted on the corner of the building. The clock was also a town landmark for many years before, during and after the war. A few minutes later, I turned left on 'J' Street and two blocks further along I stopped in front of Ellen's home. Howard went to her front door and rang the bell. Ellen appeared almost immediately and joined Howard as they returned to the car and climbed into the rear seat. Thus it was that I became their chauffeur for the balance of our journey that April day in 1943.

0930 Saturday
17 April 1943
Ellen Reed's Home

"Good morning, Ellen, it is so nice to see you again", I said. "Same here, Whitey, and how is Navy life agreeing with you?", asked Ellen. "Well, I really have no complaints. They feed us well and keep us so busy that the time passes by rather quickly. By the way, I called Lucille this morning and she will be expecting us to arrive around noon so timing-wise we will not have to be in a panic to reach her home on time". Placing the Ford in gear, I continued straight ahead to Vine Avenue where I turned left to return to 'A' Street for access to the main highway leading to Los Angeles. At 'A' Street, I turned right toward Pomona where, six miles later, we passed through this small California town on the fringe of the citrus belt of thousands of acres of orange, lemon, grapefruit and tangerine trees. Although none of us realized it at the time, all of the citrus trees of Pomona Valley and San Bernardino Valley would disappear beginning in 1947 at the onset of the great postwar housing boom. Continuing west, we passed through the small towns of Walnut, El Monte, Alhambra, Puente, and then I turned south on Figureoa Avenue on the eastern edge of Los Angeles. Lucille's parents rented a home at 843 West 34th Street and we soon arrived at 34th Street where I turned right toward the Smith residence. Turning into Lucille's driveway on the north side of the street right at 1200, I parked and turned off the ignition switch. "Give me a few minutes and I will see if Lucille is ready to leave." I said. "Take your time, Whitey", replied Howard. "Lucille is always punctual so it will not take me long to return with her", I said.

1200 Saturday
17 April 1943
Lucille's Home
843 West 34th Street
Los Angeles, California

Stepping up onto the porch, I rang the bell and after a brief wait, Lucille opened the front door sporting her sweet pixie smile. "Hello, Whitey, what a wonderful surprise to see you here in Los Angeles", announced Lucille. As she spoke, I took her in my arms and gave her a loving kiss, which she returned placing her arms about my neck. "How nice to hold you in my arms again, sweetheart. I have missed you so very much", I whispered in her ear. About that time, Lucille's mother came to the front door and bid me to enter. She was a very attractive lady and her name was Stella. "Whitey, won't you come in and stay awhile?", she asked. "Thank you for the kind invitation Mrs. Smith, but Howard and Ellen are waiting in the car so I had best take a rain check on your kind invitation till another time. We are planning to drive to the 'Roller Drome' in Hollywood and go skating. I promise to bring Lucille home at a reasonable hour", I said. "Very well, Whitey, but next time plan on staying overnight with us for an entire weekend", said Mrs. Smith. "When the Navy is willing, I will surely take you up on your generous offer, Mrs. Smith", I said smiling all the while.

Taking my hand, Lucille said, "Good-bye, Mother, and I will be home by eleven o'clock". "Have a very nice time you two", she replied. Walking out the front door, I led Lucille to the passenger side of the Ford's front seat and opened the door for her to enter. After closing the door, I walked to the driver's door and climbed in. Lucille slid over and it was a pleasant sensation to feel her warm body pressing against mine. "Hello, Howard and Ellen, how nice to see you after such a long time", said Lucille. "Hi, Lucille, and how do you like living in Los Angeles by now?", asked Ellen. "Actually, I am still living in Ontario with Whitey's parents until I graduate from Chaffey High School this fall. So it is a rather back-and-forth existence at the moment. To tell you the truth, when I am in LA, I miss Ontario and all the friends that I grew up with and then left behind. If the war had not come along, I would still be living there permanently", lamented Lucille. Amid other conversational pleasantries, I started the engine and backed out onto 34th Street and turned toward Figureoa Avenue where, upon reaching it, I turned left in the direction of Hollywood. The traffic on Figureoa Avenue was very light so we made good time traveling to Hollywood and the Roller Drome Skating Rink.

1240 Saturday
17 April 1943
Hollywood Roller Drome

Thirty minutes later, I was parking the Ford in the Hollywood Roller Drome parking lot. I left my driver's seat and hurried around to open Lucille's door as Howard and Ellen stepped out of the rear seat. Taking Lucille's arm, I led her to the ticket booth, where I purchased our tickets and then waited for Howard to get their tickets and follow us inside. The Hollywood Roller Drome was a very popular place with servicemen and women in those wartime days and the rink was already full of civilian and military skaters. An organist was playing from his mezzanine perch, and we hurried to lace up our skates and get out onto the hardwood floor. The organist announced a 'couples only skate' and began playing the popular song, 'IT HAD TO BE YOU'. With our arms about each other, Lucille and I skated along in silence enjoying each other's company as well as the thought-provoking music. By then, Howard and Ellen were on the floor skating together.

By 1400, I was getting hungry. "Lucille, would you care to have something to eat?", I asked. "Now that you mention it, I am a little hungry", she replied. "Let me flag down Howard and Ellen and then we can skate over to the concession stand and find out what is on the menu". Howard came skating by and I waved him over and Ellen came right behind him. "Lucille and I are hungry. Could you folks use something to eat?", I asked. "I certainly could, How about you Ellen?", asked Howard. "By all means, my cornflake breakfast disappeared a long time ago", complained Ellen. "Yes, I have an 80-year old, railroad conductor friend who constantly complains about the fact that 'You just don't get much mileage out of cornflakes'", I joked. With everyone in agreement, we skated to the concession area where Lucille and I decided to have hot dogs, french fries and cokes while Howard and Ellen decided on hamburgers, french fries and cokes. When the food was delivered, we all sat down around a vacant table and relaxed while we ate.

The organist continued playing, treating one and all to a medley of WWII love songs. Howard and Ellen finished first and skated back onto the floor. For our part, Lucille and I were content to continue relaxing and enjoying the quite rare pleasure of each other's company. My Navy duty had brought to an end our weekly skating and motion picture dates and we both missed them very much. "Lucille, you haven't changed your mind about our getting married after the war, have you?", I timidly inquired. "No, Whitey, I absolutely have not changed my mind, nor will I, for I love you so much", confirmed Lucille. Her words filled me with a warm and contented feeling inside. "I love you so much too, and can hardly bear being away from you. I feel like I am being cheated of every hour that we are apart", I complained. "I agree with you, Whitey, for when you are away I find myself being so extremely lonely."

"Lucille, do you realize that it is only two hours from Los Angeles to San Diego by train on the Santa Fe Railroad. If I send you a ticket, do you think that your mother would permit you to travel there for a weekend? I can arrange a nice hotel room for you near the railroad depot. If she will not permit you to travel alone, perhaps your sister Lisa could accompany you", I suggested. "That would be such a wonderful treat. Let me ask her and see what happens", replied Lucille. "It will be too late for you to ask her today, so I will call you tomorrow and you can tell me what her decision is", I said. "I will say a prayer that Mom will approve and hope for the best", said Lucille. The announcer called another 'couples only' skate so Lucille and I left the food concession area and skated onto the floor, arm in arm. Deep in our own private thoughts, we did not notice Howard and Ellen waving from the gallery where they were resting.

By 1630, we were all getting tired from skating after three hours on the floor and decided to leave and find a movie that we would enjoy. After turning in our skates, we walked to the parking lot and took our places in the Ford V-8 sedan.

1700 Saturday
17 April 1943
The Strand Theater
Hollywood, California

There were many theaters from which to choose so I started the engine and drove slowly down Hollywood Boulevard while my friends studied the brightly lighted neon theater marquees. In the end, we all agreed that "The Wizard of Oz" was the best choice available so I turned into the parking lot of the Strand Theater and parked the Ford. By then it was approaching 1730 and the sun was descending slowly in the west and twilight was approaching. Taking

Lucille's hand as she stepped out of the Ford, I led the way to the theater box office, where I purchased four tickets, deciding along the way to treat Howard and Ellen. At that point my Navy pay was burning a hole in my pocket. The movie had not yet begun and with the bright house lights blazing, we found few patrons present as we selected a row of seats halfway back in the auditorium and walked to the center of that row. Lucille sat to my right while Howard and Ellen sat to my left. Within five minutes, the house lights dimmed and the Fox Movietone Newsreel began the program with their distinctive 'Eyes and Ears of the World' theme song. Lowell Thomas narrated the European and South Pacific war scenes. The newsreel was followed by a Mickey Mouse cartoon and then the 'Wizard of Oz' lead-in credits commenced to roll. Since I had seen the film several times, I decided to pay more attention to Lucille than I did to the screen. Placing my arm around her shoulder, I pulled Lucille close to me and whispered in her ear, "I love you more than life itself". She turned toward me and I kissed her sweet lips. The divine fragrance of her perfume left me breathless. I was extremely disappointed when the film ended, for it meant that my brief weekend interlude with Lucille was already coming to an end.

The house lights came up brightly and I reached for Lucille's hand and helped her to stand. Lucille led the way down the aisle, while Howard and Ellen followed close behind. Leaving the lobby of the theater, I noticed that the sun had set and Hollywood Boulevard was bathed in artificial light. Here and there, powerful carbon arc searchlights could be seen sweeping the evening sky as enticements to the public-at-large to view the latest films of Hollywood Motion Picture Producers. The stark beams touched the edges of filmy clouds floating overhead setting them aglow. My stomach told me that it was time to eat again so I raised the issue with my companions. "Are any of you folks as hungry as I am?", I asked. "I'm so hungry that my stomach is growling", agreed Howard. "I'll second that motion", chimed in Lucille. "You will not get any argument from me!", agreed Ellen. "Then that leaves us with only the matter of deciding where to eat. On our way to the skating rink, I noticed that there was a Rafferty's restaurant about six blocks before we reached the rink. "Let's try it out", offered Howard. Ten minutes later I turned into Rafferty's brightly illuminated parking lot and allowed one of several valets to park the Ford. Getting out of the car, I quickly walked to Lucille's door and opened it, at the same time extending my hand which she gently grasped. Holding hands as we were, I assisted her in stepping over the running board and took the occasion to steal a kiss.

1900 Saturday
17 April 1943
Rafferty's Restaurant
Hollywood, California

With Lucille on my arm, we entered the restaurant just ahead of Howard and Ellen and found the Maitre d' ready to seat the four of us. As it turned out, we were favored by being placed in a small alcove away from the other diners. A very nice touch, I thought. A waiter appeared and filled our water glasses, and at the same time distributed menus around the table. "The sky's the limit, Lucille; order anything that your heart desires. And that goes for you and Ellen too, Howard", I said. "What a wonderful menu; so many choices", observed Lucille. "All things considered, I am going to order a house salad and the petite sirloin steak with side dishes of green beans and mashed potatoes", said Lucille. "Have you decided yet, Ellen", asked Howard. "Yes, I am going to be different and order the freshwater trout, cole slaw and a baked potato", replied Ellen. "I am going to order a "T" bone steak along with home fries and green beans and a house salad", reported Howard. "For my meal I am going to order their rack of ribs with side dishes of navy beans and baked apples as well as a house salad", I said. At that point the waiter arrived, pad in hand, to take the four food orders. At the same time, he took our drink orders which consisted of four cokes. Although the waiter offered wine as our beverage, we all declined.

While we waited, I reached over and took Lucille's hand in mine and enjoyed feeling the supple warmth of her skin. At the same time, she moved her chair ever so slightly toward me to gain a more comfortable position. "Ellen, do you and Howard have any wedding plans yet?", asked Lucille. "No, nothing firm yet, but we have talked about it a great deal. I expect that we will wait until the war is over before we take the big step", replied Ellen. "With the uncertainties of war, we plan to just wait", clarified Howard. "It turns out that Whitey and I find ourselves caught up in the same dilemma. We love each other so very much, but have decided to wait until the war is over to get married". Fifteen minutes having passed, the waiter, accompanied by an attendant, arrived with our food orders. The food was excellent and all conversation essentially ended as we consumed our meals. It turned out that we had selected a very fine restaurant for, without exception, all of the meals were excellent. While we relaxed at the end of our meals, the waiter appeared to take orders for dessert. "Ladies and gentlemen, here is our dessert menu", said the waiter handing each person a folded page containing glossy color photographs of each dessert. "I can take your orders now or come back later", said the waiter. "I have already decided. Please bring me one of your hot fudge sundaes", requested Lucille. "I really shouldn't, but I am going to order the strawberry shortcake", said Ellen. "Your apple pie has whetted my appetite so I would like to have that dessert a la mode", I said. "Put me down for a piece of cocoanut cream pie", concluded Howard. "It will just take a few minutes to fill your orders and I will return", said the waiter as he departed in a hurry. True to his word, the desserts arrived on a wheeled pastry cart about ten minutes later. Checking the grandfather clock standing in a corner nearby, I realized that the timing of our meal was working out perfectly. By the time our desserts were eaten, there would be just enough time to return Lucille to her home before 2300, as I had promised her mother. The waiter brought our check and I paid for the meals, following through on my decision to treat Howard and Ellen for which they offered their sincere appreciation.

2230 Saturday
17 April 1943
Leaving Rafferty's Restaurant

I presented my claim check to a valet and he brought the Ford to us immediately. We all climbed into the Ford and I again treasured the pleasant sensation of Lucille's hip pressing against my own. As we departed Rafferty's parking lot, Lucille placed her arm around my shoulder and I was doubly blessed by her presence. I disliked thinking about the fact that our date was ending and I would be returning to Ontario and leaving Lucille behind. Pulling out into traffic on Hollywood Boulevard, I turned east to eventually connect with Figureoa Avenue to travel south toward Lucille's neighborhood. We reached 34th Street, and I turned right and a block away, pulled into Lucille's driveway. Lights were on in her home so I walked to her side of the car and opened the door. Taking her by the hand, I assisted her in leaving her seat. "Howard and Ellen, I have enjoyed our time together today so much and hope that we can have a chance for a repeat performance sometime in the not too distant future", said Lucille. "It has been a lovely day, Lucille, and please let us know the next time you plan to visit Ontario; it would be so nice to get together again", replied Ellen. "Lucille, just keep in mind that this war cannot last forever, so eventually, your marriage to Whitey will happen", consoled Howard. "I know that what you say is true, but it is so difficult to be patient", replied Lucille. "So long till next time", were Lucille's parting words as I walked her to her front door. Climbing the three steps of the porch, Lucille hesitated at the front door giving me an opportunity to take her in my arms and kiss her sweet lips for the last time that day. Holding her close, I was excited by the pressure of her ample breasts pressing against my chest. How exceedingly lovely Lucille is, I thought. "I will call you tomorrow, sweetheart, to learn what your mom decides about your traveling to San Diego", I said. "Please do, and call around noon, if you will", replied Lucille, and with that she opened the front door, and, waving good-bye, disappeared inside. By then, it had been a very long day and I was not looking forward to the long drive to Ontario. Nevertheless, I appreciated having had the opportunity to spend the day with the love of my life.

2300 Saturday
17 April 1943
Lucille's Home
843 West 34th Street
Los Angeles, California

With Lucille safely inside her home, I walked to the Ford, started the engine, and headed east down 34th Street toward Ontario. Reaching Figureoa Avenue, I turned left toward downtown LA and the main highway leading toward San Bernardino County and the many small towns east of Los Angeles. As I drove along, it was quiet in the back seat as Howard and Ellen snoozed with their arms around each other. That was fine with me, since I really did not feel much like conversation at that moment anyway. It was then after midnight and traffic was extremely light allowing me to drive the posted speed limit without any interference from other drivers. As I drove along, I relived the day's events in my mind's eye and said a prayer that Stella Smith would take kindly to my suggestion that Lucille be allowed to travel to San Diego on the train. The train depot is only a short distance from boot camp and I expected to be able to meet Lucille when her train arrived. Only time will tell, I told myself.

The miles passed quickly by and we were soon entering Ontario's city limits. In the middle of town I turned left on Vine Avenue retracing the route to 'J' Street and Ellen's home. Turning right onto 'J' Street, I reached over the front seat back and touched Howard's knee to wake him. "Where are we, Whitey?" asked a sleepy Howard. "We are only a block away from Ellen's house, so I thought that I should wake you", I said. "Wow, what a quick trip", marveled Howard. "Yes, sleeping in a moving automobile will do that to you sometimes. It comes under the heading of a 'state of confusion'", I observed with a smile. At that point, Howard leaned over and kissed Ellen and she awoke with a smile on her lovely face. "Time to wake up, sleeping beauty; we are almost home, sweetheart", said Howard. "I can't believe that we got here so fast", mused Ellen. I pulled to a stop in front of Ellen's home and left the engine idling. Howard opened the back door and helped Ellen to her feet as she left the car. "Good-night, Ellen, and I really enjoyed your company today", I said. "It was my pleasure, Whitey, and have a nice rest of the weekend", finished Ellen. Holding on to Ellen's arm, Howard walked to the front door where the porch light was on. Ellen opened the front door and hesitated, while Howard gave her a good-night (actually a good-morning) kiss, since it was then about 0130 hours.

Returning to the Ford, Howard climbed into the front passenger seat. "Well, it has been a mighty long day, Whitey", observed Howard. "Yes, it has and I plan to sleep in this morning. Although it has been a long day, it was wonderful to spend some quality time with Lucille", I said. By then, we had reached Euclid Avenue where I turned south toward Dessau Street. We reached Dessau Street ten minutes later and I turned right along the north side of DeAnza Park and then left when I came to Fern Avenue and we were almost home. As we passed by the South Side Mutual Water Company pump house on Fern Avenue, we could hear the hum of the monster electric motor and the "slap", "slap", "slap" of the splices in the 30-foot long leather drive belt that rotated the deep-well pump that was feeding water to one of the farmers in the neighborhood. When Daddy raised an acre of corn or other produce, he relied on Mr. Swain (or one of his four sons) to turn on the pump at the appointed hour. A network of concrete irrigation pipes served all of the lots on Elm, Locust, Maple and Francis Streets in those years. All of the properties were in a zone classified as agricultural. Two blocks south of the Pump House, I turned right on Elm Street and soon stopped in front of Howard's home. "Thank you again, Whitey, for the good time and your treating us to the movie and that great meal in Hollywood", said Howard. "You are most welcome, Howard, and when I get liberty again and can visit Ontario, perhaps we can double date again", I replied. "Just give me a call and I can be ready most any time. So long for now, Whitey", and with that Howard walked to his front door and disappeared inside.

I drove past the next three houses and then turned left into Daddy's driveway and turned off the Ford's engine at the street so that I could put the car away in the garage without disturbing the sleeping family. It was easy to do, as the driveway had a slight, natural slope toward the garage. I allowed the car to coast down the driveway and stopped it just short of the garage doors, set the emergency brake, and then got out and opened the doors. With the doors open, I released the brake and, with very little physical effort the Ford coasted into the garage where I placed the transmission in first gear and then closed the garage doors. The house was dark as I walked up on the back porch steps; however, there was a dim nightlight shining over the kitchen sink. Using the key that Mom had given me that morning, I opened the door and entered the house as quietly as I could. After locking the door, I walked down the hallway to my room, put on my night clothes, brushed my teeth, and then fell into bed. I was bone tired and needed the rest. In no time at all, I was dreaming of my day in Los Angeles with my sweetheart, Lucille. My dream was one of confusion as it was from another time after the war when Lucille was all dressed up in her wedding finery and the minister was preparing to marry the two of us. Organ music was playing and as I looked up the aisle Lucille was walking toward me by her father's side. At that point, the dream ended and I found myself at home in my bed.

1200 Sunday
18 April 1943
459 West Elm Street
Ontario, California

When I awoke, I was surprised to find that it was almost 12 noon. I hurried into the bathroom to take a shower and dress for the day. Walking into the kitchen, I found Mom and Dad reading the morning paper. "Good-morning, Melvin", said Mom. "Did you have a nice time in Los Angeles yesterday?", asked Daddy. "Yes, it really was a wonderful day. We went skating at the Roller Drome, saw a good movie and had a wonderful meal in the evening at Rafferty's Restaurant. It was well worth my late arrival back home. I suggested to

Lucille that she might consider coming to San Diego on the train for a weekend visit and she told me that she would ask her mother for permission, and I am supposed to telephone her about this time to find out what the answer is. So if you will excuse me, I will go call her now", I said. Walking to the elderly wall-mounted telephone in the hallway, I removed the receiver and waited for the operator to answer, "Number, please". I gave her Lucille's number and waited for ring-back tone. At the end of the second ring, Lucille answered somewhat breathlessly. "Hello", came her sweet voice in my ear. "Hello, sweetheart. How are you this morning after such a long and busy day yesterday?", I asked. "I feel great, especially since Mom has approved my request to visit you in San Diego. And all by myself, I might add". "That is the most wonderful news; when do you plan to make the trip?", I asked. "I have thought about that very thing and I decided that I would travel to San Diego next Friday. We can have two full days together over the weekend, and I can return home on Monday", revealed an excited Lucille. "Lucille, I don't know if I can mail you a ticket in time for you to receive it before Friday. Do you have enough money to purchase the ticket and I can reimburse you when you arrive in San Diego?", I asked hesitantly. "That is no problem", said Lucille. "Just as soon as you have made your reservations, would you please call my mom and let her know? I will call her to learn your arrival time and be at the Santa Fe depot waiting to meet you", I said. "Yes, I'll call your mom tomorrow after I have made my reservations", replied Lucille. "Well, it seems that our prayers were answered after all, sweetheart", I said. "Yes, they were and I am so happy that we will get to be together again in only a week's time", enthused Lucille. "I can't wait for next Friday to get here. In the meantime, please take good care of yourself, and know that I am thinking about you and that I love you with all my heart", I said. "Whitey, I will be counting the hours until we meet again", promised

Lucille. "Good-bye till Friday then", I said. "Good-bye, Whitey, and I love you too" said Lucille as she hung up her telephone and I did the same.

Walking back into the kitchen with a smile on my face, I told Mom and Dad the good news. "Son, have you decided when you will drive to San Diego today?", asked Daddy. "No, I really had not given too much thought to that unhappy aspect of my weekend liberty. I guess my only thought is that I would rather not be making the trip after dark since I have never driven to San Diego before. With the way the roads are laid out, I don't expect to get lost, but I do think that a daylight trip would be preferred", I replied. "Yes, I agree with your assessment and I would suggest that you leave around 4 p.m.", said Daddy. "I know that the distance is about 120 miles so I expect the travel time to be about two hours. I will take you up on that suggestion. A 4:00 p.m. departure should see me in San Diego in time to have sunshine most, if not all, of the way. On that basis, I am going to take the Ford uptown and have the engine oil changed and fill up the gas tank", I said. "Let me go with you and we can give the business to Wade Weeks at his Shell Station on East 'A' Street", said Daddy. "That sounds fine to me", I replied. It turned out that Wade Weeks was a lifelong friend of my Dad's from a time when they were both young boys growing up in the cotton fields of Buffalo Gap, Texas. As I thought about Daddy's relationship with Wade, it finally dawned on me that before we moved to Elm Street, Daddy used to trade at Wade's Shell Station when it was located on Bon View Avenue and 'A' Street on the east side of Ontario. After our move, that location was just too far out of the way for Daddy to continue to trade there. Wade's present Shell Station was located next door to the only hotel in Ontario and it was named after the town, 'Hotel Ontario'. So, Wade's Shell Station was quite close to the center of town. Walking to the garage, I opened the doors, and backed the Ford out while

Daddy came out of the back door of the house, closed the garage doors and climbed in beside me. It would be a special treat to spend some quality time with my father before I had to leave for the confines of Navy life in San Diego. Joining the Navy had deprived me of my home life as well as my love life and I had come to resent that fact. Taking the same route that I had traveled on my Saturday trip to LA, I soon turned right on 'A' Street by the Ford Lunch Restaurant and drove two blocks east to Wade's Shell Station at the corner of 'A' Street and Lemon Avenue.

1400 Sunday
18 April 1943
Wade Weeks' Shell Station
Ontario, California

Driving into the station, Wade met us and I said, "Mr. Weeks, I need an oil change and my fuel tank filled up". "I can do both right now. Just drive your Ford onto the hoist and I'll get started", replied Wade. Noticing my Dad in the front seat Mr. Weeks said "Hello, Percy, and how are you today?" "I couldn't be better now that I have son Melvin home for a few hours", replied Daddy. "I know what you mean; my oldest son is off in the South Pacific chasing Japs someplace and I don't know when we will get to see him again", complained Mr. Weeks "He is in the Navy and has been gone for a year as a Gunner's Mate on a destroyer and it is about time for him to come home on leave as far as I am concerned", exclaimed a discouraged and no doubt lonely Mr. Weeks. " My wife writes to him frequently but it isn't the same as him being here at home."

With the car on the hoist, I got out of the Ford and prepared to watch an expert in action. Daddy also got out of the car on his side to admire his friend at work and engage him in small talk. The first thing that Mr. Weeks did was to operate the valve that admitted compressed air into the pneumatic cylinder of the hoist to raise the Ford. With the car raised about six feet in the air, Mr. Weeks rolled his zerc grease gun under the car and proceed to grease all of the fittings in the steering linkage and suspension spring shackles. Ford automobiles, with their transverse suspension spring system, were notorious for their squeaking undercarriages. I pretty well solved that problem by keeping a squirt can full of penetrating oil handy in the trunk of the car and I squirted the springs at least once a week. As a result, my Ford had very few squeaks. With all the grease points attended to, Mr. Weeks rolled his waste oil collection tank under the Ford and drained the old oil while the engine was still hot from our trip to his station. Once the old oil was removed, Mr. Weeks reinstalled the plug in the crankcase pan and then lowered the hoist. Once the Ford was on the floor of the station bay, Mr. Weeks lifted the driver side hood and removed the oil filter cover as well as the spent Fram C-4 Oil Filter Cartridge. Mr. Weeks had the new filter cartridge in place and the filter cap reinstalled in a couple of minutes and then he proceeded to add five quarts of 30 weight premium Shell oil. The engine of my Ford was in excellent mechanical condition and never required the addition of any oil between oil changes every 3,000 miles. With the oil in place, Mr. Weeks started the engine and checked beneath the car as well as under the hood for any leaks, and after he was satisfied that there were none, he shut the engine down. Allowing enough time for the warm oil to drain back into the crankcase, Mr. Weeks pulled the dip stick, wiped it clean and again checked the oil level. It registered a pint low so he added a pint and the oil job was finished.

"Okay, Melvin, back your car off the hoist and pull it over to the pumps and I'll fill your tank", said Mr. Weeks. Watching for adequate side clearances at the hoist entry, I carefully backed up and pulled alongside the first pump.

Mr. Weeks was already there and quickly removed the fuel tank cap and began pumping regular grade 87 Octane Shell gasoline into the Ford after I had shut the engine down. Quite soon the fuel gauge on the dashboard registered full and I was ready for my two-hour return trip to San Diego. Daddy followed his friend around and I overheard them discussing some long-forgotten incident from their days as young boys growing up in the cotton fields of Buffalo Gap, Texas. Their camaraderie was palpable. "Well, Melvin, that comes to $3.50 for the Fram filter cartridge, grease job, oil and gasoline", said Mr. Weeks. "Mr. Weeks, I consider that a bargain, especially since all I had to do was stand around and watch an expert in action", I joked. "Next time you are back in town, stop by and I'll be glad to help in any way that I can" offered Mr. Weeks. "I will be certain to do that, Mr. Weeks", I replied.

1500 Sunday
18 April 1943
Leaving Wade Weeks' Shell Station
Ontario, California

By that time, Daddy had climbed into the front seat beside me and we were ready to return home. "Good-bye, Wade. I'll see you around", said Daddy through his open window. "So long, Percy, it was so nice to see you again. We should get together more often than we do", said Wade. "I agree", replied Daddy as I eased the Ford down the driveway from Wade Weeks' station and merged into the westbound traffic lane on 'A' Street. Wishing to see more of Ontario than I had for several months, I continued west on 'A' Street passing the Ontario Hotel, the Ford Lunch Restaurant and then crossed over famous double-drive Euclid Avenue. When Canadian George Chaffey laid out the city of Ontario in the late 1800's, he provided a double drive highway extending 11 miles from Ontario to the Foothills of the 10,000 foot high Mt. Baldy to the north. Italian Pepper trees lined the two paved streets and grass was planted between the rows of trees in the center median. It made a very beautiful thoroughfare and is still a striking feature in the cities of Ontario and Upland, California, today. In the early part of this century a horse-drawn trolley ran on rails all the way to the base of the mountains from Ontario. The trolley featured a trailer on which the horse rode on the return trip after reaching the north end of the line. Gravity returned the trolley to Ontario. Use of the trolley was discontinued after the automobile came to Ontario and diminished trolley rider ship to below the break-even point. This was the unhappy result of some forms of change that otherwise might be seen as progress.

Continuing west on "A" Street, we passed the Van De Kamp Bakery and I noticed the tantalizing fragrance of fresh baked yeast bread in the air. Further on, we passed Mr. Wheeler's auto upholstery shop where the red leather upholstery in my Ford had been installed a few years earlier, and then we passed the Western Auto store next door to the M.K. Smith Chevrolet dealer's showroom and used car lot. When I reached Vine Avenue the signal turned red so I stopped, shifting the transmission into neutral as I braked at the red light. I preferred to take the car out of gear to avoid the needless wear and tear on the clutch throw-out bearing that would otherwise occur. Daddy spoke up about that time and said, "Melvin, do you see that Methodist Church on the northeast corner here?" Our stop had placed us adjacent to the front doors of the church. "When your mother and I were first married in 1924, I was working for a building contractor and was part of the 15- man crew that installed those six tall columns across the front of the church. When that job was finished, your Uncle Faye Fenwick happened to be a foreman at the General Electric Plant on Main Street, and he was instrumental in getting me hired at what was then referred to as the 'Flat Iron Plant' in 1925, just before you were born." This was a bit of family history that I had never heard before. "Wasn't Mom concerned about you having to perform work at such a height?", I asked Daddy. "If she was, she never mentioned it to me." "Well, I am not an accurate judge of heights, but it seems to me that the tops of those columns must be at least 50 feet in the air", I said. "That is a good estimate, Melvin, but I was never concerned about my safety because there was plenty of scaffolding surrounding our work area along with strong safety fences and applying the plaster to the columns was a relatively easy task. Interestingly enough, the columns look as good today as they did in 1925, 18 years ago", said Daddy.

The signal light turned green and I shifted into first gear and then through second gear on my way to high as we drove west on 'A' Street. At the corner of 'A' Street and San Antonio Avenue, next to the 'Jim Dandy Food Market', I turned left when I remembered that Elm Street dead ended into San Antonio Avenue a mile or so ahead and I could get back home more directly that way. We crossed over the Southern Pacific and Union Pacific railroad tracks again and continued down the avenue passing the two Selfrige Company citrus packing houses between the tracks. Oranges and lemons were still big crops in those pre-war days. Although Daddy was quiet on the way home, I could sense from his demeanor that he was pleased that he and I could at least spend a few hours enjoying each other's company. Passing by the 400-acre Armstrong Nursery propagating plant, we arrived at the Elm Street connection and I turned left toward 459 which was the equivalent of one city block away. Arriving at Daddy's driveway, I turned in and parked adjacent to the front concrete porch that my brother, father and I had built a few years earlier. The minutes were ticking away and it would soon be time for me to leave. "Daddy, I'm going to go in and pack my things and get ready to head out for San Diego", I said. "I hate to see you go, Son, but I realize that you don't have any choice in the matter at this point", replied Daddy. Leaving Daddy at the Ford, I slipped through the front door and walked to my bedroom and packed my extra uniform, shoes and remaining clothes for the return trip to San Diego. Marvin and Ida Mae were away playing with their neighborhood friends so I didn't get a chance to tell them good-bye. Passing through the kitchen, I gave Mom a big hug and kiss and she walked with me out the back door and around to the front porch where the Ford was parked. Daddy was still there, now with an Eastman Kodak Box Camera, and he took several photographs as I was preparing to leave. I hugged Mom again and then placed my arms around my father to tell him good-bye. Although he worked hard every day at the General Electric Company, as well as caring for his farm, he seemed more frail than I remembered in times past. At that point he was 42 years old. "Good-bye, Daddy, I'll try to get back in a few weeks for another weekend visit and I thank you for accompanying me to Wade Weeks' Shell Station", I said. "You are more than welcome, and Mom and I will look forward to that day, Son, and you be sure to take care of yourself", replied Daddy. "I have always done what you tell me to do and I see no reason to change now", I joked. Letting Daddy go, I gave Mom one more hug and kiss and climbed into the Ford and started the engine. Backing out of the driveway, I turned west toward San Antonio Avenue for the road to San Diego lay in that direction. I could see Mom and Daddy waving good-bye until I turned the corner at San Antonio Avenue and lost sight of them behind a nursery greenhouse.

1600 Sunday
18 April 1943
Leaving Home for San Diego

I turned north on San Antonio Avenue and drove to 'A' Street where I turned left toward Pomona six miles away. In the middle of Pomona, I noticed a favorite hangout, 'Mel's Diner'. The diner specialized in selling fifteen-cent hamburgers and it was always a busy place. I stopped in and bought two hamburgers, plus a coke, which I would consume along the way to San Diego. Getting back on the highway, I soon reached the western boundary of Pomona where I turned south to pick up the Brea Canyon Highway to retrace the route that my helpful angel, driving her Pontiac sedan, had followed in bringing me home to Ontario three days earlier. As I approached La Habra, I came upon the oil fields with their derricks and engines pumping crude oil out of the ground. Passing through Brea, I soon came to Santa Ana and then Orange, and later San Juan Capistrano and then San Clemente on the coast road which I followed the remaining distance to San Diego. By the time I reached Oceanside, I had finished the hamburgers, but was still hungry, so I stopped and bought a sandwich and a coke at a roadside diner and continued driving while I ate my food.

During my travels while hitchhiking last Friday, I had not paid much attention to the names of the many small towns that I had passed through. It was a different story on the return trip. All of the names were strange to me, but I tried to memorize each of them for I knew that on future liberty trips to Ontario I would be passing through them again and again. After Oceanside, I came to Carlsbad, Solano Beach, Del Mar, La Jolla and then finally San Diego and the Navy boot camp. As soon as I saw the boot camp main gate, I knew exactly where I was. I drove by the entrance gate and then drove beyond it for three blocks before turning right on a side street that seemed like a good candidate for parking in the local neighborhood. It was far enough removed from the boot camp gate to avoid casual perusal by Navy personnel, but close enough for convenient access when I needed the Ford, which would be this coming Friday, to pick up sweetheart Lucille at the Santa Fe Railroad Depot. I parked the Ford making certain that I did not infringe upon someone's driveway, locked the car and then, bag in hand, walked the few blocks to the entrance gate where I reported in from liberty. Upon showing my liberty pass, the shore patrol petty officer passed me onto the base where I soon found my barracks and went to my bunk and crashed till morning reveille.

0800 Monday
19 April 1943
Navy Boot Camp
San Diego, California

Although I slept soundly enough, I did not really feel rested when reveille broke the silence early Monday morning. Rousing myself, I headed for the shower and then dressed for the day not remembering what was in store for us recruits that day. It turned out to be more marching drills on the grinder where we spent from 0900 to 1200 hours marching to the music of the Navy band. Being in the second platoon and among the shortest recruits, it was impossible to stay 'in step' and still maintain the proper alignment and spacing with the taller men at the front of each column. In essence, the shorter men, like myself, had to more or less 'skip along' to increase our stride to have some semblance of order among the rows at the end of the second platoon that included me and a couple of dozen other short sailors. I never did learn the reason that the Navy had for placing the tall sailors at the front and us short guys at the rear of the columns. Precision marching was a fetish with the Navy for reasons never quite explained to our satisfaction; but we did our best to accommodate the company commander's wishes. We tried all the more diligently when it was learned that the company winning the marching drill contest, to be held in a week, would be given extra liberty privileges. Unfortunately, as we would learn later, the prize would go to another company, worse luck.

1300 Monday
19 April 1943
Navy Boot Camp
San Diego, California

Between 1300 and 1600 today, the company was exposed to marine knot-tying exercises. From that activity, I learned to tie the bowline knot which, in my lifetime, came to be the most useful knot I have ever known. The bowline knot is exceedingly strong and has the unique characteristic of being easily untied, regardless of how much tension has been applied to the knot. It is also an exceedingly secure knot too, inasmuch as it will never slip or "self destruct" like some of the other knots that we were taught to tie.

After we were dismissed for the day, I hurried over to the Boot Camp Communications Office to place a telephone call to my mother. I was anxious to learn when Lucille would arrive. On the Navy Base, long distance telephone calls were placed by an attendant and then connected to a designated telephone booth when the called party was on the line. After giving Mom's telephone number, I sat down in a chair next to the designated telephone booth to wait. Five minutes later, the telephone rang and I hurried to answer. "Hello", I said. "Hello, Melvin, how nice to hear your voice!", replied my mother. "Same here, Mom. Are you feeling well?", I asked. "Oh, yes, I feel fine and so does Daddy.

I expect that you want to learn of the schedule for Lucille's arrival", she offered. "Indeed I do. I don't want to leave her stranded alone at the Santa Fe Railroad Depot on Friday", I replied. "It turns out that Lucille's train #409 arrives in San Diego at 7 p.m.", (1900 Navy time) said Mom. I quickly made an entry in my pocket notebook so I would not forget the details of what Mom had told me. "Thank you very much for running interference for me on this. There simply wasn't time enough to handle this by means of letter writing", I said. "Not to worry, Son, I am only too happy to assist young love in any way that I can. And when you see Lucille on Friday don't forget to give her our love", concluded Mom. "I will be certain to do just that, Mom. I am sorry that I have some other things that need my attention so I must hang up now", I said. "Dad sends his love and we will talk again soon, Melvin. Take good care of yourself", said Mom as she hung up her telephone. With the line having gone dead, I hung up the receiver. I left the booth and walked to the attendant to await notice of the cost of the long distance call. A short time later, I learned that the call cost me $1.25 which I gladly paid and then returned to my barracks. Although I usually wrote Lucille a letter every day, I elected to forego that nicety today with the realization that she would arrive here in just four days. She would likely not receive any letter written today before she left home. Even though I would be seeing Lucille in just a few days, I longed to hear her voice and took the occasion after speaking with Mom to call Lucille's telephone number at home. It turned out that she was not home so after a brief conversation, I told her mother to please give Lucille a kiss for me.

1830 Friday
23 April 1943
Santa Fe Depot
San Diego, California

The next four days passed by in a blur as the recruits of Company 43-119 went about the business of becoming productive sailors in Uncle Sam's Navy. On Friday, with the duty day having ended and the liberty period having commenced, I packed my small bag and headed for the main gate. Arriving there, I offered my liberty pass to the duty shore patrol petty officer and he waved me through. Leaving the main gate, I turned in the direction of my 1936 Ford automobile. I found the Ford safe and sound exactly where I had left it five days earlier, albeit somewhat the worse for wear due to a coating of dirt and dust that had been blown in by the prevailing westerly winds on the peninsula and turned into mud by the moisture delivered in the early morning fog banks each day. One evening next week, after Lucille has gone home, I will take the Ford and have it washed and waxed, I decided. The battery was fully charged during the return trip from Ontario a week earlier so I started the engine and allowed it to warm up for a few minutes before putting it in gear and slowly easing away from the curb. Because of its Spanish Style Architecture as well as its age, the Santa Fe Railroad Depot serving San Diego is listed on the nation's National Register of Historic Landmarks. I found it directly and parked in the adjacent parking lot designated for patrons. I actually had arrived a few minutes early, so I left the Ford and walked to trackside where I sat down on a bench among other individuals waiting for the arrival of Train #409 scheduled to arrive at 1900. And, right on time, the presence of the train became apparent from the engineer blowing his piercing air horn for several grade crossings a few blocks west of the depot. Smoke could be seen rising from the diesel electric engines and the sleek streamline shape of the red and silver Santa Fe ALCO (American Locomotive Company) Diesel Locomotive loomed out of the trackside haze as the train rolled noisily into the depot amid the roar of its noisy engines and the metallic screech and hiss of its air brakes.

After the train had stopped, three coaches away, I noticed the conductor place his step box on the depot platform and instantly realized that that was the door where Lucille would appear, so, avoiding other individuals lining up to meet loved ones, I hurried along the platform to wait for Lucille by the step box. I waited impatiently as about 30 passengers left the doorway, but where was Lucille? In due course the passengers leaving the coach vestibule became fewer and fewer; then I saw Lucille move into the vestibule and I waved excitedly to her. Lucille waved back behind a huge smile and, carrying her overnight bag, she climbed down the coach steps. I hurried to the steps, brushing in front of the conductor, and relieved her of her bag and set it down on the platform while, at the same time, sweeping her into my arms and giving her a resounding kiss and whispering in her ear "You are so beautiful and I love you so much." I then said aloud. "Welcome to San Diego, sweetheart". "It is so nice to be here, Whitey", Lucille replied. "Come this way, my Ford is just on the other side of the depot". Taking her arm and carrying her bag, I led Lucille to my car. I placed her bag in the trunk after opening the passenger side door and helping her inside. Climbing behind the steering wheel, I said, "Our hotel, the Chalfont Arms, is what travel agents term a residential hotel and is only a block away. This hotel caters to both long term tenants as well as folks who just want a room for a few nights. I took the liberty of booking two rooms, so I won't have to run back and forth between the hotel and the Navy Base". "What a wonderful idea, Whitey. That has to mean that I won't have a chance to become lonely during my stay", enthused Lucille. "That is exactly what I had in mind when I set up your accommodations. The travel agent at the Navy Base was quite helpful to me in setting up our rooms. She was able to obtain rooms for us that cost less than the civilian rate for similar accommodations. So, being a U.S. Sailor was worth money in my pocket", I said with a grin.

1930 Friday
23 April 1943
Chalfont Arms Hotel
San Diego, California

With the initial pleasantries behind us, I started the engine and slowly moved the Ford out into local traffic heading toward the Chalfont Arms Hotel, a block east of the Santa Fe Depot. Arriving at the hotel, I drove down the private parking ramp and parked beneath the hotel in the space reserved for guests along the rear wall of the basement parking garage. Walking to Lucille's side, I opened her door and assisted her as she stepped out of the car. "The elevator is over there", I said, pointing to my right. "You can wait there while I get our luggage from the trunk". Carrying the bags to the elevator door, I pushed the call button and a minute later the elevator doors opened. "We're on our way", I said, easing Lucille in beside me. The door closed and I took the privacy of the empty cab as an opportunity to steal another kiss from my sweetheart which she enthusiastically returned.

The door opened on the main floor lobby and we left the elevator as I carried our luggage to the registration desk. I filled out the registration cards for the two rooms and paid the clerk the required room charges. "Here are your keys, you will find your rooms on the fourth floor, oceanside. The view is nice from there", observed the clerk. A bellman was summoned and we followed him to the elevator where we all entered. The bellman selected the fourth floor. After a very brief ride the doors opened, and he led us to his right down a long hallway. Coincidentally, Lucille's room number turned out to be #409, the same as her Santa Fe train number. Opening Lucille's room first, the bellman deposited her bag as she entered and then he opened my room #410 right next door. As he handed me the room keys, I tipped him as he left and he pulled the door closed behind him. There was a connecting door between our rooms and I gently tapped on it and Lucille opened her side again beaming her sweet pixie smile. "Here is the key to your room", I said handing over the key. "Did you have anything to eat on the train or should we go out and have a meal now?", I asked. "No, Whitey, I haven't eaten a thing since leaving LA; I was just too excited enjoying the ocean front scenery passing by to think about eating; I didn't want to miss a thing", replied Lucille. "Well, then, after you have had a chance to freshen up, we will go out for a nice meal. Take your time for there is no rush this evening", I advised. I pushed the connecting door almost closed, but not latched, so Lucille would have the privacy that young ladies prize so highly. For my part, I entered the bathroom and washed my face and checked to see that my dress blues uniform was presentable (which it was) and then splashed some 'Old Spice' aftershave lotion on my face.

Ten minutes later, Lucille tapped on the connecting door and pushed it open wearing a colorful halter-top dress and comfortable patent leather shoes. The glossy shine on her shoes would be the envy of any sailor in the Navy. A 'spit and polish' Navy shine could never equal the gloss that I saw on Lucille's patent leather shoes at that instant. What a wonderful sight to behold, I thought to myself. "How beautiful you look this evening, Miss Smith. It will be my pleasure to squire you around this town, or any other for that matter", I joked. "Why, thank you, kind sir, and I want you to know that flattery will get you everywhere", smiled an extremely happy Lucille Smith. Taking her hand, she passed through my door and I paused to lock it and checked that hers was locked as well. With everything secured we walked to the elevator where I pushed the call button.

The elevator soon arrived bearing an elderly couple who moved aside as the door opened and we entered. "Good evening" I said. "Hello, and that is a mighty beautiful young lady that you have beside you this evening", the gentleman complimented. "Oh, Albert, stop that. Can't you see that you're embarrassing the young lady?", said Albert's wife. "Of course, that was not my intention; I was merely putting into words what I perceive to be a very visible fact", replied Albert. "Thank you, sir. I appreciate your kind thought and do not find it offensive in the least", offered Lucille. "Thank you, young lady", replied Albert with a vindicated smile on his face. The elevator door opened again and the elderly couple stepped out first and we followed. "Are you hungry for anything special, sweetheart?", I asked. "No, not this evening.", replied Lucille. "In that case then, let's patronize the hotel restaurant and see how we like it", I suggested. The Shalfont Arms lobby was brightly illuminated and on the far side we could see other dinner guests entering the Flying Pig Restaurant. A very unusual name for a restaurant, I thought. I hoped that we were not making a mistake in our decision to have our meal in the hotel.

2030 Friday
23 April 1943
Chalfont Arms Hotel
Flying Pig Restaurant

For reasons that we never learned during our short stay at the Chalfont Arms, the restaurant was named the

'Flying Pig' and replica winged pigs were hanging from every conceivable place, along all four walls, surrounding every window, from the ceiling fans and lighting fixtures, over the fireplace mantle; and each table sported a winged pig at its center where it watched over the salt and pepper shakers as well as the sugar and catsup bottle. The Maitre d' met us at the entrance and led us to a table in the rear that offered at least a small amount of privacy. Leaving two menus he said, "I will return in a few minutes and take your orders." After he left, a wine steward arrived, but both Lucille and I declined to take any wine. Neither of us care for alcoholic beverages. Soft drinks are more our style. "Do you see something on the menu that catches your eye, honey?", I asked. "Yes, the listing of chicken and dumplings just caught my eye and I think that is what I will order, along with a house salad", replied Lucille. "The menu lists a shrimp salad and I think I will have that along with an order of onion rings since I am not too hungry", I said. True to his word, the Maitre d' returned and took our orders. Although there were a number of guests seated in the restaurant, none were close to our table. "Tell me, Lucille, what was the price of your train ticket?", I inquired. "Well, Whitey, it only came to 23 dollars and since you are paying for the two rooms, why don't you just let me pay my own train fare?", Lucille asked. "Thank you for the kind offer, sweetheart, but I promised to pay and here is your money", I said, handing over a twenty and three one-dollar bills. "Thank you, Whitey, but you really didn't have to do that", admonished Lucille with a frown. "No, my Daddy has always taught me that a promise is a promise to be kept so now we are square the way it should be. And on top of that, my mother says that one needs to learn to become a gracious receiver so as not to spoil the pleasure of another individual who feels disposed to give you a gift", I concluded. "And before I forget, Mom asked me to pass along her own and Dad's feelings of love for you." "Why, thank you, Whitey, it was sweet of her to share her own and your father's feelings toward me. I really consider myself blessed to be allowed to stay with them while I finish my schooling in Ontario."

At that time, the meals arrived atop a mobile food service cart and were served with a flourish. We ate in silence and enjoyed the food as well as each other's intimate company. What a treat it was to have my very own sweetheart in San Diego sitting across the dinner table from me. I had had enough of the company of sailors to last me for a while. Life couldn't get much better than this, I thought to myself. When she had finished eating I asked Lucille if she would care for some dessert. She declined and so did I. I paid the check and we left the 'Flying Pig' quite favorably impressed with the quality of the food and especially the excellent service. When we left the restaurant, I suddenly realized that the day had ended and that it was too late even to find a motion picture to view. "Sweetheart, it seems that we have run out of time this evening. Shall we call it a day and make some plans for tomorrow?", I asked. "Yes, I am a little tired anyway and would not be up to much more activity today", admitted Lucille. We walked to the elevator where I pushed the call button. The next elevator arrived quickly enough and once inside I pushed the button for the fourth floor. Getting out on the fourth floor we walked to our rooms where I kissed Lucille good-night at her door, and hugged her tightly as I repeated my favorite refrain, "I do love you so much".

When I released her, Lucille entered her room and locked the door saying "Good-night, Whitey" as the door latch 'clicked' into place. The stress of the day had taken its toll on me as well, and I was glad to merely enter my room and 'hit the hay' after brushing my teeth. I lay there for some time musing over what tomorrow might bring and thought that we might take the time to drive to Tijuana, Mexico, and do some sight-seeing along the way. The hotel bed was comfortable enough and sleep came easily with the knowledge that my very own Lucille was nearby and soon I would see her in my dreams.

0900 Saturday
24 April 1943
Chalfont Arms Hotel
San Diego, California

I had purposely not left a wake-up call with the hotel operator, but nevertheless the bright sunshine streaming into my room brought me wide awake anyway. It was already late by Navy standards, so I hopped out of bed and headed for the shower. Before entering the bathroom, however, I stopped long enough to enjoy the beautiful San Diego view of the blue Pacific Ocean from the window of my room. I could see breakers pounding the foaming surf and gaily-colored umbrellas sticking out of the sand with swimmers relaxing beneath them. Many picnic coolers were present and children were raiding them for cold drinks and sandwiches. Anxious to see Lucille, I literally tore myself away from the wonderful view and continued into the shower. The warm water felt good on my skin and I finished up with a stimulating cold-water rinse. Toweling dry, I grabbed my toothbrush and brushed my teeth.

The care of my teeth has always been exceedingly high on my priority list of routine personal hygiene tasks. The reason for this dates back to the year of 1935 when I saw my father lose all of his teeth to an incurable case of pyorrhea. Daddy was only 35 years old at the time, and on two successive weekends in June of that year the family accompanied Daddy to Long Beach, California (about a 50-mile drive one-way from Ontario) where his dental work was performed. All of his upper teeth were pulled on one weekend and his lower teeth on the following weekend. Mom packed a picnic lunch each weekend and we children played on the rings and long slide in a nearby park while Daddy was treated. After his gums had healed sufficiently, he received his temporary dentures which turned out to be his permanent teeth for he never followed up to obtain his permanent dentures. Whether this circumstance was caused by a lack of money, I do not know. But over the years, whenever his dentures would cause his gums to become irritated, he would merely take out his pocketknife and scrape away a small amount of material to relieve the irritation caused by friction. Of all things, his dentist's advertised name in radio commercial messages was 'Doctor Painless Parker'. My father could testify to the unhappy fact that losing all of one's teeth did not happen painlessly!

With the morning necessities attended to, I put on my dress blues uniform and was ready for whatever the day would bring. Walking out of the bathroom, I heard Lucille tapping on the connecting door so I yelled "Come on in, I'm dressed for company", Lucille replied "So am I", as she pushed the door open and walked in wearing a snazzy pair of slacks and a beautiful matching halter top blouse. "I have to say this, sweetheart, you certainly are a sharp dresser", I concluded, in all seriousness. "Thank you, my dear. It does my heart good to know that you appreciate the way that I dress", replied Lucille, smiling happily at the compliment.

"If you are so inclined, I thought that we might drive over to Tijuana, Mexico, for some sightseeing", I offered. "Oh, Whitey, I have never been there before, and to visit there sounds like so much fun", replied an excited Lucille. "Next question, shall we have breakfast in the hotel or eat along the way?", I asked. "Let's get on the road and eat along the way", replied Lucille, obviously in a hurry to live life to its fullest. Leaving our hotel rooms, we locked the doors and took the first elevator to the basement level where the Ford had resided overnight. Arriving at the car, I unlocked Lucille's door and she climbed in and I closed the door, but not before stealing my first kiss of the day. Climbing into the driver's seat, I started the engine and backed out of the parking space, turning as I did toward the exit ramp. Once we had reached curbside of the local street, I turned south toward Mexico expecting to follow the coast road all the way to the custom's station at the Mexican border. After the traffic thinned out beyond San Diego proper, I placed my arm around Lucille's shoulders and she moved closer to me and I was in heaven again. Ten miles beyond the San Diego city limits we saw the sign for 'Mom's Diner' peeking out from beneath a gigantic Chinese Elm tree and we quickly decided to pull in. The place appeared brand new and was clean as a pin. The primary structure was one of those stainless steel prefabricated enclosures that was designed to resemble the appearance of a railroad dining car and the shiny metal exterior glistened in the morning sun. A few fluffy white clouds were reflected, with some distortion, in the shiny metal exterior walls. Once inside we were met by a spotless black and white decor. Lucille and I took a booth as an elderly lady came to take our food orders. I recall wondering at the time as to whether or not she was the 'MOM' of 'MOM's Diner'. As it turned out, we never learned the answer to that question. Lucille checked the menu and ordered bacon and eggs and two pancakes. As hungry as I was, her meal sounded delicious to me and I doubled the order requesting milk to drink. Lucille merely wanted water to drink. The meals were delivered quickly enough and we were soon enjoying filling our tummies. When we had finished eating, I paid the cashier, leaving a tip on the table for the waitress, and we returned to the Ford and resumed our southbound journey. It was a beautifully clear, sunny day and we could see a wide expanse of ocean as we drove along not far from shore. In the distance we could see a group of six sailboats moving parallel to the shore with billowing sails in a stiff breeze.

1300 Saturday
24 April 1943
Tijuana, Mexico

After driving another 45 minutes we reached the custom's station at the border crossing, and were merely waved through the checkpoint without being stopped. I remembered later that it was only when leaving Mexico that one is stopped for any necessary U.S. Customs declaration payment. Once in Tijuana I drove slowly around town where we enjoyed observing a totally different culture. Most of the Mexican men were wearing wide brimmed sombreros while their ladies were attired in bright, multicolored blouses and skirts. Eventually, we decided to park and walk along the uniquely festooned streets with their colorful banners and native flags moving lazily in the warm breeze. I parked the Ford in an open area amid a dozen other cars from the U.S.A. and went to the passenger side to help Lucille out. As I did so, the method in my madness was to steal another kiss, which I did. Lucille understood the game and was an active participant to my absolute delight.

I held Lucille's soft hand, and as we walked along we came to a large area of gaily-decorated outdoor booths, with colorful flags flying, where local artists and artisans offered samples of their work for sale. There were silversmiths, coppersmiths, artistic painters, woodworkers, pewter metalsmiths, as well as rug weavers and basket makers and other crafts persons offering their wares from colorful individual booths. I noticed Lucille eyeing a pair of earrings of silver and turquoise. "May I purchase those earrings for you?", I asked. "I really love them, but they seem awfully expensive to me", replied Lucille. I spoke with the dealer, who was also the craftsman maker, and we agreed upon a price of ten dollars for the pair, which I thought was a bargain. Placing them in her hands, I said "Please put them on and enjoy them, sweetheart". Carefully, one ear at a time, Lucille placed the rings on her shapely ears. They looked beautiful against her soft, velvet skin. The dealer had a mirror in his display and I held it up in front of Lucille so that she could more fully appreciate how lovely her new earrings really were. "Oh, Whitey, thank you so very much. The earrings are even lovelier than I could have imagined", bragged Lucille. "You are more than welcome, darling, for it is my distinct pleasure to provide gifts for my one and only sweetheart", I replied. After more than three hours of visiting different booths we decided to return to the car and conclude our Mexican adventure. Arriving at the Ford, I unlocked the passenger-side door and helped Lucille into the car, stealing another kiss as the price of admission. Her pixie smile was ever in attendance. Lucille's demeanor was such as to make her an extremely easy person to L-O-V-E I thought. Taking my place behind the steering wheel, I started the engine and re-entered the local street traffic heading toward the California border crossing and the custom's checkpoint. There was a long line of automobiles returning to California so it took us the better part of an hour to arrive at the booth of a custom's agent. However, I did not object to the delay for, after all, I had my very own sweetheart beside me and the passage of time really was of no consequence to me at that moment. Finally pulling up to the custom's booth and stopping, the agent said, "Good-afternoon folks, and do you have anything to declare?", he asked in a very friendly voice. "The only purchase that we made was my fiancee's earrings which cost $10", I offered. "Well, sailor, you will be happy to know that you did not spend enough money to owe Uncle Sam anything", joked the U.S. Custom's Agent. "Have a pleasant trip home", he called as I drove through the gate into California 'The Land of Milk and Honey'.

As we traveled along the coast road, with the Pacific Ocean stretching to the far horizon, the sun was dropping ever lower in its westward journey, and I was most happy that we were returning to San Diego while there was still plenty of sunlight. "Lucille, what do you think about our returning to the hotel area and finding a movie that we haven't seen?", I asked. "I would like that very much. I don't get to see movies all that often anymore now that the Navy has taken you away. So, let's do it", agreed Lucille happily. I drove the posted speed limit and we were back in San Diego by 1730. Our Mexican sojourn was so much fun and kept us so busy that we had even forgotten to eat lunch, and that fact was about to catch up with us. In the block surrounding the hotel there were three theaters. After checking them all out, we elected to go see "Casablanca," starring Humphrey Bogart. After parking the Ford in the basement of our hotel, Lucille and I walked up the automobile ramp to the street and continued along the avenue and came upon a pushcart vendor selling hot dogs, and the fragrance of cooking meat was so overwhelming that I purchased one hot dog for each of us, as well as two cokes with which to slake our thirst. By the time we reached the motion picture theater, we had eaten our food. The movie began at 1830 and Lucille and I arrived at the theater in time to be seated before the film began. As in Hollywood previously, I had already seen the film, so I was more interested in making love to Lucille than in paying attention to the movie itself. I did not, however, make a nuisance of myself nor did I intrude upon Lucille's enjoyment of the film.

I held Lucille close throughout the film and she acknowledged my presence from time to time by turning her head so that I could kiss her lips. When the film ended, we were still hungry and stopped by the 'Flying Pig' restaurant and ordered ham and roast beef sandwiches to take to our rooms. We observed the fact that the 'Flying Pig' was doing a brisk Saturday evening business.

2100 Saturday
24 April 1943
Chalfont Arms Hotel
San Diego, California

Lucille and I returned to our rooms with the sandwiches, and a bottle of coke for each of us. We set up the impromptu meal on a small table in my room in front of a soft and very comfortable oversized leather-covered couch. The sandwiches were accompanied by potato chips and bread-and-butter pickles, and to our near empty stomachs it was a veritable feast, what with the effect of our hot dogs having long since disappeared during the movie. When we had finished the sandwiches, I called room service and ordered two pieces of apple pie for our dessert. The pie arrived within 15 minutes, and it was very delicious and a fitting end to our otherwise limited meal. I tipped the bellman who delivered the pie, and he left with a smile on his face. With our meal consumed, I turned on the hotel provided FM radio to a local 'easy listening' station which, at that moment, was playing mostly WWII love songs. Quite apropos, Lucille and I both thought. Tramping around Tijuana the entire day had taken more out of us than either of us had realized, and relaxing on the couch with her head on my lap, Lucille fell fast asleep. The music continued to play and I became drowsy myself, and did not attempt to resist the urge to sleep. Leaning back against the soft couch cushion, I closed my eyes and drifted off into a dream world. When I was awakened later, as Lucille stirred in her sleep, my wrist watch was indicating 0100 and I realized that I had been sleeping for about four hours. Now somewhat rested, I was afraid to move for fear of waking Lucille. In the end, however, I decided that it would be best to wake her anyway so she could climb into the soft bed in her room and sleep more comfortably for the rest of the night. Gently cradling Lucille's head, I slowly scooted sideways along the couch cushion, eventually escaping, and then I lowered Lucille's head onto a small pillow that I obtained from the head of my bed. Still, Lucille did not wake up, so I obtained a blanket from the closet and covered her up deciding, on my own, that her sleep should not be interrupted.

For my part, I was still tired and went to the bathroom and brushed my teeth and dressed for bed. Walking from the bathroom, I could see that Lucille was still in a calm but deep sleep. I decided to leave the small desk lamp illuminated, so that if she awoke later on, Lucille would be able to see where she was and would not become frightened in a strange location. Before climbing into bed, I checked once again to make certain that the blanket over Lucille was covering her completely. I also decided to leave the radio playing as I found the music to be soothing and restful. Checking her one last time, I was satisfied that Lucille was comfortable and then I climbed into bed and relaxed. It was then going on 0200 hours. In no time at all, I began to dream about our Mexican journey and lapsed into a dreamy unconscious state.

Perhaps an hour or so later, I was awakened by a movement next to me in bed. I roused myself enough to realize that Lucille had moved from the couch into my bed and was then quietly relaxing beside me. Since the bed was 'king size' we were not crowded. At first, I did not know what to think since I had never visualized a circumstance where a beautiful woman was in my bed at night. Lucille cuddled close to me and I placed my arm around her and felt the warmth of her body against mine. She lay still and I was afraid to move for fear that it was all just a dream and would instantly disappear if I moved at all. But, it was not a dream as my arm around her soft body could attest. Not knowing exactly what to do, I merely lay still and tried to get back to sleep myself. Although the spirit was willing, my brain simply would not calm down enough to allow sleep to overtake me. So, I just lay there and listened to Lucille's slow, steady, breathing.

An hour passed by, and then two, and still Lucille was in a deep sleep. But that was fine with me, for at least I could rest in this comfortable position with my arm wrapped loosely around Lucille. The time was going on 0400 the last time I looked and dawn would soon be breaking. At last, I decided to make one final attempt at sleeping and I began breathing deeply, thinking that an increased supply of oxygen in my lungs might aid my quest for sleep. Whether or not it helped I do not know, but I was finally able to fall into what I would describe as a fitful sleep. It was an uncomfortable sleep inasmuch as the dream that presented itself seemed too farfetched to be real. Some time later, Lucille turned in bed and laid her hand on my face. I was awake instantly. "Are you feeling all right, sweetheart?", I said. "Oh, yes, I feel fine and thank you so much for covering me up with that nice soft blanket". "You are quite welcome, darling", I replied. As we spoke, I eventually became aware of the fact that Lucille was absolutely naked. Since she was facing me, the warm skin that I had been feeling for lo these many hours was actually that of Lucille's slender back. "Whitey, I want you to make love to me", pleaded Lucille. "Lucille, do you realize what you are asking?" I inquired, more than a little dumbfounded. "Yes, I do. I just know that I love you so much that I will not be satisfied until we make love to each other whether married or not", replied Lucille. "Well, Lucille, you need to know that I am a virgin and may not understand just exactly how a man should treat a woman at such a time", I replied. "The truth of the matter is, then, that we are both virgins", admitted Lucille. "As the saying goes, it will be fine if we just do what comes naturally", encouraged Lucille. "And, for the record, I know that I am not in season so there is no fear of my becoming pregnant".

The butterflies in my stomach were creating an unremitting storm that seemingly would not soon subside.

I had been in love with Lucille for so many years that I had finally lost track of the number, but I had never gotten beyond daydreaming about making love to her one day in the distant future after we were married. With her naked charms here in my bed, it seemed that the time for day dreaming had finally ended and the real world was about to take over. There was enough light from the small desk lamp that I could see her wonderful face and I moved my hand up the small of her back and pulled her head toward me until our lips touched; what a magical sensation as my heart rate doubled at once. With our lips together, we explored each other's tongue while I also explored with my hands the tender breasts now facing toward me. The divine fragrance of her perfume captivated me. I thought, nothing ventured, nothing gained, as I rolled Lucille onto her back while at the same time, I slipped out of my PJ's. Next, I kissed her plump breasts, noticing as I did that her pink nipples became erect at once and her breathing came in short gasps. Lucille moved closer to facilitate my caressing her warm body with my hands. My heart was beating so hard that I thought it would burst, and during a dreamy kiss, Lucille pulled me on top of her and we made love for the very first time. As it turned out, Lucille and I reached our sexual climax simultaneously and it was a supremely exquisite sensation. In the following moments, I lay still, nestled beside Lucille's warm body, as she gasped to regain her own breathing stability. "Well, I know the answer now, Whitey, You are a great lover despite the newness of it all and our virginal limitations", smiled a spent but contented Lucille. "Was one time enough for you, Lucille?", I asked. "I think so; why don't we get some more sleep and then try for a repeat performance later on". "That suits me just fine" I said, as I gazed at Lucille's lovely body while continuing to fondle her firm breasts. By then, the world outside was turning bright and Lucille and I snuggled closely together, spent as we were, and closed our eyes to all but the arms of Morpheus.

1100 Sunday
25 April 1943
Chalfont Arms Hotel
San Diego, California

Lucille was the first to leave her dream world and become fully awake. She found herself totally immersed in a sense of awe at her all-consuming love for me, and mine for her. Her sleep, although inadequate, had totally rejuvenated her body. It was her impression that such a quality of intense love could not help but energize a person's body. As she lay there studying me as I continued in a peaceful sleep, she moved to lay her hand lightly upon my chest to see if that act would wake me. For my part, the touch of her warm, soft hand brought me awake immediately. I slowly opened my eyes and allowed them to feast upon my sweetheart laying naked in bed beside me. "Wow, what a sleep I had. If that is what love can do for you, I want lots more of it", I exclaimed, wearing a supremely contented smile. "You won't get any argument from me on that score for I agree with you wholeheartedly. I suspected that making love to you would be wonderfully nice, but I found that making love with you far exceeded my expectations, I'm here to tell you", said Lucille "You know, another surprising revelation is the fact that I really love how your body feels next to mine. It is almost as though there is electricity passing between the two of us as we are making love", I revealed. Fully awake now, Lucille and I enjoyed the warmth of our relationship, and then Lucille posed a question. "Honey, do you think that there is any reason why we should get up and get dressed today?", she asked somewhat timidly. "With the day already half gone, the answer to your question has to be 'not only no, but hell no'", I joked. "We will not starve because we can order our meals from room service and I can just pull on a housecoat to let them deliver the food", volunteered Lucille. "Then let there be more love in the world and we shall help make it", I replied.

And that is exactly what the two lovers did for the rest of the daylight hours of Sunday; they made love again and again to their hearts content and mutual delight. Toward sundown, Whitey remembered that he had to be back on the Navy Base by 0600 the following morning and thus could not see his sweetheart off at the train station. "Lucille, I regret to tell you that I have to return to the Navy Base by 0600 in the morning so I will be unable to see you off at your train. Would you be agreeable to going to sleep now and I will leave a wake-up call for 0430 at which time I will 'love you to pieces' and then be on my way back to the Navy and you can take a taxi to the train station", asked Whitey. "That's what I love most about you, Whitey. It just goes to show that I am in love with a person with innovative, yet very practical ideas. That is a fabulous idea and I'm all for it", concluded Lucille. "No sooner said than done", quipped Whitey as he called the hotel operator and left a wake-up call for 0430. "Oh, the sacrifices we make for the sake of love", joked a happy and contented Lucille. "I can tell you that I will not have to be rocked to sleep this evening", smiled Whitey, and he was serious. "Me neither", responded Lucille. Falling into bed Whitey leaned over and gave Lucille a good-night kiss on her lips and each of her lovely breasts. "What a way to end such a memorable day, and I loved it", smiled Lucille. With the lights turned out, the lovers were asleep almost as soon as their heads hit their pillows.

0430 Monday
26 April 1943
Chalfont Arms Hotel
San Diego, California

Promptly at 0430, the hotel operator rang the telephone in Whitey's room. He quickly answered the call and then ran into the bathroom to answer nature's call, brush his teeth and then quickly took a shower. Hurrying as fast as he could, Whitey towel dried and then left the bathroom for his sweetheart to attend to similar needs. Lucille, somewhat sleepily, followed Whitey's lead. Returning to bed, Lucille and Whitey embraced, after which Whitey commented in a joking manner, "I have the feeling that this lovemaking session comes under the heading of 'having one for the road". "Yes, you might say that", agreed a giggling Lucille. With time being of the essence, Whitey kissed Lucille on her mouth and breasts and for the next two hours, they made love in their own private paradise. Lucille felt tingling waves of ecstatic pleasure run up and down her spine and Whitey could feel the shivers of repetitive pleasure course through Lucille's body as they satisfied each other's passion.

As the climax of their lovemaking subsided, Whitey lay next to Lucille and kissed her sweet lips. "I would love to spend the entire day with you, like yesterday, sweetheart, but duty calls", said a forlorn Whitey. And with that, Whitey ran into the bathroom and jumped into the shower for his second bath of the morning. Fifteen minutes later he was dressed and packed for his departure. Before leaving, Whitey gave Lucille money for her taxi and train fares, and included enough for her meals on board the train, and thanked her for making the trip to San Diego, and more importantly, making his life worth living by her loving him. Holding Lucille tightly in his arms, Whitey kissed her for the last time and wished her a safe journey home. "Whitey, I want to thank you again for the beautiful gift of my new earrings." "You are more than welcome, sweetheart, and I assure you that I positively enjoyed purchasing them for you Please write to me when you can, and I will do the same. And remember that you are my one and only sweetheart, and I love you so much", were Whitey's parting words. Whitey returned to the Navy base in a daze with visions of Lucille dancing before his eyes as he drove along the deserted San Diego street in front of the hotel. Not long after, having parked his car near the Navy boot camp in the same place as before, Whitey walked to the main gate and was on hand for the routine morning muster of his platoon. However, his mind was still playing back the memories of the most fantastic weekend of his young, 18-year old life. More than ever, he wished that the war was over so that he and Lucille could be married immediately. During the weeks that followed Lucille's visit, Whitey experienced great difficulty concentrating on the lessons being offered by his boot camp instructors. During this period, in the absence of anyone using his nickname of "Whitey", his personal identity slowly reverted to Melvin Eugene Hacker, Apprentice Seaman, Serial Number 565-16-19. He made daily telephone calls to speak with his sweetheart and learned that her trip home had been lonely, but otherwise uneventful. Of course, he and Lucille continued to correspond by letter continuously.

0800 Monday
10 May 1943
U. S. Navy Point Loma Radar School
San Diego, California

I survived boot camp as an apprentice seaman with no other structural Navy rating, but happily received orders to attend the Navy RADAR Training School located in San Diego, California, on the nearby Point Loma Peninsula. In fact, the school was just a short distance down the street from where I had been parking my 1936 Ford. This peninsular coastal location was an ideal vantage point for teaching the new RADAR technology as it provided an unobstructed view of the surrounding ocean, and any ships traveling along the coast served as real-time moving targets for the students to practice their target tracking fundamentals. All the students were housed in a barracks on the boot camp grounds and hauled by Navy bus to and from the school each day. The close proximity of the Navy Boot Camp also facilitated students being shuttled between the school and boot camp for meal service as well. Because the RADAR technology was extremely new and absolutely SECRET, the school was under the protection of heavily-armed security guards 24 hours a day. Students were not permitted to discuss any aspect of their training with their family or friends and were required to report any unsolicited contact by any individual seeking information about the school and its activities. At the same time, students were not allowed to remove any technical, operational or other RADAR documents from the school for study at their barracks or elsewhere. All necessary study time was accommodated during normal school hours of operation from 0800 to 1700. Fortunately for me, no one ever attempted to query me about RADAR and its technical details at all.

One of the fringe benefits that I enjoyed most while attending the RADAR school was the 24-hour-a-day access to a machine dispensing bottles of Coca Cola. No matter when our duty times were assigned, Coke was always available. The neat, but unusual, aspect of the school's Coke machine was that its thermostat was set to such a low temperature that the glass bottles that we received from our five-cent coin deposit were filled with frozen 'coke slush'. In the absence of cups or other containers, the slush guaranteed that the 'coke slush' would stay cold for a very long time making ice cubes unnecessary. I found that a frozen bottle of 'coke' would stay cold for at least an hour. It is interesting to note here the fact that, 64 years later, 'coke slush' is a widely available frozen delight in many 'fast food' places.

A typical RADAR System in 1943 was comprised of a six or seven-foot tall relay rack in which slide-out drawers were provided for maintenance access to the various tubes, blowers, and other electronic components of a given system. Due to the extremely high radio frequencies involved, energy to and from the remotely mounted rotating antennas was conveyed through rigid wave guides (essentially rectangular or circular metal pipes that were silver plated on their interior surfaces to minimize the loss of radio electromagnetic energy to the greatest extent possible). To safeguard against moisture penetration of the wave guide and the attendant degradation of the reflected signal, a small compressor applied a few atmospheres of pressure of an inert gas to assure that any leak that occurred would be revealed more or less instantaneously and send the electronic technicians on a hunt for the leak. The standard leak detection kit consisted of a small bottle of a mixture of liquid soap and water and a small artist's paintbrush. If the compressor continued to turn on frequently, technicians would visit each wave guide coupling and apply a liberal coating of soapy water and observations would be made for the telltale bubbles that would reveal the presence of a leak. Fortunately, leaks were a rare occurrence.

The radio frequency energy of the 1943 systems was generated by magnetron vacuum tubes. These special tubes were mounted within an extremely strong horseshoe permanent magnet that radiated the magnetic field that was required for proper magnetron operation. In addition to the associated relay rack, each RADAR system was provided with an operator control console (about the size of a small student desk) that included indicator cathode ray tubes which permitted the operator to interpret the reflected signal received from any target detected by the RADAR beam of high frequency radio energy. The word RADAR is a contraction of the phrase 'Radio Detection and Ranging'. Thus, RADAR operates on the basis of a radio transmitter sending out thousands of extremely brief but powerful pulses of radio energy per second, and between pulses, when the transmitter is silent, an extremely sensitive receiver is automatically activated to provide an indication of any energy that is reflected back from a target that is encountered by the focused radio beam. Knowing the time that the pulse left the antenna and the speed with which a radio beam travels (186,000 nautical miles per second), the distance to a given target is easily and automatically determined. Its direction from the ship is read off directly from the RADAR beam compass rose showing exactly where the remotely mounted antenna is pointing.

When RADAR systems were initially introduced into the fleet in WWII, there were medical concerns relative to the health impact of the high frequency radio energy upon members of the RADAR operating crew. For this reason, we were initially required to wear radiation sensitive badges while on duty. These badges were processed from time to time and reviewed by Navy doctors to ascertain whether or not the observed radiation exposure represented a health hazard. After 12 months, use of the badges was discontinued when it was determined that no health hazard existed. Nevertheless, warnings were posted prohibiting RADARmen from exposing themselves to the intense radio energy field existing at the output end of the wave guide mounted at the center of the rotating tower-mounted antenna. Typically, RADARmen were prohibited from visiting the RADAR antenna while a system was turned on.

Mounted on the RADAR control console are two cathode ray tubes that serve the same function as the 'picture tube' of a television set. One is designated as the 'A' scope and allows the operator to quickly determine the distance to a given target appearing on the scope as well as its location. When an operator observes an unknown target, the antenna drive motor is turned off and the beam is manually swept back and forth over the target, while the operator observes the 'A' scope while looking for a peak reading of the target's reflected energy. The peak reading occurs when the antenna is pointing directly at the center of the target, at which time the operator reads the compass bearing of the target on the associated compass rose. At the same time, the operator turns a crank to align the range step in the trace with the reflected target, and then reads off the distance on the associated counter calibrated in yards. The distance and direction are called out to the duty RADAR man responsible for plotting targets at the moment. The second indicator on the console is also a cathode ray tube, but it is arranged to give a polar (aerial) view of the ocean area surrounding the ship. This CRT is known as a PPI scope or 'Plan Position Indicator'. The radio beam is represented on the PPI scope as a white line originating at the center of the scope that rotates in synchronism with the tower mounted RADAR antenna. The persistence of the phosphors applied to the inner surface of the PPI scope is such that any target that is detected by the system remains visible on the screen after the beam passes by, and the target intensity is refreshed with each subsequent sweep of the target by the RADAR beam. A movable reticule is provided around the perimeter of the scope so that the relative bearing of a given target can be quickly determined and reported to the officer of the deck as well as the duty RADAR man responsible for plotting all targets. Compass bearings of targets are usually reported with reference to their location with respect to the bow of the ship. Considering the bow as zero degrees, a target off the stern would be identified at

180 degrees, while a target off the port beam (left side of the ship for readers not familiar with nautical terms) would be at 270 degrees, while the starboard equivalent would lay at 090 degrees. Although the antennas are normally switched on to rotate continuously, the operator may, at any time, turn the drive motor off and turn a hand crank to manually move the antenna as mentioned above. Manual scanning is employed to obtain a more accurate range and bearing of a given target once it appears on the PPI scope and target tracking has been initiated. It should be noted that the ship is depicted in the exact center of the PPI scope at the origination of the beam trace. There is a rough range feature built into the PPI scope that permits an operator to turn a switch that causes equally spaced range markers to be overlaid on the CRT. The markers show up as bright concentric circles and permit an operator to estimate the range to a given target without having to stop the antenna from rotating. This is a particularly useful feature when the screen is filled with many targets and it is necessary to quickly evaluate the threat potential of the nearest target. Of course, where maximum accuracy is required, manual scanning of a target is employed for target plotting purposes. RADAR operators are trained to identify various types of targets such as aircraft, surface ships, buildings, land masses, large birds and submarine periscopes, to name a few of the potential targets.

As mentioned earlier, RADAR classes also took their meals at the boot camp commissary. Schooling at Point Loma involved learning the technical theory of RADAR as well as its operation, and included nighttime duty assignments where we were required to man fire control RADAR equipment in the midnight to 0700 timeframe several times each week. Fire Control RADAR differed from Surface Search RADAR in that it contained a feature identified as 'lobeing' that increased the accuracy in pointing the antenna at a target. The lobeing system separated the RADAR beam into two separate beams of energy. Rather than depend upon returned target intensity, the lobeing system presented two target indications on a scope and the antenna was merely moved until the target indications were of equal height to obtain an exact position of the target.

All students were taught the operation of Surface Search RADAR (with an effective range of slightly more than the horizon approximately 25 miles distant), Air Search RADAR (with an effective range of several hundred miles) and Fire Control RADAR that was limited to a range of about 25 miles). Interestingly enough, I was never assigned to a ship that was equipped with Fire Control RADAR. The reason for that circumstance was the fact that troop transports, (on which I served my entire Navy career), were not equipped with guns that were larger than five inches and were always under the protection of capital ships of the Line that were equipped with the latest in Fire Control RADAR technology.

With the curriculum emphasis on RADAR operation, the School did not teach any technical subjects dealing with RADAR maintenance. The single exception to this rule was found in the indoctrination of new operators in the important necessity of performing daily inspections and cleaning of the air filters associated with the RADAR systems. Cooling air for the magnetron tubes required filtering to prevent airborne contaminants from entering the electronic equipment. Inspection and cleaning of the filters was a daily task, the results of which were entered into the RADAR equipment maintenance log, with filter replacement being dependent upon the number of hours of filter use. The accumulation of dust and dirt in our filters always amazed me inasmuch as one would expect to see very little contaminants far out to sea as we generally were. Nevertheless, air borne foreign matter was always present in our shipboard environment.

0800 Tuesday
6 July 1943
San Diego, California
Santa Fe Railroad Depot

Upon graduating from the Navy RADAR School, I was promoted to the rating of third class RADARman and given orders to travel to San Francisco to report aboard the U.S.S. Zeilin, which was an attack troop transport (APA-3). My journey began at the Santa Fe Railroad Depot in San Diego (the same depot where I had met sweet Lucille lo those many weeks before). Traveling from San Diego to San Francisco turned out to be a memorable, albeit distasteful, experience in and of itself. I received a travel voucher for coach passage on the Santa Fe Railroad between San Diego and Los Angeles, where I transferred to what was to have been a Pullman sleeper coach continuing on to San Francisco via the Southern Pacific Railroad. However, upon arriving at the Los Angeles Union Station, the conductor of my train on the Southern Pacific Railroad claimed that there had been a mix-up in my orders for travel and that I would be carried in coach class as there were no empty sleeper compartments available on the train. To this very day, I believe that the railroad company merely sold my compartment to some civilian who was willing to pay an extra fare price for what should have been my sleeping compartment. Adding insult to injury, the coach to which I was assigned was equipped with 12 flat wheels occasioned by a heavy-handed engineer applying his brakes too energetically somewhere along the line, causing the wheels to lockup and slide on the rails, thus burning flat spots in each of the twelve wheels on which our coach was suspended. In transit, the thumping chorus of those flat wheels sounded as though there were a dozen or more angry blacksmiths pounding on anvils beneath the coach floor. Absolutely no one among the 75 servicemen and women riding in that coach got any sleep that July night in 1943. Fortunately, I had kept my sea bag with me and decided to remove my pea coat, roll it up into a pillow, and then laid my blanket on the dirty floor between two seats and rested the best I could. How I longed for a pair of ear plugs with which to exclude the wheel noise penetrating the floor of the coach.

With the train schedules being as irregular as they were, I was unable to see Lucille when I passed through Los Angeles. However, I was able to call her on the telephone and we enjoyed a 30-minute conversation during which I again professed my undying love for her, and at the same time Lucille pledged her love to me. Wedding plans were discussed briefly, but not finalized at that time. Twelve hours later, the train pulled into the Southern Pacific Depot, and I had arrived in San Francisco, finally bringing my nocturnal ordeal to an end.

I had mailed the keys to my 1936 Ford home from San Diego (along with directions on how to find it) and the following weekend Mom and Dad drove to San Diego with brother Marvin and sister Ida Mae, and brought my car home for the duration of WWII. In a later letter, Daddy remarked about the quality of his drive home from San Diego in my Ford. He was favorably impressed by the spunkiness of the V-8 engine since he was used to driving only six-cylinder and four-cylinder Chevrolet automobiles. My mother took over the driving duties in Daddy's 1931 Chevrolet on the return trip to Ontario.

From the Southern Pacific railroad depot I boarded a municipal trolley car carrying my sea bag and pea coat for the ride down Market Street to San Francisco Bay. The weather was clear but very hot, as one would expect in the month of July. I relaxed and enjoyed the brief trip to the shore of San Francisco Bay where I exited the trolley. I soon located a Shore Patrol petty officer and inquired as to the location of the U.S.S. Zeilin. He turned me around and pointed to a pier about a block away where my ship was then tied up. As I approached the U.S.S. Zeilin, I noticed a line of 25 U.S. Army artillery pieces on the dock and they were being hoisted aboard. It appeared that a crew of about 15 sailors attended to the loading operations giving hand signals to winch operators high above the dock beside the U.S.S. Zeilin's forecastle. The U.S.S. Zeilin was tied up at the end of Market Street at a pier that was quite close to the San Francisco to Oakland Ferry Building.

Saluting the colors as I approached the quarterdeck, I requested permission to come aboard from the Officer of the Deck. The Officer of the Deck gave me directions to the executive officer's office and I went there immediately to deliver my orders. After turning in my orders, I checked in with the duty RADAR officer, Lt. (jg) Warren R. Davenport, who directed me to find a berth in the 7th Division's compartment near the ship's fantail. I then busied myself unpacking my gear and getting settled into my new 'home away from home'.

Responding to an earlier admonition of a 20-year Regular Navy sailor, with the hash marks to prove it, I selected a vacant top bunk and applied my mattress cover along with my standard Navy issue wool blanket, and finished making up my bunk. The 'old salt' mentioned that securing a top bunk near a ventilating duct brought with it the best of all possible worlds. Number one, no one would soil my mattress cover by stepping on it, and number two, opening a duct cover plate would supply plenty of fresh air when the compartment became stuffy from crewmen smoking below decks. I appreciated receiving the benefit of such knowledgeable and important information.

The following day, I was introduced to my coworkers in the RADAR Gang. My arrival brought the number of RADARmen on board to 25. During the introductory process I met a gentleman by the name of Marshall Herron who became my friend for life. Of course, in 1943, we were merely two 18-year old kids just starting out along life's journey.

Melvin Eugene Hacker in 1943 during his assignment to the U.S.S. Zeilin (APA-3) as a RADARman. This photo dates from September 1943 following the Kiska, Alaska Invasion. He is wearing his first campaign ribbon. There would be six more to follow during WWII.

Marshall R. Herron RADARman on the U.S.S. Zeilin (APA-3).

The entire Percy Hacker family as it existed in the year of 1931.

Left to right in photograph are, Harold Ray Hacker, Marilee Ruth Hacker and Melvin Eugene Hacker; each holding a rabbit from our father's rabbit hutches hidden behind the palm frond wall. Circa 1936.

Della L. Hacker on the right and husband Percy Eugene Hacker on the left. Date of photo is April, 2nd 1944.

Melvin Eugene Hacker taken at Chaffey Union High School in 1942, his senior class year.

The entire Percy Hacker family as it existed in the year of 1944. The persons standing in the rear are Harold Ray Hacker, Marilee Ruth Hacker and Melvin Eugene Hacker. In the front row left to right are Percy Eugene Hacker, Marvin Dean Hacker, Ida Mae Hacker, and Della Leonard Hacker.

Seaman First Class Melvin Eugene Hacker while he was assigned to the U.S.S. Zeilin attack troop transport (APA-3). Circa 1944.

Melvin Eugene with his arm around his sister Marilee Ruth Van. This photo dates from 1944 when Melvin was home on leave from the U.S.S. Zeilin (APA-3).

THE ALEUTIAN ISLANDS OPERATIONS

While exploring the ship that first day, I found it to be almost fully loaded with troops of the U.S. Army's 7th Division and their war material for a mission that included delivery of those troops and equipment to the Aleutian Islands where the invasions of Adak and Kiska Islands would be carried out. It appeared militarily, at the time, that the Japanese had established outposts among those and other Aleutian Islands. For historical completeness, it is appropriate that I cover the Zeilin's participation in the invasion of the Aleutian Island of Attu at this point, even though this invasion occurred prior to my joining the ship's crew.

THE U.S.S. ZEILIN SUPPORTS THE ATTU INVASION

Thursday & Friday, 4 & 5 June 1942

After the battle of Midway on these dates, the Japanese Supreme Command sent an invasion force of more than 3,000 troops to occupy the Aleutian Island of Attu.

Thursday, 18 February 1943

Commanded by Rear Admiral C. H. McMorris, two cruisers and four destroyers spent the day shelling Japanese installations on Attu.

Friday, 31 March 1943

On this date, the American Pacific Command issued a directive for the invasion of Attu. At that time, it was specified that the operation would take place on 7 May 1943 and would be directed by Admiral Kinkaid, Commander of Task Force 16 of the U.S. Northern Pacific Fleet. Scheduled under him would be Rear Admiral Rockwell who would command the combined operations landing force, with General Albert E. Brown heading the U.S. 7th Division. This was an unexpected task for the 7th Division inasmuch as the Division's troops had been training for months in desert fighting

Thursday, 15 April 1943

Today, infantry units of the 7th Division began the combined operations for the capture of Attu Island. Plans called for the troops to be taken first to Adak and Dutch Harbor where several platoons would embark on a destroyer and two submarines for a commando reconnaissance raid on Attu.

Monday, 26 April 1943

Commanded by Rear Admiral C.H. McMorris, a squadron of three cruisers and six destroyers shell Japanese installations on Attu. This effort was concentrated on the harbors at Chicagof and Holtz Bay.

Friday, 30 April 1943

Comprised of numerous battleships and cruisers as well as destroyers, the convoy transporting the main body of the 7th Division for the Attu landing reaches Cold Harbor. The U.S.S. Zeilin is a member of the 21 troop transports making up the convoy.

Tuesday, 4 May 1943

Extremely bad weather delayed the convoy's departure for an additional day. Because of the unfavorable winds and extremely cold temperatures, it became necessary for day 'X' to be set back by three more days to Tuesday, 11 May 1943.

Tuesday, 11 May 1943

Troop transports finally approach the island of Attu and commence their unloading operations. Unloading the troops and their materiel was severely hampered by freezing weather and the dense fog banks that prevented landing craft coxswains from seeing their assigned beaches. At times, it seemed that operations came to be a case of the 'blind leading the blind'. The lack of shore visibility extended the time that was required to move the troops and their supplies to their assigned beaches. Eventually, conditions improved, and during the next six days the U.S.S. Zeilin finished unloading its troops and their equipment. This endeavor was accomplished by moving the ship to a more suitable beach on the other side of the island. Fortunately for the American troops and Navy personnel, the Japanese did not fire on the landing beaches as they did in so many other WWII invasion sites. No doubt poor visibility contributed to this circumstance. The soldiers of the Japanese garrison on Attu fought an aggressive defense of their positions, but eventually, the American 7th Division troops surrounded them in the Sarans Valley. Counter attacks by the Japanese were beaten back and the Americans consolidated their north and south units on the island. For his steadfast prosecution of the difficult landing operations associated with his ship, the U.S.S. Zeilin Captain, Thomas B. Fitzpatrick, was later presented with the Legion of Merit commendation.

Monday, 17 May 1943

Having completed its work at Attu, the U.S.S. Zeilin set sail for San Diego with a stop at Adak along the way. In the Attu engagement, the U.S.S., Zeilin added yet another battle star to its growing list of WWII commendations. No crewmen were lost or injured in this engagement. However, the landing craft coxswains were extremely happy to return aboard ship to escape the freezing weather that had confronted them during the invasion. The poor condition of the rocky landing beaches caused significant damage to many of the U.S.S. Zeilin's Higgins boats. Replacements would be found upon the ship's arrival in San Diego.

Sunday, 30 May 1943

With all organized Japanese resistance eliminated, Attu is secure. 500 men of the Japanese garrison committed suicide with hand grenades after the battle had ended. 2,352 Japanese dead were counted. American losses in the battle were put at 550 dead and 1,140 wounded.

Tuesday, 8 June 1943

The Japanese Supreme Command orders the island of Kiska abandoned. At this time, the island is being shelled daily by American warships to prevent the arrival of any supplies. During this period, daily aircraft bombing runs were also carried out by U.S. Navy and U.S. Air Force planes.

Thursday, 22 July 1943

On this date, Japanese installations on Kiska were bombarded by two battleships, five cruisers and nine destroyers. Although it was unknown to the key invasion planners; by this time the Japanese garrison on Kiska had already been evacuated. This evacuation was successfully carried out surreptitiously by the Japanese and no resistance from U.S. ships was encountered.

0900, Thursday
29 July 1943
U.S.S. Zeilin departs San Francisco

With a full load of troops and their equipment, the U.S.S. Zeilin and its convoy depart San Francisco for the Aleutian Islands invasion of Kiska. With the Japanese having initially taken control of Attu, Adak and Kiska islands, a United States military decision was made to eliminate the threat posed by the Japanese penetration of the American hemisphere. The first step in accomplishing this objective was the elimination of Japanese forces from the island of Attu as described above. Taking this island had the effect of cutting off Kiska from being resupplied with provisions and troops. The elimination of Attu as a threat commenced on 11 May 1943 and continued for 20 stressful days under exceedingly adverse weather conditions. No Zeilin casualties were suffered in landing the occupying United States troops and none were incurred by any of the other participating troop transports.

The convoy for the Kiska invasion steamed single file beneath the Oakland Bay and Golden Gate bridges on its way to open Pacific Ocean waters west of San Francisco. What a thrill it was for me to see the Golden Gate bridge from the surface of San Francisco Bay. Although I had seen photographs of the single-span Golden Gate suspension bridge over the years, seeing it with my own eyes was one of the most awe-inspiring moments of my life. Once in open water, away from the normal shipping lanes, the troop transports and their protective screen formed up into a coherent combat unit. The outer screen contained numerous destroyers while the next ring contained three battleships, and inside them was a ring of cruisers. At the core of the convoy were the 30 amphibious troop transports. This operation was a combined American/Canadian undertaking and included a total of approximately 34,000 troops distributed among the 30 troop transports.

On the first night out, I was assigned to be on watch from 1800 until midnight. Four RADARmen were assigned to the watch so that both surface and air search RADAR sets could be operated. Standard practice was for an operator to be on a machine for 30 minutes, at which time he would be relieved for 30 minutes. This regimen was employed to minimize the eye strain inherent in long-term observation of the RADAR cathode ray tubes hour after hour. During the duty period, the RADARmen would notify the duty RADAR officer of any contacts detected in order for this information to be passed along immediately to the officer of the deck. In addition to watching for targets of conflict, RADAR operators scan for land mass appearances to aid the ship's navigation officer in determining the U.S.S. Zeilin's exact position on Naval charts of the region that the ship is passing through. In support of the RADAR equipment, the U.S.S. Zeilin's RADAR shack was also equipped with an auxiliary unit designated as a DRT (Dead Reckoning Tracer). This electromechanical machine was comprised of DC and AC electric drive motors, fine pitch brass gears and slip disc analog, variable rate transmission elements. The DRT also contained a target projector that was electrically synchronized with the ship's gyro compass circuits, such that the moving target was locked into and moved on the same relative course heading that was being traversed by the ship itself. Thus, if the ship was sailing on a heading of 360 degrees, (due north), the DTR target moved in a straight line toward the bow of the ship which at that moment corresponded to a course line of 360 degrees on the DRT. Of course, the target projector would have to be reset from time to time to place it in a usable area of the associated translucent tracing paper plotting record. Provision was made in the design of the machine to adjust the mechanism controlling the movement of the ship's target projector such that its DRT movement corresponded to an exact scale representing the current speed of the ship in knots per hour. The normal U.S.S. Zeilin cruise speed was about 17 nautical miles per hour.

The drive motors, gear trains and selsyns (rotary transformers) of the DRT are covered by a large piece of plate glass over which is stretched translucent tracing paper. When tracking an unknown target is in progress, ranges and bearings are recorded as pencil dots on the tracing paper, and at each mark the position of the target projector is also marked to show the position of the U.S.S. Zeilin at the instant the fix is taken. At the same time, the target distance and bearing from the Zeilin is marked to scale on the paper. In less than five minutes this routine will reveal the course and speed of an unknown marine or aircraft target. If the target is equipped with military IFF equipment (Identification, Friend or Foe), it can be identified as Friend or Foe.

At 2345 our relief crew arrived early so I and the other RADARmen on duty headed for our compartment in the stern of the ship and a good night's sleep. It turned out that my compartment was located directly above the twin propellers that provided propulsion for the U.S.S. Zeilin. At 17 knots, the propellers imparted a synchronous rumble to the 7th Division compartment. Interestingly enough, the subdued noise never seemed to cause the crew to lose any sleep.

Entering my compartment, I grabbed my toothbrush, soap and a towel and headed for the showers under the red night-vision illumination condition. After sundown, the entire ship is rigged for running under night-vision conditions so that any call to general quarters after sunset will be effectively manned by crew members whose vision is essentially unimpaired.

Taking a shower on the U.S.S. Zeilin was always a challenge in our compartment due to the effect of being at the stern of the ship where upward and downward movements of the hull translated into magnified movements that made standing quite difficult. Add to that, a slippery floor and getting a shower becomes a study in flailing gymnastics. However, in time one becomes adept at responding to the moving deck and few sailors end up slipping and falling in the shower. With my shower finished, I climbed into my bunk and relaxed for a good night's sleep with hopes of dreaming of sweetheart Lucille.

Before attempting to sleep, I decided to pen a few lines to Lucille. Although the light was poor, the night vision illumination was sufficient for writing on white, lined paper.

0900 Friday
6 August 1943
Adak, Aleutian Islands

Accompanied by its screen vessels and the other troop transports, the U.S.S. Zeilin steamed into the harbor at Adak and would spend four days during which time the ship would be refueled and provisions taken aboard to feed the ship's company as well as its military passengers. Similar reprovisioning was provided for all of the companion troop transport ships in the convoy as well as all screen vessels.

0100 Sunday
15 August 1943
Approaching Kiska Island

After leaving Adak and steaming for three days in calm seas, I am part of the duty RADAR crew as the U.S.S. Zeilin approaches Kiska Island. The profile image of the island is clearly visible on the SG-2 surface search RADAR that I am operating and the beach designated for our landing craft is well defined. Minute by minute position marks are passed to the officer of the deck and the designated 3,000 yard departure reference point approaches. When the 3,000 yard offshore point is reached, the officer of the deck commands "all engines stop" and the anchor is deployed by the deck crew. The other troop transports in the convoy have found their anchorages as designated in the order of battle plans and have dropped their anchors as well. The weather is calm with some light fog in the vicinity. Under cover of darkness, the convoy is deployed according to plan, just off Kiska Island.

0500 Sunday
15 August 1943
Off Shore of Kiska Island

The troop transports are stationed in a line 3,000 yards offshore at anchor. The battleships, cruisers and destroyers are stationed at a distance of 5,000 yards offshore. All ships have been at general quarters stations for the past ten hours. Orders are given for the troops to move to their debarkation stations for off-loading into their respective Higgins landing craft boats. At the same time, shelling of the shoreline installations commences by the battleships, cruisers and destroyers. Listening to the undulating sound of the shells passing overhead, accompanied by the sound of their lethal whine, gives one an eerie sensation, and then, a few seconds later, the shells are heard again as they explode on their targets on shore. Star shells descending on tiny parachutes brightly illuminate the target area.

At the end of one hour, the shelling of the shoreline installations is terminated and the loading of the Higgins boats commences. All coxswains on the U.S.S. Zeilin have manned their posts and their boats are lowered from the Welin boat davits into the cold Alaskan water and moved to the cargo nets to receive the U.S. and Canadian troops. Once loaded, the Higgins boats move independently to their assigned landing beach destinations. Although the troops were prepared for stiff Japanese opposition, none is forthcoming and the taking of Kiska island continues on a peaceful note; the entire Japanese garrison having been previously evacuated. It turned out that there were approximately 91 casualties during the invasion of Kiska Island that resulted from separated Army groups stumbling upon each other and mistakenly believing that they were Japanese enemy soldiers. Several days passed before word could be effectively circulated that there were no Japanese soldiers on Kiska.

0700 Sunday
15 August 1943
Off Shore of Kiska Island

The tank lighters are off-loaded from the U.S.S. Zeilin and filled with tanks, heavy vehicles, artillery guns and ammunition, and moved to the beaches for unloading. The beaches themselves were quite rocky, and as was the case at Attu Island, considerable hull damage occurred to some of the landing craft. Later in the operation, the U.S.S. Zeilin and the other transports were moved to a more suitable beach on the opposite side of Kiska Island where unloading operations were commenced again. Within 24 hours, all supplies were delivered to the beach and the convoy prepared to withdraw. The troops and their equipment and supplies were delivered as scheduled and the U.S.S. Zeilin then set sail for San Diego.

1200 Tuesday
17 August 1943
Departing Kiska Island

However, two days into the voyage to San Diego, while still in Alaskan waters, the U.S.S. Zeilin encountered an extremely severe storm that came close to causing the ship to capsize. It was payday and the Navy paymaster had set up his operation in the vacant troop officer's mess. All of the compartment tables had been raised to the overhead ceiling and pegged there. The ship was rolling crazily as the line of sailors moved in alphabetical order to the paymaster's table, which was the only one that had not been raised to the ceiling of the compartment. To keep from being thrown about the deck, sailors waiting in line to be paid clung in pairs to the nearest pipe stantion as they waited their turn. My turn came and I left the nearest pipe and grabbed hold of the edge of the table top at the paymaster's position and received my money (The Navy paid in cash in those wartime days). With the ship rolling as severely as it was, there was little conversation in the pay line. Sailors were interested only in getting their money and quickly getting back to their own compartments where they could 'sack out' and ride out the storm until their duty time arrived. At the peak of the storm, 30-foot seas were buffeting the ship and the spray coming over the forecastle blew half the ship's length (almost 300 feet) and each wave inundated the flying bridge. Needless to say, posted lookouts were called in for safety reasons. The duty RADARmen were hanging on to their positions as best they could and feeding reports to the bridge of any targets ahead of the ship. The bow of the U.S.S. Zeilin was plunging wildly and the forward guns were buried in salt water with each dip of the bow.

On the bridge, Captain Fitzpatrick kept a sharp lookout and gave orders to the helmsman to steer the course producing the least interference with the ship's passage. Eventually the storm abated and the U.S.S. Zeilin settled down on the still choppy waters. George Abernathy, a quatermaster friend, later told me that he happened to be on duty on the bridge at the peak of the storm and had occasion to observe the Clinometer Pointer when an extreme oscillation of the hull occurred. He told me that the ship rolled over to a 45 degree port list. When he reported that fact to Captain Fitzpatrick, the Captain merely groaned his displeasure as he continued to hold on tightly to one of the wheel house chairs welded to the deck. George confessed that he was fearful that the ship would not recover from that extreme roll.

1100 Sunday
3 September 1943
San Diego, California

When the U.S.S. Zeilin arrived in San Diego, a Marine Engineering Company was called in and their analysis determined that the original design for the conversion of the civilian Cruise Liner S.S. President Jackson to the Attack Troop Transport U.S.S. Zeilin (APA-3), for the Navy, included a design error causing the ship's center of gravity to be close to an out-of-limit condition. The C/G shift was caused by the additional weight of the eight Welin boat davits required to carry a quantity of 24 Higgins landing craft boats as well as the considerable weight of the boats themselves. There were four boat davits located on the upper boat deck on both port and starboard sides of the ship. Each davit nested three Higgins boats. The combined weight of the davits themselves, plus the weight of their 24 Higgins boats in place, raised the center of gravity of the U.S.S. Zeilin to a critically dangerous point. The problem was solved upon the ship's return to San Diego by the addition of many tons of ballast in the form of readymix concrete that was pumped into the bottom of several cargo holds. Although this adaptation had a minimal effect on the carrying capacity of the ship, it did not appear on later cruises to decrease the ship's efficiency in future invasions. During later cruises in the South Pacific, the U.S.S. Zeilin encountered severe monsoon-type storms and associated heavy seas, and rode them out without any adverse incident. While the ship was being modified, Mom and Dad brought

Lucille to San Diego and we enjoyed a brief two-day reunion and took pleasure in consuming some very tasty meals before they had to return to Ontario.

0900 Sunday
12 September 1943
Departing San Diego

On this date, the U.S.S. Zeilin set sail for Pearl Harbor on the second of her cruises in South Pacific waters. As the ship passed by Point Loma, I could see the antennas of the Navy RADAR School where I had trained following boot camp. I could not help but feel that a new page was turning in my life's journey. Gone were the carefree and fun-filled days of my youth to be replaced by the regimentation and unknown hazards of wartime Navy life in the South Pacific. In the years before I joined the ship, the U.S.S. Zeilin had participated in the invasion of Guadalcanal in the Solomon Islands. In that engagement, the ship was damaged by a Japanese dive bomber whose bomb caused the loss of her starboard propeller with no loss of life among her crew. When originally built as a cruise liner, the ship had been designed and equipped with twin propellers, and thus, following the attack, the ship was able to limp back to Espiritu Santo for temporary emergency repairs utilizing only her port propeller. With a seaworthy condition obtained at Espiritu Santo, the U.S.S. Zeilin returned to the United States for more permanent reconstruction improvements. Of course, it was a slow trip home what with only the port propeller able to function. The distance from San Diego to Pearl Harbor is approximately 2,100 miles. With both propellers in operation, the U.S.S. Zeilin cruises at a speed of approximately 17 knots. Traveling 24 hours per day, the U.S.S. Zeilin covered the distance to Pearl Harbor in about seven days. During this cruise I busied myself writing responses to the many letters that I had received while the ship was tied up in San Diego. Of course, I concentrated on sending words of encouragement to my sweetheart, Lucille.

1200 Sunday
19 September 1943
Entering Pearl Harbor
Hawaiian Island of Oahu

The view from the signal bridge of the U.S.S. Zeilin, as the ship moved into the inner harbor at Pearl, was awesome. The hulk of the Battleship Arizona could be seen still sitting in the mud the same as it had been since 7 December 1941. Although the fires had long since been extinguished, much salvage and cleanup work on the U.S.S. Arizona and other sunken ships in the harbor remained for the years ahead. With the U.S.S. Zeilin tied up at its assigned dock, mail was brought aboard and letters written en route from San Diego were taken ashore. When mail call came, I counted 10 letters from my mother and another 10 from my sweetheart, Lucille. And, happily, I found many of the letters contained photographs to be mounted in my growing Navy photograph album.

Upon arrival at Pearl Harbor, the U.S.S. Zeilin was refueled and provisions taken aboard in preparation for the invasion of the Atoll of Tarawa in the Gilbert Islands. With our final destination of Wellington, New Zealand, a stop would be made along the way at Espiritu Santo in the New Hebrides Islands chain for fuel and other supplies before continuing on to Wellington, New Zealand, where troops of the Second Marine Division would be embarked.

During our stay in Pearl Harbor, the ship's company enjoyed several days of liberty and the opportunity to leave the Navy behind for a few hours. Sightseeing was a favorite activity as was seeking out good restaurants to enjoy foods not available on board ship. During this time, the quality of food in the mess hall improved significantly. Fresh milk was available, replacing the staple of powdered milk when the ship is at sea. In addition, tubs of fresh pineapple slices were prepared for the crew. Fresh eggs replaced the powdered variety, and breakfasts comprised of biscuits and bacon or sausage and eggs cooked to order, were enjoyed by all hands.

While in Honolulu on liberty, I visited a local photographic studio and had my picture made to send to my family and especially to Lucille. I mailed the photographs to Mom and Dad and in Lucille's case sent along a letter reminding her of our vows to be married after the war ended. In later correspondence, we went so far as to plan some of the details of our wedding as well as selecting a few potential names for children that we might have. They included both male and female names. With the long voyage ahead of the U.S.S. Zeilin I spent considerable time writing replies to the various letters that came aboard upon our arrival at Pearl Harbor. I definitely did not want my letters to Lucille to be delayed at all.

0800 Friday
24 September 1943
Depart Pearl Harbor
for Espiritu Santo in
the New Hebrides Islands

It was a blue-sky day as the U.S.S. Zeilin and its protective convoy screen bid good-bye to a very pleasant stay in Pearl Harbor and got underway on the voyage to Espiritu Santo. Absent the usual load of 1,000 or more military troops, the trip to the New Hebrides Islands would be a pleasant one for the crew. Fresh water hours would not be imposed and the decks would remain clear of human bodies lining the rails feeding the fish due to seasickness attacks.

Inasmuch as the U.S.S. Zeilin's route of travel to New Zealand approached islands still held by Japanese forces, escort destroyers and other ships accompanied the U.S.S. Zeilin and were responsible for maintaining a SONAR watch for the presence of any Japanese submarines during our voyage to Espiritu Santo. The standard war-zone zigzag course changes were made throughout the voyage and the RADAR gang maintained a sharp lookout for the possible approach of any enemy aircraft or surface vessels as well as submarine periscopes. No such incidents occurred during this leg of our cruise to New Zealand. The RADAR gang maintained its usual eight-hour per day duty schedule en route and experienced only one equipment failure in the SG-2 surface search RADAR where the magnetron vacuum tube became inoperative. RADAR officer Lt. (jg) Warren Davenport and first class electronic technician Kenneth Fonticello succeeded in bringing the RADAR back on line within thirty minutes of the failure. As was my custom, I was on hand to peer over their shoulders as the Lieutenant and Ken explored the innards of the SG-2 system. It was my hope that, one day I could become an electronic maintenance technician. Following the advice of my father, I learned plenty by merely observing the experts in action as well as pouring over the well-documented Navy technical manuals.

0900 Wednesday
6 October 1943
Arrived at anchorage in
Espiritu Santo,
New Hebrides Islands

Upon arrival at Espiritu Santo, working parties were set to bring aboard food and other provisions and refuel the ship. Refueling was accomplished by bringing a Navy tanker alongside the ship and taking aboard a large diameter fuel line through which oil for the boilers was transferred to the near empty U.S.S. Zeilin fuel tanks. Due to the proximity of the Japanese forces on nearby islands, around-the-clock watches were maintained by the RADAR Gang, utilizing both air and surface search RADAR systems. As it turned out, no enemy targets were detected. No liberty could be granted at Espiritu Santo because the local civilian enclave was not large enough to accommodate the ship's company of the U.S.S. Zeilin and all of its support vessels.

However, the usual 'bum boats' of the local native population visited the U.S.S. Zeilin and the other ships daily, hawking their wares of seashell necklaces, cat-eye earrings and other native trinkets. 'Bum boats' are small native skiffs made from coconut or other tree trunks and usually have lateral, outrigger supports to provide stability as they are either rowed with very large oars or propelled by colorful sails. While anchored at Espiritu Santo, swimming was a favorite activity of the crew during off-duty hours.

0500 Friday
8 October 1943
U.S.S. Zeilin and screen vessels depart
New Hebrides Islands

The U.S.S. Zeilin is underway again, under fair skies, on an approximately 1,150 mile leg to Wellington, New Zealand. Travel time is estimated to be about five days. Thus far, no general quarters alarms have been set since we left Pearl Harbor and none are anticipated on the trip to Wellington since the convoy is moving away from Japanese forces. Daily routines involve mustering at quarters primarily to assure that no men have been lost overboard accidentally overnight. Notwithstanding the fact that lookouts are posted 24 hours a day and the RADAR sets are operating 24 hours per day as well, physical head counts of all personnel are important tasks for the crew and division officers. In fair weather, motion pictures are shown on the upper boat deck in the evening after the day's duty shifts have ended. In the main, the movies are musicals. During my three-year Navy career I was never able to determine why the persons responsible for supplying the amphibious forces with motion picture films elected to give us a heavy diet of musical movies. On rare occasions the ship was able to trade with another ship and obtain an adventure film such as 'Frenchman's Creek'. Evening time is also utilized by the ship's company to write letters to loved ones back home to be mailed at the next port-of-call. Of course, all mail leaving the ship is subject to examination by Navy censors to prevent transmission of any sensitive military information. Following breakfast, I stopped by the RADAR Shack and could see the coast of New Zealand registering on the Surface Search RADAR system. The harbor at Wellington was dead ahead only 50 miles away. Notwithstanding the 50-mile distance, the fragrance of flower blossoms, trees and inhabited land was pleasantly noticeable in the breezes flowing over the U.S.S. Zeilin's decks.

0800 Wednesday
13 October 1943
U.S.S. Zeilin ties up at the wharf
in Wellington, New Zealand

The crew of the U.S.S. Zeilin is fortunate in the fact that the ship's company includes a Navy commodore who is responsible for planning and executing the upcoming invasion. Because of his presence, the crew usually knows ahead of time where and when the U.S.S. Zeilin will be scheduled to leave port and the intended destination after leaving port. While in port at Wellington, liberty is granted to both port and starboard sections of the crew. During the visit to Wellington, I learned that the New Zealanders certainly know how to prepare fine breakfasts. The standard bill of fare that I observed for breakfast was steak and eggs, with potatoes on the side. What a stomach pleaser that sort of meal represents.

On one of my liberty visits to Wellington, it was a special treat to patronize a motion picture theater and sit in a plush loge seat for a change. The 1942 film showing that evening was 'Journey into Fear' starring Agnes Morehead. While watching the movie, I was reminded of the wonderful evening that Lucille and I spent in a San Diego theater following our trip to Mexico while I was still in boot camp. I clearly recall how delicious the warm butter-covered popcorn tasted that evening. And, wonder of wonders, Coke soft drinks were available in Wellington. As I was walking along the docks returning to my ship following the movie, I was surprised to be hailed by a boot camp friend by the name of Alexander Lemon. We enjoyed catching up on events in our lives since leaving San Diego, and we agreed to meet again following the completion of invasion training exercises slated to begin in the next few days.

Working parties are set to reprovision the ship in preparation for exercises during the coming weeks. The troop transport flotilla will take on members of the Second Marine Division who will be transported to the Tarawa Atoll in the Gilbert Islands for an invasion scheduled for November, 1943. For the past several days, the commodore has been hosting officers from other attack transport ships as well as the Marine officers who will be in command of the invasion force on the beach to assist in the planning phase of the invasion. The whine of Cummins Diesel Engines never leaves the air as the many landing craft ply the harbor transporting Navy and Marine officers to and from the U.S.S. Zeilin. Of course, the U.S.S. Zeilin quarterdeck was an extremely busy place as the visiting officers and their staffs arrived and departed the ship. Lieutenant Thompson was on hand to maintain order and see to it that the higher ranking visitors were accorded the proper Navy recognition as befit their rank. Members of the U.S.S. Zeilin boat crew were kept busy parking the visiting Higgins boats as well as dispensing diesel fuel as well as motor oil.

0500 Tuesday
19 October 1943
U.S.S. Zeilin departs with convoy and screen
for Hawkes Bay, New Zealand

The U.S.S. Zeilin has been joined by fifteen additional attack troop transports, several aircraft carriers, heavy cruisers and a plentiful supply of destroyers. Hawkes Bay was selected to permit the Marines to practice the method of climbing down cargo nets and boarding the Higgins landing craft that wait alongside the transports to take them to shore. In the planning phase, designated beaches are given code names (usually color such as Red Beach one, Red Beach two, etc.). Once we arrive at Hawkes Bay, the troops will make practice landings on designated beaches along with their vehicles. The crew of the U.S.S. Zeilin and the other transports get their workouts along the way as well. There is a coxswain for each Higgins boat and he is furnished with a chart that directs him to the appropriate beach to drop off his load of troops or support equipment. The coxswain is also equipped with two-way FM radio communicators to allow for a change of orders, if necessary, once he leaves the U.S.S. Zeilin for his designated beach. In addition to the personnel carriers, there are tank lighters and LST's to bring the tanks and heavy artillery to the enemy beachhead. The tanks and jeeps and other rolling stock are unloaded during the exercises to verify that the support material for the troops is delivered on time to the place where it is assigned to go. With three days of training exercises under their belts, the Marines and support personnel are ready to return to Wellington to stand down for a few days. With all of the heavy guns, tanks and support vehicles reloaded into the cargo holds of the various transport ships, the convoy gets under way and returns to Wellington. Mail call is held soon after the ship docks in Wellington, and I am impressed by the number of letters that arrive for me. Mom usually sends along a letter from home each day and, of course, Lucille sends a love letter each day as well as reporting on her high school activities and ever-present loneliness. I could tell her about my loneliness, but, instead, I attempt to convey a positive upbeat flavor in my letters to her and emphasize the pleasant days that we will enjoy together after the war when we are married.

1600 Thursday
21 October 1943
Familiarization exercises conclude and the
convoy returns to Wellington, New Zealand

As before, the ships of the convoy are reprovisioned and refueled at Wellington harbor in preparation for their run to the invasion site. At the same time, the ship's company and the Marine troops go on liberty and relax for a few days before the convoy departs for Tarawa. Under the direction of Lt. (jg) Warren Davenport, routine maintenance procedures are applied to each U.S.S. Zeilin RADAR set and proper operation is verified. Similar routines are applied to SONAR, Fire Control RADAR and related equipment aboard the screen vessels. With the simulated invasion landing exercises having been successfully completed, the Marines busy themselves with the tasks of cleaning and lubricating their weapons as well as securing their vehicles in the cargo holds in preparation for the voyage to Tarawa. Vehicle fuel tanks are topped off and the ammunition loads for the various weapons are distributed according to plan. Bulk small arms ammunition for the invasion site remains safely stored in its respective armory pending arrival at Tarawa and release for distribution to the Marine platoons.

Mail call is perhaps the single most important daily event in crew members' lives once the ship arrives in port. Today I received a dozen letters from my mother along with eleven letters from Lucille. I also received a care package from Mom that included homemade cookies and peanuts that were shipped in sealed Mason jars to maintain their freshness. Of course I shared the booty with my friends in the RADAR gang. Since it appeared that the U.S.S. Zeilin would be getting under way soon, I spent a few hours today writing letters to my parents as well as sweetheart, Lucille. In her latest letter, Lucille advised me that she had acquired her wedding dress and urged me to hurry home and marry her on my next leave from the U.S.S. Zeilin. Those words were music to my eyes. She also advised me that her mother and father approved of her wedding plans and encouraged her to tell me to hurry home. I busied myself for several hours in writing a reply to her not so surprising announcement, but had to tell her that I could not speculate on how long it might be before I could return to Los Angeles on leave. I went on to say that I would advise her at the earliest possible moment once I received orders to return to the States. With our first major South Pacific invasion in the offing, it was doubtful in my mind that I would be lucky enough to return to the States on leave any time soon. Nevertheless, I acknowledged Lucille's happy thoughts in a letter and requested that she thank her parents for their positive support of our plans to be married upon my return home.

0900 Monday
1 November 1943
U.S.S. Zeilin departs Wellington,
New Zealand, in convoy

In the order assigned by the commodore commanding the operation, all of the troop transports, supporting aircraft carriers, battleships, cruisers, destroyers, mine sweepers, oil tankers and submarines depart Wellington's harbor and the convoy forms up at sea. The heading from Wellington to Espiritu Santo is slightly west of north, being approximately 355 degrees. The convoy will travel to Espiritu Santo where it will refuel and reprovision and depart on a schedule that will see it arrive off the shores of Tarawa in the nighttime hours of Saturday, 20 November 1943.

The Tarawa Atoll, one of the Gilbert Islands, is approximately 2,000 miles southwest of the Hawaiian Islands and lies just north of the equator. It is 105 miles south of the Makin Atoll. Tarawa Atoll is made up of several low coral islets, the largest of which is Betio (two miles long and 2,400 feet wide). Early in WWII the Gilbert Islands were captured by the Japanese who then built their strongest defenses on Tarawa Atoll. These defenses are comprised of steel, coral and concrete pill boxes, trenches, barbed wire entanglements tunnels and the whole of the revetments being backed up by artillery of various sizes and types. In addition to the defenses installed on Betio Atoll, the Japanese also built an airfield there. During the cruise from Wellington to Espirtu Santo, the prescribed war zone zig zag navigation patterns are followed day and night. Continuous RADAR surveillance for surface and air contacts is maintained, as is SONAR surveillance for the presence of enemy submarines. RADAR is also employed to assist in navigating through the numerous small islands encountered along the route of passage, particularly during nighttime hours. The usual eight-hour duty time for RADARmen was revised to six hours on duty and six hours off in anticipation of the four hours on and four hours off duty cycle when the U.S.S. Zeilin arrives at the invasion site.

1300 Monday
8 November 1943
Convoy anchors at
Efate, New Hebrides

With the troop transports anchored in their assigned locations, work commences to refuel all ships, and working parties turn to in moving necessary food and other supplies from storage to all of the ships in the convoy. At the same time, fuel supplies are delivered to the transports and screen vessels. During the next several days Navy and Marine officers will travel to the U.S.S. Zeilin for strategic consultation meetings with the commodore to finalize the conduct of the coming invasion. In addition, the time is used to develop any contingency plans felt to be necessary. Timing for the arrival of the troops at their respective beaches is finalized, as is the routine to be followed in the removal of wounded troops from shore and return to the U.S.S. Zeilin which, once troops are off-loaded, converts into a temporary hospital ship. At the proper time, the U.S.S. Zeilin will depart the invasion locale and expedite its arrival and rendezvous with the assigned Navy hospital ship scheduled to receive its casualties from the invasion. During the period of time that the convoy is anchored at Efate, as well as during its transit to Tarawa, extensive Naval and U.S. Air Force aircraft bombing runs are being made at Tarawa to soften up the defenders of the Atoll. Upon arrival at Tarawa, battleship, cruiser and destroyer naval gun fire will be directed against shore-based batteries of the Japanese defenders.

1000 Saturday
13 November 1943
Convoy departs New Hebrides Islands

With the proximity of Japanese ships along the route of travel, general quarters condition is set aboard all ships of the invasion fleet upon their departure from Efate. In this emergency mode, shipboard personnel perform their duties utilizing a four-hour on duty and four-hour off duty schedule. This operational mode assures that an immediate response will be possible should an enemy threat appear. Of course, all ships maintain radio silence and communicate ship-to-ship via signal flags during daylight hours or shielded flashing lights at night. As before, the standard war zone zigzag pattern is followed by all ships. Any course change required en route is synchronized with the zigzag pattern to assure, to the extent possible, that inadvertent collisions between any ships do not occur. While in transit during daylight hours, Marine personnel take advantage of open deck areas (including cargo hatch covers) for calisthenics exercises in the interest of maintaining their physical fitness at a peak performance level. It is a time of waiting and sober contemplation of the arrival at the distant Atoll. For the past few hours the Tarawa Atoll has been registering on the U.S.S. Zeilin Surface Search RADAR, although the signal is weak and not a solid lock-on yet.

2400 Saturday
20 November 1943
Approaching Tarawa Atoll

The invasion convoy is approximately twenty nautical miles from its destination at the Tarawa Atoll and the scene within the U.S.S. Zeilin RADAR shack is tense. The RADAR shack is a steel-enclosed room approximately twenty-five feet on each of its four sides and is situated immediately behind the navigator's chart room which opens on to the bridge. Each of the four legs of the 75-foot high tower supporting the associated RADAR antennas is welded to a corner of the RADAR shack roof. Although somewhat cramped for space, the duty section and all off-duty RADAR operators are stationed in the RADAR shack whenever a general quarters condition is set.

The U.S.S. Zeilin RADAR equipment is comprised of one type SC-2 Air Search RADAR and one type SG-2 Surface Search RADAR. The room is not air-conditioned, and, with the equipment being based upon vacuum tube technology, the RADAR sets generate a significant amount of heat. This heat combines with the high temperatures characteristic of the equator to challenge operator tolerance of the physical environment. In other words, it gets hot as hell in there and we RADAR operators sweat profusely.

As the convoy moves closer to Tarawa, the PPI scope displays the position of the troop transports as three rows of bright dots, one row on the portside of the U.S.S. Zeilin and one row on the starboard side and a third row in line with the U.S.S. Zeilin itself for a total of 16 troop transports. There are five dots in each outside row and six in the center row. The image shows that all of the transport ships are exactly on station as are the screening vessels distributed in semicircular arcs in front of the convoy. As the transport ships arrive at their mooring locations, the screen vessels move to seaward to commence their bombardment of the Atoll.

The Tarawa Atoll itself is characterized as a loose collection of coral islets that lay in the general shape of an equilateral triangle with Betio located in the base of the triangle. The base of the triangle runs east and west for a distance of about 20 miles between the southern corners of the triangle. The eastern boundary of the triangle extends in a northeasterly direction for a distance of approximately 25 miles. However, the small islets are not large enough to be fortified. Betio holds down the southwestern corner of the triangle and its major axis runs east and west for a distance of approximately two miles. On the PPI scope, Betio is located slightly off the port bow of the U.S.S. Zeilin. Range and bearing information is continuously fed by the duty RADARman to the officer of the deck as he navigates to the ship's assigned mooring place 3,000 yards offshore. At the designated point, the officer of the deck signals the engine room to secure the engines and the deck hands on the forecastle deploy the anchor.

Prior to the arrival of the invasion convoy, the original plans called for the last minute bombing of the Atoll by a squadron of B-24 Liberator bombers. However, this raid never took place for the reason that the squadron assigned to the task suffered so many casualties during a raid on Japanese positions on another island the previous day that it had neither the personnel nor serviceable B-24's with which to conduct the Tarawa raid. As it turned out, it is doubtful that the absence of this bombing run had a significant impact on the outcome of the invasion.

0359 Saturday
20 November 1943
Convoy arrives off Tarawa Shores

Shelling of the Japanese beach defenses commences immediately. The noise created by the firing of the heavy Naval guns is ear shattering. The U.S.S. Zeilin, anchored 3,000 yards off its designated beach, prepares to launch its landing craft. It is a moonless night; however, the star shells fired by the various ships have the effect of turning the night into day. Japanese fire is returned from the Atoll, but, initially at least, it does not reach the location of either the

U.S.S. Zeilin or the other capital ships raking the Atoll with shell fire. This will change later on when heavier, eight-inch guns of the Japanese are brought into play and become a threat to the U.S.S. Zeilin and other transports, whereupon they withdraw to a safer distance.

In transit, Marine troops visit the mess hall for their final meal on board the U.S.S. Zeilin and at 05:00 they move to their boat boarding stations for off-loading. The U.S.S. Zeilin crew is busily engaged in placing the tank lighters in the water followed by the APC's (Armored Personnel Carriers). The cargo hatch covers have all been removed and the main deck is a beehive of activity. At 0600 all coxswains report to their Higgins boat stations and prepare to be lowered from the Welin Boat Davits into the water on both port and starboard sides. Once in the water, the boats move to the cargo nets to receive their Marine passengers. At this time, Captain Fitzpatrick salutes the departing Marine troops by playing a recording of the 'Marine Hymn' over the U.S.S. Zeilin's public address system. The approaching dawn is apparent in the eastern sky and the air is still being rent by the almost unbearable noise of the heavy Naval guns firing at targets on Tarawa. The formerly black night is giving way to a gray haze; not so much fog as it is smoke from the continuous firing of the heavy guns of the battleships, cruisers and destroyers as well as smoke rising from burning targets on the Atoll itself. The Atoll is becoming visible and star shells are no longer required to illuminate targets for the gunners on the various ships. At 08:30, the beach master releases the first wave of Higgins boats and the invasion begins. Boats from the U.S.S. Zeilin and all other transports move toward their assigned beaches on the Atoll. A sudden calm settles over the convoy as the gunfire from the battleships, cruisers and destroyers ceases. However, the noise of Japanese machine-guns is clearly audible across the 1.7 miles of water separating the U.S.S. Zeilin from its designated beachfront. This gunfire commenced when the first landing craft came within range of the Jap gunners. Even in the face of the pounding taken by the Atoll from aircraft bombs as well as Naval gunfire, too many Japanese soldiers survived to oppose the American troops.

On top of that eventuality, there was an unfortunate natural occurrence during the Tarawa invasion that was not fully anticipated by invasion planners. As a result of a marginal tidewater level, (occurring on only two days out of every twelve month interval) a submerged coral reef caused the Higgins boats to run aground some distance from shore. Thus, the Marines on board each Higgins boat found it necessary to leave the limited protection of the landing craft and wade to shore while fully exposed to the Japanese gunners. Firing from protected positions the Japanese troops decimated the initial and some of the subsequent waves of Marines. As previously mentioned, regardless of the earlier aircraft bombing and Naval gunfire that morning, the majority of the Japanese troops on Tarawa survived to exact their vengeance on the Marine invaders. Nevertheless, the attack by the United States 2nd Marine Division prevailed only after three days of the bloodiest fighting yet encountered in the Pacific theater. United States Marine and Navy losses were estimated to be 3,500 killed and missing and 2,085 wounded. The Japanese losses totaled more than 5,000 men. On the first day of the Tarawa invasion, 5,000 young Marines moved from the Navy transport ships to their designated beaches, but by nightfall 1,500 had perished without ever getting close enough to even see their enemy.

After delivering its cargo of wounded Marine personnel to the waiting Navy hospital ship cruising nearby, the U.S.S. Zeilin was dispatched to Guadalcanal to pick up a load of Army and Marine troops to train them for the invasion of the the Japanese held island of Saipan.

AUTHOR'S NOTE:

Notwithstanding the fact that the U.S.S. Zeilin remained at Tarawa for five long, dangerous days, those of us who remained on duty aboard ship had exceedingly little knowledge of the unmitigated hell facing our Marines on shore. It was only while researching background information for this book that I finally gained a meaningful perspective of the trials and suffering that confronted the Marines during the Tarawa invasion. The eye witness account contained in Robert Sherrod's book "Tarawa" - "The story of a battle", written in 1944, tells it all from the point of view of an individual who was there as the battle happened. When the battle took place, Robert was a War Correspondent for Time Incorporated. Another book listed in my bibliography titled, "Bloody Tarawa" the 2nd Marine Division, November 20 - 23, 1943" is a 1998 version of the epic battle for Tarawa Atoll. It is replete with many official Marine Corps photographs taken during the invasion. It is now almost 64 years since the battle of Tarawa was fought and it is still difficult for me to comprehend the human suffering, both Japanese and American, that occurred on that small South Pacific island during a period of three days.

Melvin E. Hacker
October 2007

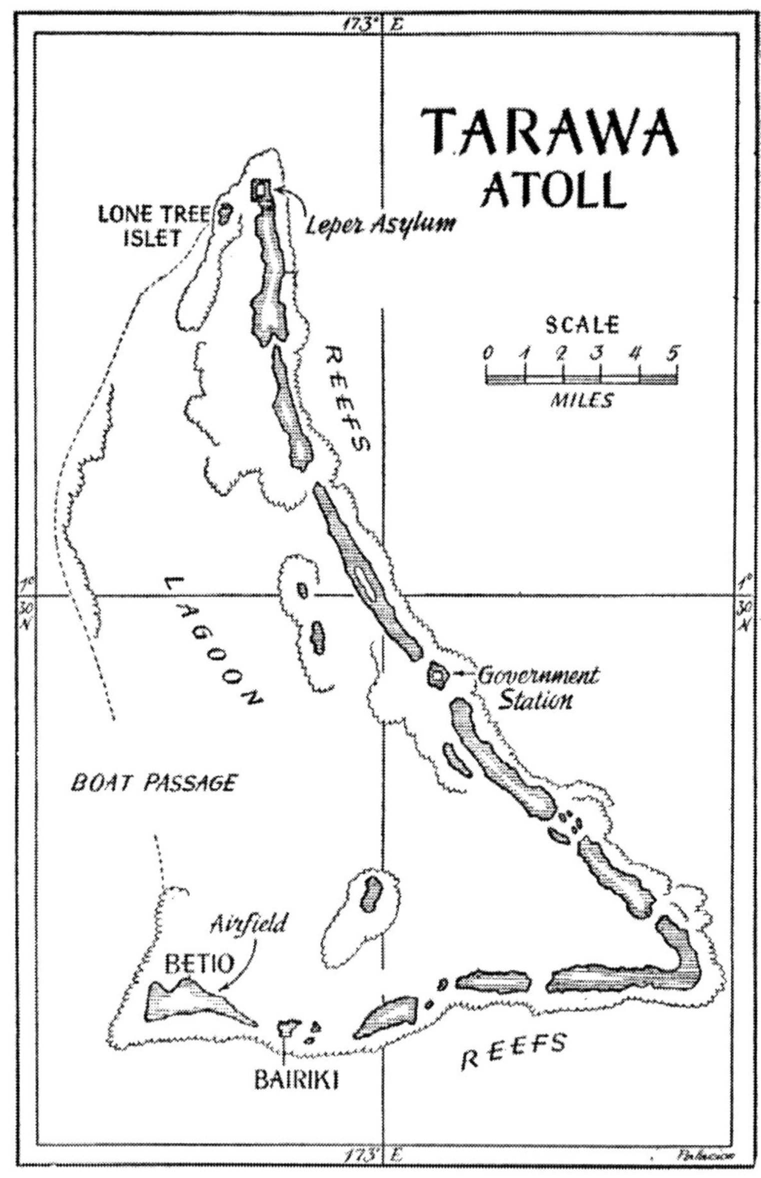
TARAWA
ATOLL
LONE TREE
ISLET
Leper Asylum
SCALE
0 1 2 3 4 5
MILES
REEFS
LAGOON
Government
Station
BOAT PASSAGE
Airfield
BETIO
BAIRIKI
REEFS
173° E
1° 30 N

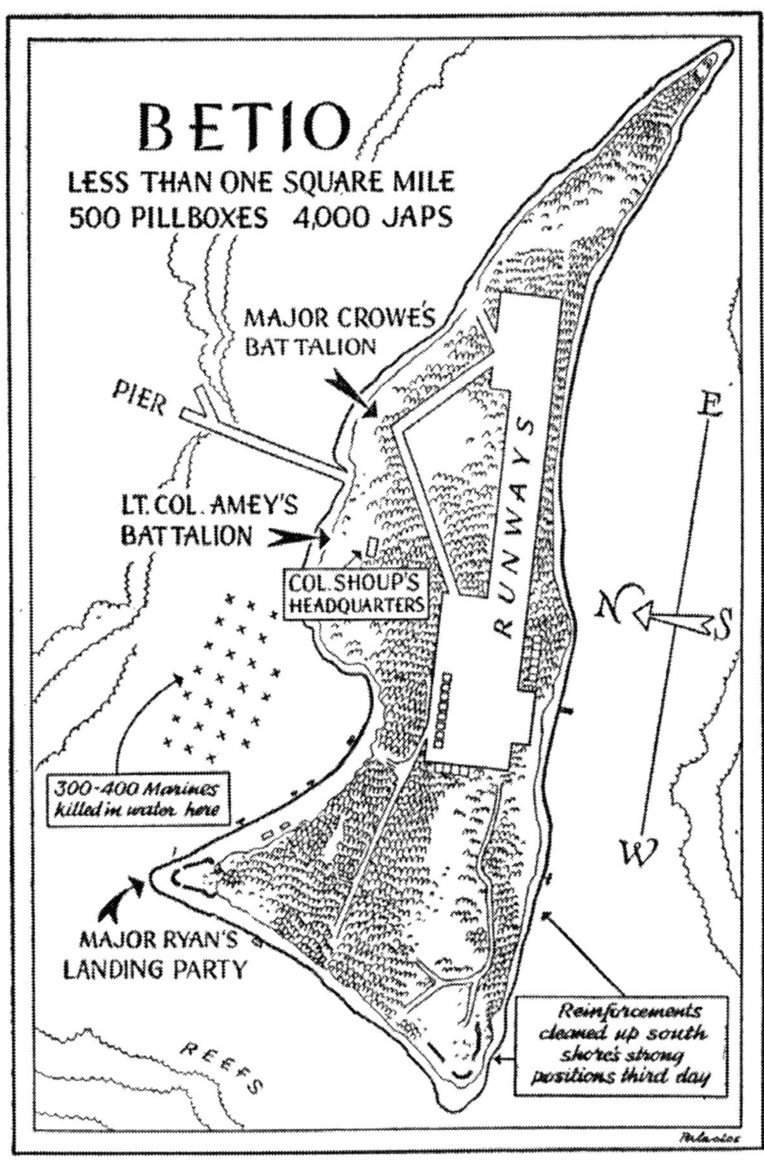
BETIO
LESS THAN ONE SQUARE MILE
500 PILLBOXES 4,000 JAPS
MAJOR CROWE'S BATTALION
PIER
RUNWAYS
E
LT. COL. AMEY'S BATTALION
COL. SHOUP'S HEADQUARTERS
N
S
300-400 Marines killed in water here
W
MAJOR RYAN'S LANDING PARTY
REEFS
Reinforcements cleaned up south shore's strong positions third day

MAP OF PACIFIC OCEAN LOCATIONS WHERE THE U.S.S. ZEILIN ENGAGED JAPANESE MILITARY FORCES--- MAP IS NOT TO SCALE.

National Archives Photo #80-G-50921: Attu Invasion, May 1943
Soldiers unload landing craft on the beach at Massacre Bay, Attu on 13 May 1943. LCVPs in foreground are from U.S.S. Zeilin (APA-3) and U.S.S. Heywood (APA-6).

National Archives Photo #80-G-50827: Attu Invasion, May 1943
Soldiers pull an ammunition cart along the beach at Massacre Bay, Attu, 12 May 1943. One of the LCVP's in background is from U.S.S. Zeilin (APA-3).

USMC #67706: U.S. Marine Corps
Tarawa Operation November 1943
Marines and sailors study a relief model of Betio Island Tarawa, while en route to the invasion of that place.

U.S.S. Zeilin (APA-3) seen in this view with her wartime camouflage paint job.

National Archives Photo #80-G-54399: Tarawa Invasion
20 November 1943. Invasion leaders on the bridge of U.S.S.
Maryland (BB-46), watching the landings.
Taken circa 20 November 1943. In foreground is
MGen. Julian C. Smith, USMC. Radm. Harry W. Hill
is beyond him, wearing two star helmet.

Harold Ray Hacker and Melvin Eugene Hacker (left to right). Melvin at this time was a Third Class RADARman assigned to the U.S.S. Zeilin while Harold was an Apprentice Torpedoman.

CHAPTER TWO

CALVIN JOINS THE NAVY AND GETS MARRIED

0500 Friday
5 December 1941
Des Moines, Iowa

Born into an Iowa farming family in March 1925, Calvin Honeycut was up at the crack of dawn attending to his chores on a beautiful December morning. His parents raised corn and oats on a 1,600 acre farm twenty miles west of Des Moines, Iowa, the state capitol. Calvin attended Lincoln High School in the city and he rode the bus to school each day. A tall, redheaded fellow of Irish descent, Calvin enjoyed sports and was a member of the Lincoln track team in which he excelled in the broad jump, high hurdles and 400-meter relay race.

Calvin's family kept several Jersey milk cows and it was his responsibility to see that they were fed and milked before he could leave for school. For this reason, he was up and moving at 5 a.m. so that he could finish his chores, eat his breakfast and take a shower before the school bus arrived around 7:00 a.m. The Honeycuts lived on one of the main roads leading west out of Des Moines and Calvin caught the bus on its return trip to school out in front of his home.

On this fifth day of December the weather was clear and cool with the temperature seemingly stuck at 41 degrees F. Although the temperature was above the freezing mark, it nevertheless called for a winter coat to be worn against the chilling breeze blowing from the west. As he left the front porch of his home, Calvin could see the yellow school bus as it rounded a bend in the road about a mile west of his driveway. Walking briskly he timed his arrival at the bus stop to coincide with the driver bringing the bus to a stop. When the doors opened, Calvin climbed on board and took the vacant seat next to his best friend, Lowell Evans, who was also the heir of a dedicated farming family.

"How goes the battle, Lowell?", asked Calvin. "It would be going a lot better if I could understand algebra better than I do", responded Lowell. "Mathematics comes easy to me so why don't you stop by on your way home from school this afternoon and I will be pleased to help you over the rough spots", offered Calvin. "Many thanks, Calvin, but my folks expect me to be home right on time to help in harvesting our crop of winter wheat. Perhaps over the weekend we could get together", suggested Lowell. "As far as I know, I am free on Sunday, so just give me a call when you want to come over", replied Calvin.

From there, the conversation drifted to other mundane topics such as their girlfriends, and before long, the bus pulled to a stop at Lincoln High School. The air brakes hissed and the doors opened and Calvin and Lowell followed the other students off the bus. "So long, Lowell, I have to hurry over to take an 8 a.m. chemistry exam. I'll catch up with you this afternoon on the way home. Have a great day", and with that exchange Calvin trotted off to his classroom. When it was over, Calvin felt good about his chemistry exam. He was well prepared and felt that he had 'aced' the exam. It would do his grade point average a lot of good to bring in an 'A' for a change. Although he was a diligent student, Calvin still had to struggle with some of his classes, mathematics not being one of them. From chemistry, Calvin moved to his Mechanical Drawing Class where, unbeknownst to him or his classmates, another exam was lurking. However, this one was a surprise sprung on the entire class by Mr. Thompson without prior notice. After the morning pleasantries, Mr. Thompson said, "All right, class, each of you please take a clean piece of 8 1/2" by 11" paper and tape it to your drawing board. Then get out your protractor and 'T' square together with a 45-degree triangle. You will need these items to complete the following test." Mr. Thompson went on to describe the test parameters as follows: "Examine the cube that I am holding in my right hand. Notice the small circle on face 'A' near one edge and consider where, and on which face of the remaining faces marked 'B', 'C', 'D', 'E', and 'F', a corresponding hole would appear if you were to drill a one quarter-inch hole perpendicular to face 'A'". At this point, Mr. Thompson drew a sketch of the cube on his blackboard and labeled each of the faces so that his students would have a common understanding of which face was which. He also provided the dimension of the distance from the corner of the cube to the center of the marked circle on face 'A'. "When you have completed your work, please bring your test papers to my desk."

At this point, Calvin laid out the standard top, front, and side- views of the cube on his paper. Having done that, he marked the identity of each face as well as the dimension that Mr. Thompson had given the class regarding the location of the small circle. Recording the small circle on side 'A', Calvin determined by projection that the hole would exit side 'C' and he applied the correct dimension of the distance of the hole from the edge of the cube. The mechanical drawing class was given the entire period of one hour in which to complete the exam and Calvin and most of his classmates had finished the assignment well before the bell rang for the next period class to begin. Mr. Thompson graded the papers as they were handed in and Calvin was pleased to see 100% A+ marked in Mr. Thompson's notation as he returned the exam paper to Calvin.

Calvin's next class was study hall, and he spent the

available time reviewing current events for an examination review scheduled for his first class after lunch, which was U.S. History and Civics. For some time past, Calvin had been aware that some of his classmates were leaving school to enlist in various foreign armed forces, but he had not given any thought to his own involvement in the war raging in Germany and Europe as a whole. While reviewing a series of current events reports, he was surprised to find a U.S. Navy recruitment advertisement on the facing page of an article describing the Navy's efforts to protect ship convoys sailing to Great Britain bringing troops (volunteers) and airplanes and other war materials in support of the British people who were already at war with Germany. As he studied the article, Calvin began to realize that some of his departed classmates had volunteered to serve as pilots in Great Britain's Royal Air Force.

Calvin's study for his next class was interrupted by the bell signifying that lunch time had arrived. Since he had not brought his lunch, Calvin hurried to the school cafeteria where he grabbed a hamburger from the self-service line along with a piece of apple pie and a soda, and then scanned the room for a place to sit. In the far corner, Calvin noticed Lowell sitting alone and he hurried over to join his friend. "Lowell, I see that you survived your morning classes all in one piece", remarked Calvin.

"Survived is the correct terminology, Calvin, because there were no quizzes or exams this morning, merely lectures on the tough topics yet to come. The really interesting thing is the fact that we were told that our next series of exams will all be open-book tests for all classes", Lowell reported happily. "You have to be very careful with open-book exams", cautioned Calvin, "because they usually contain a good many 'trick' questions that are intended to derail your thought processes. In the open-book test domain, 'haste makes waste', so remember to take your time as you carefully study each question before you list your answer."

"I know whereof you speak, Calvin, so I plan to take my time and avoid making 'stupid mistakes'", replied Lowell. "Do you and Cathy have any plans for the weekend?", asked Calvin. Cathy Lewis being Lowell's high school sweetheart. "As it turns out, Cathy and I plan to see a movie Saturday evening. Why don't we make it a double date with you and Mary Jane?", replied Lowell. Mary Jane Thomas had been Calvin's sweetheart since their freshman year in high school. They were definitely 'going steady'. "Lowell, let me speak to Mary Jane to see if she has any plans. And by the way, will you be able to use your parents' car?", asked Calvin. "I have already cleared the transportation needs with my dad and he said 'okay' to my request," Lowell replied with a knowing smile.

"I will see Mary Jane in my next class and will speak with her about your plans, and rather than call you on the telephone this evening, I will tell you on the bus on the way home this afternoon whether or not we can join you and Cathy", and having finished his lunch, Calvin flashed a smile and headed off to his next class.

Calvin's afternoon classes became a blur. Mary Jane had told him that she would love to double-date with Lowell and Cathy to see the latest movie at the Bijou Theater so Calvin was walking around on 'Cloud Nine'. The last class of the day came and went and Calvin returned his unneeded books to his locker, and then hurried to the bus passenger pickup zone. His bus had arrived and was loading when he arrived at the loading zone. Climbing aboard Calvin noticed Lowell sitting in the rear of the bus and navigated down the narrow aisle to join him.

"Things are all set for Saturday night, Lowell. Mary Jane is excited by your invitation to double-date", noted Calvin. "That is great news, Calvin. Cathy and I will pick you up at 6:30 p.m. for the 7:00 p.m. show and then we can pick up Mary Jane on the way into town. It promises to be a fun evening", concluded Lowell.

About this time, the bus driver warned of his imminent departure and the students who had been loitering in the aisle speaking to friends, quickly took their seats. It was not a full load that afternoon with at least a dozen seats being unoccupied. This circumstance was occasioned by the fact that there was an after-school football game and many bus riders had elected to stay and watch the game. Extra curricular activities had to take a back seat in Calvin's and Lowell's lives since their responsibilities to their farm families had to come first.

"Calvin, do you think that I could visit you around 1:00 p.m. tomorrow for some assistance with my algebra questions? It is easier to ask you now rather than call you on the telephone later." "As far as I know now, that should be a good time. I will have finished all my chores and we can get a few hours of tutoring in before we have to pick up the girls", replied Calvin.

Although Calvin was the last student to board the bus on the morning run, he was the first off in the afternoon run. At this point, the bus stopped at Calvin's driveway and he bid Lowell good-bye and climbed off the bus. After the bus departed, and before walking up the driveway to his home, Calvin checked their mailbox and found the day's mail waiting to be taken to the house. A quick scan of the contents confirmed that there was no mail for him that day. Not that he was expecting anything for he was not in the habit of corresponding with any 'pen pals' or ordering any items from the many unsolicited mail-order catalogs that made their way into the Honeycut household.

The sun was sinking low in the western sky as Calvin stepped up on the front porch of his home. His dog, Skippy, ran barking to greet him with his tail wagging and placed his paws on Calvin's knee waiting to have his ears rubbed.

With that ritual behind him, Calvin opened the front door and shouted a greeting to his mother and father. From the kitchen came the wonderful aroma of a fried chicken dinner, soon to be dished up. Calvin could hardly wait, for he was famished.

5:00 a.m. Saturday
6 December 1941
Honeycut Farm

Regardless of the fact that it was Saturday, Calvin was up at the usual early morning hour to attend to his cows. Milking the cows was a 365-day per year requirement that could not be left unattended. However, after breakfast Calvin busied himself completing his own homework assignments for his high school classes. He enjoyed getting the work done early and not having to concern himself about such tasks for the remainder of the weekend.

Calvin had finished all of his assignments by the time Lowell arrived around 1:00 p.m. There was a knock on the front door, and Mrs. Honeycut greeted Lowell and led him into the kitchen where Calvin had arranged a chalkboard on which to write the problems that seemed to be troubling Lowell. As Calvin's mother closed the front door, Skippy darted into the house amid a shouted warning to Calvin. From the beginning, Skippy had not been a welcome guest inside the Honeycut home. His tenuous home with the Honeycuts remained in effect only as long as he remained outdoors where he bedded down at night in the hayloft inside the barn. Calvin snagged Skippy as he scampered through the kitchen and deposited him on the back porch out of harm's way.

"Lowell, would you care for a glass of Orange Juice?" asked Mrs. Honeycut. "Yes, please, I would enjoy that very much.", replied Lowell. "How about you, Calvin?", his mother inquired. "No, thanks, Mom, because I'm nursing a glass of warm chocolate milk at the moment." After delivering Lowell's Orange Juice, Mrs. Honeycut left the boys alone in the kitchen as she busied herself with chores of her own in the laundry room.

Lowell produced his algebra book from his briefcase and opened it to the chapter of concern. Calvin quickly reviewed the material and then set about developing sample problems on the chalk board to illustrate the principles that were eluding Lowell. The boys spent the next two hours in deep concentration, taking each element on a step-by-step basis until Lowell was thoroughly infused with the knowledge that he needed to not only catch up with his class, but maintain a satisfactory proficiency necessary to earning a good semester grade. Neither boy having had any lunch, they set aside their math studies to fix themselves some peanut butter and jelly sandwiches about 3:00 p.m. A gallon of cold milk had been taken from the refrigerator with which to quench the thirst that always accompanies peanut butter sandwiches.

"Lowell, are you comfortable with the results of our work thus far, or do you think we need to plow ahead a little longer?", asked Calvin. "Thanks, Calvin, I really think I've finally got it. You have been such a good friend to help me out this way".

"That being the case, let me make a suggestion. If it is okay with you, let me take a quick shower and get dressed and I can accompany you as you return home in your dad's car and it will not be too long before we will need to go to town and pick up the girls for the movies", remarked Calvin. "That is an excellent idea, and while you are showering I will go over this math chapter one more time to reinforce what we have been studying", replied Lowell. With that said, Calvin hurried to his room to lay out his clothes and then took his shower. By the time Calvin had dressed, it was close to 4:00 p.m. Calvin sought out his mother to tell her that he and Lowell were leaving for Lowell's home and that he would not return home until after the movie was over, probably around 11:30 p.m. "Drive carefully, Lowell, and do you need any money, Calvin?", asked Mrs. Honeycut. "No, thank you, Mom, I have all that I need to pay for my own and Mary Jane's ticket with enough to spare for popcorn and a coke. Thank you for the kind offer anyway", shouted Calvin as he and Lowell walked out the front door and down the porch steps.

Sitting in the Honeycut's driveway was a shiny, green, 1931 Chevrolet four-door sedan, sporting black fenders, that belonged to Lowell's father. Although it was ten years old, it looked brand new. It had a straight, six-cylinder engine and represented dependable General Motors transportation. Lowell climbed behind the wheel, and after checking that the gear shift was in neutral, started the engine as Calvin climbed in beside him in the front passenger seat. Although Calvin had obtained his driver's license in early 1941, he had yet to save enough money to purchase his own automobile. During the past year, he had been studying manufacturer's literature and had come to the conclusion that he preferred the appearance of Ford automobiles as opposed to those of the General Motors Company. His preference was shared by many of the high school senior boys for the school parking lot was populated by a large number of 1934, 1935, and 1936 Ford coupes, pickup trucks and four-door sedans. Although the 1940 and 1941 models were being sold, few school boys had the money required for such a costly purchase. The boys were attracted to the Fords not only by their modern lines, but also by the strong V-8 engines beneath their hoods. Calvin's goal was to accumulate enough money to purchase a used Ford by the end of the current school year.

Pushing the clutch to the floor, Lowell selected the reverse gear and gently released the clutch. As the car began to move backward, Lowell turned the steering wheel to cause the Chevy to perform a "U" turn in the wide driveway. This maneuver lined the Chevy up to meet the highway at the end of the driveway. Shifting into low gear, Lowell again eased the clutch out and the car slowly moved down the long, tree-lined driveway toward the highway where he braked to a full stop. After looking in both directions for oncoming traffic, he put the car in low gear and turned right toward his home. The transmission hummed as Lowell shifted through second gear on his way into high gear. Notwithstanding the fact that the highway was a secondary road, it was well maintained by the state and the Chevy was soon cruising effortlessly along at 50 miles per hour.

From his seat on the passenger side, Calvin watched as the flat Iowa countryside flashed by. During the day the temperature had warmed up to about 50 degrees with the full sun shining all day. Although Calvin had ridden his bicycle to Lowell's home previously, he did not know the exact distance. "Hey, Lowell, how many miles is it until we reach your house?", asked Calvin. "Oh, I clocked it on the way over and it is right at 10 miles, driveway to driveway, so we will be there in about 24 minutes or so", replied Lowell. "Is it okay if I turn on the radio?", asked Calvin. "Sure thing, I could go for some nice music right about now myself", replied Lowell. Calvin turned on the radio and rotated the tuning dial until the strong AM signal of a local Des Moines station eliminated the static that assaulted their ears between stations. The disc jockey announced that he was playing 'Sweet Lorraine' by the Glenn Miller Orchestra and the two riders relaxed and enjoyed the song. Three minutes later, Jimmy Maxwell, the disc jockey for Station WEBB, announced his next selection which was a listener request for 'Has Anybody Seen My Gal?' The boys smiled as the song began to play and Calvin tapped his index finger on the ebony window frame of his door to the rhythm of the music.

As the boys traveled west, the afternoon sun was setting and Lowell reached down and turned on the Chevy's headlights to combat the lengthening shadows. Several cars had passed them on the two-lane highway traveling in the opposite direction on their way to Des Moines or other points east. Jimmy Maxwell continued his banter and played at least six additional songs by the time Lowell slowed the Chevy and turned left into the Evans' driveway on the south side of the highway. He stopped by the mailbox and Calvin jumped out and retrieved the day's mail. Like most farm houses in the area, the Evans' home was situated about a quarter mile from the highway. As was the case with Calvin's driveway, Lowell's parents' driveway was also tree lined. The intent of the closely spaced fir trees was to ward off winter time snowfall, to the extent possible, to minimize the need to plow the driveway.

The boys arrived at the Evans farm at about 4:30 p.m. and Lowell parked the Chevy next to the house and set the parking brake as he stepped out of the driver side door. Turning off the radio, Calvin climbed out of the automobile and joined Lowell who was climbing the porch steps. As he opened the front door, Lowell made their presence known by calling out a greeting to his father who responded with a hearty, "Come on in and stay awhile". "Good evening, Mr. Evans And how are you doing today?". "I am pleased to report that I am hale and hearty with not a single thing to complain about. How about yourself, Calvin?", asked Mr. Evans. "Like you, I'm 'fit as a fiddle' and looking forward to a nice evening with Lowell and Cathy", said Calvin.

"Yes, Lowell told me about your plans when he requested use of the family automobile", said Mr. Evans. "Mr. Evans, I want you to know that this is a dutch treat activity this evening and we will see to it that your vehicle is returned with more gasoline in its tank than when we left". A smile crossed Mr. Evans face with that remark having been made.

"If you will excuse me, Calvin, I will go shower and get dressed so that we can go pick up the girls on time", and with that Lowell left the living room. "Calvin, make yourself comfortable while I go to the kitchen to help Martha with our evening meal. Can I get you anything to drink while you wait?", inquired Mr. Evans. "No, thank you, Mr. Evans. Lowell and I have pretty full tummies at the moment what with all the peanut butter and jelly sandwiches and milk that we consumed just before we came over here. I appreciate your kind offer though", replied Calvin with a smile. Mr. Evans then went into the kitchen to help his wife; the two of them would be dining alone this evening.

Calvin found an overstuffed chair and made himself comfortable with a copy of the latest issue of the National Geographic magazine whose lead article happened to be filled with photographs of farming activities peculiar to the state of Iowa. He enjoyed refreshing his knowledge of the topography of the state and the locations where the best crops were grown and of which varieties. A farm boy could never know too much about such things.

5:50 p.m. Saturday
6 December 1941
Des Moines, Iowa
The Evans' Farm

Lowell entered the living room dressed 'fit to kill'. In his 'Sunday Go-to-Meeting' clothes he was quite the dapper young man. He had that freshly scrubbed look and his blond hair was well brushed and shined brightly in the glow of the wagon wheel light fixture hanging from the ceiling of the living room. "Well, Calvin, I see that you have been entertaining yourself while I dressed", commented Lowell. "Yes, indeed I have. And I have learned a few things about Iowa that I did not know before, especially about which crops are best suited to the soil of our state and which crops bring in the most money. There is lots of food for thought in that National Geographic magazine", replied Calvin. "Well, lay the farming aside for now, as we need to leave to pick up Cathy and then Mary Jane in town." It turned out that both of the girls were city dwellers so the boys had about a 30 mile drive ahead of them to reach their dates.

By that time, Lowell's parents had finished their evening meal and were relaxing in their living room, and the boys bid them good evening, and stepped out on the front porch. The sun had set and it was quite dark with only the yard security lights illuminating the porch railings. They walked over to the Chevrolet and climbed in. Moving the gear shift into neutral, Lowell started the engine. As with the Honeycut farm, the Evans front yard was spacious, and Lowell turned the Chevy in one sweeping maneuver; and the car was then pointed toward the highway, invisible though it was a quarter mile away in the darkness. With the headlights turned on, navigation between the tree lines was simple. At the highway, Lowell braked to a full stop and waited for a single westbound automobile to pass before pulling out and turning right toward Des Moines. No cars were ahead of them so Lowell increased his speed to sixty miles per hour and the Chevy hummed along in a relaxed, unstrained mode.

Within thirty minutes, the boys reached the city limits and Lowell stopped at the first Shell gasoline station on Main Street where an attendant filled the Chevy's fuel tank, washed their windshield, and the boys split the cost of the fuel between themselves. At 18 cents per gallon, the six-gallon fill-up cost them each the grand sum of 54 cents.

Leaving the service station, Lowell continued east, and three blocks later turned right onto Grove Street and stopped at the curb of the third house on the right. The porch light was on. "Calvin, you hop in the back seat while I go get Cathy." "I'll be there by the time you return", observed Calvin. Aside from the porch light, the neighborhood was well illuminated by the adjacent city street lights.

Lowell made his way to the front door and rang the doorbell. Almost immediately, the door opened and Cathy was standing there. "Hi, Lowell. My, don't you look spiffy all dressed up in your fine clothes". "Thank you, Cathy, I guess I do look a little different than when I wear my jeans to school", offered Lowell. At that point, Cathy's father came to the door and stood beside her. "Good evening, Mr. Lewis, and how are you this evening?", asked Lowell. "The Mrs. and I are fine, but the question is, how are you?" said Mr. Lewis in a friendly voice. "Couldn't be better, Mr. Lewis, especially since Cathy and I and my friends Calvin and Mary Jane are headed out to see a nice movie at the Bijou Theater." "Sounds like a fun evening for sure, Lowell, but please have Cathy home by 11:30 p.m.", said Mr. Lewis. "No problem on that score, Mr. Lewis. In fact, there will be enough time after the movie is over for us to stop by Jackson's Drive-In for a hamburger and a milk shake." offered Lowell.

"Sounds like a good plan, Lowell. Now you and Cathy run along and enjoy yourselves". "Good night, Daddy", Cathy called over her shoulder as she and Lowell ran across the front lawn to the Chevy. At the car, Lowell opened the front passenger door and Cathy stepped in. Calvin spoke first saying, "Hello, Cathy, how are you this evening?" "Couldn't be better, Calvin, and I am so happy that you and Mary Jane could join us." "Thank you so much for inviting us. It promises to be a fun time". By then Lowell had entered the driver's side door and started the Chevy's engine. "Calvin, how do we get to Mary Jane's home from here?" "Well, the best way would be to just go straight ahead for three blocks, and then turn right on Lemon Street, and travel another two blocks and turn right on Laurel Street. She lives on Laurel, second house from the corner on the right", said Calvin.

"Sounds easy enough to me, Let's see if I can dead reckon us from those directions without getting lost", joked Lowell.

With less than five blocks to travel, Lowell pulled up in front of Mary Jane's home in about five minutes and they found Mary Jane standing on the front porch waiting with her mother. Calvin opened his door, climbed out and hurried up to the porch. "Good evening, Mrs. Thomas, and you too, Mary Jane. My, Mary Jane, don't you look stunning this evening". "Why, thank you, Calvin. And as the saying goes, 'flattery will get you everywhere'". "Calvin, it is so nice to see you again. It has been ever so long since the last time you were here", remarked Mrs. Thomas "Yes, ma'am, with it being harvest time on the farm I have been kept pretty close to home lately That will all change now that winter is upon us and I will have more free time", explained Calvin. "Well, you two run along so you won't be late for the show and have a nice evening", said Mrs. Thomas. "Same to you and Mr. Thomas, and I promise to take good care of Mary Jane, and bring her home on time", said Calvin. Following that exchange, Calvin led Mary Jane to the Chevy and held the door open for her to step inside. Carefully closing the door, Calvin walked to the opposite side of the car and climbed into the back seat. Without further adieu, Lowell pulled away from the curb and headed for downtown Des Moines via Main Street. In less than ten minutes Lowell was parking across the street from the Bijou Theater whose marquee listed the films that were playing. The double feature program included, "The Wizard of Oz" and "The Grapes of Wrath". These were preceded by a Fox Movietone Newsreel and a Mickey Mouse cartoon.

Lowell and Calvin purchased their own and their girlfriends' tickets from the young lady in the ticket booth, and the foursome entered the theater lobby, stopping first at the refreshment stand. "Mary Jane, what is your pleasure this evening" asked Calvin. "Oh, I think a bag of popcorn would be nice, along with a medium-size coke", said Mary Jane. To the waiting attendant, Calvin said "Two large popcorns and two medium cokes, please". The attendant returned almost immediately with the desired items and announced, "That will be 35 cents, please." Calvin handed over the money and Lowell and Cathy stepped forward to place their order. "Cathy, what is your preference this evening?", asked Lowell. "I have a sweet tooth so I am thinking that I will choose to have a package of Walnettos (small squares of smooth carmel-flavored candy flecked with walnuts) and a medium-size coke, if that's okay", said Cathy. "By all means, and I am going to treat myself to a bag of salted peanuts and a medium coke", said Lowell. Having heard the order, the attendant handed over the desired items and asked for 40 cents in payment, proving that candy was more expensive than popcorn. With their purchases in hand, the friends walked past the attendant, who took their tickets and tore them in half, returning stubs as proof of payment of the admission price of ten cents per person. Lowell led the way up the stairs to the mezzanine floor where their loge seats were located. Once there, he moved to the center of the first row that he had selected for the best view of the movie screen. Being in the first row, they would not be bothered by the heads of anyone sitting in front of them, which was often the case on the main floor. The house lights dimmed and the projector flashed the Fox Movietone News logo on the screen as the sound track played the 'Eyes and Ears of the World' Fox Movietone theme song. Both Calvin and Lowell slipped their arms around their girls who nestled their heads on the boys' shoulders. The newsreel devoted the major part of its footage to scenes from various war fronts in Russia and Great Britain. Scenes showing destroyed buildings in London caused by German bombers, also showed sad Londoners going about their daily lives, and Lowell Thomas' distinctive voice narrated the entire reel of film.

Lowell Thomas reported that on November 6, 1941, President Roosevelt made a direct appeal to the emperor of Japan for peace, while on the European Front, scenes were shown of German and Russian tanks and troops fighting in and around Moscow. In Russia, loyal troops attacked the German line north of Moscow and penetrated it up to eleven miles. Clips were also included showing massive groups of British bombers taking off from English air fields. Although Calvin was aware of the war in Europe from his studies in school of world current events, it was one of those out-of-sight,-out-of-mind sort of things. Seeing the events up close on a big screen placed the war in a much different and more personal perspective. Calvin realized that soldiers and troops in general were dying along with the pilots and crews of the various countries' bomber and fighter airplane fleets. Calvin was happy when the newsreel ended, as were Mary Jane and Cathy. Lowell himself did not attach any particular significance to the newsreel. He was two years younger than Calvin, so was that much more removed from any immediate concern about being drafted for military service.

The Mickey Mouse cartoon played next and the resulting laughter helped relieve the tenseness brought on by the Newsreel War coverage. The double feature films seemed to end all too soon. Calvin enjoyed savoring the closeness of Mary Jane's warm body as well as the fragrance of her exotic perfume. (At least, it struck him as being exotic). In a similar manner, Lowell enjoyed the presence of Cathy's head resting on his shoulder. Both boys wished that the movies would go on forever. However, the end of the second feature came and the house lights were turned up, and a rather full house of patrons arose and began exiting the theater. Sitting in the first row of the balcony, as they were, meant that the friends would have to wait a short time for the aisles to clear before they could leave the theater. While still seated,

Calvin said, "Jackson's Drive-In gets my vote for an after movie refreshment stop. Is that satisfactory with the rest of you guys and gals?" "That sounds fine to me", replied Mary Jane. "And I'll second the motion" chimed in Cathy. Lowell observed, "I will make it unanimous because I am really hungry. Those peanuts didn't last nearly as long as I thought they would. My stomach is empty and growling". Calvin noticed that the aisles were clear and said, "Okay, the aisles are empty so let's clear out of here." On the landing at the top of the stairs leading to the lower lobby, the boys assisted the girls in putting on their coats and then the boys slipped into their own coats. With the hour approaching 10:00 p.m. the outside temperature was cold at 35 degrees and dropping.

Once out of the theater, the foursome crossed Main Street to Lowell's father's car. Calvin opened the door for Mary Jane and helped her step inside. Walking around to the other rear door, he climbed in himself and was pleasantly surprised when Mary Jane scooted over and pressed her hip against his. Considering this action to be an invitation, Calvin reached over and grasped Mary Jane's left hand. It was soft and warm to his touch and caused a pleasant thrill in his brain. Lowell opened the door for Cathy and then walked around the car and climbed behind the steering wheel. Calvin observed that Cathy scooted over next to Lowell as soon as he was settled in and put her arm around his shoulders. "Look out Mr. Jackson, here we come", said Lowell. With that, he started the engine and smoothly accelerated to 20 miles per hour as he pulled away from the curb on Main Street and left the brightly illuminated Bijou Theater behind with its Marquee still blazing brightly above a few late evening patrons.

Jackson's Drive-In was located on the edge of Des Moines at the intersection of Main and Locust Streets. It was constructed in a 'U' shape with marked parking spaces on each side of the legs of the 'U'. The kitchen was located in the structure that joined the legs of the 'U' to provide ready access for the roller skating waitresses. The waitresses served their customers from roller skates and their number varied with the time of day. With the time approaching 10:00 p.m. (the busiest time of day), and a major quantity of customers present to be served, there was no shortage of waitresses. However, there was a shortage of parking places. As Lowell turned into the access driveway all parking spots were occupied; however, fortuitously a shiny red 1940 Ford convertible coupe backed out of a space next to the kitchen and Lowell immediately took its place. "There must be a guardian angel watching over us tonight", commented Lowell. "How lucky can we get?", agreed Calvin. The boys rolled down the windows on the left side of the car, leaving just enough glass exposed for the portable trays to hook on when their food was delivered. At the same time, Calvin pulled two wool blankets from storage behind the rear seat and handed one to Lowell. Keeping one for himself, he smoothed it over Mary Jane's legs as well as his own to offset the chill of the breeze coming through the lowered windows. Calvin enjoyed the pressure of Mary Jane's warm leg against his own.

Jackson's parking spaces were overbuilt with a substantial roof with which to ward off rain or snow during inclement weather, and each space included an illuminated menu board from which customers could choose their favorite food and drink. "Mary Jane, what catches your fancy?", asked Calvin. "I'm very hungry too, so I think I will choose a chili dog, french fries and a chocolate milk shake." replied Mary Jane. "That sounds like a winner to me, but I am going to opt for a vanilla milk shake", said Calvin. At this point Cathy spoke up and announced that she would order a hamburger, french fries and a strawberry milk shake. "I'm going to order the same thing", said Lowell. Jackson's Drive-In prided itself on being the home of the 15 cent hamburger. About the time the friends had decided upon their respective choices of food, a waitress skated up to the driver's window and asked, "May I take your orders, please?" The waitress wore a badge proclaiming her name to be Mary Catherine. "Yes, Mary Catherine, there are four of us and we wish to order two hamburgers with french fries and two strawberry milk shakes plus two chili dogs with french fries and one chocolate milk shake and one vanilla milk shake, and that is our complete order", said Lowell. "Thank you, sir. I'll give your order to the kitchen right away" and with that Mary Catherine skated to the order window and clipped her order sheet to the 24-inch diameter stainless steel merry-go-round that held all the food orders for the cooks to prepare. While they waited for their food, the friends discussed the movies that they had seen, but elected to forego any discussion of the 'war' topic. After all, why spoil a perfectly lovely evening dwelling on such an unhappy subject. Within ten minutes, Mary Catherine returned with two trays and hung one on each of the front and rear driver-side windows of the Chevy. After a quick glance Calvin said, "It is all here and just as we ordered, and is complete with napkins, salt and pepper and catsup and a breath mint for each of us. They didn't miss a thing. Thank you, Mary Catherine." "You're welcome I'm sure, and that will be $1.20", replied Mary Catherine. Calvin produced $1.45 and said, "Mary Catherine, please keep the change and we'll flash our lights after we've finished". "Thank you, sir, and enjoy your meals", and with that the waitress skated away to her next customer. Calvin, Mary Jane, Cathy and Lowell ate in silence savoring their last meal of the day. The food and drink were satisfying and the meal was a perfect way to end an enjoyable night on the town. By the time Lowell flashed his headlights, time was running out to return the girls to their homes without being late.

Mary Catherine quickly skated over and collected the empty trays just as Lowell started the engine of the Chevy.

Slowly moving out of his parking place, Lowell noticed a brand new 1940 Maroon Lincoln Zephyr Club Coupe pull into the space that he had just vacated. Then Lowell turned up Main Street in the direction of Mary Jane's home. Calvin held Mary Jane close and inwardly wished that the trip home would last an hour or more. Everyone was silent while their heads were illuminated sporadically by the headlight beams of oncoming cars. In due course, Lowell pulled to the curb in front of Mary Jane's home and Calvin opened his door, stepped out, and walked around to let Mary Jane exit the Chevy. "Thank you for a wonderful evening, Lowell and Cathy, I wouldn't have missed it for the world", said Mary Jane. Calvin took her arm and led her to the front porch where the light was still on. Turning her around to face him, Calvin said, "Mary Jane, I want you to know how very much I enjoyed being with you this evening and I look forward to being with you again very soon. I also want you to know how very much I love you". And with that, Calvin placed his arms around Mary Jane's waist, pulled her toward him and kissed her full on her mouth. Mary Jane returned the kiss and said, "Oh, Calvin, I have loved you since the very first day we met and I am so proud that we found each other". At that point, the front door opened and Mary Jane's mother was standing there and invited Calvin to come in for a hot chocolate. "I'm sorry, Mrs. Thomas, I'll have to take a rain check as I am riding with Lowell and he has to get Cathy home on time, but many thanks for the kind invitation anyway. Good night, Mary Jane, and I'll see you in school on Monday", said Calvin as he left the porch and ran back to Lowell's car and jumped into the back seat. Mary Jane waved as Lowell slowly moved the car into the street and turned in the direction of Cathy's home. Sadly, Calvin returned Mary Jane's wave and relaxed into the rear seat cushion never feeling more lonely before in his entire life; at the same time pulling the wool blanket over his legs. In those prewar days, the rear seats of automobiles were not heated.

Ten minutes later, Lowell pulled to the curb in front of Cathy's home and applied the parking brake as he turned off his engine. Then, he opened the driver's side door and walked around to Cathy's door and opened it. At the same time, extending his arm, Cathy clasped his hand and the two of them walked to Cathy's front porch arm in arm. The city street lights illuminated the porch, as did the light coming through the glass in the front storm door panel. Cathy knocked on her door, and between the time she knocked and some one arrived to open it, Lowell reached over and gave Cathy a significant hug and resounding kiss, which she also returned energetically. When the door opened, Mr. Lewis greeted the couple and invited Lowell to come in for some refreshment. Lowell replied, "Many thanks, Mr. Lewis, but I will have to decline your kind invitation this evening because my friend Calvin is waiting in the car and we both have very early farm chores to attend to in the morning. Perhaps I can take advantage of your hospitality at another time." "Absolutely, Lowell, stop by any time that you are in the neighborhood", said Mr. Lewis. "Thank you, Mr. Lewis, that is mighty kind of you", replied Lowell. "Well, Cathy, thank you for being my date this evening and I look forward to taking you out again very soon", and with that Lowell stepped off the porch waving good-bye to Cathy. Cathy stood on the porch waving until the Chevy was out of sight.

In only a few minutes, the Chevy was speeding west on the main highway leading to the boys' homes. It was going on 11:30 p.m. and it had been quite an eventful evening. "I don't know about you, Lowell, but I had a magnificent time this evening, and the best part of it all was getting to kiss Mary Jane good night", said Calvin. "Yes, Cathy and I noticed that you two were pretty cozy in the back seat and that performance on the front porch left nothing to be desired", said Lowell. "Look who's talking. I didn't notice Cathy shoving you away when you kissed her before her father came to the front door. I would say that she has more than a 'little crush' on you", observed Calvin. "Yes, you're right, Calvin. I love Cathy and she loves me and that is all that counts", said Lowell. The time and miles passed quickly by and soon Lowell turned the Chevy into Calvin's driveway and pulled up to his front porch. The yard lights were still illuminated as Calvin stepped out of the front passenger seat which he had taken while Lowell was saying good-night to Cathy. "Lowell, I can't thank you enough for the pleasure of your and Cathy's company this evening, and please thank your father for being so kind as to let us use his Chevrolet", said Calvin. "No problem, Calvin, and we'll do it again very soon. See you in school next Monday", called Lowell as he turned the car around and moved off down the long tree-lined driveway. As Calvin stepped up on the porch steps, Skippy ran up to greet him. Calvin stopped long enough to rub Skippy's ears and then sent him on his way to the barn for the rest of the night.

Calvin entered the front door and found that a nightlight had been left on for him. Locking the front door, he turned off the nightlight and quietly walked upstairs to his bedroom; his parents had already retired for the night. Calvin put on his PJ's, brushed his teeth and climbed into bed with tantalizing thoughts of Mary Jane circulating in his mind. He hoped that he would dream about her in his sleep.

1200 p.m. Sunday
7 December 1941
Des Moines, Iowa

Calvin and his parents were on their way home from church following the 11:00 a.m. service. The family car was a 1939 Dodge four-door sedan and Calvin was driving. Mr.

Honeycut reached over from the front passenger seat and turned on the radio which happened to be tuned to Station WEBB with Jimmy Maxwell announcing the titles of records that had just previously been played. 'In the Mood', 'I'll Be Seeing You', and 'That Old Black Magic' were the tunes that the Honeycuts had just missed. A few minutes after the radio was turned on, the normal programming was interrupted by the first sketchy news reports that Japanese government airplanes were attacking United States ships and naval installations located in Pearl Harbor on the Island of Oahu in the Hawaiian Islands. By the time they arrived home, President Franklin Delano Roosevelt was speaking to the nation's citizens decrying the sneak attack and articulated his soon to be famous 'Day of Infamy' speech. Thus, after staying on the neutral sidelines for several years, the United States finally joined World WarII with the declaration of war with Japan. Although it was noon in Des Moines, Iowa, it was only 0800 in Pearl Harbor and the attack was still in progress.

Calvin parked the Dodge in its garage and the family hurried to their house and turned on their Philco Console Radio to continue learning about the attack. The announcer reported that the Battleship Arizona had been sunk along with several others and a few cruisers. The death toll of Naval personnel was unknown in the early reports and few of the attacking planes were shot down by Naval gunners, caught off-guard as they were.

Calvin took the time to telephone Lowell to learn whether or not he and his family were aware of the disaster happening in Hawaii. "Hello, Lowell, are you aware that the Japanese are attacking Pearl Harbor in the Hawaiian Islands?", asked Calvin. "Yes, we have been following the story on the radio for about an hour now. Such a terrible event. And it was surprising to us for President Roosevelt to declare war against Japan so quickly", observed Lowell. "But, really, Lowell, what else could he do with such tremendous loss of life, much less the loss of so many ships of the Navy and airplanes of the Army Air Force", asked Calvin. "Well, perhaps you're right, but from where I sit, I have the distinct feeling that both of us will be drafted into the military along the way", responded Lowell. "You'll get no argument from me on that point. I have been thinking about the draft for some time now and have decided that I want to control my own destiny and not have it determined by a local draft board clerk", Calvin observed. "Well, I think I will get back to the radio and see what else there is to learn. See you on the bus in the morning, Calvin" and with that, Lowell hung up the receiver of his telephone.

Calvin returned to the living room where his parents were still gathered around the radio. Mr. Honeycut brought Calvin up-to-date on the latest information, and they spent the entire afternoon around the radio which, to them, seemed to be a gigantic magnet preventing the family from pursuing any other endeavors. In late afternoon, Mrs. Honeycut went to the kitchen and made some sandwiches and brought them into the living room along with some ice cold milk to drink, and the family enjoyed the makeshift meal in front of the radio. The radio announcer reported the sinking of the battleships U.S.S. Arizona, U.S.S. California, U.S.S. West Virginia, and the U.S.S. Nevada. In all, eight battleships were either sunk or damaged. And those numbers did not include the destroyers and cruisers that were damaged. From the radio reports, it was easily understood that, militarily, the Japanese had brought the United States to its knees. It was estimated that it would take many years to replace the destroyed ships and repair the other damage caused by the Japanese attack.

Eventually, the Honeycuts turned off their radio and went to bed, for tomorrow was another day on the farm and there were early morning chores ahead. Calvin got into his

PJ's and lay awake in bed on his back attempting to visualize what impact the declaration of war would have on his young life. No clear picture emerged and he fell fast asleep dreaming of his sweetheart, Mary Jane.

0700 Monday
8 December 1941
Des Moines, Iowa

Calvin was waiting in his usual spot the next day when the school bus braked to a stop at his driveway. The doors opened and he bounced up the steps looking for Lowell. He spotted him in the rear of the bus and walked down the narrow aisle as the driver eased the bus back onto the highway and continued toward Des Moines. "Hello, Lowell. How are you doing this morning?", asked Calvin. "I'm doing just fine, but I certainly wish that I had a crystal ball so I could see what is in store for me and my life as a result of the Japanese attack on Pearl Harbor", replied Lowell. "I am sorry to report that my crystal ball is as cloudy as yours, but I can report one decision that I made last night. I have decided that I will never let my eighteenth birthday arrive only to find that my life is at the mercy of some faceless individual in the local Des Moines, Iowa, draft board. I want to control my own life, especially from the point of view of choosing which branch of the military service that I will serve in", said Calvin. "Sounds like a reasonable approach to me. How do you plan to go about deciding the matter?", asked Lowell. "Well, for one thing, the Fox Movietone newsreel that we saw Saturday night tells me that being a soldier is not the way to go. Don't you recall those scenes of the soldiers who were under attack hiding in muddy foxholes in Germany?", inquired Calvin. "Yes, I paid close attention to those and other scenes", said Lowell. "The way I see it at this point, neither of us has a chance to go to Officer's

Candidate school; we're just too young and I doubt that we can obtain a deferment for that purpose either. On that basis, it seems that we only have a couple of choices. Either we enlist in the Navy or the Marines. And at the moment, I am leaning heavily toward the Navy for the reason that a person will have three square meals a day and a clean, dry place to sleep at night. I'm not saying that there will not be any danger, there always is danger in any war. But, all things considered, the Navy seems the most attractive service to me", Calvin said, catching his breath. "Well, Calvin, you won't get any argument from me. I have had similar thoughts since yesterday. Why don't we take some time off from school today and talk to the Navy recruiters in town?", asked Lowell. "You just passed your course in mind reading, Lowell. Those are my thoughts exactly", remarked Calvin. During their conversation, the bus had reached Lincoln School and the boys exited the bus along with the other bus-riding students who lived west of Des Moines.

Calvin and Lowell walked to the School Admissions office and obtained passes for late class arrival, explaining to the attendance monitor what their mission was all about. She eagerly provided the needed documentation and the boys left the school grounds. As it turned out, the Navy Recruiter's office was only six blocks from school and the boys covered that distance in about fifteen minutes. Hanging in the window of the Navy Recruiter's office was a poster admonishing any reader to 'Join the Navy and See the World!' Beneath the text was a photograph of a U.S. Navy cruiser tied up to a dock in some exotic foreign port, with sailors present along with a number of shapely, young girls languishing in the foreground.

Taking several deep breaths, Calvin and Lowell pushed the door open and stepped inside. Although they should not have been surprised, they had not expected to find so many other boys their ages having come to the same conclusion and were already standing in a long line of potential recruits. "Well, Lowell, it appears that we are not alone in our endeavor, if that is of any consolation", said Calvin. "Let's take a number and wait it out", said Lowell. Having made their decision, the boys took sequence number tags and sat down on benches provided in the waiting area. Several pieces of Navy PR literature were available on a table so the boys helped themselves and began to read about the requirements for becoming a sailor.

It immediately became quite clear that neither of the boys was qualified to join the Navy since neither one had reached his eighteenth birthday. However, they soon read the proviso that parents could consent to boys having reached the age of 17 to join the navy by signing certain Early Enlistment Permission Forms. "Well, Lowell, it looks like we were 'saved by the bell' on that one", observed Calvin. "I know that my folks will resist my desire to enter the Navy, but I think that I can give them the benefit of my logic in choosing to do so", said Lowell. "I think that you are correct. Your parents seem to me to be reasonable folks and I am certain that they would want only what is best for you and, to my way of thinking, being drafted into the Army is definitely not the proper choice for any number of reasons", replied Calvin.

A Navy petty officer called out Number 10, which happened to be Calvin's number, so he stood up and was waved toward an open office door. Walking inside Calvin was greeted, "Hello, I'm Chief Petty Officer Roland Jones, and who might you be?", Jones said in a friendly voice. "My name is Calvin Honeycut and I and my friend Lowell Evans came in today to learn how we might join the Navy", replied Calvin. "Very well, then why don't we have Lowell come on in and I can give you two the story together", responded Chief Jones. With that, the chief called his assistant and asked him to go fetch Lowell from the waiting line and bring him to his office.

After Lowell arrived in his office, Chief Petty Officer Jones asked him and Calvin how old they were, and upon learning that both boys were underage, pulled several copies of the appropriate Navy Under Age Enlistment Form from his desk drawer. "Well, men, I want to make joining the Navy as easy as I possibly can for you. But the simple fact of the matter is that I cannot do anything absent the approval of your parents because you are not 18 years old. So what I want you to do is to leave here with these forms, take them home, discuss the matter with your parents, and if they are in agreement, return here tomorrow with your parents, and then I can swear you into the Navy", advised Chief Jones. "Is there a telephone number that we can call you on in case there are some questions that our parents raise that we cannot answer?", asked Calvin. "By all means. Please call us on Greenwood 62400. That number is manned 24 hours per day and the duty officer will be pleased to answer any questions that you or your parents might have", replied Chief Jones. Both Calvin and Lowell wrote the telephone number on the back of the forms that they had received. "You will notice that I have given you two sets of the same form. One set is for you to retain for your personal records and the other will become part of your official Navy Personnel File. "I want to thank you for coming to see me today, and I look forward to seeing you both tomorrow", said Chief Jones, and with that he escorted Lowell and Calvin to the front door and bid them good-bye. Once outside, the boys congratulated themselves on their good fortune and carefully held the manila envelopes marked U.S. NAVY in large blue letters into which Chief Jones had deposited the magic Under Age Enlistment Authorization Forms. "Hey, Calvin, did you notice that Chief Jones called us men?", said Lowell. "Yes, I did, and he is correct. If we are old enough to fight for our country, we have to be men, don't we?", asked

Calvin. "There is no doubt about it in my mind. Let's hurry back to school and tell the girls what we have planned", said Lowell. "Why do I have the distinct impression that neither Mary Jane nor Cathy will appreciate what we are preparing to do?", said Calvin. "Well, as far as I am concerned, I think that Cathy and Mary Jane will be proud to have a couple of good-looking sailors hanging around", replied Lowell. "That may be true, but just how long do you think that we will be 'hanging around' once we are inducted into the Navy?", asked Calvin. "Not too long I would expect, but Chief Jones told us that we could expect to come home on leave after we have finished boot camp, so I guess I would lean on that old saying that says 'Absence makes the heart grow fonder', Lowell said with a sly smirk. "I hope that you are right, Lowell, because I really had not given any thought to my feelings about leaving Mary Jane behind", mused Calvin. In about fifteen minutes the boys arrived back at school and entered their respective classes and presented the authorized absence slips to their teachers.

1200 Monday
8 December 1941
Des Moines, Iowa
Lincoln High School

The boys had missed all of their morning classes and returned just as the lunchtime bell had rung. Heading for the cafeteria they expected to find Cathy and Mary Jane either in line or already seated. Calvin decided to have a hamburger and joined the appropriate line. The line moved slowly and he could hear the chatter all around him. Everyone of the students in line was talking about the Pearl Harbor disaster. Inwardly he was thinking, 'yes, you guys can talk all you want about the attack, but I have gone and done something about it'. He was, indeed, proud of himself. Moving his tray along he soon had his hamburger, then grabbed a coke and chips, paid the cashier and stood looking around for Mary Jane. He soon spotted her sitting alone near one corner of the cafeteria. He waved at her and she waved back and motioned for him to join her. Calvin did not see Lowell so he walked over to Mary Jane's table and sat down. "Good day, Mary Jane, and how are you today?" asked Calvin. "I'm just fine, but I missed you during our English class; where were you?", queried Mary Jane. "Well, Lowell and I had some personal business to attend to so we were not in school this morning. Mary Jane, haven't you heard about the Japanese Naval Forces attacking Pearl Harbor?" asked Calvin. "Oh, of course I have, that is the only thing one can get on the radio for the past 24 hours. But what has that got to do with anything?", complained a sullen Mary Jane. "Well, what it has to do with anything is the fact that Lowell and I are planning to enlist in the Navy and help America win the war", blurted Calvin. Mary Jane had a surprised expression on her face as though she could not believe the words that Calvin had just uttered. "You can't be serious, Calvin, giving up a nice safe place in school to go to war", moaned Mary Jane. "Mary Jane, you need to realize that eventually I will be drafted into one of the armed services, whether I like it or not, and I have elected to make a choice that I can control and not be victimized by the ruling of some draft board clerk who knows nothing in the world about Calvin Honeycut or what he desires. I have given a lot of thought to this action as has Lowell, and this morning Lowell and I visited the Navy Recruiter's office and obtained the necessary enlistment papers which my parents will have to approve before I can enlist", said Calvin. "Well, Calvin, I hope that they tell you 'no!'", said Mary Jane unhappily. "Please, Mary Jane, try to understand that I am only trying to do the best that I can in a difficult time for our country", said Calvin. "Calvin, please excuse me, I can't discuss this matter any further", and with that Mary Jane stood and walked quickly out of the cafeteria. By then, Calvin had lost his appetite and decided to throw his food into the refuse container and leave the cafeteria himself.

Outside, in the fresh air, Calvin spotted Lowell, and flagged him down. "Well, how did it go when you told Cathy about our plans?", asked Calvin. "Probably about as well as things went when you told Mary Jane", Lowell said with a bitter frown. "Cathy was furious and not inclined to be the least bit understanding", said Lowell. "Tell me about it, Lowell; I ran into exactly the same thing", said Calvin. "Women are strange critters, I guess, but I am not going to change my mind. I suppose the only apprehension I really have is the possibility that my parents will not approve and thereby deny me the opportunity to fight for my country", said Lowell. "If I would admit it, I have the same uncertainty in my heart, but all we can do is try", observed Calvin. The afternoon classes all ended up being a blur in the boys' minds. But finally it was time to take the bus home. The ride home for Calvin was unremarkable. He watched the other kids on the bus and heard them talking about the declaration of war and was proud of the fact that he and Lowell had already taken action to volunteer their services. In what seemed like no time at all, the bus stopped at Calvin's driveway, and he told Lowell good-bye and wished him luck as he stepped off the bus. Calvin stood and watched as the bus continued out of sight down the highway, and then, the day's mail in hand, he trudged slowly up his driveway secretly dreading the thought of telling his parents of his desire to join the Navy.

Although the temperature was above freezing, Calvin shivered as he walked up the Honeycut driveway, climbed the porch steps, and opened the front door. Entering the living room he heard the radio playing softly and his father was sitting in his favorite easy chair enjoying the music.

"Good afternoon, Dad, how are you feeling?", asked Calvin. "Couldn't be better, Son" replied Mr. Honeycut. "Is mother about? I have something important that I need to speak to both of you about", asked Calvin. "Well, as far as I know she is out gathering eggs from the henhouse and will return momentarily", volunteered Mr. Honeycut. Five minutes later, Mrs. Honeycut came through the front door with a basket full of fresh white and brown eggs. "Hello, Mother", said Calvin. "Hi, Calvin, I didn't know that you were home from school" said Mrs. Honeycut. "Yes, I just walked in a few minutes ago and I need to speak to you and Dad for a few minutes, if you have the time". "Let me put these eggs away in the refrigerator and then we can talk", said Mrs. Honeycut.

Mrs. Honeycut returned from the kitchen and announced, "The floor's all yours, Calvin". Calvin cringed inwardly at first, and then steeled himself to the session ahead. "I really don't know exactly how to approach this subject, so I will just say it the way it comes to my mind. First of all, America is in a war, not of its own choosing. It was forced upon the United States by the cowardly sneak attack of the Japanese nation. With our country moving to a war footing, I am bound to be drafted and I have given a great deal of thought to the merits of waiting to be drafted versus enlisting. Enlisting appeals to me because I can, to a limited extent, control my own destiny. Instead of being forced to take whatever assignment, go to whatever branch of the military that might come my way from a draft board. By enlisting I will have the ability to select the military service of my choosing, not someone else's. So today, both Lowell and I visited the Navy recruiting office in Des Moines and obtained copies of the necessary early enlistment papers inside this envelope that I am carrying. Of course, the papers are worthless without your signatures because I cannot enlist before I am 18 years of age. In choosing the Navy, I have done so on the basis that I will have a dry and clean place to sleep every night and will also have three square meals a day, and not have to live in foxholes in the earth like soldiers of the Army do. In seeking to enlist, I realize that it will place a burden on you, my parents, but eventually I will be taken by the draft anyway and I am hoping that you will see your way clear to agree to my enlistment", concluded a relieved Calvin, now happy that the worst was over.

At this point, Calvin's father spoke up and said, "Well, Calvin, that's calling a spade a spade for sure, and I can't say that we are all that surprised. We know that, in time, as you said, the draft will get you, but we appreciate the rationale you have outlined and know it to be true. Your mother and I have already discussed this matter and decided early on that if and when the time came and you made up your mind to enlist, that we would support you in every way possible. Not that we want to lose a son, but because we, like you, are as patriotic as the next family and want to do our part for America. Your mother and I will be pleased to go with you to the Navy recruiter's office and sign your enlistment papers", concluded Mr. Honeycut. Calvin's mother spoke up next and said, "Calvin, you know that we love you and want the best in life for you. Hopefully, your Navy duty will merely be an interlude that will come and go and represent happy memories for you in your adult years. We shall miss you with all our hearts, but trust in God to keep you safe". "Thank you, Mom and Dad, and I will do my very best to be a credit to you both as I do my service for my country", said Calvin. "In the morning, I will drive you to school and on the way we can stop by the Navy Recruiting Office and deliver the signed enlistment papers", said Mr. Honeycut. By then, it was bedtime and Calvin went to his room, put on his PJ's and climbed into bed. His thoughts were of Mary Jane and her not unexpected negative reaction to the news about him joining the Navy. He disliked having to contemplate leaving her behind, but did not see any way of avoiding his enlistment. He was soon slumbering in a restless, uncomfortable dream. There were visions of Mary Jane angrily criticizing him for enlisting in the Navy and, worst of all, threatening to throw him over and take up with another high school boy. Calvin was overjoyed when his alarm clock forced his distasteful dream world to evaporate amid the sustained ringing of his alarm clock.

0800 Wednesday
10 December 1941
Honeycut Farm
Des Moines, Iowa

With his morning chores having been completed, Calvin collected his schoolwork and Navy enlistment forms and waited in the living room for his parents. Without Calvin having realized it, his father had walked out the back door, started their 1939 Dodge, and driven it around to the front door. "Come on, Calvin, Dad's waiting out front for us", called his mother as she walked briskly through the living room and out the front door. "Be right there", shouted Calvin as he ran to catch up with her. Outside, Calvin opened the front passenger door for his mother to enter and then climbed into the rear seat clutching his important Navy papers as his father slowly released the clutch and the Dodge moved down the long, tree-lined driveway toward the Des Moines highway. The school bus had long since passed by and there was no conflicting traffic when the Dodge reached the highway. Mr. Honeycut was quiet on the drive to Des Moines as was Calvin's mother. Unbeknownst to Calvin, his father already knew the location of the Navy Recruiter's Office and drove directly there, where they arrived at about 0830. Mr. Honeycut parked the car at the curb and Calvin jumped out and opened the front passenger door for his mother.

0830 Wednesday
10 December 1941
Navy Recruiting Office
Des Moines, Iowa

As the family entered the Navy Recruiting Office, Calvin noticed that the lines of prospective Navy recruits were substantially longer than they had been the previous day when Lowell and he had come by. Calvin waved shyly to two of his classmates who were moving slowly along in one of the lines of prospective sailors. This morning, the Honeycuts had an appointment with Mr. Jones and were taken to his office as soon as they arrived.

When the door was closed, Calvin said, "Mr. Jones, I want to introduce my father, Arnold Honeycut, and this is my mother, Marcella Honeycut", said an extremely proud Calvin. "I am pleased to meet you folks", replied Petty Officer Jones. "Yesterday, I explained to Calvin and Lowell how our enlistment procedures are arranged, and I am pleased to see that, as parents, you are of a mind to support Calvin in his quest to become a sailor in the U.S. Navy", said Chief Jones. "Here are the signed forms that you gave to me yesterday, Mr. Jones, and you will note the original signatures of my father and mother in the positions called for on the forms", said Calvin. "Thank you Calvin. Let me glance over the paperwork briefly and then I will send you down the hall for a physical examination", remarked the Chief.

"The paperwork is in order and while you wait for Calvin to finish his physical exam, would either of you care to have a cup of coffee or a soft drink?", asked Chief Jones. "A coke would be nice", replied Calvin's mother. "Coffee sounds better to me", said Arnold "and I like it black." The Chief buzzed his petty officer assistant and the requested beverages were provided within five minutes. The Chief then beckoned Calvin to follow him into an adjoining room where a Navy doctor was just finishing with another recruit's examination.

"Calvin, this is Doctor Rassmussen and he will determine whether or not your physical condition meets Navy requirements". "Hello, Calvin, and how are you feeling this morning?" asked the doctor. "Actually, I have butterflies in my stomach at the moment if you want to know the truth of it", replied Calvin "This exam is quite simple and will not take long, so please relax while I check your blood pressure and other vital signs", suggested the doctor. "Calvin, when you are finished, please bring your paperwork back to my office and you will either be a sailor or remain a civilian", advised Chief Jones. "Thank you, Mr. Jones", replied Calvin, who at the same time felt a distinctly foreboding feeling about the impending physical examination. Chief Jones then departed the examination room and returned to his office.

"Calvin is being examined by our Navy doctor and will return as soon as the examination is completed. When Calvin returns, we will know whether or not he is a sailor or will remain a civilian. My offhand impression is that Calvin will pass the exam with flying colors. By the way, has Calvin expressed any preference as to the kind of Navy assignment he might desire?", inquired Chief Jones. "No, not to my knowledge", replied Mr. Honeycut. "Calvin is quite adaptable and has always displayed plenty of initiative in solving problems around the farm. He understands how to handle electricity and has an interest in radio communications. But whether he would express a desire to pursue any of these specific disciplines, is better left up to him for a decision", concluded Mr. Honeycut. "I appreciate having your insight, Mr. Honeycut, and what you say is quite true. Calvin will have the opportunity, if he is accepted, to select a specific craft to pursue and he will be trained in his chosen endeavor at a Navy school following his orientation at the Great Lakes Naval Boot Camp near Chicago, Illinois", stated Chief Jones.

Thirty minutes later, Calvin knocked at the door and came back into Chief Jones' office carrying the doctor's report which he handed over to the Chief. "Well, Calvin, you will be happy to know that you have passed your physical and are 100% acceptable for duty in the United States Navy. You are not color blind and health-wise are in excellent condition", stated Mr. Jones." During the next ten minutes, the Chief swore Calvin into the Navy and concluded with, "Mr. and Mrs. Honeycut, on behalf of the U.S. Navy, I wish to thank you for your affirmative response to Calvin's desire to enlist and he is now officially in the U.S. Navy, although he is free to return home with you with this travel voucher that will allow him to travel by airplane to the Great Lakes Naval Training Center to arrive no later than noon 15 December 1941. There, he will join a new company of sailors that will form at that time. Do you have any questions?", the Chief went on to say. "There is one thing that I am curious about", said Calvin. "All right, and what might that be?", asked Chief Jones. "When I finish boot camp training, will there be any time in which I might return home for a few days?" asked Calvin with a smile. "When your boot camp training is complete you will be given 10 days delayed orders before you must report to your next duty assignment", replied the Chief. "That sounds fair enough to me", replied Calvin. "Here is your travel voucher, Calvin. Take good care of it because it is the same thing as money. Unless you have any more questions, then, we are finished with the necessary paperwork and you are free to leave", said Chief Jones. "Thank you for your kind assistance to our son, Mr. Jones, and I am certain that he will make a splendid addition to the Navy in whatever position he is assigned", said Calvin's father. "I couldn't agree more", replied the Chief.

1030 Wednesday
10 December 1941
Lincoln High School
Des Moines, Iowa

After leaving the Navy Recruiting Office, Calvin's father drove the family to Calvin's school where he removed his books from his locker and then visited the school Guidance Office to turn them in. Leaving in mid-term, as he was, his grades would be recorded as incomplete; however, in the future, a ruling by the Iowa State Legislature would see him gain credit for his completed high school studies as well as his Navy service to the point that he would be issued his High School diploma.

Calvin visited each of his teachers and told them good-bye, but he was too late to catch Mary Jane before she had left school for the day. With Calvin's withdrawal business at school complete, the family returned home.

1300 Wednesday
10 December 1941
Honeycut Farm
Des Moines, Iowa

When he arrived home, Calvin called Lowell to check on how his parents had reacted to his proposal to enter the Navy. As it turned out, Lowell's parents were unalterably opposed to his early enlistment even if it meant exposing him to being drafted into the Army at some future date. Calvin felt sorry for him, but realized that he was not in any position to influence Lowell's parents one way or the other.

Next, Calvin called Mary Jane to find out if he might come over and speak with her about the day's events. Mary Jane was not at home, so Calvin left a message for her to call him when she returned home. It wasn't until about

7:00 p.m. that Mary Jane returned his call. "Hello, Mary Jane, are you busy this evening?", asked Calvin. "Actually, I'm on my way out the door to visit some friends", replied Mary Jane. "Oh, I have something important to discuss with you so could we get together some time tomorrow?", asked Calvin. "Well, how about our having lunch in the cafeteria together?", asked Mary Jane. "It is a rather personal matter, so could I pick you up and take you to a restaurant for lunch instead?", asked Calvin. "Yes, I could do that; pick me up in front of the school at noon", said Mary Jane. "Fine, I'll be waiting for you and many thanks, Mary Jane, and have a good evening", concluded Calvin.

Later, Calvin went to bed and pondered just what he would say to Mary Jane and how he would say it. Her brusk response on the topic of war in the cafeteria earlier in the week made him exceedingly apprehensive. He finally realized that there would be no easy way of breaking the news to her. After all, she already knew that he had gone to the Navy Recruiting Office to explore the possibility of enlisting. All he could do was profess his undying love for her and hope that she would understand, if not now, then eventually, and still be willing to be his sweetheart and, hopefully, be willing to write to him once in a while wherever the Navy might send him. With his myriad thoughts turning over in his tormented mind, Calvin finally relaxed and fell asleep.

0500 Thursday
11 December 1941
Honeycut Farm
Des Moines, Iowa

Awakened by his alarm clock at the usual hour, Calvin hopped out of bed and quickly dressed and headed for the barn and his Jersey cows. Milking the cows was one chore that, he decided, would not be missed in his new Navy life. When the milking was done and the cows put out to pasture, Calvin went in the house to shower and get ready for whatever the day might bring. After breakfast, he went to the living room and picked a comfortable chair and removed from his school tote bag some of the Navy literature that Mr. Jones had given him when he enlisted. In addition to learning something about the history of the U.S. Navy and its traditions, Calvin learned some of the details about the boot camp to which he had been assigned. He had never done much traveling in his life and he was intrigued by the prospect of flying from Des Moines to Chicago on a commercial airplane.

Satisfied that he had learned enough to find the Navy's Great Lakes Training Center, Calvin sought out his father to request permission to use the family automobile with which to pick up Mary Jane for their lunchtime date. Of course, his father was only too happy to permit Calvin to use the car, but could offer little guidance regarding the matter that Calvin necessarily had to discuss with his sweetheart. Arnold felt that the discussions should only involve the two hearts of Calvin and his sweetheart, Mary Jane.

1200 Wednesday
10 December 1941
Lincoln High School
Des Moines, Iowa

And so it was, that at the appointed hour, Calvin was waiting as Mary Jane walked out the front door of Lincoln High School. By the time Mary Jane had reached the car, Calvin had exited his side and was waiting by the open front passenger door. "Hello, Mary Jane, I'm so happy to see you.", said Calvin as pleasantly as he could. "Hi, Calvin, right on time I see.", replied Mary Jane, somewhat coolly, as Calvin assisted her in stepping into the front seat. After closing the door, Calvin hurried to the driver's side and took his place behind the steering wheel. Calvin started the engine, shifted into low gear and gently released the clutch as the car began to coast down the slight incline toward the avenue. "What sort of food would you like, Mary Jane?", asked Calvin. "Well, now that you ask, Armondo's is a nice Italian place only a block away and it is also very quiet; why don't we go there?", asked Mary Jane. "Armondo's it is", said Calvin, turning the car in the direction of the restaurant. Five minutes later Calvin parked behind Armondo's and quickly went to Mary Jane's door and opened it for her to exit. Calvin reached for her hand as she maneuvered over the car's running board and then stood on the pavement.

Gently taking her elbow, Calvin led Mary Jane toward the restaurant entrance. Inside, the motif was pure Italian and the fragrances of meals being prepared was enough to whet any appetite. The Maitre d' seated the young couple in a private corner of the sparsely-filled restaurant. It was early and the normal midday lunchtime crowd had yet to arrive. A waiter appeared and took their drink orders. After the waiter departed, Calvin took a deep breath and began, "Mary Jane, you know that I love you with all my heart and I am the last person in the world who would ever want to intentionally hurt you, but there are events that come into a person's life, that on occasion, cannot be avoided. From your remarks of the other day, I know that you are opposed to the war that our nation is now engaged. Nevertheless, the war is not going to go away unaided and it eventually will affect the lives of every American citizen, whether they like it or not. In recognition of that fact, I have withdrawn from high school and joined the Navy. I will be leaving Des Moines in time to arrive at the Navy's Great Lakes Naval Training Center by noon on December 15 for a period of 12 weeks. Then, I will come home on leave for ten days prior to my reporting to a new assignment, which is as yet unknown.

I pledge my heart and soul to you and hope that you can see your way clear to continue to return my love as you have done so perfectly in the past", concluded Calvin.

"Calvin, you have taken my breath away, and I hardly know how to respond. The thought of losing you to a war, however just in concept, is almost beyond my comprehension. I do love you so very much and had hoped that one day we might be married and raise a family. Of course, I will make myself content to wait out the lonely months until you return. There is no other boy in my life but you and that is the way it shall remain. Let us cram as many dates into your remaining time as we can", said Mary Jane with a smile. The waiter returned with their drinks, but neither Calvin nor Mary Jane had looked at the menu. "Take your time and I will return in a few minutes for your orders", said the waiter. "Mary Jane, you have made my heart so proud. I will cherish every minute that we can be together between now and the 15th. But for now, let's choose our meals", said Calvin.

The waiter returned and took the young couple's orders and departed immediately for the kitchen. In his absence, neither Calvin nor Mary Jane felt like talking so they merely sipped their drinks and observed the lunchtime crowd filling up Armondo's dining room. Ten minutes later the meals were delivered, but neither Calvin nor Mary Jane professed much of an appetite as a result of the stress of the occasion. After picking at their food for a time, Mary Jane suggested that they ask the waiter to bring them some 'take-out' containers and save the food for later in the day. "That is an excellent idea, Mary Jane, and I apologize for the circumstance that has dissipated our hunger", said Calvin. "Nonsense, Calvin", admonished Mary Jane with a fleeting smile. Calvin caught the waiter's eye and requested several 'take-out' containers.

The waiter returned and promptly transferred the uneaten food into individual containers, and gave Calvin the check for their meals. Calvin placed the money and a suitable tip in the waiter's leather folder with Armondo's embossed prominently in gold letters. "Shall we go, Mary Jane?" asked Calvin. "Yes, let's leave, but I do not feel as though I can face my classmates this afternoon. Would you mind taking me home? I'll worry about getting an excused absence slip later", replied Mary Jane. Calvin placed the food containers in the restaurant bag the waiter had provided and took Mary Jane's arm and led her out of the restaurant. Outside a winter sun was shining brightly as Calvin opened the car door for Mary Jane to step in. Climbing behind the steering wheel, Calvin started the engine, engaged the transmission and turned toward the parking lot exit ramp and then turned in the direction of Mary Jane's home.

1400 Wednesday
10 December 1941
Mary Jane's Home
Des Moines, Iowa

Less than fifteen minutes later, Calvin parked at the curb in front of Mary Jane's home. "Calvin, I would ask you in, but I think that I need to be alone for a time to digest all that you have told me", said Mary Jane. "I understand perfectly, Mary Jane, but would it be okay if I came over, say around 7:00 p.m., and we could eat our take-out food at that time?" asked Calvin. "Yes, that is a good idea and I will look forward to seeing you then. Perhaps at the same time we can make a plan for the days that you have left", said a hopeful Mary Jane. "It will be fun to make a plan with you, Mary Jane", offered Calvin. Calvin then opened his door and walked around to let Mary Jane leave the car. He took her arm and walked with her to her front porch and said, "So long for a while", at the same time kissing her lightly on her pink cheek as they parted company.

By the time Calvin was back in his car, Mary Jane was

already inside her house. Calvin drove home at a moderate rate of speed since he was in no hurry to reach the farm. He didn't relish the thought of speaking with his parents about his lunchtime session with Mary Jane. He, like Mary Jane, merely wanted to be alone with his private thoughts to attempt to sort them out into some meaningful form. Mary Jane's remark about marriage, and a family, had come 'out of the blue' as a total surprise to him, for although he loved her dearly, he had never gotten that far in his view of their future life together. Since she raised the issue, he felt obliged to decide just how he felt about the prospect of fatherhood. For example, should they consider marrying while the war is going on or should a safer path lay in the deferral of any marriage until the war ended? Calvin could not decide on the spur of the moment. As Calvin drove along the highway in the afternoon sunlight, his thoughts of Mary Jane seemed more and more important to his life's ambition. In the end, he decided that having a family had to represent the pinnacle of any relationship between a man and his wife. And, raising a family was something that he could become accustomed to.

1600 Wednesday
10 December 1941
Honeycut Farm
Des Moines, Iowa

Calvin arrived at the Honeycut Farm driveway and turned in toward the house after stopping long enough to pick up the day's mail delivery. Traveling up the driveway he decided to speak with his father about taking the car that evening, hoping that his parents had not already made plans for its use themselves. After parking the car in its garage, Calvin went into the house through the kitchen door where he found his mother preparing the family's evening meal.

"Mom, I need to mention that I will not be here for dinner this evening. I have been invited to have dinner with Mary Jane. Will that be a problem?", asked Calvin. "No, the meal that I have prepared is not dependent upon the number of mouths present at the table", replied his mother. Calvin could hear the radio playing softly in the living room so he assumed that his father was there and there was no time like the present to check out his need for the family automobile. Walking into the living room, Calvin greeted his father, "Good afternoon Dad, and how was your day?", asked Calvin. "Well, I finished all the planting of the winter wheat crop and I am happy to report that none of the machinery broke down in the process", reported Mr. Honeycut with a satisfied smile. "By the way, I am interested in knowing how things went with your talk with Mary Jane today?" Calvin had expected something like this inasmuch as he had sought his father's counsel as to how best to approach the subject with Mary Jane. "Let me just say that she was less than thrilled at the prospect of my leaving Des Moines more or less permanently for the duration of the war. However, in the end she, being the reasonable person that she is, allowed as to how she would wait for me no matter how long I might be gone to war", stated Calvin. "We left it on the basis that we would talk some more about it this evening at her home. Do you and Mom need the car this evening?", queried Calvin. "No, as far as I know now, we're staying home this evening, so help yourself to the Dodge", replied Mr. Honeycut. "I am to be at her place at seven o' clock for dinner, but I should not be out too late. Mary Jane's telephone number is in our directory in case something should come up and you would need me to come right home.

On another subject, Dad, I want to thank you and mother again for doing me the kindness of allowing me to enlist in the Navy. Having your blessing means more to me than you will ever know", said Calvin. "My son, that is what parents are for, to help their offspring get started off in life and this is a golden opportunity for you to learn what life is all about. My father did the same thing for me when I went to join the Army in the first World War", said Mr. Honeycut.

Calvin went to his room and took a shower and then dressed for his dinner date with Mary Jane. He didn't feel that he could actually identify what was going to happen, such as would be the case if they were merely going out on a Saturday night movie date. But, at the same time, he realized that it would be one of the most important meetings of his life. At 6:30, Calvin told his parents good-bye and then backed the Dodge out of its garage and continued on down the long driveway to the highway leading into Des Moines. He had allowed just the right amount of time to reach Mary Jane's home and pulled to a stop at the the curb in front at exactly 7:00 p.m.

1900 Wednesday
10 December 1941
Mary Jane's Home
Des Moines, Iowa

Pulling to the curb in front of Mary Jane's home, Calvin set the parking brake and stepped out of the car and locked the doors. With wintertime upon the countryside, it was dark long before seven o'clock, but the street lights provided plenty of illumination for the sidewalk leading to Mary Jane's front door. Calvin walked to the front door and rang the doorbell. He could hear the musical chimes sounding off beyond the glass-front door. Mary Jane opened the door and invited him in. "Mother and Father went to the Bijou Theater to see a movie so we are alone this evening", said Mary Jane. "I don't mind telling you that I am relieved to hear that. Did you tell them that I am now a sailor?", inquired Calvin. "No, I felt that you would want to do that yourself in your own good time and I should just keep mum on the subject", replied Mary Jane. "Thank you for that courtesy, Mary Jane. It was sweet of you to be so considerate", complimented Calvin. "Calvin, I have already heated up our food, so come into the kitchen, I'm starved!", said Mary Jane. "If you want to know the truth of it, I am ravenous myself", admitted Calvin.

Walking into the kitchen, Calvin found their food nicely arranged with a tall, red candle burning in the center of the table and a bouquet of red carnations decorating the table as well. "Wow, Mary Jane, you shouldn't have gone to so much trouble", said Calvin. "It was no trouble at all, Calvin, for I enjoy making things appear as professional as in a restaurant", said Mary Jane. "From my perspective, you certainly have succeeded", observed Calvin. "Thank you." said Mary Jane, with her dimpled grin showing.

Mary Jane served the components of their meal and the two proceeded to enjoy the food that they had missed at lunch- time that day. Calvin helped himself to the cold milk in a pitcher on the table while Mary Jane drank sweet iced tea. The main course was lasagna together with salad and warm garlic bread and farm fresh cow butter. (while the cow butter was a special treat to Mary Jane, it was 'old hat' to Calvin who routinely enjoyed farm-fresh cow butter that his mother made.) With their meal finished, Mary Jane served cherry pie a la mode for dessert. "What a delightful way to wind up a delightful meal with such a delightful and caring young lady", observed Calvin. "Why, thank you, kind sir, you always say the nicest things", replied Mary Jane. Having finished his meal, Calvin stood up and began to clear away the plates from the table and place them in the sink. However, Mary Jane had other ideas. "Guests are not allowed to do the dishes in this house, Mr. Honeycut", scolded Mary Jane. "That habit is merely something that is inbred into farmers' children. They are taught from early childhood that when they leave a dinner or breakfast table, they leave with something in their hands and head for the sink", reported Calvin. "Well, thank you for the kind thought, but our next stop is in the den to let our dinner settle a while."

The Thomas' den was a comfortable room with a tidy, but pleasantly 'lived-in' appearance. There was a nice crackling fire blazing in the fireplace, and Calvin placed another log on the fire before he sat down and took a place on the long leather couch as Mary Jane sat down beside him. He enjoyed the sensation of the pressure of her warm body against his own. The warmth of the radiant heat emanating from the fireplace gave Calvin an unbidden, exhilarated feeling throughout his body. Calvin placed his arm around Mary Jane's waist and pulled her closer to himself. "Mary Jane, you made a remark during our restaurant discussion at lunch time that has been running through my mind all afternoon, and that was when you mentioned the possibility of marriage and having a family. Although I have secretly considered that topic ever since I have known and loved you, I have never had enough nerve to discuss the topic with you personally. Why do you suppose that is?", asked Calvin behind a friendly smile. Turning and looking directly into his eyes, Mary Jane said "I think that it has to do with one's priorities as much as anything".

Calvin couldn't resist the temptation any longer and gave Mary Jane a long, lingering kiss. She did not resist, but put her arms around Calvin's waist and returned his kiss. "I guess where I am going with this conversation is to explore your thoughts about whether or not we should get married soon or wait until after the war is over", explained Calvin. "I suspect that our parents would tell us to wait, but it is our lives that we are talking about here and I am amenable to making the choice to marry now and let the future take care of itself", observed Mary Jane. "After all, we have been in love for the past four years and I feel that we are mature enough to accept the consequences of marrying, and beyond that I believe that we are exceedingly compatible", said Calvin. "We have the choice of either having a church wedding or eloping", said Mary Jane. "Under the State of Iowa laws, we are both of age and really do not require parental consent; however, to keep peace in the two families I suppose that we should at least attempt to obtain their approval. Here I am running off at the mouth and just realized that I have neglected to ask you the most important question of the day, Miss Thomas, Will you marry me?", said Calvin with a happy smile radiating from his lips. "I thought that you would never ask that question and the answer is YES!", cried Mary Jane.

Lost in each other's arms, Mary Jane and Calvin enjoyed the release of unabated kissing. Eventually they came up for air and smiled at each other. "May I make a suggestion, Mary Jane? What would you think about my coming over in the morning and asking your parents for your hand in marriage and, at the same time, letting them know that I am now a sailor in Uncle Sam's Navy. At the very least, I have a steady income and can support you and any children that we might have", added Calvin. "I think that that would be the best approach possible. If they have a serious objection, then we can decide whether or not to elope", replied Mary Jane with a meaningful smile.

By then it was going on 9:30 p.m. and Calvin had to hit the road for home. "Sweetheart, I am so sorry to have to leave you at a time like this, but duty calls and 5:00 a.m. comes around mighty soon. What time should I plan on seeing your folks in the morning?", asked Calvin. "Dad and Mom like to sleep-in so why don't you plan on coming over around 9:00 a.m. and I will stay home from school tomorrow", replied Mary Jane. Mary Jane walked Calvin to the front door and the two enjoyed a parting kiss and Calvin felt as though he was walking on air as he reached his car and started the engine. Pulling away from the curb he waved to Mary Jane who was waving from her front door. What a strange day, Calvin mused as he drove along the highway toward home. "Here I thought I had lost my sweetheart at lunch time, and end up the day asking her to marry me and, best of all, she said YES! What a glorious day in my life!" Arriving home, Calvin found his parents in bed so he quietly got into his PJ's, brushed his teeth and fell into bed. The cows would be calling all too soon. In the morning at breakfast he would tell his parents that he and Mary Jane were planning to be married. He realized that the biggest question of the moment was whether or not Mr. and Mrs. Thomas would give their consent.

0800 Thursday
11 December 1941
Honeycut Farm
Des Moines, Iowa

Calvin came downstairs from his room to find his mother preparing breakfast for the family. "Good morning, Mom", said Calvin. "Hello, Son, and how are you this fine morning?" asked his mother. "I couldn't feel better. Is Dad coming to breakfast?", asked Calvin. "Yes, he'll be along in a few minutes, he's out checking on a newborn calf that came into the world last night", said Mrs. Honeycut. Calvin's father walked into the kitchen about then and Marcella carried eggs, bacon, biscuits and gravy to the table. Calvin helped by bringing milk and butter from the refrigerator. The family took their places around the harvest table amid meaningless 'small talk'. After his father had said the morning blessing for their meal, Calvin thought it best not to spring his surprise on his parents early in the meal for fear of upsetting them to the point that they might not be able to finish their meal. When his mother and father were mostly finished, Calvin took a deep breath and decided to begin. Win, lose or draw, he had to tell them of yesterday's events at Mary Jane's house.

"Dad and Mom, I spent some time with Mary Jane last evening, mostly to try to soothe her hurt feelings caused by my joining the Navy. As you know, Mary Jane and I have been going steady since our freshman year in high school. We fell in love when we first met and nothing has changed that fact during the intervening years. We consider ourselves to be quite compatible and enjoy a relationship that is pleasant and rewarding. What I am leading up to is the fact that, last evening, I asked Mary Jane to marry me and she told me that she would do so. I plan to visit the Thomas' this morning and ask them for Mary Jane's hand in marriage. With my Navy pay I will be able to support Mary Jane while she stays in school to finish her senior year. She told me that she never planned to go to college, so that is not an issue. I have to admit that I had not seriously considered marriage heretofore, but the entry of our country into wartime conditions made me realize that these are no longer normal times. I dislike springing this matter on you two as I have, but there is a scarcity of time in which to make things happen", finished Calvin.

"Calvin, your mother and I have been aware of your love for Mary Jane and we have always approved of her social demeanor and maturity in general. About the best advice that we can give you is to wish you luck and encourage you to perhaps think a bit more about the life you will leave Mary Jane upon your departure for the Navy. You don't yet know what your permanent duty assignment will be so it may be unfair to Mary Jane to enter into a marriage at this time of uncertainty", cautioned Mr. Honeycut. "Calvin, you know that your father and I love Mary Jane as much as we love you and want you both to be happy in your life's pursuit, but, as your father has cautioned, perhaps you two should consider putting off your marriage until after the war is over", observed Mrs. Honeycut.

"Thank you for your counsel, Dad and Mom, but Mary Jane and I spent hours last night repeatedly going over all the alternatives, but in the end decided that we should take happiness where we can find it together. To do that, with Mr. and Mrs. Thomas' permission, we are planning to be married after I come home on my ten-day leave following boot camp. We thought about just eloping and getting married, but decided that that would be unfair to Mary Jane's parents as well as my own. In making our plans, we have assumed optimistically that the Thomas' will not object to my marrying Mary Jane. Only time will tell. Mary Jane told me to be at her house at nine o' clock this morning to speak with her parents, so I had best leave or run the risk of being late. Dad, could you drive me there, or if you do not need the car this morning, could I borrow it?", inquired Calvin. "We won't need the car, Calvin, you go ahead and use it" said Mr. Honeycut. "Thank you, Mom and Dad again, for your kind words of wisdom.", said Calvin as he left the kitchen and walked to the garage. Skippy met Calvin on the way to the garage and begged to have his ears rubbed and Calvin was only too happy to oblige. Skippy then bounded off after a stray cat and Calvin climbed into the Dodge and started the engine.

On the way into town, and in his mind's eye, Calvin went over various approaches that he could take to convince Mr. and Mrs. Thomas to approve his request to be allowed to marry their daughter. In the end, he elected to merely make a straight forward exposition of the facts as he had done with his parents. No need to 'guild the lily' he thought. When Calvin arrived outside the Thomas home, he was surprised to discover that he had no recollection of passing any of the major landmarks on his way to town. This circumstance had to have been the result of his total concentration on the meeting just ahead. With that realization Calvin took several deep breaths and decided that the best thing for him to do was to merely relax and take a leisurely walk to Mary Jane's front door.

0900 Thursday
11 December 1941
The Thomas Home
Des Moines, Iowa

Calvin rolled to a stop at the curb in front of Mary Jane's home right at nine a.m., parked and walked slowly to the front door. He assumed that Mary Jane would be standing by the door waiting for him to arrive. Calvin pushed the door bell button and heard the familiar chimes sound-off through the glass-front door as he had the night before. No sooner had he taken his finger off the button than the front door was immediately flung open and Mary Jane stood there smiling out at him.

"Good-morning, Mary Jane. Did you sleep all right last night?", inquired Calvin. "To tell the truth, I didn't sleep well at all last night because I was too 'keyed up', said Mary Jane. "But come on in, don't just stand there on the porch", admonished Mary Jane with a smile. When he stepped into the living room, Calvin could hear Mary Jane's parents speaking to each other in the kitchen. "Do your parents know that I have come to speak with them?" asked Calvin. "Yes, they do, but I did not tell them what the subject of your interest might be", smiled Mary Jane. "Well, as we expected, my parents suggested that we wait until after the war is over to get married", Calvin whispered into Mary Jane's ear so that her parents could not possibly hear his statement". "Come with me, Calvin, let's go into the kitchen. Mom and Dad, Calvin is here", announced Mary Jane. "Hello, Calvin", Mr. Thomas said in a friendly voice. "Good morning, Mr. and Mrs. Thomas, and how are you this morning?", asked Calvin. "On such a nice sunshiny day, how could we be anything but thankful and glad to be alive", said Mrs. Thomas. "I'll certainly have to agree with that sentiment. If it were a little warmer I'd swear it was springtime with such a blue sky outside", observed Calvin.

Calvin took a deep breath, exhaled and then began. "Mr. and Mrs. Thomas, is this a convenient time for me to speak with you this morning?", asked Calvin, with no small amount of trepidation. "Calvin, we are retired folks and have all day at our disposal, so forge ahead" smiled Mr. Thomas. "Very well, sir. To begin with, I am certain that both of you know that I love your daughter Mary Jane more than life itself. We have been sweethearts for the past four years in high school and have concluded that we were made for each other. We see eye-to-eye on most things and otherwise are totally compatible in our likes and dislikes. After the Japanese attacked Pearl Harbor, I felt obliged to join the Navy to be of service to our country. My parents approved of my action and signed the necessary enlistment forms to allow me to enlist even though I am a few months shy of my 18th birthday. In fact, I became a sailor last Tuesday and will be reporting to the Navy's Great Lakes Boot Camp near Chicago, Illinois, on December 15th for three months of training. Following that assignment, I will be given ten days delayed orders to permit me to come home on leave prior to traveling to my next duty assignment which is unknown at this time." Calvin intentionally hesitated at this point to let what he had revealed be fully comprehended by the Thomas parents.

"Last evening, Mary Jane and I discussed our lives and what we could see of the future, both near-term and long-term. During that discussion, I expressed my love for your daughter and asked her to be my wife. Amazingly enough, she accepted my proposal of marriage and that is why I am here this morning. I am here seeking your approval to marry

Mary Jane sometime during my leave following boot camp; probably around the middle of March. Mary Jane and I are comfortable with our desire to be married and hope that you will find it in your hearts to look favorably upon my request", concluded Calvin.

"Calvin, speaking for Mary Jane's mother as well as myself, we have always considered you to be one of the family. That you elected to join the Navy to fight for your country is commendable and to be admired and we congratulate you on your action. However, we feel that there will be uncertain times ahead for Mary Jane if you two should marry before the war is over. Without having had an opportunity to discuss your proposal privately, we would like to suggest that you and Mary Jane take some time to evaluate your desired plans between now and when you return home on leave. At that time, Mrs. Thomas and I will give you and Mary Jane our final decision." concluded Mr. Thomas.

"I want to thank you and Mrs. Thomas for giving me the courtesy of listening to my proposal. I personally appreciate your concerns and I am certain that Mary Jane feels the same way", concluded Calvin. After bidding the Thomas' good-bye, Calvin took Mary Jane's hand and the two of them walked out the front door and down to Calvin's car where they stood silently holding each other tight for some time. At length, Calvin broke the silence by saying, "Mary Jane, don't be discouraged. We have three wonderful days to enjoy each other's company before I have to leave town. Let's make the best of a bad situation and just fall back and regroup. Although we might perceive your parent's decision to withhold an immediate approval as a failure, the door is still open, as I see it. And, alternatively, we still have available the option to elope in March should your parents continue to withhold their approval. In between then and now, we will just have to carry on a campaign to convince them that what we propose to do is the right thing for our ultimate happiness, war or no war", enthused Calvin.

"Oh, Calvin, I am so disappointed. I just knew that my folks would acquiesce to your splendid proposal of marriage. I love you all the more for the things that you said to my father and mother. And I agree. Should it turn out that they are unwilling to give us their blessing in March we will merely travel to some Justice of the Peace and become man and wife on our own" said Mary Jane, with tears welling up in her eyes. "We can even get Lowell to be "best man" and Cathy to stand up for me as my maid of honor", stated Mary Jane, ever so sadly. "But back to us, what are you doing this evening? Do you plan to go to school today? If not, would you feel like returning home with me and spending some time on our farm and perhaps we could go to the movies this evening if you are so inclined", asked Calvin. "I have no plans for this evening and "NO!" I do not plan to go to school at all today, or any other day until you are gone, and "Yes" I would love to accompany you back home to the Honeycut Farm; it will be a treat to see your parents again. Let me run in and tell my folks where I am going and I'll be right back". Mary Jane ran into her house as quickly as she could and was back in less than five minutes smiling her satisfaction at being able to accompany Calvin to his home. "Mom and dad thought that it was a good idea for me to spend some time with your folks. Imagine that?", said Mary Jane quite unbelievingly. Calvin held the door open as Mary Jane stepped in. Then Calvin hurried around to the other side of the car and climbed in behind the steering wheel, happily noting the fact that Mary Jane had scooted over and was pressing her body against his and placed her arm around his neck. After starting the engine, Calvin pulled the Dodge out into traffic and headed west out of town. It was a sunny day and Des Moines never looked so clean and elegant in the bright sunshine. And with his sweetheart by his side, all was right with Calvin's world. He would enjoy the presence of Mary Jane's company at his father's farm for the entire day. What a blessing, Calvin thought to himself. Thirty minutes later, Calvin turned into the Honeycut Farm where he drove up the long driveway and into the garage and parked. With his hands not otherwise occupied, Calvin turned and gave Mary Jane her first kiss of the day. "What a pleasant surprise, Mr. Honeycut", said Mary Jane.

1200 Thursday
11 December 1941
Honeycut Farm
Des Moines, Iowa

"If you don't mind, I would like to go in the house and tell my folks a little of what happened at your place. Is that okay?", asked Calvin. "By all means, let's do that. I think that it would help me to talk about it and get the disappointment behind me", said Mary Jane. As the couple stepped out of the Dodge, Skippy ran up looking for Calvin to rub his ears. "Mary Jane, in case you have not met him before, this is my dog, Skippy. He is a Shelty and is mighty handy around the farm in herding the cows when it is milking time", concluded Calvin. "Hello, Skippy", said Mary Jane, kneeling down to pet the dog. Skippy seemed to enjoy the attention and licked Mary Jane's hand. After sending Skippy on his way, Calvin and Mary Jane proceeded to the house.

"Knock, knock" yelled Calvin loudly as he and Mary Jane entered the kitchen. It was lunch time and Calvin's parents were seated around their harvest table. "Hello, Mr. and Mrs. Honeycut" smiled Mary Jane. "Why, hello to you, Mary Jane", said Mrs. Honeycut. "It's so nice to see you again. Please pull up a chair and join us" chimed in Mr. Honeycut. Calvin grabbed a chair for Mary Jane and then one for himself "We're just having sandwiches", said Mrs. Honeycut. "And there are plenty of 'makins' along with lots of fresh baked bread. Would you care for some sweet iced tea, Mary Jane?", asked Mrs. Honeycut. "That sounds so tasty; yes, I really would enjoy having some. Thank you", replied Mary Jane. During the conversation, Calvin had quickly made himself a ham sandwich and also one for Mary Jane.

"Dad and Mom, we want you to know that Mary Jane's parents are considering my proposal of marriage, but have requested that we continue to think about the possibility until mid-March when I return to Des Moines from boot camp. At that time, they will be prepared to give us their final decision. We think that their proposal is a fair compromise and I thanked them for allowing me to personally make my proposal to them", said Calvin. "Yes, and Calvin did a magnificent job of explaining what the two of us have in mind. Both of us thought that you would want to know how things stand", said Mary Jane. "Why, thank you, Mary Jane, for taking us into your confidence" said Mr. Honeycut. "We know that it must be a great disappointment to you, but in the end, it never hurts to give a lot of thought to the consequences of acquiring a partner for the rest of your life", added Mrs. Honeycut. "Truer words were never spoken", added Mr. Honeycut. "With my departure a mere three days away, Mary Jane and I want to spend as much time together as we can, so we came here first and plan to spend this afternoon on the farm and take in a movie this evening. Dad, is there anything that I can do to assist you this afternoon?", asked Calvin. "No, Calvin, thank you for the kind offer, but things are very well under control on the farm at the moment. Perhaps Mary Jane would like to see the new calf that was born last night", suggested Mr. Honeycut. "Oh, yes, indeed, I would enjoy that very much", said Mary Jane. Having finished their sandwich, Mary Jane and Calvin stood and Mary Jane said, "Thank you very much for the nice luncheon and refreshing tea." "You're quite welcome, my dear", replied Mrs. Honeycut. "We'll be out by the barn if you need us", said Calvin. Taking Mary Jane by the hand, he led her out the kitchen door and across the yard to the whitewashed fence surrounding the corral. Opening the gate, Calvin led Mary Jane into the manger where the newborn calf was having its dinner, courtesy of its Jersey mother. "What a sweet little calf", exclaimed Mary Jane as she knelt down to rub its tiny head. "My dad believes that Jersey cows are the best so those are the only milk cows that we own", said Calvin. "They certainly have lovely blonde-colored fur" observed Mary Jane.

From the manger, Calvin took Mary Jane across a meadow to a pond located about a quarter mile north of the barn. The spring-fed pond was full of crystal clear water and large catfish could be seen swimming in lazy circles, and an occasional one leaped out of the water in pursuit of an insect. Surrounding the pond, perhaps 40 feet from the shoreline, was a dense stand of oak trees. "My dad and I thin the trees on occasion when we need to replenish our supply of wood for our fireplaces", volunteered Calvin. The sloping shore of the pond was covered with a lush green grassy carpet. The grass was dry on this sunny day and Calvin and Mary Jane sat down to enjoy the solitude. The soft grass felt just like a thick carpet of wool fibers beneath their backs as they lay down to absorb the sun's rays.

"Are you content, Mary Jane?", asked Calvin. "Oh, yes, Calvin; this is such a lovely place to enjoy each other; it is almost like being in another world. I am so happy that you invited me to accompany you to your home. Being alone with you is the answer to one of my prayers", continued Mary Jane. Calvin reached over and touched Mary Jane's long blonde hair. "Mary Jane, you are so beautiful that it makes my heart skip a beat when I look at you", confided Calvin. "I'll give you the rest of my life to stop saying nice things like that. By the way, you're no slouch in the physical department yourself. I just love your red hair. Not that it is a secret, but the color of your hair is what first attracted me to you", revealed Mary Jane with a grin. Laying beside Mary Jane, Calvin reached over and turned her body toward him and planted a lingering kiss on her soft, red lips. As he held her, he could feel her firm breasts against his chest and the sensation sent ecstatic chills through his body. For her part, Mary Jane felt her pulse quicken under the pressure of Calvin's lips upon hers. Their embrace continued and Calvin thought that he had arrived in heaven and was holding an angel in his arms.

Time passed by and the sun slowly made its way descending lower in the western sky. Still, Calvin and Mary Jane enjoyed their lovemaking in their own private little world. Eventually Calvin stood up and then reached down to help Mary Jane to her feet and held her tight for one last delicious kiss. It was time to think about leaving for town if they were to get to the Bijou Theater before the 7 o' clock movie began.

The couple strolled leisurely back to the farmhouse where Mary Jane said her good-byes to his parents and Calvin obtained permission to use his father's car to take Mary Jane out on a date. Calvin backed the Dodge out of the garage and opened the front passenger door for Mary Jane to enter. As before, and happily so for Calvin, Mary Jane scooted close to him and put her left arm around his shoulders. For his part, Calvin reached for Mary Jane's other hand and she held his hand in her lap throughout the trip to town. Heaven again, twice the same day, Calvin thought. It was only 5:30 p.m. when Calvin turned down the street on which the Bijou Theater was located. He was hungry and was certain that Mary Jane was too. Without asking, Calvin stopped at Jackson's Drive-In where they each ordered a hamburger, coke and french fries. "This should tide us over till we get into the Bijou and can get some popcorn", said Calvin. "No doubt about it, I was famished after our afternoon on the farm and I thank you for thinking about food. I also want to thank you again for making my day such a delightfully special one", said Mary Jane. "If it was pleasant for you, it was doubly pleasant for me, and I look back upon it with some regret with the realization of all the days that we have missed being together this past year and now there are only three days left", lamented Calvin. "Never fear, sweetheart, for we shall make the rest of them exceedingly memorable indeed", promised Mary Jane. With their meal consumed, Calvin asked Mary Jane if she should call home and let her parents know where she was. She agreed that that was an excellent idea and made the call. Her parents appreciated the courtesy and, indirectly, complimented Calvin for his thoughtfulness again.

1800 Thursday
11 December 1941
Jackson's Drive-in
Des Moines, Iowa

With their meal having been consumed, Calvin started the engine of the Dodge and then departed Jackson's Drive-In for the Bijou Theater, parking across the street at a parking meter that, for the lateness of the day, did not have to be fed any coins. Calvin and Mary Jane walked across the street and directly to the ticket booth where Calvin bought two tickets. Tickets in hand, the couple walked into the lobby and received back their stubs showing any later official of the theater that they had, indeed, paid their 10-cent admission fee. For that evening's program, Calvin elected to sit in the loge section on the lower floor about ten rows from the rear of the theater. Stopping midway from either wall, Calvin sat down alongside Mary Jane. As it turned out, neither Mary Jane nor Calvin were hungry when they passed the refreshment stand in the theater lobby for their Jackson's

Drive-in food had not had time to digest. Calvin, in an aura of contentment, wasn't the least bit interested in whatever movie was playing either. He planned to concentrate his attention on Mary Jane to the exclusion of anyone sitting beside, in front of or behind them. In other words, he planned to carry on his lovemaking with his sweetheart to his heart's content. The houselights were dimmed and Calvin took Mary Jane's hand in his and kissed her fingers, one-at-a-time while at the same time placing his right arm around her shoulder while, on the screen, coming attraction previews were playing. Mary Jane responded by placing her head on Calvin's shoulder and snuggled closer to him. Occasionally, Mary Jane would turn her head toward Calvin and he would oblige her by tenderly kissing her sweet lips. He left it up to her as to whether or not the images on the screen were of any importance. Mostly, she agreed with him that the transient images flashing on the theater screen were really not that important to their lives, what with time to enjoy each other being so short. Eventually, the motion picture ended and the houselights came on brightly signaling to the audience that it was time to depart.

As their row emptied, Calvin and Mary Jane stood and walked slowly to the lobby and out across the street to where their transportation waited. Calvin assisted Mary Jane by opening her door and then hurried to the driver's position. Starting the engine, Calvin reluctantly engaged the transmission and pulled away from the curb. It was but a short distance to Mary Jane's home and Calvin disliked the prospect of having to drive home alone to the farm. Parking in front of Mary Jane's home, Calvin noted that the front porch light was on and that there were other lights illuminated within the house. "It appears that your parents are waiting up for you, Mary Jane." "No, I don't think so, as late as it is they're certain to be in bed already." With that having been said, Calvin opened Mary Jane's door and helped her over the nearby curb and they then walked to the front porch. Mary Jane had her own key and proceeded to unlock the door while Calvin waited. "Mary Jane, may I come by in the morning and pick you up? We'll find something fun to do like roller-skating or going to Johnson's Penny Arcade. And there is even Axelson's Indoor Carnival up the road in Leroy Township", offered Calvin. "Stop by as early as you wish; I will be up and dressed and I know that my parents will approve. Those all represent exceedingly fun activities to me and I just love roller-skating", continued Mary Jane. With their next day's program decided, Calvin pulled Mary Jane close and gave her a lingering kiss, again noticing the delightful pressure of her firm breasts against his chest. How he longed to be kissing them in addition to Mary Jane's sweet lips. But that would have to wait for another time. "Goodnight, Mary Jane, and I thank you from the bottom of my heart for letting me love you. You are the light of my life", proclaimed Calvin. "Calvin, please don't forget that that is a two-way street. You are certainly the light of my life too", observed Mary Jane. By then, Calvin was opening the driver's door to his car and called out, "See you tomorrow, sweetheart", as Mary Jane waved. Calvin started the car and turned toward the highway to home as Mary Jane entered her home and turned off the porch light.

On the way home Calvin relived the events of the day including the pleasant interlude when he and Mary Jane were kissing each other on the banks of his father's spring-fed pond. Memories like that were wonderful in the extreme, thought Calvin. Occupied as he was with thoughts of his sweetheart, Calvin failed to notice his driveway flash by until some distance beyond when his mind came back to earth. Well, that's a good one on me, he mused, as he turned the car around and retraced the short distance to his driveway. "I never knew what the power of love could do to a person", he repeated quietly to himself.

The yard light illuminated his access to the garage and he parked the Dodge in its usual stall and went into the darkened house. Quickly changing into his PJ's, Calvin climbed into bed and relaxed for the first time that day. His life was hectic, but somewhat more simplified now that the Thomas' had set their ground rules for himself and Mary Jane to follow. Mid-March could not get here soon enough to suit him, thought Calvin. With visions of Mary Jane in his mind, Calvin fell into a deep sleep. It seemed, in his dream, that the war was over and Mary Jane and he were married and making love on their honeymoon. About the time that the dream was fully developed, Calvin was awakened by his alarm clock.

0500 Friday
12 December 1941
Honeycut Farm
Des Moines, Iowa

The alarm clock sounded and Calvin roused himself from a tantalizing dream about Mary Jane and their married life together. His cows awaited without, so he hurried to dress and attend to his morning milking chores. His father had yet to inform him as to his plans for the milking chore after Calvin left for the Navy. The herd was not large enough to warrant installation of a mechanical milking system, so perhaps his father would contract with one of the neighbor boys, Lowell, for instance, to handle the work. It was Calvin's hope that his father would make a decision soon as he disliked the prospect of leaving for Chicago with the issue still unresolved.

0900 Friday
12 December 1941
Honeycut Farm
Des Moines, Iowa

With his chores finished, Calvin returned to the kitchen where he found his mother busily preparing breakfast. "Good morning, Mom", said Calvin. "Good morning, Calvin, and did you sleep well?", asked Mrs. Honeycut. "As a matter of fact, I slept very soundly and felt quite rested by the time the alarm went off", replied Calvin. "Good for you, Calvin, I was afraid yesterday's events might have been a bother to you", said his mother. "I have to admit to some disappointment in the Thomas' position, but I can certainly appreciate their concerns and am willing to live with the ground rules that they have established", observed Calvin. "Well, Calvin, that reaction tells me that you have a level head on your shoulders, which I have always known", said Mrs. Honeycut. "Thank you, Mom, for the vote of confidence, and incidentally, as soon as I have eaten my breakfast, I plan to leave and spend the entire day with Mary Jane. We are going roller-skating and probably drive over to Leroy Township and check out their winter carnival. Is there something that I can do for you or Dad before I leave?" "No Calvin, nothing for me, but you had better check with Dad to see what he might have in mind", suggested Mrs. Honeycut. "Okay, I'll do that, but where is Dad at the moment?", asked Calvin. "Last I knew, he was down at the barn checking on the new calf", offered Mrs. Honeycut. Calvin left the kitchen and walked down to the barn. Opening the corral gate, Calvin found his father feeding the young Jersey mother cow and the new calf standing on shaky legs was getting its morning meal from its mother. "Good morning, Dad. It looks as though the new arrival is hale and hearty", said Calvin. "Yes, it is, and for that I am exceedingly thankful. There is nothing worse on a farm than having sickly animals around", observed Mr. Honeycut. "Dad, I promised to spend the day with Mary Jane, but I wanted to check with you to see if there was something that I could do to help you before I left", said Calvin. "No, Son, things are still under control here and there isn't anything that I need help with at the moment and, by the way, go ahead and use the Dodge. If we need to go anywhere, we can always use the pickup truck", offered Mr. Honeycut. "Many thanks for the kind offer and you and Mom have a nice day", replied Calvin. "I'll return home well after dark, so don't plan on waiting up for me" advised Calvin. "No problem, Son, and enjoy yourself with Mary Jane today" said Mr. Honeycut.

Calvin was already wearing his dress clothes, so he opened the garage door and backed the Dodge out of its stall and headed down the driveway toward the Des Moines highway. Arriving there, he found no conflicting traffic as he turned east and continued on his way to Des Moines, thirty minutes down the highway. Again, he was blessed with a blue-sky day and a temperature around 50 degrees. Thank goodness, freezing weather was still somewhere in the distant weeks ahead. Driving past the Des Moines "City Limits" sign, Calvin slowed the Dodge slightly to the posted speed limit. No sense in starting the day off with a traffic citation he thought to himself. As he drove along the Des Moines streets leading to Mary Jane's home, Calvin's thoughts unexpectedly brought Lowell to mind. It was such a personal disappointment that he and Calvin could not enter the Navy together.

1030 Friday
12 December 1941
Thomas Home
Des Moines, Iowa

Five blocks away, Calvin pulled up in front of Mary Jane's home and parked. No one was outside, so he got out of the car and walked to the front door where he pushed the doorbell button. The now familiar sound of the musical chimes filtered through the door and the sound had become a comforting welcome sign for him. The front door opened and Mary Jane smiled out through the storm door pushing it open as she said, "Please come in, Calvin. You look so handsome this morning in your nice suit". Whereupon she caught Calvin by the arm and gave him a lingering kiss. "Thank you for the kind words, Mary Jane, and you look mighty stunning yourself with your pretty angora sweater, color-coordinated slacks and shiny patent leather shoes. Are your parents home at the moment?", asked Calvin. "No, they had an errand to run so they left about an hour ago", reported Mary Jane. "Well, then, lets hit the road and have some fun", said Calvin. Helping Mary Jane on with her coat, Calvin pointed her toward the front door which he pulled closed as they walked out on to the front porch. Mary Jane reached behind Calvin and locked the front door.

Reaching for the car door handle, Calvin pulled the passenger door open and held Mary Jane's hand as she stepped in. Hurrying around to the driver's door Calvin wondered what they should do first. "Mary Jane, I am undecided. Why don't you decide what we should do this morning. My first thought was to take you roller-skating, but going to the carnival over in Leroy Township seems mighty attractive to me as well. What is your preference?", asked Calvin. "Since we went skating last week, why don't we vote in favor of the carnival. We could spend all day there having fun", smiled

Mary Jane. "Okay, then, the carnival it is, even though the temperature is about 50 degrees, I wish that it was warmer so the outdoor amusement rides would be more comfortable. And I am happy to note that you have your heavy coat with you to keep you warm", complimented Calvin. "It is still quite early so perhaps the sunshine will warm things up a bit later on.", offered Mary Jane.

With their decision having been made, Calvin started the engine and slowly released the clutch as he guided the Dodge out into light traffic in front of Mary Jane's home. Leroy Township was about 50 miles north of Des Moines so Calvin headed for Highway 97, where forty-five minutes later found the couple passing the city limits sign. Following the directions observed on a large billboard, Calvin brought the Dodge to a stop in the large carnival parking lot which was quite full of the automobiles of other Des Moines patrons. Calvin was thrilled over the fact that Mary Jane had kept her arm around his shoulder throughout the entire trip. Stepping out of the car, Calvin was struck by the delicious fragrance of cooking food being carried on the slight breeze blowing from the carnival. After helping Mary Jane exit the Dodge, Calvin said, "I'm so hungry, would you mind if we bought some food before we continue down the midway?" "Not at all, Calvin, since I didn't have much breakfast myself. I could go for a hot dog or something else right about now", agreed Mary Jane. Hand in hand, the couple walked to the nearest sit-down restaurant which happened to be "Joe's Diner", and went inside. Before they were seated Calvin took their coats and hung them on a coat rack near the entrance. Seated at a small table with menu in hand, Calvin could smell the fragrance of onions on a grill and he thought that he would order liver and onions and a piece of apple pie. "What catches your fancy, Mary Jane?", asked Calvin. "I think that I will order the chicken and dumplings and a piece of lemon pie", said Mary Jane. "I've decided on the liver and onions plus a piece of apple pie and a glass of milk" said Calvin. At the same instant, Calvin realized that onions were not a suitable dish for couples intent on kissing, so he changed his mind and ordered pork chops. A young waitress appeared and took their orders and inquired about a drink for Mary Jane. Calvin had ordered a large milk. "Oh, milk will be fine for me too", replied Mary Jane.

Calvin smiled at Mary Jane seated across the table from him, and she responded with a dimpled grin. "Mary Jane, it seems that I spend every waking minute thinking about you and dreading the passing hours that will eventually see me going to Chicago and leaving you behind. The only happy and bright aspect in all this is the realization that I will be gone for only 12 weeks and then return to marry you, hopefully with your parents' consent", lamented Calvin. "Please don't be unhappy, Calvin, we're together now and that is what really matters, isn't it? And to cheer you up a bit, while you are away I will select my wedding outfit and have that all taken care of by the time you return", offered Mary Jane. "That is wonderful news about details that had not yet even occurred to me, Mary Jane", admitted Calvin. The waitress appeared with their food orders and they enjoyed their food in silence while thinking about their forthcoming marriage in three months. With her pie having been consumed, Mary Jane asked, "Where to from here, Calvin?" "Well, I thought it would be nice to meander down the midway and check out some of the galleries and games of chance", replied Calvin. "Perhaps, Calvin, you could win me a memento of our trip here today", asked Mary Jane. "That is a distinct possibility", agreed Calvin. After paying for their meals, Calvin helped Mary Jane on with her coat and then slipped into his own. With their coats "zipped up" Calvin and Mary Jane walked out of the restaurant to join the throng of patrons attending the carnival. It was a festive occasion and a Wurlitzer organ was playing familiar circus music on the merry-go-round, perhaps 400 feet ahead. Mary Jane was inclined to hurry to the Merry-Go-Round, but, at the same time, she wanted to enjoy seeing Calvin win her a memento of today's visit to the Mercy Brothers Carnival. Souvenir stands were everywhere on the carnival grounds so mementos were easy to come by. Nevertheless, Mary Jane fretted about the prospect of leaving the Carnival without one.

1300 Friday
12 December 1941
Leroy Township, Iowa
Mercy Brothers Carnival

As Calvin and Mary Jane walked along the midway, barkers were busily haranguing passersby encouraging them to stop and try their luck at various games of chance. Passing by a booth that displayed a large quantity of teddy bears and other stuffed animals, Calvin thought that he might have enough talent to win one of the cuddly animals for Mary Jane. The barker was delighted to explain the rules to Calvin and encouraged him to take something home for his 'lady friend'. The game involved throwing several baseballs at six metal bottles (about the same size as quart size glass milk bottles) the bottles were stacked on a small round table placed about twenty feet from a barrier rope. One was allowed to touch the barrier, but not lean over it to reduce the distance to the target bottles. The bottles were arranged in three layers. Three bottles on the table, two bottles on the two middle bottles of the three and a single bottle on top of the middle row. It looked simple enough to Calvin, and with his baseball experience, he felt that he was a sure winner. "That'll be 25 cents for three balls. And remember, the bottles must all be on the ground around the table, none can be left on the table", clarified the barker. Calvin paid the man and studied the waist-high table and the bottles sitting on it. By this time, a crowd had gathered around Calvin and Mary Jane to observe what was happening.

Having decided that he had psyched himself up sufficiently, Calvin wound up and threw his first ball for a clean miss. A low murmur of disappointment arose from the assembled crowd. "You'll do better next time", encouraged Mary Jane. Calvin took his next ball and aimed for the center bottle of the bottom row. Miraculously, the ball took the center bottle away and the stack fell to the floor, all, that is, except a single bottle laying in the center of the circular, fabric-covered table. The crowd yelled their approval at Calvin's good fortune, but he wasn't a winner yet. Lining up his last ball, Calvin aimed to hit the center of the bottle hoping to spin it off the table. Winding up in a pitcher's stance, Calvin let the ball fly and smiled with extreme joy as the bottle tumbled to the floor and he was, after all, a winner for Mary Jane. "See how easy it is, folks; who wants to be next" cried the barker, and there were several takers ready to replace Calvin. "And now, 'missy', you can choose any of the animals on these shelves over here", the barker called to Mary Jane. "Oh, Calvin, I am so proud of you", cried Mary Jane. Mary Jane studied the supply of stuffed animals and eventually selected a cuddly foot-tall red teddy bear. "Calvin, I'm going to name him Sir Calvin to remind me of you and the day that you beat the bottles", beamed Mary Jane. "I am absolutely honored", smiled a proudly contented Calvin Honeycut. Wishing not to have Mary Jane encumbered while they enjoyed the rest of the carnival, Calvin hurried back to the Dodge and placed Sir Calvin in the trunk and quickly returned to the midway and Mary Jane. From the bottle gallery, the couple wandered hand-in-hand down the midway and came to the merry-go-round, and the music was still playing. Purchasing two tickets, Calvin helped Mary Jane onto a horse just as the merry-go-round was ready to start. Calvin climbed on the horse next to Mary Jane. After a full load of children and adults was on board, the merry-go-round began to turn. Both Calvin's and Mary Jane's horses were articulated and moved up and down as the merry-go-round turned. The Wurlitzer organ played a rendition of 'I Love You Truly', and Mary Jane yelled over to Calvin "They're playing my song". "Mine too", replied Calvin. "It's a special performance just for the two of us, I'm convinced", yelled Calvin. All too soon the ride ended and Calvin lovingly lifted Mary Jane from her horse and lowered her to the platform. "It's a shame that such good things come to and end before they should", lamented Mary Jane. "It doesn't have to end, Mary Jane, for I can get some more tickets and we can ride again", offered Calvin. "Thank you anyway, Calvin, but I don't think so, the spell is broken", replied a downhearted Mary Jane. Located next to the merry-go-round was the tilt-a-whirl ride with many potential riders lined up at the ticket booth "Mary Jane, I am sorry to report that the tilt-a-whirl ride does bad things to my stomach so I have learned to avoid it" commented Calvin. Mary Jane replied. "Calvin, I suffer from the same malady on that ride and I have learned to merely observe other folks having fun on that ride. Calvin and Mary Jane spent fifteen minutes as tilt-a-whirl observers before moving on to another ride.

1700 Friday
12 December 1941
Leroy Township, Iowa
Mercy Brothers Carnival

Continuing on down the midway, Mary Jane and Calvin came to an extremely tall, twin-wheel ferris wheel for which Calvin bought four tickets for two rides each. Evening was coming on all too soon as the couple waited for their turn to step into a seat. Eventually, the ferris wheel stopped and it was their turn to climb aboard. Calvin handed over their tickets to the attendant and soon the wheel was turning, lifting them high into the twilight sky. The ferris wheel was one of the new, double-wheel designs and at the top of highest point, Calvin thought that he could see the lights of Des Moines. As the ferris wheel revolved, Mary Jane snuggled against Calvin and he placed his arm around her shoulders. Their heavy winter coats protected them from the slight breeze blowing in from the west. "How beautiful the lights are from up here", murmured Mary Jane. "Yes, it definitely seems as if we are in another world", agreed Calvin. The ferris wheel traveled round and round as the young lovers savored the presence of each other's company. The wheel stopped from time to time to let other riders get off, and when their seat came to the attendant on a final turn, Calvin handed over their second pair of tickets and they went for another ride. On the last turn of the wheel, Calvin leaned over and gave Mary Jane a long kiss as their seat descended for them to exit the ride. "Thank you, Mr. Honeycut. This has to be the finest ferris wheel ride that I have ever experienced", smiled Mary Jane. "Me too", agreed Calvin.

"Do you think that we should consider returning to Des Moines about now?", asked Calvin. "It seems to me that we just got here and I dislike leaving so soon", answered Mary Jane. "Yes, this has to be one of the most memorable and absolutely special days of my entire life", said Calvin. "I just wish that it could go on forever", replied Mary Jane. With darkness now complete, Mary Jane and Calvin returned to their car and climbed in. Calvin turned on his headlights as he started the engine and then drove the Dodge from the carnival parking lot. Once on the highway, Calvin turned on the heater. Although it had been some time since they had eaten at "Joe's Diner" Calvin and Mary Jane decided to wait until they reached Des Moines to have their evening meal. Turning south on Highway 97 Calvin ran the Dodge up to 60 miles per hour and the countryside flew past their windows. Off to the right side of the highway there was a slightly rosy tinge in the western horizon marking the spot where the sun had recently set. Commercial development was very spotty in that part of the state so traffic was quite light on the two-lane road.

Mary Jane had taken her usual position against Calvin's side with her arm around his neck. Calvin enjoyed the warmth of her body and turned from time to time to smile his pleasure at her company. "Mary Jane, since we have a little time before we arrive back in Des Moines, do you have any special activity that you would like to suggest for tomorrow?", asked Calvin. "Yes, now that you ask, I think that it would be especially nice to go dancing at the Lido after our evening meal tomorrow. There will be a special band playing all the latest songs and the food there is excellent." "That sounds fine to me, but what about during the day? Surely we won't be dancing all day", joked Calvin. "Right you are, that is definitely an evening activity. During the afternoon, why don't we go roller skating at the 5th Avenue Roller Rink", suggested Mary Jane. "That sounds like a winner to me", agreed Calvin. From two miles out, they could see the glow of lights emitted by Des Moines' tall office buildings in the night sky. About that time they passed a city limits signpost, and Calvin slowed the Dodge down to the posted 40 miles per hour speed limit. Commercial businesses now lined both sides of the highway and Calvin looked for the street leading to the Willard Hotel.

2000 Friday
12 December 1941
Des Moines, Iowa
Willard Hotel

On his own motion, Calvin had decided enroute that the Willard Hotel was the place for them to have their evening meal. "Mary Jane, I thought that the Willard Hotel would be a nice place for us to have our evening meal. Is that all right with you?", asked Calvin. "Yes, it certainly is. The Willard is a high-class place and boasts of a very fine menu", replied a contented Mary Jane. While Mary Jane was speaking, Calvin turned the Dodge into the Willard parking lot. Two valets immediately opened Mary Jane's and Calvin's doors after Calvin had put on the parking brake. Calvin was given a claim check as he walked around the car and took Mary Jane's arm. Ten steps away they entered the lobby to find the restaurant door off to their right. Arriving at the maitre d' station, Calvin and Mary Jane were greeted by a waiter who addressed them with just a hint of a German accent in his speech. "Good evening, sir and madame, please accompany me this way and I will seat you", said the maitre d'. Calvin and Mary Jane followed along, a pace behind, and were pleased to observe that they were placed off to one corner where their conversation would be quite private. Floor attendants quickly filled their water glasses and offered menus to both Calvin and Mary Jane. "My, such fine service", observed Mary Jane. "Yes, the quality of the organization is quite evident in the hotel personnel we have encountered thus far", said Calvin. After studying the menu for a time, Calvin asked, "What catches your fancy this evening, Mary Jane?" "I'm inclined to order the petite prime rib with green beans and mild horseradish", replied Mary Jane. "For my meal, I plan to order the stuffed pork chops and mashed potatoes with apple sauce on the side", said Calvin. Their waiter returned as if on cue and took their drink orders first and then their food orders, and quickly withdrew to his station near the front of the restaurant.

"Mary Jane, I just realized that I haven't told you that 'I love you' in the past hour, so I want to remedy that oversight", boasted Calvin. "Calvin, I do so love you. There is a new song playing on the radio these days with the title of 'It Had To Be You' and it is a perfect love song for us. It will no doubt go to the top of the popularity charts very quickly. It is truly a song for wartime lovers", boasted Mary Jane. With absolutely poetic timing, 'It Had To Be You' began playing over the restaurant public address system loudspeaker just over their heads. Mary Jane looked over at Calvin and grinned sheepishly, with her grin changing to a fully developed, dimpled smile.

Their food orders were served. The young lovers ate leisurely and in silence, enjoying each other's company and savoring the flavorful food. When the dishes of the main course were cleared away, the waiter appeared to take their dessert orders. The waiter offered several different pies together with a choice of puddings and various flavors of ice cream. "For my dessert, I would prefer to have bread pudding", requested Mary Jane. "I would like to have a piece of coconut cream pie", said Calvin. "Thank you for your orders and your selections will be right out", said the waiter. True to his word, the desserts appeared as if by magic on a tray delivered on a serving cart to their table. By then, the time was approaching ten thirty p.m. and it was time to think about getting Mary Jane home before her parents became uneasy. Calvin paid the waiter, leaving a generous tip for the staff, and taking Mary Jane's arm, escorted her back through the lobby where they pulled on their coats and then continued into the foyer where the valet station was located. Handing over his claim check, a valet hurried out the front door to retrieve their 1939 Dodge sedan. Mary

Jane and Calvin noticed their car arrive and walked through the front doors of the hotel. Outside, valets held the front doors open and Mary Jane entered the passenger side, while Calvin handed the valet on his side a tip generous enough to share with the other valet. "Thank you for taking good care of my car", said Calvin to the valet. "You're most welcome, sir; we aim to please", offered the valet.

Before he drove the car out onto the street, Calvin noticed that Mary Jane was pressing against his side again, to his secret delight, and she rested her hand on his thigh. Ten minutes later, Calvin parked the Dodge at Mary Jane's home and escorted her to the front door, but not before retrieving Sir Calvin from the trunk of the Honeycut Dodge. As on other dates, the lights were on inside the house attesting to the fact that her parents were home. Extracting her door key and giving it to Calvin, he unlocked the front door while at the same time collecting Mary Jane in his arms for a good-bye kiss. For the first time, he felt Mary Jane's tongue graze his tongue and he enjoyed the sensation quite breathlessly. "I do love you so much, Mary Jane", breathed Calvin into her soft ear. "Good-night, Calvin, and thank you for such a wonderful day", Mary Jane said, gently clutching Sir Calvin in her arms. "It was my absolute pleasure, I assure you, and I look forward to picking you up in the morning for a repeat performance", breathed Calvin. "I'll be waiting with bells on", said Mary Jane. As before, Calvin felt a tingling sensation in his chest where Mary Jane's breasts were touching him. "Good-night, sweetheart", said Mary Jane as she went into her house and locked the front door. Calvin made his way back to the Dodge and started the engine and quietly drove toward the west heading back to the farm.

On the way home Calvin relived the day's events including his extraordinary luck at winning Sir Calvin for Mary Jane at the carnival bottle game. How could I have been so lucky, Calvin wondered to himself. Surely it must have had something to do with Mary Jane's magnetic personality. On the other hand, Calvin may have had the assistance of a fairy godmother. Thirty minutes later Calvin turned up the Honeycut driveway at the end of which he parked the Dodge in its stall and went into the house. He slipped quietly into bed hoping to dream of his sweetheart again.

0900 Saturday
13 December 1941
Des Moines, Iowa
Honeycut Farm

With his cows milked and breakfast behind him, Calvin showered and dressed to pick up Mary Jane for another exciting day with his sweetheart. Of course, at that time he had no inkling of just how exciting the day would become. As usual, he sought out his father and verified that his use of the Dodge would not inconvenience his parents. His father affirmed the fact, that should a need arise, he and his mother could always use their pickup truck, so not to worry. And cheerfully said, "Go to town and have a nice day with Mary Jane". Calvin happily skipped out to the garage stopping just long enough to give Skippy's ears a brief rub. Climbing into the front seat, Calvin started the Dodge and backed it out of its stall. Heading down the driveway to the highway, Calvin could visualize Mary Jane waiting in her front room for him to arrive. Thirty minutes later he parked in front of the Thomas home and ran up to the front door and rang the door bell. The musical notes of the chiming signal reached his ears as in every previous visit. Mary Jane opened the front door and greeted him with a come-in wave motioning him to enter, which he did. Once inside, Mary Jane grabbed him around the neck and gave him a resounding kiss before he knew what was happening. "I have been waiting all night to do that", she breathed softly into his ear.

"Come on into the kitchen; Mom and Dad are there". Following Mary Jane, Calvin entered the kitchen and greeted her parents as they sat at their kitchen table. "Good morning, Mr. and Mrs. Thomas, and how are you doing this nice sunshiny morning", asked Calvin. "We are just fine, Calvin, and hope that you are the same", said Mr. Thomas. "You won't get any complaints from me. I feel fine and really have nothing to complain about", said Calvin with a smile. "How are your parents?" asked Mrs. Thomas. "They are well and enjoying a holiday of sorts, what with all the winter wheat planting having been completed", acknowledged Calvin. "Well, it turns out that we are traveling today, so we will expect you to take good care of our Mary Jane", said Mrs. Thomas. "You need have no fear on that requirement, Mrs. Thomas", replied Calvin. "My sister over in Redbluff is having a birthday party and it is more or less a command performance for us to be there", revealed Mr. Thomas. "Mary Jane and I will start the day at the 5th Avenue Roller Rink for a few hours of skating and after that we will have lunch and just play the afternoon by ear", offered Calvin. "We expect to arrive home quite late, Mary Jane, so there is no need for you to wait up for us", said Mrs. Thomas. "Okay, Mom, I'll probably just end up the day playing some of the records that I just bought", offered Mary Jane. "Well, if you folks will excuse us, Mary Jane and I will be on our way", concluded Calvin. "You kids have a nice time", called Mrs. Thomas as Calvin and Mary Jane walked through the living room and out the front door. "You do the same", replied Calvin from the living room. Just before reaching the door, Calvin took the opportunity to clasp Mary Jane to his bosom and give her a firey kiss, tongue-to-tongue and all. On the porch, Mary Jane said, "Calvin, I just love the way you kiss me." "Likewise, I am certain", responded Calvin. Leaving the porch, Calvin led Mary Jane to the Dodge where he opened the front passenger side door. Mary Jane entered and Calvin took his place behind the steering wheel and started the engine.

1000 Saturday
13 December 1941
Des Moines, Iowa
5th Avenue Roller Rink

The 5th Avenue Roller Rink was only a few short blocks from Mary Jane's home, so in less than 10 minutes Calvin was parking the Dodge in the ample parking lot. By then it was after ten a.m. and the skating rink was open for business. Both Calvin and Mary Jane owned their own skates, and Calvin pulled them, in their cases, from the trunk of the Dodge. The two lovers walked leisurely to the ticket window and Calvin purchased their admission tickets. Once inside they found that they had the rink virtually to themselves, what with only two other couples skating on the huge hardwood floor. Calvin helped Mary Jane on with her skates and then set about lacing his own. With the getting-started tasks complete, Calvin and Mary Jane moved out to the center of the rink. Some very pleasant organ music was playing on the sound system and attracted several other skaters onto the floor. Calvin moved next to Mary Jane and put his arm around her waist and they skated along together that way. Another popular WWII song was playing, titled 'I'll be Seeing You', and although it was a beautiful song, the music made Mary Jane feel sad knowing that the next day Calvin would be leaving. But that was tomorrow, and today was today to be enjoyed to the fullest by them both.

Calvin and Mary Jane were accomplished skaters due to their regular sessions at the rink. They entered the dancing contests for rexing couples, and also liked to participate in the waltz competitions. On a Saturday morning, however, the rink was merely there for open skating with the special contests reserved for the evening hours. That fact notwithstanding, Mary Jane and Calvin skated along in their own private world, totally oblivious to all of the other skaters.

"Calvin, I have a surprise for you. Would you like to hear about it now? It seems that 'Sir Calvin' gave me the answer to our dilemma while I slept with him last night", continued Mary Jane. "Oh, is that right? Then please tell me all about this divine revelation", responded Calvin. "The secret that 'Sir Calvin' disclosed to me was in the form of an angelic and silent message from within my being. The message that I received revealed to me the fact that obtaining Mom and Dad's approval for our marriage lies totally within ourselves. That is, we need to take an active part and guide my parents in the direction that we most desire", emphasized Mary Jane smiling happily all the while. "That may be all well and good, Mary Jane, but I am having some difficulty following the thread of your conversation", said a somewhat perplexed Calvin Honeycut. With a dimpled blush, Mary Jane smiled and said, "Calvin, all we have to do is make ourselves a baby and we will automatically receive my parents' consent to marry", concluded Mary Jane. When her statement finally sank in, Calvin was thunderstruck at the implication of Mary Jane's divine prophecy. "I don't disagree that that is one way of making things happen, but are you certain that it is the best and most prudent way?", asked Calvin, still quite skeptical. "Oh, yes, Calvin, don't you see; it is the best and most perfect God-given, solution. I have consulted the fertility tables that deal with such things and found that my body is in the ideal part of my season to be most receptive to conception", spoke Mary Jane with a voice of authority.

Calvin did not immediately comprehend the significance of Mary Jane's analysis. "Now that we have solved the problem, let's go to my home and turn our love for each other into a baby", cooed Mary Jane. At that, the two lovers left the rink floor and removed their skates placing them in their carrying cases and walked to the Dodge where Calvin placed the cases in the trunk again. Calvin's mind was in a whirl as he started the Dodge. Three hours had passed by so Mary Jane's parents should be long gone from their home. But, he had questions about himself; he was still a virgin and not experienced in such matters. "Mary Jane, you need to know that I am a virgin and may not be able to perform in the manner that you desire", revealed Calvin. "Oh, Calvin, we will just do what comes naturally since I am a virgin too. With 'Sir Calvin's' assistance, how could we possibly fail in our objective?"

1200 Saturday
13 December 1941
The Thomas Residence
Des Moines, Iowa

Excitedly, the two lovers ran to the front door where Mary Jane unlocked it and hurried inside, at the same time making a quick, but thorough, search to confirm that her parents were actually gone. The house was quiet as well as empty. "Calvin, you can read today's newspaper while I take a shower, after which you can do the same", smiled an excited Mary Jane. Calvin's thoughts were so confused as to leave him with the uncomfortable feeling that his brain was completely addled. How could what was about to transpire mean that he was of sound mind and living in the real world? Of course he would love to have a child of his very own, but having one as a means of coercing two adult parents into agreeing to an action that both he and Mary Jane strongly desired seemed preposterous in the extreme. But, at the same time, he realized that Mary Jane was correct, given the time constraints imposed upon them both by his Navy enlistment. Primarily for this reason, Calvin was prepared to participate in Mary Jane's plan. After all, the message had come from Sir Calvin and the angel involved had given Mary Jane all the assurance that she needed to take the contemplated action, reasoned Calvin.

Twenty minutes later, Calvin had not touched the newspaper and Mary Jane stood in the doorway leading to her bedroom wearing her pink terry cloth bathrobe. "I placed one of Dad's bathrobes in the bathroom for you to use", offered Mary Jane. Calvin rose from the couch as if moving in a deep trance and slowly made his way to the bathroom off the hall, kissing Mary Jane on her lips as he passed by. Clearing his mind of adverse thoughts, Calvin did not hurry with his shower. The warm water felt wonderful on his skin and erased the perspiration that had been generated by the physical exertion of his roller skating exercise. He used Mary Jane's shampoo and gave his hair a good going-over, finishing up with a conditioning treatment to make his red hair more manageable. His shower finished, Calvin towel dried and stepped out of the shower enclosure onto the adjacent absorbent floor mat. Borrowing a comb, Calvin combed his hair and pulled the flannel bathrobe about him at the same time connecting the brass buckle of the narrow green belt. Calvin opened the bathroom door to find Mary Jane waiting for him. She took his hand and proudly led him to her bedroom where she had already turned down the bedspread. "My, aren't we efficient", observed Calvin noticing that Mary Jane had also turned on her clock radio to the music of an 'easy listening' station'. "I just believe in being prepared", remarked Mary Jane.

Standing in front of him, perhaps an arm's length away, Mary Jane allowed her robe to slide to the floor revealing her voluptuous breasts, slender legs, flat tummy, and her blond pubic hair. "Mary Jane, your sensual beauty leaves me breathless", whispered Calvin. Pulling the brass buckle loose from his green belt, Calvin allowed his own robe to slide to the floor as he stepped forward and took Mary Jane in his arms and kissed her passionately. Releasing his grip slightly, Calvin gently laid Mary Jane on her bed and then crossed over to the opposite side and took his place beside her. At the same time, he pulled the top sheet over their trembling bodies. Calvin felt the heat of his erection in his groin as he kissed Mary Jane again. "Oh, Calvin, at last it is going to happen. I have been waiting a lifetime to be with you", mused Mary Jane. Calvin could no longer resist the temptation and gently pulled their naked bodies together and felt the pressure of her tender breasts against his chest. During another passionate kiss, Mary Jane explored Calvin's tongue with her own. Soon thereafter, Calvin took Mary Jane's left breast into his mouth and gently stroked the rosy nipple with his tongue and marveled at the fact that her nipple instantly assumed an erect attitude caused by his caress. From her prone position, Mary Jane pulled Calvin on top of her and took him within her body. For the remaining hours of that Saturday afternoon, Calvin and Mary Jane made love to their heart's content. Laying on Mary Jane's bed with the cool air surrounding his heated body, Calvin marveled at this turn of events in his young life. It was amazing to him what joining the Navy had accomplished, he pondered to himself. He had been in love with Mary Jane for four years, but had never considered making love to her out of wedlock. Nevertheless, over the afternoon hours, Calvin and Mary Jane made love to each other numerous times. In the end, with their orgasms fully satisfying each other's passion, Mary Jane confided, "Calvin, I can assure you that your lovemaking leaves nothing to be desired. Although I have never had sex before, I certainly could not have wanted nor found a more worthy partner." "Mary Jane, it seems to me that it all goes back to something you said along the way, all we have to do is what comes naturally".

After they had showered and dressed, as they were leaving Mary Jane's bedroom, Calvin acknowledged the presence of 'Sir Calvin' looking down from his perch on Mary Jane's chest of drawers. As they reached the Thomas den, a curious Calvin asked, "When will we know whether or not we have succeeded in our objective?" "Well, probably not for at least a month or two since I do not plan to see a doctor right away, but will merely wait to see if my menstrual periods are interrupted", replied Mary Jane. "We will definitely know before you come back to Des Moines in March and if we did not succeed the first time, we will merely try again. Sweetheart, I only wish that we had more time", said Mary Jane. "Our time together this afternoon has been such a wonderful interlude", said Calvin. Mary Jane locked the front door and Calvin drove them to Jackson's Drive-In for a meal of hamburgers, french fries and cokes. Mary Jane was strangely quiet, seemingly lost in her own reverie with dreamy meditative, though private, thoughts flowing through her mind. "Do you have any regrets at this point, Mary Jane", asked Calvin. "Oh, no, Calvin, how could I? After all, it was my idea based upon 'Sir Calvin's' and the angel's revelation to me. I could never have any regrets especially if what we have attempted proves to be successful and we ultimately get ourselves a baby or two. After all, there are twins on my side of the family, you know", said an extremely happy and contented Mary Jane.

The day was over by the time they had finished their meal, and Calvin had driven Mary Jane home. Walking her to her front door, Calvin was struck by the fact that he would not be able to have sex with Mary Jane again for three months. Mary Jane unlocked the door and turned to Calvin with a smile as he pulled her as close to him as their clothing would permit. "Mary Jane, I will not see you again until March unless you can talk your Dad into bringing you to the airport around 7 a.m. tomorrow morning when the plane leaves for Chicago. So let me say good-bye to you now and once again tell you that I love you more than life itself and look forward to marrying you in March." "Thank you, Calvin. I'll be ready, willing and able. Even if I have a baby in my tummy by that time, we can still make love while you are home", said Mary Jane. "That's extremely good news anyway", replied Calvin. Taking one more kiss for the road, including searching Mary Jane's tongue, Calvin walked to his car and started the engine. Waving to his sweetheart, who waved back from her porch, Calvin pulled into traffic and headed for home. Arriving home thirty minutes later, Calvin parked the car in its stall and walked into the kitchen. Mother Honeycut was there doing dishes. "Twelve weeks and then I will come home for ten days. I can't wait for the time to go by", said Calvin. Your Dad has already gone to bed so we'll be up early to see that you get to the airport before 7 a.m." "Many thanks, Mom." Is there anything that I can do for you before I hit the hay?", asked Calvin. "No, I'm finished here. You just go on to bed", said Mrs. Honeycut. Calvin climbed the stairs to his room and laid his exhausted body down with visions of the day's events dancing in his brain. He would dream dreams that he had never dreamed before on this night of nights. After Calvin dressed in his nightclothes and climbed into bed, he lay on his back and contemplated the pleasant prospect of becoming a father. He was elated at the possibility, but concerned about the prospect of being separated from Mary Jane by his Navy duty commitment. Closing his eyes, Calvin visualized Mary Jane in all her pristine beauty as they made love in her bedroom, and fell to sleep with that image being all too real in his dream.

0600 Sunday
14 December 1941
Honeycut Farm
Des Moines, Iowa

The cows had been milked for the last time and Calvin had showered and dressed for his trip. Mr. Honeycut was calling from the kitchen for everyone to hurry to the car so as not to miss Calvin's flight. Calvin and his mother responded to find the Dodge parked next to the house with the engine running and Mr. Honeycut in the driver's seat. Mrs. Honeycut slid in beside her husband as Calvin took the rear seat as his father drove off down the driveway. Calvin looked out through the rear window at his boyhood home as it was fast receding into the distance. He concentrated on that image to the exclusion of everything else at that moment. Calvin only gave up the image when his father turned on to the road to Des Moines and he could see his boyhood home no longer. Then, Calvin checked to see that he had his plane ticket voucher and placed it in his jumper pocket. Forty minutes later, Mr. Honeycut parked at the airport and helped Calvin carry his luggage inside and get checked in at the Lake Central Airlnes counter. Upon presenting his voucher, Calvin was assigned a window seat on the Douglas DC-3 airplane that would carry him to Chicago.

Although Calvin thought that there was a slight chance that Mary Jane might come to see him off, it was a forlorn hope that would not be fulfilled. At 6:40 a.m. the passengers were boarded and Calvin said his good-byes to his parents and took his seat. Calvin waved through the tiny window to his parents as the pilot started the engines and moved the DC-3 off to the main runway at Des Moines. With both engines howling, the DC-3 roared along the length of the main runway and became airborne near the distant end. This was Calvin's first airplane ride and he enjoyed the smoothness of the climb-out to their cruising altitude. During the hour-long ride to Chicago's Midway Airfield, Calvin's thoughts drifted back to his last day with Mary Jane. What a wonderful wife she would become. Calvin decided that he would write her a letter as soon as he could after reaching the Great Lakes Naval Training Station. He enjoyed watching the earth slip by his window and wondered about the source of the lakes and highways that seemed never ending. At length, the stewardess offered her passengers soft drinks or coffee. Calvin decided on a coke since it reminded him of home and Jackson's Drive-In.

0800 Sunday
14 December 1941
Chicago, Illinois
Midway Airport

The Lake Central flight landed around 0800 and taxied up to the terminal and parked, at which time the pilot shut down his two engines. Calvin deplaned and began his search for the Navy Shore Patrol office as his orders required. Ten minutes into his search he saw the Shore Patrol office and presented himself to the duty chief petty officer to whom he offered his travel orders. "Well, sailor, you're just in time for the next bus to your destination". Returning Calvin's orders, the chief said, "Walk out through that blue door there and climb into the waiting Navy bus. It is about an hour ride to the training station so get on board and make yourself comfortable. The bus leaves in ten minutes."

As Calvin entered the bus, he could see that he had plenty of company, for at least 40 or 50 recruits had preceded him. He grabbed a vacant front seat behind the driver's seat and waited. There was little conversation among the other recruits and he appreciated being left alone with his own private thoughts. About 0830, the Navy driver entered and announced that, "Anyone not going to the Navy's Great Lakes Training Station should exit the bus now". There was no response to that admonition. The driver closed the door, started his engine and engaged the transmission, and the bus departed the Midway Terminal. It turned out that the training station was some 60 miles north of Chicago on the shore of Lake Michigan. Calvin settled down to enjoy the ride and see some new country. From time to time he caught glimpses of the lake as the bus traveled north on local Illinois roads. Around 1000 Calvin was able to see the training station through the bus windshield. The entry gate was manned by Shore Patrol guards who waved the driver through the gate area. The bus pulled up and stopped in front of an administration building marked 'Receiving Barracks.'

Calvin and the other recruits left the bus and entered the barracks. Inside the door was a long counter behind which a number of uniformed sailors waited for the incoming busload of green recruits. A storekeeper chief petty officer called out the name of each recruit from the bus driver's passenger manifest. "All right, sailors, as I call your name, form a line in front of a station (of which there were ten) and you will be issued your sea bag, shoes, uniforms, and blanket and other clothing." When Calvin heard his name, he answered "here" and walked over to station #3 which was vacant at that time. "What is your shoe size, sailor?" inquired the storekeeper third class. "Seven and one half", replied Calvin. As he handed Calvin his sea bag, the storekeeper told him, "As soon as you have received all of your Navy-issued gear, visit station #11 and receive a stencil with which to mark your name on all items including the sea bag, shorts, socks, handkerchiefs, blanket, hats and all clothing except your blue uniforms. And be especially careful when you stencil your whites so that you pick a place where the black ink will not bleed through and ruin them for the inspections that will be coming along in the summer time. Do you have any questions?" inquired the storekeeper. "None at the moment", replied Calvin. With his stenciling completed, Calvin loaded his new possessions into his sea bag and lined up with the other recruits at the end of the room by the exit door. A first class petty officer soon called the recruits to attention and ordered them to follow him into the adjoining room. Upon entering, Calvin could see that they were due for a Navy-style haircut. A dozen barber chairs and attendant barbers awaited the new recruits. Several of the recruits had overly long hair, and the barbers joked with the recruits asking, "Would you like to keep that hair?" Of course, the individual replied in the affirmative at which point the barber promptly cut off the hair to Navy regulation length and handed the severed hair to the disappointed recruit, the joke being lost on the recruit in question. With the haircuts finished, the new recruits were marched by a petty officer to the mess hall where lunch was being served. The newly stenciled sea bags were piled by the door. "Please form up outside at 1300", was the parting remark of the petty officer. Lunch consisted of breaded pork chops, apple sauce with dessert of apple pie with cheese topping. "Well, at least we will be eating regularly here from the looks of it" observed the recruit sitting next to Calvin. "By the way, my name is John Harris and I hail from Topeka, Kansas". "I'm Calvin Honeycut and my home is in Des Moines, Iowa. Pleased to meet you, John.", replied Calvin. "Maybe we will have an opportunity to be in the same barracks if we're lucky", offered John. "It is a possibility, and I suppose we will find that out soon enough when we muster at 1300", said Calvin.

Calvin and John finished their meal and took their dirty trays to the dishwashing station and placed them on the conveyor belt after which they made their way to the front of the mess hall, retrieving their sea bags along the way. Several recruits had preceded them outside and were, even then, lining up in ranks to await the petty officer for further instructions. John and Calvin took their places at the end of the line. Within a couple of minutes, the first class petty officer appeared and he was accompanied by a chief petty officer. "Good afternoon, sailors. I have the pleasure of introducing Chief Petty Officer Albert Johnson who will be your company commander during your stay at the Great Lakes Naval Training Station. In that regard, you need to know that you are members of Company 41-162. This nomenclature means that you are part of the 162nd Recruit Company formed here in 1941. Please memorize that identity as you will need it in the future for various purposes, not the least of which is receiving your mail from home. In addition, you are required to memorize your Navy serial number that is listed on your admission papers which you received when you checked in at the receiving barracks. This serial number will serve you throughout the period of your Naval career", advised the chief petty officer. Next, Chief Johnson cleared his throat and launched into his presentation. "Sailors, let me be the first to welcome you to the Navy's Great Lakes Training Station, where you will learn about the Navy and your responsibilities over the next twelve weeks. At the end of that time you will either be assigned to a ship or other duty station including the possibility of being sent to another Navy training facility for specialized training on various weapons, marine engines or other important disciplines. Perhaps the most important attribute for you to cultivate here is that of paying attention to all of your instructors. They are here to do a job, but that job will not be successful without your complete cooperation and diligent attention to all matters pertaining to the Navy and its traditions. For your information, my company is housed in Barracks number 26A which is about one block to your left, toward the shore of Lake Michigan. When I dismiss you, please take your sea bags to the barracks and place them on the bunk which has been previously assigned to you by the duty yeoman. There is a bulletin board in the vestibule and the bunk assignments are posted thereon. I should mention that some of you are assigned to the ground floor while others are assigned to the second floor. In addition, each recruit is assigned the use of a locker during his stay on this base. The arrangement of each floor is identical, including the location of the bathroom facilities, study desks and lecture rooms. That should be sufficient information to get you started today and I look forward to seeing you all on the Grinder in front of the barracks promptly at 0700 in the morning. As a parting remark, I encourage you to become acquainted with the 24-hour system of military time keeping. This will become quite important as you progress in your seamanship lessons. Company Recruits ATTENNNTION! DISSSSSMISSED", concluded the Chief.

Calvin and John grabbed their sea bags and headed for Building 26-A at a leisurely pace. Covering the block in about five minutes the boys entered the vestibule and worked their way through the crowd of other recruits toward the bunk assignment posting. Upon reaching the bulletin board, they discovered that they were assigned to adjoining bunks on the second deck. "What a pleasant surprise," said John. "It can't get much better than this", observed Calvin. They climbed the stairs and placed their sea bags on their bunks and stowed some personal items in their nearby lockers. "John, it has been a long day for me, but before I turn in, I want to go write my girlfriend a letter. Do you care to join me?" asked Calvin. "Yes, Calvin, I need to drop a few lines to my parents to let them know that I arrived safe and sound", replied John.

The leisure room was on one end of the barracks and the boys went there and found open spaces at several desks all of which were equipped with nice lamps to illuminate their stationery. Calvin sat back and thought about his letter before placing anything on his paper. He was in awe at all that had happened to him this day and wanted to tell Mary Jane about it. At length, he put pen to paper and began.

Great Lakes Naval Training Station
Company 41-162
Sunday, 14 December 1941

My Darling Mary Jane:

It is evening now and I wanted to take a few minutes to tell you again how much I love you and how much you mean to me and my life.

The trip to the Navy Training Base was uneventful and since arriving, we have all been issued Navy clothing and assigned to our barracks. I really do not know what is in store for me, but am certain that tomorrow will reveal the fact that I have plenty to learn. Please take care of yourself and remember that we have a date twelve weeks from now and I am praying that our plans for our future will materialize in the manner in which we desire.

Should the plans that we made not work out, I want you to be ready to elope with me as soon as I return to Des Moines. When I leave to go overseas, on whatever assignment I am given, I want to know that you are my WIFE and will be waiting for me when I return! And, darling, how I ache to hold you in my arms and kiss you!

I guess that is all for this time so write to me when you can at the above address.

ALL MY LOVE FOREVER,
YOUR LOVER, CALVIN

P.S. For as long as I live, I will never forget the Wonderful interlude that we shared last Saturday.

With his letter finished, Calvin placed it in an envelope, wrote the word "FREE" where the stamp would normally be placed, and addressed it to Mary Jane at the same time marking it 'PERSONAL' in large letters. Calvin would post it in the morning on his way to breakfast. To be on the Grinder at 0700 meant that he would have to rise at 0600, shower and run to the mess hall to be on time.

0600 Monday
15 December 1941
Great Lakes Naval Training Station
Chicago, Illinois

With the clock approaching 0600, it was quiet in the barracks save for the sound of soft snoring here and there. Amid the quiet bunks, a bugle sounded loudly and the master at arms began shouting at the top of his voice "Reveille!, Reveille!, Reveille! All right, all you sailors, climb out of those 'fart sacks' and hit the deck running". Pandemonium broke out and Calvin jumped up and ran to the bathroom, toothbrush in hand. After finishing his morning toilet chores, he ran back to his bunk, quickly made it up and then dressed. About this time, John returned and did the very same thing. "Do you think that this bedlam happens every day, Calvin?", asked John rather tiredly. "I am not certain, but it wouldn't surprise me to find it to be so. Come on, let's run over to the mess hall", invited Calvin. "Be right with you", replied John. Clutching his letter to Mary Jane, Calvin headed for the stairs leading to the vestibule. The previous day, Calvin noticed a mailbox next to the mess hall and he dropped his letter in as he passed by. Their breakfast consisted of fresh milk, pancakes, and bacon and eggs. Calvin particularly enjoyed the fresh ice-cold milk. He and John finished about the same time and had just enough time to return to their barracks, brush their teeth, and still get to the Grinder by 0700.

0700 Monday
15 December 1941
Great Lakes Naval Training Station
Chicago, Illinois

Company 41-162 formed up on the Grinder with only a few stragglers hurrying to catch up from breakfast. Company Commander Johnson called for attention and then the company yeoman called the roll. Subsequent roll calls would be the responsibility of the platoon leaders, yet to be selected. There were no absentees among the 100 men. Following roll call the recruits were separated into two platoons of 50 men each. Individuals were then lined up in four rows according to size, with the tallest at the front of the lines and the shortest at the rear. At five foot six inches, Calvin found himself near the center of the ranks, with John two men behind him in the first row of the second platoon. "In the future, I will expect you to fall in according to your placement in your platoon, so pay attention to who is next to you and assume the same location whenever the platoon is formed up", said Chief Johnson. "Physical fitness is important to the Navy so we plan for a calisthenics drill at the beginning of each day. Platoon leaders will be appointed in each platoon to set the drills and assure that everyone participates. This is not an elective activity. You will not be excused from calisthenics", advised the company commander. "Along the way, you will be taught how to march, the most important aspect of which is keeping in step. Marching practice will commence tomorrow after calisthenics", advised the Chief. In preparing to march, spacing is the second most important aspect. Toward this end, you will be taught how to dress right and left so that uniform spacing is achieved in the marching configuration. When you reported for duty, you were each issued a copy of the sailors' bible, 'The Blue Jacket Manual'. This book will answer many of your questions about the Navy and provide information that you will study in future weeks. Following lunch today, please muster here for a tour of the Navy's obstacle course. This facility is intended to further fine-tune your physical fitness. This concludes the morning announcements company ATTENNNNTION! DISSMISSED".

With no classes assigned until 1300, Calvin and John went to the ship's store to purchase a few items. Calvin needed more stationery and toothpaste while John merely wanted some ice cream for his sweet tooth. From there they returned to the barracks and Calvin decided to write a letter to his parents. "John, I'm going to write a letter to my parents. Do you need to communicate with anyone?", asked Calvin. "Not today since I wrote my folks yesterday, but thanks for the invitation anyway, Calvin". "See you later", replied John.

Moving to the study hall area, Calvin selected a desk and began to write.

After he finished his letter, Calvin ran over to the mess hall and deposited it in the mailbox to go out the next day.

1500 Wednesday
17 December 1941
Des Moines, Iowa

Mary Jane hurried home after school hoping that she had received a letter from Calvin. Checking her mailbox at home, she found the letter that he had written to her on Sunday evening. All smiles, she ran into the house as she ripped the envelope open to read his words.

Moving slowly to her bedroom, Mary Jane sat down at her desk, turned on her student lamp, and prepared to write a reply to Calvin. Stationery in hand, she leaned back in her chair and recalled their time together last Saturday. How sublime that entire day had turned out to be. She could still recall the fragrance of Calvin's after-shave lotion and the fresh fragrance of his glorious red hair. That Calvin continued to profess his love for her sent chills up and down Mary Jane's spine. She thought that she would just die if he ever changed his mind about loving her. But after four years of loving each other she knew that that thought was a totally foreign and meaningless one. And there are those lovely, magnetic words, "I want to know that you are my WIFE and will be waiting for me when I return". Becoming Calvin's wife was all that she could think about since his departure last Sunday. She had already surreptitiously purchased suitable clothing and a new pair of shoes for their wedding and had secreted them in her 'Hope Chest'. Should her mother happen to notice the garments, Mary Jane was prepared to tell a little 'white lie' to protect their secret. Mary Jane was home alone as her retired parents were on one of their frequent shopping excursions. Taking pen in hand, Mary Jane began her letter.

655 Laurel Street
Des Moines, Iowa
December 17, 1941

My Darling Sweetheart:

Your letter just arrived and I hasten to reply to tell you that I cannot wait to become your wife. Lately, that is all that I think about. In fact, I have already purchased my wedding outfit and a new pair of shoes. My purchases are secreted in my Hope Chest for safe keeping. Since you left, I have attended school every day, but it is no fun any longer with you not being here! How I wish that you were here so that I could kiss your sweet lips.

Mom and dad are out shopping and as soon as I finish this letter, I plan to run to the corner and drop it into the Post Office mailbox. I need to tell you how sorry I am for the fact that I could not be at the airport to see you off last Sunday. Since I do not have a driver's license yet or a vehicle, I was trapped at home. Nevertheless, I will be there with bells on when you return in March! Please be certain that you let me know what your arrival time is and which airline you will arrive on.

Like you, I have fond memories of our last day together and will never forget your love for me! And, by the way, 'Sir Calvin' sends his love too. I love you so much, Calvin, and will for the remainder of my *life! Write me when you can and I will do the same.*

ALL MY LOVE AND KISSES.

YOUR SWEETHEART,
MARY JANE

Having finished her letter, Mary Jane placed a stamp on the envelope corner and left the house to place it in the mailbox on the corner for Uncle Sam to deliver. Receiving Calvin's letter had given Mary Jane a new outlook on her young life and it was one of contentment and comfort in the knowledge that she would soon be Mrs. Calvin Honeycut. What a wonderful way to start a new life, she thought. She returned home and began to complete her homework assignments for the next day's high school classes. School could be such a drag when one was so in love.

1400 Wednesday
17 December 1941
Des Moines, Iowa

At the Honeycut farm, mail was delivered on what the post office defined as "Rural Route #2" and all mail boxes were identified by individual number. The Honeycut box was number 46. Calvin's father had been to the feed store and drove up shortly after the mailman had delivered the day's mail. Expecting to see the usual pile of 'junk mail,' Calvin's father was all smiles when he recognized his son's handwriting. He quickly retrieved the mail, returned to his pickup truck, and excitedly sped up the driveway to his house. Skidding his truck to a stop in a cloud of dust, he jumped out and left his truck on the run heading for the kitchen where he knew that his wife would be.

"Mother, gather 'round, we have a letter from Calvin" said Mr. Honeycut. Quickly putting her work aside, Marcella sat down at the kitchen table as her husband read Calvin's letter out loud.

Great Lakes Naval
Training Station
Company 41-162
Monday, 15 December 1941

Dear Mom and Dad:

Just a few lines to let you know that I arrived safely at the Naval Training Station and am pretty well settled in. I have an entirely new wardrobe courtesy of the Navy with my name stenciled on each item of clothing except my blue uniforms. I also have two brand new pairs of black Navy shoes that I have shined up via the "Spit and Polish Method". My new friend, John Harris from Topeka, Kansas, taught me how to polish shoes up to Navy specs.

We have bunks next to each other on the second deck of our barracks. The food here is great, but I don't expect to gain much weight because the Company is required to do Calisthenics every morning. On top of that we will have to run over an obstacle course on occasion.

I was wondering if you have spoken to Mary Jane since I left. She didn't make it to the airport that morning when I left, but we got to say our good-byes the previous day, thank goodness. If you see her, tell her that I send my love. Till next time, My thanks TO BOTH OF YOU again for letting me become your sailor boy!

Your Loving Son,
Calvin

When he looked up from his reading, Calvin's father noticed tears in the corners of Marcella's eyes. Rising from the table, he walked over and placed his arms around her and said "Cheer up, Marcella, Calvin is in good hands and will make a fine sailor". "I know, Arnold, but only yesterday he was a tiny boy" she said with a tender smile. "Why don't we sit down and send him a letter?", asked Arnold. "Yes, I would enjoy that. You dictate and I'll do the writing", said Marcella.

1600 Wednesday
17 December 1941
Des Moines, Iowa

In a halting voice, Arnold began:

Mr. & Mrs. Arnold Honeycut
Rural Route #2, Box 46
Des Moines, Iowa
17 December 1941

`Dear (Sailor Boy) Calvin:

Your mother and I were thrilled to receive your letter and learn of your safe passage to Chicago. Congratulations on getting to know some new friends; no doubt there will be others as time goes by. It is also nice to know that the Navy is feeding you so well.

As to your questions about Mary Jane, we have not seen her since you left, but have spoken to her on the telephone several times. We know that she is lonely and is trying to keep busy with her school studies as a substitute for the loneliness. However, she is a strong person and will provide you with plenty of support when you eventually become Man and Wife.

We continue to be in good health and the farm is moving into its winter doldrums now that cold weather is upon us. You take care of yourself and write to us now and then. Please know that we miss you as much as Mary Jane does.

All our love,
Mom and Dad

With the letter finished, Arnold walked to her side and embraced Marcella. "Let's send this via Air Mail in the morning", said Calvin's father. "That will be the best way", agreed Calvin's mother. By then, it was bedtime so they climbed the stairs looking forward to some well-earned rest.

1000 Friday
19 December 1941
Des Moines, Iowa
Honeycut Farm

With Christmas just around the corner, Arnold and Marcella had set aside this day to be devoted to buying gifts for Calvin and Mary Jane. So it was that they spent the entire day in Des Moines and had the presence of mind to have their purchases shipped directly to the recipients by the respective department stores that they patronized. The store's sales personnel assured Arnold that the gifts would be delivered before Christmas. This approach simplified the Honeycut's lives inasmuch as they were relieved of the prospect of gift wrapping as well as delivery responsibilities.

While shopping in Grove's Department Store the Honeycuts encountered Mary Jane and her mother who were also shopping for Christmas gifts. The timing of their meeting was quite propitious inasmuch as the foursome elected to eat their lunch together. By that time, Arnold and Marcella had finished their shopping and left Mary Jane and her mother to continue shopping when they had finished their lunch.

0800 Saturday
20 December 1941
Great Lakes Naval Training Station
Chicago, Illinois

With no training sessions scheduled for the weekend, John and Calvin decided to get in the Christmas Spirit by sending a few gifts to their families and girlfriends. Although the selection available in the Ship's Store was somewhat limited, the boys were able to locate suitable gifts and have them shipped to their parents and girlfriends. Fortunately, the Ship's Store stocked a number of lovely jewelry items that the boys could choose from. There was a professional Christmas wrapping service operating in the Ship's Store and this service also took care of the shipping requirements. At the end of the day, the boys left the base on liberty for a few hours to enjoy a motion picture at a local cinema. During the movie, Calvin could not help but think back to the last movie that he and Mary Jane had seen together in Des Moines. Those memories were enchanting and would no doubt last him a lifetime. In his imagination he could still feel the pressure of Mary Jane's arm around his shoulder.

1200 Thursday
25 December 1941
Great Lakes Naval Training Station
Chicago, Illinois

Today's noontime meal in the mess hall was especially delicious what with lots of turkey and dressing to be had along with mashed potatoes, brown gravy, biscuits, green beans and a green salad. For dessert there was apple pie ala mode topped with cheddar cheese. Calvin and John ate their meal together and then returned to their barracks where they enjoyed opening the Christmas gifts that had arrived from home. "Calvin, take a look at this 35 mm Kodak camera that Mom and Dad sent me", said John. "Wow, John, that certainly is a beauty", observed Calvin. "Yes, it is, and it came with four rolls of film for good measure", said John. Then it was Calvin's turn to open one of his packages. "How about this flashlight, John?", said Calvin. "It came with spare batteries and will be a great asset when I go on night duty on board ship", said Calvin. At the end of two and a half hours the boys gathered their presents and placed them in their lockers as their evening meal time had arrived. Among the gifts were winter gloves, sweaters, watch caps, (almost duplicates of those issued by the Navy upon their arrival at boot camp) candy peanut clusters, shoe polish, stationery and each boy received a photo album. "When we return from supper, I plan to call home to see what Mom and Dad are up to", said a lonely Calvin. "This is the first time I have ever been away from home at Christmas time", lamented John. "Same here, John, and I hope that it will not be too long to get a telephone call through to my folks" said Calvin. "I plan to do the same", replied John.

One hour later found the boys, with full stomachs, waiting outside the telephone booths for their calls to be completed. Calvin's call came in first and he picked up his receiver and said, "Hello" from afar, Calvin heard his father's voice reply, "Hello, Calvin, what a wonderful surprise. And you will be happy to learn that we have shared our Christmas meal with your prospective mother and father-in laws and future wife. Hold on while I get Mary Jane", said Mr. Honeycut.

Mary Jane was breathless when she said, "Hello, my husband-to-be. What a wonderful treat it is to be able to speak to you on this special day." "Mary Jane, I am almost speechless for I had no idea that your family would be at the farm", said Calvin. "Oh, yes, we have been here since early this morning and have enjoyed opening the gifts that you sent as well as the ones that we brought for your Mom and Dad", replied Mary Jane. "And before I forget, I want to thank you so much for the beautiful gold locket that you gave me. The locket is so special and I can't wait to talk your mother out of a photograph of you to place inside", said Mary Jane. "Mary Jane, I enjoyed receiving your gifts as well as they made this lonely day feel closer to home", remarked Calvin. "Calvin, your mother is waiting patiently to speak to you and here she is." "Mary Jane, before you go I want you to know that you are always on my mind and I love you so much", interrupted Calvin. "Same here, Calvin. I love you to pieces and can't wait for you to come home" said Mary Jane.

Mrs. Honeycut came on the line at this point. "Calvin, we are so thrilled that you took the time to call home. We have had a wonderful day enjoying the friendly company of your future in-laws", reported Mrs. Honeycut. "It is so nice that the two families were able to join each other on this special day of the year. I am only too sad that I cannot be there to join in the festivities", replied a lonely Calvin. I am here with John and he is speaking with his parents at this time". "Please tell John that we send our best wishes for the Holiday season", said Calvin's mother. "I will certainly take care of the matter, and before I hang up, can I tell Mary Jane good-bye?", asked Calvin.

"Oh, Calvin, it is so sad that we have to conclude this telephone call", complained Mary Jane. "I know, sweetheart, but soon I will be home and we can speak face-to-face and I can kiss those sweet lips of yours", Calvin offered with a sigh. "Calvin, I can hardly wait. Good-bye till next time", and then Mary Jane was gone.

Calvin hung up his receiver and then waited for John to conclude his call. After John had terminated his call, Calvin said, "John, my mother wants you to know that she and Dad wish you the best for this Holiday season", offered Calvin. "I also have the same greeting to extend to you from my parents", said John "That was mighty kind of them", replied Calvin. The evening is fast disappearing, so I think that I will go back to the barracks and hit the hay", concluded John. "That is the best idea I have heard for a while", replied Calvin. And thus ended the two friends' Christmas day of 1941.

0700 Wednesday
14 January 1942
Great Lakes Naval Training Station
Chicago, Illinois

At this point, Calvin and John as well as all members of Company 41-162 had successfully completed one-third of their training program. They had been exposed to structured classes in Naval history and wartime tactics, emergency abandon ship procedures, parade ground marching, etiquette, tying of marine knots, as well as respect for the Naval hierarchy of the chain of command. Classes were also given in signaling communications via semaphore signal flags as well as flashing light Morse code communications. Classes in radio communications were given to reveal any innate talent on the part of some of the recruits for assignment to radio operations, a most important function affecting ships at sea. Weekly visits to the base obstacle course kept the men in fine physical condition. Periodic examinations were given to verify that the individual topics of concern were understood by the recruits.

Classes in the care and use of high-powered rifles were held in protected gunnery ranges that were also heated against the freezing days of winter. Sharpshooter ratings were earned by many of the new recruits in training sessions that were held daily. Seamanship classes in the use and operation of landing craft boats and engines and other boats, such as captain's gigs, were part of the curriculum. Marine engine maintenance aptitude tests were given for the purpose of identifying potential candidates for specialized training in mechanics and other disciplines, such as RADAR operation and repair. The attributes of specialty ratings for electricians, yeomen, quartermasters, signalmen, machinist mates, gunners mates, cryptographers, firemen, and many more special disciplines were offered to the recruits as career opportunities for consideration in their long-term association with the Navy.

Although the various ratings were exposed to the recruits by the end of their first month of duty, firm commitments to a given rating would not be solicited until the final month of their boot camp experience, which was still some eight weeks in the future. In the meantime, the two platoons would be given training in standing various types of shipboard watches such as hazardous condition lookouts (a 24-hour per day requirement of shipboard life while at sea.)

1900 Wednesday
14 January 1942
Des Moines, Iowa

It was shortly after an early lunch that Wednesday when Mary Jane sensed that conditions were changing within her body. She realized that her menstrual period that should have occurred toward the end of December was conspicuous by its absence. Her heart rate quickened as the import of this revelation registered in her mind. So, 'Sir Calvin' was right after all, she thought to herself. With that discovery having been made, the next question was: how could she verify whether or not she was pregnant. Having given the prospect considerable thought over the past few weeks, Mary Jane already knew the answer to the question. It was obvious that she could not consult her family doctor without revealing the matter to her parents. Thus, she struck upon the tactic of seeking out the doctor who had treated her following her bicycle accident many years before in which her hymen was ruptured. She knew that Dr. Wilson was still practicing and resolved to seek an appointment as soon as possible. Mary Jane's parents left the house unexpectedly to run errands, whereupon she looked up the telephone number for Dr. Wilson and called his office. Since he was an OB GYN specialist, it was not necessary for her to specify a reason for requesting an appointment. The doctor's assistant advised Mary Jane that she could be seen at 3:45 p.m. that same day. Leaving a note for her mother purporting to go on a shopping trip downtown on her bicycle, Mary Jane mounted her bicycle and headed for the doctor's office. Fortunately, the doctor's office was in a commercial section of Des Moines only a mile away, and Mary Jane was certain that she would see no one who would recognize her. Entering the doctor's office, she signed in as Mrs. Calvin Honeycut and had thought to place a gold band on the ring finger of her left hand. Within ten minutes, the doctor's nurse called her into one of the treatment rooms and had Mary Jane disrobe and dress in a hospital gown. The doctor entered, and with the nurse standing by, said, "Good morning, Mrs. Honeycut, and how are you today?" "I feel fine, but have a question on which I need your assistance", requested Mary Jane. "All right, but first let me take your blood pressure and temperature", said Doctor Wilson. With the nurse's help, the doctor began his examination. "Just what is your question, please", asked the doctor. Well, I missed my menstrual period last month and I am wondering if I am pregnant", admitted Mary Jane. "With the proper test, that will be an easy question to answer. Please accompany the nurse so that you can provide a sample of your urine", requested Dr. Wilson. With the sample having been secured, Mary Jane returned to the treatment room. "Mrs. Honeycut, the test will take overnight so you may dress and return home, but call me tomorrow afternoon and I will give you the results." Leaving the office, Mary Jane paid her bill and rode her bicycle home in time to arrive before her parents, and she had the presence of mind to destroy the note that she had left for her parents.

Mary Jane was confident that she already knew the answer to the pregnancy test results and went to bed smiling and fell asleep dreaming of Calvin and their family-to-be. At 3:00 p.m. on Thursday, Mary Jane left her home and rode her bicycle to a nearby pay telephone booth from which to call the doctor. After the nurse put the doctor on the line, Mary Jane identified herself and the doctor advised, "Well, Mrs. Honeycut, there is no doubt that you are indeed pregnant and should expect to have your child about the middle of September. Congratulations", concluded the doctor. "Thank you very much, Doctor, and I will plan to visit your office on whatever schedule you feel is appropriate", replied Mary Jane. "Initially, monthly visits will suffice. However, as things develop I will modify the schedule to fit your needs", advised Dr. Wilson. "Thank you very much, Doctor, and I will call your office later for my next appointment", concluded Mary Jane. "Very well, Mrs. Honeycut, and be sure to watch your diet for I do not like my patients to gain too much weight", commented the doctor as he hung up his telephone. Mary Jane felt giddy with maternal happiness, and she was more than comfortable with the outcome of her angelic revelation. Now all she had to do was to write a letter to Calvin to inform him of his upcoming fatherhood. Mary Jane hoped that Calvin would be as thrilled as she was at the prospect of beginning their very own family.

1900 Friday
16 January 1942
Des Moines, Iowa

655 Laurel Street
Des Moines, Iowa
January 16, 1942

My Darling Calvin,

I consulted a newborn infant doctor yesterday and learned today that I am pregnant with your baby. I was told to expect delivery in the September time frame. So all of our work was not in vain, was it? I hope that you are as happy about this state of affairs as I am. I love you so much and am so pleased that I will be the one to bear your first child! Please write to me and tell me that you share my happiness. Of course, I do not plan to say anything to my parents until you return home in March.

And at that time, I think that it would be prudent to consult your parents first to seek their counsel on the best way to approach my parents.

Hurry home, Darling, for I am waiting for you!

You have my eternal LOVE!

YOUR SWEETHEART AND WIFE TO BE!
MARY JANE

Mary Jane mailed her letter via Air Mail on Saturday morning which meant that Calvin was unlikely to receive the good news until Monday, January 19, 1942. Nevertheless, Mary Jane was certain that Calvin would be overjoyed at the news contained in her letter. Beyond that it was just a matter of time before Calvin could come home and marry her.

0900 Monday
19 January 1942
Great Lakes Naval Training Station

Between classes on Monday morning, both John and Calvin waited for mail call. When their names were called out, they stepped to the head of the line and accepted their envelopes. John received a letter from his parents while Calvin received two letters, one from his parents and one from Mary Jane. He elected to read his parents' letter first.

Noticing the date of January 17th, Calvin wondered where his parents' letter had been languishing along the way. But, this was wartime, wasn't it, and no doubt delays in mail delivery were commonplace. After reading his parents' letter Calvin opened Mary Jane's letter and quickly scanned its contents ending up in an indescribable euphoria at the news of the baby. Mary Jane had written to tell him of their good fortune.

Although Calvin attempted to remain calm and casual after learning the spectacular news, his inner emotional turmoil was betrayed by the huge smile on his face. "I assume that you received some good news from Mary Jane", questioned John. "Yes, you might say that; she is already making plans for our first date when I get home in March". (Calvin dared not reveal the true purpose of her letter.) John, our next class doesn't begin until 1300 so I am heading back to the barracks so I can reply to Mary Jane's letter", advised Calvin. "Okay, Calvin, I'll catch up with you at the obstacle course at 1300", said John. "See you there", Calvin called as he ran toward his barracks where he settled into one of the writing room desks, Calvin relaxed and calmed his mind. What could he say to the momentous announcement revealed in Mary Jane's letter? Of course, he would have to acknowledge 'Sir Calvin's' contribution to this wonderful news as well as the unseen angels that informed Mary Jane of THE PLAN. The news contained in Mary Jane's letter sent Calvin's heart racing and it was reflected in his inability to easily control his handwriting. In the end, Calvin took time out to wash his face and obtain a cold coke to help him calm his nerves. He then began writing a reply to Mary Jane's letter.

0930 Monday
19 January 1942
Great Lakes Naval Training Station
Chicago, Illinois

Great Lakes Navy Training Station
Company 41-162
Monday, 19 January 1942

My Darling Mary Jane,

I have just returned from "Mail Call" where I received your astounding letter containing the blessed news about our baby. I cannot begin to tell you just how proud I am of you and of the profound happiness that engulfs my heart. That we will soon be wed is the 'icing on the cake'. And, indeed, 'Sir Calvin' was right all along!

How fortunate that the advice of your angel resulted in our success. Although we never discussed the issue, isn't it about time that we picked out a name for our baby? I am afraid that I do not have any suggestions at the moment except that, if the baby is a boy, I would not want him to be a 'Junior'. Tell me what you think about selecting a suitable name. Mary Jane, thank you for being willing to be my partner in life! I know that we will be happy together. I have to run so will close till next time. Take extra good care of yourself and the baby, For you are now my family. Remember that I love you with all my heart!

YOUR LOVING HUSBAND TO BE
I AM YOUR ELATED CALVIN!!!!!!!!!!!!!!

Having finished his letter, Calvin addressed the envelope, wrote 'FREE' on the stamp corner and hurried over to the mess hall to drop it into the outgoing mailbox.

1900 Wednesday
21 January 1942
The Thomas residence at 655 Laurel Street
Des Moines, Iowa

The postman brought Calvin's letter to Mary Jane in the late afternoon. She was waiting impatiently to learn of Calvin's reaction to her pregnancy. Written the previous Monday, Mary Jane opened the envelope with shaking hands to find his response.

0900 Wednesday
21 January 1942
Des Moines, Iowa

Mary Jane was overcome with joy after reading Calvin's latest letter and immediately sat down to send a reply.

655 Laurel Street
Des Moines, Iowa
January 21, 1942

My Darling Husband to be!

I just received your most recent letter and hasten to send this reply. First of all, your idea about selecting a name for the baby is an excellent one. However, I would prefer that we develop a suitable name together. With at least eight months in which to select a name, that task really isn't something that is time sensitive. I have obtained several books containing potential names for boys and girls from which, I believe, we can find a suitable candidate or candidates. Notice that I haven't given up on the possibility of having twins, you see)

Thank you for your kind words about ourselves being your family. Your words strike me in my core of love as being very protective; just what I would expect of you as a father.

Please concentrate on getting through your training as fast as possible and come home to us. I love you so much, darling, that mere words are inadequate to give meaning to my feelings for you. Again, please hurry home for I miss you so much

Your lonely wife to be.

MARY JANE

Writing the letter to Calvin left Mary Jane in a melancholy mood, and a few tears glistened at the corners of her eyes. To offset the depression that she felt, she placed her letter in an envelope and left the house to get it in the mail system as soon as possible. Instinctively, she never retained copies of her letters for fear that her parents might find them, although, at the same time, she was essentially inconsistent, inasmuch as she saved all of Calvin's letters, keeping them in a safe, but highly secret, hiding place.

0930 Thursday
22 January 1942
Great Lakes Naval Training Station
Chicago, Illinois

Calvin and John, along with other members of the second platoon were participating in boat-handling exercises along the shore of Lake Michigan. It was a sunny day and the surface of the lake was calm. The two boys were assigned a 25-foot powerboat along with an experienced petty officer. They were drilled in seamanship activities involving running in a straight line parallel to the lake shore as well as approaching and mooring to a dock. The boys realized early on that the mooring aspect of the exercise would be the most difficult task. In practice, each boy was given control of the boat at various times, and he was expected to approach the dock at a slight angle and at a relatively slow speed. The boat was equipped with rubber bumpers with which to protect the hull from damage. On the approach, the desired technique was to place the transmission in neutral perhaps 20 feet from the mooring dock, and then be prepared to select the reverse gear to stop the boat's forward movement perhaps four feet from the dock. Executed properly, the boat should barely 'kiss' the dock with a forward speed of almost zero miles per hour. If the approach was made too fast, it would be necessary to reverse the propeller and apply some throttle to prevent the boat from crashing into the dock.

Once contact was made with the dock, the idle crewman jumps from the boat and ties up the craft to the nearest bit on the dock. In five attempts, Calvin succeeded in accomplishing the maneuver four times. John, on the other hand, succeeded on only two out of five attempts. John was his own worst enemy in terms of timing the reversing of the boat's propeller, but they would have many opportunities to practice in the weeks ahead. The entire afternoon was spent in this exercise, and by quitting time, John had improved significantly; again proving that practice makes perfect. John's effort produced a passing grade for the afternoon's endeavor and the petty officer duly entered this fact in the platoon records. At the same time, Calvin's superior grade was also entered in the platoon records. In the coming days, Calvin and John would spend many hours honing their boat-handling expertise on the lake.

23 January 1942 through 31 January 1942
Great Lakes Naval Training Station
Chicago, Illinois

The powerboat handling exercises continued through the latter nine days of the month of January. Both first and second platoons participated in the training sessions, and all of the recruits passed this phase of their training. Powerboat training was interspersed with marching exercises to the music of the Navy band playing the music of 'Anchors Aweigh'. Marching is considered important in teaching the recruits coordination in close order drills. Marching is important for another reason and that is, on the day of graduation all companies are required to march in front of a reviewing stand occupied by Navy officers, recruit relatives and other members of the public-at-large.

1 February through 15 February 1942
Great Lakes Naval Training Station
Chicago, Illinois

With the boat-handling exercises completed, the recruits are exposed to gunnery practice utilizing machine guns of various calibers. Live ammunition is used and safety petty officers control the target ranges to minimize the occurrence of any accidents. The recruits are equipped with ear plugs to safe-guard against hearing loss due to the loud reports of the shells being fired. Calvin and John performed exceptionally well in the gunnery exercises and, in fact, Calvin performed in such an exemplary manner that the company commander elected to place a commendation in his service record. In this manner did Calvin's Navy career take a turn that he might not have otherwise expected.

15 February 1942 to 12 March 1942
Great Lakes Naval Training Station
Chicago, Illinois

The 26 days of this period of recruit training were devoted to teaching radio communications procedures as well as developing a proficiency in sending and receiving Morse code. The recruits learned the principles of code encryption, and they received a 'Hands On' exposure to handling message traffic from various Navy communication networks. It turned out that of all the training curriculum exposed to the two platoons, radio communications generated the most interest among the recruits of Company 41-162; so much so that many were recommended for advanced technical radio training following their boot camp assignment. It was in this phase that John decided that he would like to pursue radio communications as a Navy career, but Calvin was more interested in the gunnery discipline. Although Calvin passed the radio communications tests with above-average grades, he decided that radio was just not his 'cup of tea'. As they were approaching the end of their boot camp training period, Calvin recalled the documents received from the Navy recruiting officer in Des Moines and his attraction to the gunnery rating available at the Navy school located in Nevada. From his boot camp training experience, he was even more certain than ever that a Navy gunnery billet would be his first choice

10 March 1942
Great Lakes Naval Training Station
Chicago, Illinois

Following the company commander's announcement of the program for graduation day, Calvin stopped by the communications building to make two important long distance telephone calls. Call completion was a slow and lengthy process in 1942. After giving his first number to the operator, Calvin waited in the small booth for the telephone to ring. Fifteen minutes later it rang and he said "Hello". On the distant end he recognized the voice of his father saying "Hello, Calvin, how nice it is to hear your voice". Without any preliminary conversation, Calvin launched into the purpose of his call. "Dad, I am graduating from boot camp on March 15th and I would appreciate it if you and Mom would plan to attend the ceremony. The plan would be for you two to arrive on the 14th and stay at a nearby Ramada Inn that is under contract to the Navy. You would take a Lake Central plane into Midway, like I did, and then take a Navy bus to my location where I would meet you at the front gate", said Calvin. "Well, Calvin, I think that we could arrange that and it would certainly be nice to see you again", replied Mr. Honeycut. "I have money to pay for Mary Jane's ticket and I would like to have her accompany you and Mom on this trip", requested Calvin. "We will be happy to arrange that as well. Should we call Mary Jane or will you advise her of our plans?", asked Mr. Honeycut. "Dad, I plan to call her after I hang up to invite her to come to my graduation", replied Calvin. "Very well, Son, but please ask her to call us immediately thereafter so that we can get together on arrangements in the face of such a short time frame.", requested Mr. Honeycut. "Yes, Dad, I'll have her call you this evening and let you know if she will attend", confirmed Calvin. "It will be a fun trip and thank you for inviting us, Calvin", said Mr. Honeycut. "You're quite welcome and many thanks for shepherding Mary Jane and arranging for her ticket. I will give you the money for her ticket when you arrive here. Well, I guess that is all for this time, Dad. I'm looking forward to seeing you and Mom real soon. Good-bye for now", concluded Calvin as he hung up his telephone receiver.

Calvin walked over to the service desk and gave the attendant Mary Jane's telephone number. After that, he returned to the booth to await his call completion. This time, it only took ten minutes for his call to go through and for the telephone in his booth to ring. "Hello, is this the Thomas residence?", asked Calvin. "Yes, this is Mrs. Thomas, and is that you, Calvin?", asked Mrs. Thomas. "Yes, ma'am, it is, and I would appreciate your calling Mary Jane to the telephone if she is home", requested Calvin. "Just a moment, Calvin, and I will go get her". "Thank you, Mrs. Thomas", said Calvin. A few moments later, a breathless Mary Jane answered. "Is it really you, Calvin?", questioned Mary Jane. "Yes, it is, sweetheart, and how are you feeling today?", asked Calvin. "I feel fine and your call is making me feel even better", replied Mary Jane. "Listen, Mary Jane, I have something important to tell you", said Calvin. "I am graduating from boot camp on 15 March and I want you to accompany my parents on a trip to see the graduation ceremony to be held at the Chicago boot camp", requested Calvin. "Oh, Calvin, what a thrill it will be to see the place where you have spent the past three months, and best of all have the opportunity to kiss you again", said Mary Jane. As he listened, Calvin wondered if mother Thomas was nearby and could hear Mary Jane's side of the conversation. "Mary Jane, I told my father that you would call him after I hang up so he can arrange to get you a plane ticket which, by the way, I am paying for", said Calvin. "Oh, thank you, Calvin, I will be sure to call him right away and I am certain that my parents will approve of my making the trip", offered Mary Jane. "That is wonderful, Mary Jane, and I can't wait to wrap my arms around you and give you a great big kiss", enthused Calvin. "You won't get any argument from me on the kissing part, for I have longed for your kisses over these past many weeks", revealed Mary Jane. "I love you so much, Mary Jane, and I am extremely happy that our separation is about to end", said Calvin. "So am I, Calvin, I can hardly wait to see you again", said a delighted Mary Jane. "I trust that you are not having any health problems with the baby", queried Calvin. "Of course I'm not, Calvin, Everything is fine and will be even better when your folks and I reach Chicago", bragged Mary Jane. "Mary Jane, are we still on for the wedding, no matter what?", asked Calvin. "No matter what, Calvin, it is going to happen", said Mary Jane happily. "That is great news and does my heart good to hear you confirm our plans", said Calvin. "I have to run along now, but please don't forget to call my folks right away. They are expecting your call", said Calvin. "Don't worry, my love, I will call as soon as you hang up", said Mary Jane. "Sweetheart, please remember that you and the baby are my world now and I will count the days until you get here. Good-bye till then my 'wife-to-be' ", said Calvin. "Good-bye, Calvin and take care of yourself too for I love you so much", and then they hung up their receivers.

True to her word, Mary Jane immediately called the Honeycuts and arrangements for all their tickets were finalized as well as other travel plans including the Honeycuts picking up Mary Jane at her home on the day of departure. When the call was over, Mary Jane basked in the glow of her pleasant anticipation. What fun, she thought, to fly to Chicago to meet my 'husband-to-be'. Only four more days and she would get to kiss Calvin. She could hardly wait. Since it was not bedtime time yet, Mary Jane went to her room and busied herself packing the clothes that she planned to take on her trip. She decided that for a two-day trip she did not need to take too many dresses or shoes. A single pair of shoes would suffice as well as two pairs of panties along with PJ's and a tooth brush and a can of hair spray.

1900 Saturday
14 March 1942
Great Lakes Naval Training Station
Chicago, Illinois
Ramada Inn

Calvin waited impatiently by the Shore Patrol guard shack for the arrival of the Navy bus from Chicago's Midway Airfield. About 1910, he saw the headlights of the bus and stood by waiting for it to park at the receiving barracks building. Upon hearing the air brakes set, Calvin ran over to the front door of the bus and waited for it to open. When it did, Mary Jane was the first person to alight. Calvin grabbed her in his arms and gave her a long passionate kiss as Mary Jane folded her arms about him. Looking beyond Mary Jane, Calvin saw his mother and father step off the bus. Releasing Mary Jane, he immediately moved to give them both hugs and welcome them. "Welcome to the Great Lakes Naval Training Station. What a pleasure it is to have you all here", said Calvin. "We are so happy to be here, Calvin", replied Mr. Honeycut. "And how was the trip along the way", asked Calvin. "Oh, it was just wonderful with everything right on time, and the bus was right where you told us it would be", chimed in Mary Jane.

"Well, folks, the Ramada Inn is just across the street so let's get your luggage and walk over there and check in", suggested Calvin. There were only two small bags, one for the Honeycuts and one for Mary Jane. They were very light so Calvin carried both bags and led the way across the street, with Mary Jane firmly clinging to his arm and his parents following along behind. Stopping at the registration desk, Calvin had the clerk check his reservations and give him the room keys for his guests. The clerk was the model of efficiency and quickly handed over the keys and pointed the way to the elevators, since his parents and Mary Jane would stay on an upper floor of the motel.

Upon entering the elevator, Calvin selected the proper floor and the elevator soon began its upward travel. A short time later, the doors opened on the 5th floor and everyone stepped off the elevator. "Your rooms are this way", said Calvin, moving off to his right. Reaching his parents' room first, Calvin said, "Mom and Dad, why don't you freshen up and then we can go downstairs and get something good to eat", suggested Calvin. "That is the best idea I have heard for a while", replied Mr. Honeycut. "All right, I'll see Mary Jane to her room and we'll stop by in fifteen minutes and knock on your door", said Calvin. "That will give us plenty of time", said Mrs. Honeycut. Calvin and Mary Jane continued down the hall to her room where Calvin unlocked the door and followed her inside where he placed her bag on a valet in the corner of the room. With the door closed, Calvin walked to Mary Jane, turned her toward him and wrapped his arms about her waist. "Oh, Mary Jane, I have waited so long to hold you in my arms and kiss your sweet lips", whereupon Calvin gave Mary Jane another passionate kiss which she returned with her tongue grazing his. "Mary Jane, I'll take a seat here while you go freshen yourself up", said Calvin, pointing to the bathroom door. "That's a good idea and it won't take me but a minute to wash my face and put on some make-up", replied Mary Jane. "Mary Jane, you are so extremely beautiful that I hate to let you out of my sight", complimented Calvin. "Do not concern yourself, Calvin, I'm certainly not going very far for I need your love to nourish me and our baby", remarked an excited Mary Jane. Within five minutes, Mary Jane returned, but Calvin hesitated to kiss her for fear of destroying her make-up. "There is a need to worry about the condition of your make-up, Miss Thomas, when I make up for lost time kissing your sweet lips", advised Calvin. "I can hardly wait, Calvin", said Mary Jane. Calvin and Mary Jane left her room after locking the door and walked to his parents door where he knocked gently and said "We're here". "Come on in, the door is not locked", invited Mr. Honeycut. Calvin and Mary Jane entered to find Mrs. Honeycut relaxing on their bed. "Well, shall we depart for the restaurant?", asked Calvin. "Your mother would rather stay here and rest so I plan to bring her meal to her, so let's go", revealed Mr. Honeycut. With that, the trio left Mrs. Honeycut behind and strolled down the hall to the elevator. Entering the lobby, Calvin led his father and sweetheart to the motel restaurant where they were seated immediately. "This is certainly a nice place, Calvin", commented Mr. Honeycut. "Yes, the Navy spends a great deal of money here, and it shows", commented Calvin.

Menus in hand, Calvin and his guests ordered their meals with Mrs. Honeycut's meal being set up as a take-out purchase. Their food arrived within fifteen minutes, and none too soon as far as Calvin was concerned, for he was famished. "Mary Jane, how is your meal?", asked Calvin. "It is quite delicious, especially the rainbow trout. And the onion rings are tasty too", added Mary Jane. "Dad, are you managing all right?", asked Calvin. "Yes, my steak is done to a turn and the meal as a whole is quite delicious", replied Mr. Honeycut. The trio fell silent as they finished their meal and looked over the dessert menu. Mary Jane ordered a hot fudge sundae while the two men each ordered apple pie. After finishing his pie, Calvin spoke up and said, "Just a word of advice; the graduation ceremony commences at 1000 in the morning, so I suggest that you plan to arrive at the parade grounds across the street by 0930 so you can have your pick of the best available seats in the bleachers. There will be six companies graduating so it will not be a short ceremony. There will be ushers on duty to direct you to the proper seating area. Our company will be the first to graduate, and after that I will find you in the stands and join you, so please save me a seat", requested Calvin. "See you tomorrow, Calvin; I'm going to leave now and take your mother's meal up to her", said Mr. Honeycut. "Mr. Honeycut, would you please call me in the morning when you are up and around; I don't want to miss anything", requested Mary Jane. "I certainly will, and what do you say about us having breakfast about 0800?" "That sounds fine, but please give me a wake-up call anyway so I can get started on time", requested Mary Jane. "Never fear, Mary Jane, I will make certain that you have plenty of notice", assured Mr. Honeycut. Mr. Honeycut departed with his wife's take-out meal and went upstairs to deliver it. "Mary Jane, do you feel up to a little love making?", asked Calvin very quietly. "I thought that you would never ask", joked Mary Jane displaying a broad dimpled smile.

Calvin paid their check and the two lovers walked to the elevator. Riding to the 5th floor alone, Calvin pulled Mary Jane close to him and kissed her several times before the door opened on the fifth floor. Walking silently down the hall to Mary Jane's room, Calvin unlocked the door when they reached it. Walking inside and locking the door, Calvin and Mary Jane quickly disrobed and climbed into her 'king size' bed. Calvin kissed Mary Jane and caressed her lovely body with his hands from her breasts to her thighs. "Oh, Calvin, how I have longed for you to be with me these past three months", murmured a gloriously excited Mary Jane. Although highly stimulated, Calvin continued to kiss and caress Mary Jane paying particular attention to her lovely breasts whose pink nipples now stood erect. Calvin coupled with Mary Jane and they made love repeatedly for the next hour. Calvin remembered their Saturday interlude at Mary Jane's home three months earlier and that memory came back in a sudden rush. With their passions momentarily satisfied, Calvin and Mary Jane relaxed in each other's arms for an hour.

"I'm sorry that regulations forbid me from staying all night,

Mary Jane. I have to be in the barracks by 'lights out time' which is only 30 minutes from now." "That's okay, honey, we will have plenty of time to catch up on our lovemaking when we return home tomorrow", consoled Mary Jane with a knowing smile. "You're certainly right about that, but the first thing that I want to do is speak to Mom and Dad and then your parents about our marriage", replied Calvin. "Yes, you're correct about that important matter and I am certain that everything will turn out just fine and we will be married in a day or two", speculated Mary Jane. Leaning over the bed, Calvin took Mary Jane's plump right breast into his mouth and felt her shudder as he moved his tongue over the sensitive surface of her erect, pink nipple. "I'll see you at the parade grounds tomorrow", was Calvin's parting remark as he walked through the door followed by a naked Mary Jane who quickly locked the door behind him. Calvin felt as though he was floating on air as he made his way across the Grinder to his barracks and a good night's sleep. What a way to end the day, he thought; a little sex will relax the most taut and tense of bodies. Tonight he would dream of Mary Jane and their future life together. When Calvin reached his barracks he found John already in bed and snoring softly. Calvin quickly dressed in his nightclothes and headed to the bathroom to brush his teeth. When he returned, John had turned over and was no longer snoring. Calvin climbed into his bunk and relaxed for the first time that day.

0600 Sunday
15 March 1942
Great Lakes Naval Training Station
Chicago, Illinois

On this cool, end-of-the-winter-day, the recruits of Company 41-162 would graduate from the Great Lakes Naval Training Station along with several other companies.

A special program had been arranged to include the family members of the recruits at the special inspection and awards presentations that were a tradition for graduating sailors. The program was to begin at 1000 so Calvin hurried to finish his breakfast and put on his dress blues uniform along with his glistening black shoes. Calvin was ready early. At 0945 he was in his place in the second platoon on the parade grounds and he could hear the band tuning up. Calvin called over to John inviting him to join him and his family to meet Mary Jane after the ceremony. John agreed to follow Calvin into the stands since his own family was unable to attend. The music commenced and the platoon leaders guided the company onto the parade grounds for their close order drill, flags flying and the band playing 'Anchors Aweigh'. Eventually, the company turned to pass in front of the reviewing stand where everyone saluted the colors, the base commander and then exited the field. "COMPANY ATTENNNTION - DISSSSMISSED, and good luck, sailors, in your future Navy career" called out the company commander. "Boot camp" had finally officially ended. But it was not over for John and Calvin just yet.

A special awards ceremony was called to order by the base commander following the passage of the remaining recruit companies from the parade grounds. The audience was called to order by the base commander, who then called Calvin and John to his podium and presented each of them with the base commander's special commendation for their exceptionally high marks as Navy recruits. The commander announced each of the boy's post-boot camp assignments; Calvin Honeycut to attend the Navy's Gunnery School at Holman Nevada, and John Harris to attend the Navy's Radio Communications School at San Diego, California. At the same time, the base commander announced the extremely unusual appointment of each boy to the rank of third-class petty officer in their chosen fields of endeavor. Mary Jane, together with Mr. and Mrs. Honeycut, stood and yelled at the top of their lungs and were joined by all of the people in the bleachers. The roar of the crowd was deafening. Next, the base commander dismissed Calvin and John after presenting them with special certificates of appreciation for their high scholastic achievements and then continued with his program of honoring outstanding recruits of other companies on the base.

With their last boot camp event finished, Calvin and John searched the stands for Mary Jane and Mr. and Mrs. Honeycut, where they finally found them midway up in Section DD. Working their way up the steep rows of bleacher seats, Calvin and John finally reached Calvin's family. "Hello, Mom and Dad, and I would like you to meet my friend, John Harris", said Calvin. "Hello, John, we've heard quite a bit about you from Calvin and we are pleased to finally meet you in person", offered Mr. Honeycut. "Thank you, Mr. Honeycut, and I've also heard a lot about you folks from your son. So much so, that some time in the future I would like to visit Des Moines", replied John. "John, if you ever get to Des Moines, plan on staying with us, we have plenty of room", said Mrs. Honeycut. "Many thanks for that kind invitation, but with the war on, I cannot speculate on when I might be able to visit there.", said John. "No matter when it is, you will be welcome", replied Mr. Honeycut.

Turning to Mary Jane, Calvin said, "John, I want you to meet Mary Jane Thomas, the future Mrs. Calvin Honeycut". Mary Jane smiled her dimpled way as John took her hand and said, "I am so pleased to meet you, Mary Jane. I feel that I already know you from the photograph that Calvin had taped to his locker door." "Dad and Mom, as you heard during the awards ceremony, John and I have received our duty assignments and promotions just before this celebration. After 10 days delayed orders, John will travel to San Diego to attend a special radio communications school. In my case,

I have been assigned to travel to Hollman, Nevada, where I will attend the Navy's gunnery school", concluded Calvin. "Well, congratulations to both you boys, and we hope that these assignments are to your liking", said Mr. Honeycut. "Indeed they are", replied John. "Because of our excellent grades, we were allowed to pick our duty assignments. I will admit, however, that the promotions from apprentice seaman to third class petty officer came as a complete surprise", said Calvin. "No doubt these promotions will give John and me a career boost as we pursue additional training in our chosen professions. And looking on the bright side, the promotions will be accompanied by fatter pay schedules for each of us" concluded Calvin.

1400 Sunday
15 March 1942
Great Lakes Naval Training Station
Chicago, Illinois

"Dad, Mom, and Mary Jane, if we are to connect with the plane for our return trip to Des Moines, we must leave now. We will go over to the base transportation group and take the bus back to Midway airfield. John, this is where we part company and I hope that we can meet again sometime in the future", said Calvin. "I surely hope so too, Calvin, It has certainly been a great pleasure spending the last 12 weeks with you while we learned about the Navy", said John. "Good luck and happy sailing, John", said Calvin. And with that good-bye, the Honeycuts and Mary Jane walked to the transportation group building. Showing his orders to the duty shore patrol petty officer, Calvin and his family were directed to the next bus for Midway Field. Boarding the bus, Mr. and Mrs. Honeycut selected seats in the first row while Mary Jane and Calvin took two seats in the second row. Fifteen minutes later the bus was full and the driver started his engine and pulled out into light traffic in front of the Navy base. As before, the family's trip would last approximately one hour in covering the 60-mile return trip to the Chicago Midway Airport.

The noise level in the bus was such that Calvin and Mary Jane could speak freely to each other in private. Calvin appreciated this fact for he had several topics that he needed to discuss with his wife-to-be without his parents hearing their conversation. Leaning close to Mary Jane's soft ear, Calvin began. "Mary Jane, my duty orders call for me to leave for the gunnery school in Nevada at the end of my ten-day leave. My voucher specifies travel by train to the school. I will have a Pullman compartment and I would like you to plan on making the trip west with me. When we arrive at the other end, I will arrange for suitable housing for us and I am certain that we can be together whenever school classes are not in session. Would you do that for us?", asked Calvin. Placing her mouth close to Calvin's ear Mary Jane said "Oh, yes, Calvin. I wouldn't miss such a trip for all the money in the world. And you have to know that I want to spend every possible minute with you before you have to leave to board some Navy ship", happily added Mary Jane. "Mary Jane, that trip will have to serve as our 'honeymoon' since the Navy will not allow me to take any additional time off beyond my 10 day leave", complained Calvin. "Calvin, I always wanted to have a 'honeymoon' where I could look out a window and watch the world pass by", joked Mary Jane. "Then it's settled, ten days from now we will board a train in Des Moines and enjoy making love to each other all the way to Nevada", said Calvin, and he was serious. "How wonderful you make it all sound, Calvin. This is our chance of a lifetime so let's take full advantage of it. Especially since Uncle Sam will be paying for our compartment and meals", observed Mary Jane. Continuing in a soft voice, Calvin spoke to Mary Jane, "Since I will be in Nevada for several months, what do you think will happen for your physical needs of a medical nature? Do you think that Doctor Wilson can refer you to another doctor in Nevada? I don't want you to end up with inadequate treatment for the sake of our baby", said a concerned Calvin. "Calvin, I can't answer your question because I never contemplated the prospect of my needing to move to Nevada. Tomorrow, I will check with Doctor Wilson and determine whether or not he can suggest the name of another doctor out west, but I would not be too concerned because there are baby doctors all over the nation. The main problem, as I see it, is the aspect of our marriage and what my parents might do or say about it, advised Mary Jane rather timidly. "I believe that it is mandatory that we consult your parents as soon as we get home to Des Moines and then, in the morning, beard my mother and father in their den 'come what may'", counseled Mary Jane. "Yes, I believe that the plan that you just laid out is exactly what we should do". With Mary Jane so close, Calvin took the occasion to tenderly kiss her rosy cheek. "Mary Jane, have you had occasion to see Lowell or Cathy since I have been away?. asked Calvin. "Yes, I see them most every day at school, and Cathy told me that she was pleased that Lowell's parents were not inclined to allow him to join the Navy although Lowell himself looks to you with a great amount of envy". replied Mary Jane.

1500 Sunday
15 March 1942
Midway Airfield
Chicago, Illinois

The bus pulled into the Midway Field Terminal area and stopped at the Lake Central Airlines gate. The four travelers left the bus and hurried to the ticket agent's counter to check in. With little luggage and both of those being small carry-on pieces, they were assigned seats and were ready to board. Boarding took place twenty minutes later, and Mary Jane as well as Calvin were eager to return to Des Moines and get things settled in their lives. The Douglas DC-3 Transport plane took off on time and an hour later was landing at the Des Moines, Iowa Airport. Throughout the trip, Calvin and Mary Jane merely held each other and enjoyed the noisy solitude of the plane's cabin.

1630 Sunday
15 March 1942
Des Moines, Iowa
Airport

After landing, Mr. Honeycut called for his automobile and it was brought over by a valet within ten minutes. After entering their 1939 Dodge sedan, Calvin said, "Mom and Dad, will you please take us home to the farm, and by us, I include Mary Jane. We have a problem that needs resolving now and we wish to seek your advice", concluded Calvin. "Yes, Calvin, we'll go straight home since we don't need to drop Mary Jane off at her home", said Mr. Honeycut. "However, at some point, we will need to notify the Thomas' that Mary Jane is safe and sound with us", said Calvin. "You're right on that point, Son, and we shall make the notification at the proper time", concluded Mr. Honeycut.

For the remainder of the trip home, there was little discussion. Mr. Honeycut drove the Dodge directly to its stall after letting his passengers out at the house. Once inside the living room, Mrs. Honeycut asked if Calvin and Mary Jane would like something to drink. "No, thank you, Mom, I don't want any distraction from what we must discuss with you and Dad", replied Calvin. Mr. Honeycut walked in and said, "All right kids, let's have it!". Calvin decided that he should carry the ball and began to speak. "Mom and Dad, you know from earlier conversations that Mary Jane and I want to get married. When I approached the Thomas parents about my desire to marry their daughter they decided that we should wait until after I completed my boot camp training at which time they would give us their final answer. Subsequently, Mary Jane received a revelation that implied that all we had to do to obtain permission to marry was to have a baby. So to that end we decided to carry out that plan. Thus, we presently find ourselves to be prospective parents (in the September time frame) with the urgent need to marry as soon as possible. When we found that Mary Jane was pregnant, our initial thought was to elope tomorrow, but at the same time, we felt that that move would be unfair to Mary Jane's parents. So the question before the house is, what do we do now?", said Calvin. "Mary Jane, do you have an inkling as to how your parents will react to this news?", asked Mr. Honeycut. "To tell the truth, I really do not. I suspect that they will be quite hurt because we will have essentially taken away their right to decide whether or not Calvin and I should marry", said Mary Jane. "I wouldn't disagree with your observation", said Mr. Honeycut. "Dad and Mom, mine and Mary Jane's love for each other has not diminished as a result of the dilemma in which we now find ourselves, and I believe that the only thing that we can do now is to meet with Mary Jane's parents and lay it on the line and see what happens", said Calvin. "I expect that that statement isn't far from the truth, Calvin", observed Mr. Honeycut. "So on that basis, let me drive Mary Jane home and request an appointment with Mr. and Mrs. Thomas for the morning hours and let the chips fall where they may. I should tell you that Mary Jane and I have already decided that if her parents tell us that she cannot marry, we will leave town and be married by a Justice of the Peace. Notwithstanding the nature of the dilemma, we both feel that a negative response will be unacceptable", said Calvin. "Calvin, far be it for us to decide your life for you, but you will run the risk of alienating Mary Jane from her parents for the rest of her life, and that is an undesirable result. I don't disagree that something must be done and soon, but don't adopt a hard and fast position without first discussing it all with the Thomas parents", advised Mrs. Honeycut.

"Thank you, Mom and Dad, for your kind consideration, but Mary Jane and I will just have to pursue our own destiny taking into account the lives and feelings of others to the extent that we can", said Calvin. "Dad, will it be okay if I use the Dodge to take Mary Jane home?", asked Calvin. "By all means, Son, help yourself", said Mr. Honeycut.

Calvin drove Mary Jane home in silence, and, pulling up in front of her home, found the house dark. "Mary Jane, it appears as though I cannot set an appointment for tomorrow morning. Would you please ask your parents in the morning whether or not I can stop by to discuss our marriage", asked Calvin. "Of course I will, Calvin", said Mary Jane. "When you make the inquiry, don't go into any of the details as we did with my parents. Leave that chore up to me because I do not want you subjected to any vilification by either your mother or father", said Calvin. "Calvin, you need to know that I will not permit you to accept the entire burden of responsibility in this matter. In case you have forgotten, we entered into our plan by mutual consent. So when we get to speak to my parents, I plan to have my say as well as you", continued Mary Jane. "Very well, Mary Jane. Please call me as early as your folks can accommodate me so we can resolve our future course of action no later than tomorrow. Should we find the going too tough, let us beat a hasty retreat and just go get married by a Justice of the Peace", said Calvin. "Hopefully it won't come to that, Calvin", said an optimistic Mary Jane. "Come, let me see you to your door and then I am heading home", said Calvin. At the front door, Calvin kissed Mary Jane and held her tightly for several minutes. "See you tomorrow, sweetheart, and don't worry, it will all work out as we desire, you wait and see. One more thing, Mary Jane, let us adopt the strategy of only revealing the fact that you are pregnant if they tell us 'no, we cannot be married'. Absent that knowledge, they cannot claim that they were pressured into making an affirmative decision", suggested Calvin. "I like that plan very much", said Mary Jane as she unlocked her front door and went inside.

With his mind in a complete funk, Calvin looked forward to the next day with great foreboding. He drove home in a daze and was surprised when it came time to turn into his driveway and put the Dodge in its stall. Time seemed to have stood still on his trip home and he did not remember seeing a single landmark on his way home. The house was dark save for a dim nightlight as Calvin climbed the stairs to his room. He said a prayer for success in tomorrow's negotiations and climbed into bed. He did not expect this night to pass peacefully. Although Calvin fell asleep quickly enough, he found himself dreaming in a tormented scene with Mary Jane and her parents locked in a vicious argument that could not be resolved to the Thomas' satisfaction. The dream ended when he awoke the next morning to the sound of his alarm clock. Calvin did not know whether to consider his dream a prophetic omen or not. The still air carried the fragrance of bacon and eggs cooking in the kitchen so Calvin hurried to shower and dress. It was going to be a busy day and he needed food to sustain him during the forthcoming meeting with the Thomas parents.

1030 Monday
16 March 1942
The Thomas Residence
Des Moines, Iowa

At ten o'clock the next morning, Mary Jane called to tell Calvin that he should come over then, to discuss his marriage proposal. After receiving permission to use the Dodge, Calvin hurried to Mary Jane's house. When he arrived, Mary Jane was peeking out the front door. Calvin hurried up the front walk and rang the front door chimes, but found that he was too agitated to listen to the familiar melody as he had in times past, and then Mary Jane let him in. Once inside he could hear her parents talking in the kitchen. He whispered into Mary Jane's ear, "Everything will turn out all right". Walking into the kitchen, Calvin greeted Mr. and Mrs. Thomas. "Good morning, Mr. and Mrs. Thomas, and how have you been; fine I hope". "Yes, Calvin, we are in the best of health and enjoying our retirement immensely", said Mrs. Thomas. "Well, I just wanted to stop by to continue the conversation that we began at the time I left for my training at the Navy boot camp in Chicago. You will recall that I asked you to grant me the hand of your lovely daughter in marriage. As you recommended then, Mary Jane and I have spent the past twelve weeks doing a great deal of soul-searching to come to some definitive conclusion about the reasonableness of a wartime marriage. In the end, we concluded that, regardless of the risks involved, one should not shy away from the realities of life, either good or bad. So I have come again to repeat my request to be allowed to marry Mary Jane", concluded Calvin. Mary Jane chimed in with "Oh, Mom and Dad, we are so much in love, please say yes to Calvin's proposal so we can get on with our lives. Calvin has an assured income that can adequately support me and I personally cannot see the logic in waiting to marry until the war is over", pleaded Mary Jane, on the verge of tears.

"Mary Jane and Calvin, Mrs. Thomas and I have also been searching for the right answer these past weeks and have concluded that you are correct. Waiting until after the war to marry will not really accomplish anything. Therefore, you have our blessing to be married whenever you wish", concluded Mr. Thomas. Although dumbfounded as he was, Calvin moved to Mr. Thomas' side and shook his hand with thanks, and gave Mrs. Thomas a hug and kissed her on the cheek. "Thank you, Mr. and Mrs. Thomas, and I promise you that I will take the best of care of your daughter and see to it that she wants for nothing", said Calvin. "In light of Calvin's assignment to the Navy school in Nevada, we would like to 'tie the knot' as soon as possible so that I can accompany him to Nevada where Calvin will arrange for on-base housing for both of us. We can obtain a marriage license today and be married in just a few days, certainly before Calvin's leave is up ten days from now. I am not planning on a big church wedding. Once we have the license, I would prefer to just go to City Hall and have Judge Melbourne perform the ceremony. (The judge was a lifelong friend of Messers Thomas and Honeycut.) Would you object to that approach, Mom and Dad?", inquired Mary Jane. "Sweetheart, that approach sounds perfectly acceptable to me", said Mr. Thomas. "There is no reason in the world that you kids should not be married by the judge", agreed Mrs. Thomas.

"Then if you will excuse us, please, Mary Jane and I will go to City Hall and obtain a license to be married and, Mr. and Mrs. Thomas, I want to thank you again from the bottom of my heart for your compassionate understanding as well as your favorable response to our request", said Calvin. With that, Calvin and Mary Jane walked out the front door and Calvin drove to City Hall where a fee was paid and a marriage license obtained. Calvin had the presence of mind to contact Judge Melbourne's office for an appointment at noon the next day for him to perform the marriage ceremony, and at the same time waive the usual three-day waiting period in consideration of the fact that there is a war on and a sailor doesn't have an overabundance of time that he can call his own.

1300 Monday
16 March 1942
The Honeycut Farm
Des Moines, Iowa

From City Hall, Calvin drove to the Honeycut farm to advise his parents of the good news. Entering the house, Calvin shouted to his mother and father from the living room. At the time, they happened to be in the kitchen, but came to the living room immediately. "Mary Jane and I want to invite you two to a wedding ceremony tomorrow noon at City Hall. Mr. and Mrs. Thomas gave us their blessing and approved our marriage on the basis of logic, and we did not have to reveal the fact that Mary Jane is pregnant, so their decision was not made under any kind of duress", said Calvin. "Well, your mother and I congratulate you both for the manner in which you resolved your own circumstance and, of course, we are delighted and will be there with 'bells on', concluded Mr. Honeycut. Mrs. Honeycut walked over to Mary Jane and hugging her said, "Welcome to our family, my dear". "Thank you very much, Mr. and Mrs. Honeycut, for all your kind words of support. We have to leave now to tell my folks about the timing of our marriage", said Mary Jane. "Dad, will you need the Dodge this afternoon", asked Calvin. "No, Son, you can use it for the rest of the day. Your mother and I will use the pickup truck if we need to go anywhere." "Thank you so much Dad and I will take good care of the Dodge", replied Calvin. "Come Mary Jane, let's hit the road for Des Moines and brief your parents on our plans", added Calvin. "You will not have to repeat that invitation, Calvin. I'll race you to the car", joked Mary Jane.

1500 Monday
16 March 1942
The Thomas Residence
Des Moines, Iowa

Once on the highway to tell the Thomas parents about the wedding plans, Calvin said, "Mary Jane, do you think it is too short a notice to have Cathy and Lowell stand up for us tomorrow?" "There is only one way to find out and that is to call them now. Let's do that from my house as soon as possible after we tell Mom and Dad of our plans", suggested Mary Jane. Mary Jane led the way into the Thomas home and called to her parents who were in the den. "Mom and Dad, we are all set to be married by the judge tomorrow at noon. He told Calvin that he would waive the three-day waiting period, and Mr. and Mrs. Honeycut will be attending". "You couldn't keep us away with a team of mules", said Mrs. Thomas. "Calvin and I will telephone our friends, Cathy and Lowell, to see if they can attend and stand up for us", said Mary Jane. "If you will excuse us, we will get busy on the phone calls", said a relieved Calvin. "We'll keep our fingers crossed that your friends are available on such short notice", said Mrs. Thomas. Calvin and Mary Jane contacted both friends, and luckily they were available and agreed to stand up for Calvin and his wife-to-be the next day. At the same time, Calvin called the Willard Hotel and made arrangements to stay there on their wedding night. "Mary Jane, is the Willard Hotel all right with you in which to spend our wedding night? I hope so because I have already made reservations for us", revealed Calvin with a smile. "That is a wonderful gesture, Calvin and, of course, I approve", said Mary Jane. "At the same time, I arranged for a post-wedding luncheon at the Willard", said Calvin. "Wow, you have thought of everything", said Mary Jane. "Well, not quite everything. What about wedding rings;

shouldn't we leave now and go to Arnold Jewelers and pick up a wedding ring for me and an engagement and wedding rings for you?", asked Calvin. "Yes, rings are an important part of the ceremony so let's get going". Mary Jane called out to her parents to tell them that she and Calvin were leaving to go select their wedding rings, and they walked out the front door and climbed into the Dodge. Ten minutes later Calvin parked in front of the jewelry store, and an hour later they left with their rings properly sized and resting in their own, small, felt-lined boxes. "Oh, thank you, Calvin, for my rings. They are so beautiful", cried an ecstatic Mary Jane. "Mary Jane, I should tell you that I have ordered flowers for you, Cathy, your mother and my mother, and Lowell and me. And with that, I think that we have all the bases covered", said Calvin. "I agree with you; I can't think of a thing that we have missed", said Mary Jane.

"Mary Jane, with all that has happened today, we haven't taken time out to eat anything and I am starved. How about you?", queried Calvin. "Yes, I am mighty hungry too", admitted Mary Jane. "Mary Jane, while I was away in boot camp, I really missed going to Jackson's Drive-in. Is it okay if we go there now for some food?", asked Calvin. "Jackson's would be just fine, Calvin, and let's go now", replied a hungry Mary Jane. Walking out the front door of the Thomas home, Calvin was in awe of the blue sky and sunny Spring day. How could he and Mary Jane be so lucky as to finally have their wedding plans in order for tomorrow's event?

1700 Monday
16 March 1942
The Thomas Home
Des Moines, Iowa

An hour later, their stomachs comfortably full, Calvin and Mary Jane returned to the Thomas home. Night was falling and Calvin decided that he should return home for tomorrow would be an exceedingly busy and the most important day in their lives. Walking Mary Jane to her front door, Calvin said, "Sweetheart, tomorrow is the big day, so I plan to return home now and get a good night's sleep." "Yes, Calvin, you do that and I will do the same; and just think, Calvin, after tomorrow we will always be together and will not ever have to ask permission of anyone to do the things that we desire", bragged Mary Jane. "You are so correct, Mary Jane", replied Calvin. After giving Mary Jane a meaningful kiss and hugging her tightly, Calvin said, "Good night, Sweetheart. I'll see you at noon tomorrow at City Hall". "Good night, darling, and this is my last night as a single girl and I can't wait for tomorrow noon to arrive", revealed Mary Jane. Calvin started up the Dodge and turned toward the Honeycut farm, waving good-bye to Mary Jane in the process. Rolling along the highway west of Des Moines, Calvin marveled again at the events of the day. Regardless of the fact that, at one point, he was almost willing to give up in despair of getting permission to marry Mary Jane, here he was perhaps a dozen hours away from doing exactly that. And all because he had joined the Navy; will wonders never cease, he thought to himself. Calvin parked the Dodge in its stall and went up to his room. He climbed into bed and soon fell asleep dreaming of Mary Jane.

0800 Tuesday
17 March 1942
The Honeycut Farm
Des Moines, Iowa

At 0800 the next morning, Calvin's mother called him to breakfast. Quickly taking his shower, Calvin came downstairs in his bathrobe to a breakfast of bacon, eggs and biscuits and gravy. After he had eaten, he returned to his room and dressed in his Navy Dress Blues uniform and checked to see that his shoes were in their usual spotlessly shiny condition. After dressing, Calvin went downstairs to wait for his parents to dress. They had previously agreed that they should leave the farm at 1100 to allow enough time to arrive early at City Hall where they would meet Mary Jane and her parents as well as Cathy and Lowell. "Good-morning, Calvin. Are you ready for the big day?", asked his father on the way out to start the Dodge. "I'm just fine and hope that the ceremony will be a short one, and that the butterflies in my stomach calm down", said Calvin. Mrs. Honeycut walked by at that time and crossed the front porch on her way to the car, with Calvin following along. Calvin opened the front passenger door and his mother took her place beside her husband. Then, Calvin got into the rear seat and relaxed to the extent that he could. Calvin was happy to learn, upon his return from boot camp, that his father had arranged for one of his neighbor boyfriends to assume his cow milking duties. That unresolved issue had preyed on Calvin's mind throughout his boot camp duty.

1130 Tuesday
17 March 1942
City Hall, Des Moines, Iowa

It was 1130 when Mr. Honeycut pulled into the City Hall parking lot and turned off his engine. Mr. Honeycut walked to the passenger side of his car and took his wife's arm and led her into the building. where they walked immediately to the judge's chambers. Upon entering, Calvin was surprised to find Mary Jane and her parents already there, along with Cathy and Lowell. "Good-morning, everyone", said Calvin. His greeting elicited a chorus of 'good-mornings' from everyone in the room. The judge's secretary handed Calvin his carnation and his mother placed it on his uniform after she attached her own lavender orchid. Walking over to Mary Jane, Calvin said, "Mary Jane, I have never seen you appear more radiantly beautiful". "Why, thank you, Calvin and you look mighty sharp yourself in your spotless dress blues", replied Mary Jane. All too soon, the judge stepped into his office and invited the group into his chambers where the actual ceremony would be performed. Amid the buzz of conversation, everyone passed through the huge oak doors leading to the judge's chambers, where a professional photographer was waiting.

Taking his place on a low podium, the judge invited the wedding party to arrange themselves in front of him, with Calvin and Mary Jane in the center, and the matron of honor to Mary Jane's left and the best man to Calvin's right. Then the judge began. "Ladies and gentlemen, this is a solemn occasion and one that I am pleased to be involved in, for I have known Calvin and Mary Jane all their lives and it is a distinct pleasure for me to play a part in their lives as they enter the domain of holy matrimony. This is not a circumstance to be taken lightly for it portends a lifelong commitment, one person to the other. And who, may I ask, gives Mary Jane to be the bride of Calvin Honeycut?" "Her mother and I proudly claim that honor", replied Mr. Thomas who, having performed his duty, took his seat in the front row of pews beside Mrs. Thomas. "Calvin and Mary Jane, I will not give you a long-winded lecture on the duties and responsibilities that you assume in entering a married state. It is sufficient, I believe, for me to merely point out that marriage is an enterprise that commands the mutual respect of each partner for the other. By so doing, you will find that moments of tension, on whatever the issue, can be diminished by remembering to realize that we all make mistakes for which we desire to make amends. I encourage you to always be willing to discuss and accept your partner's point of view as a means of maintaining a harmonious married relationship. Calvin and Mary Jane, please join your right hands, and Calvin, please repeat after me: "I, Calvin, take thee, Mary Jane, to be my lawfully wedded wife, for better or worse, in sickness and in health, till death do us part". Calvin then repeated the phrase, word for word without a single mistake. The judge then said, "Mary Jane, please repeat after me "I, Mary Jane, take thee, Calvin, to be my lawfully wedded husband, for better or worse, in sickness and in health, till death do us part". Mary Jane proudly repeated her vows. With their vows having been exchanged, the judge said, "May I have the rings, please". Meanwhile, the photographer was, as unobtrusively as possible, recording the events in progress. Lowell and Cathy handed over the rings. Handing Mary Jane's wedding ring to Calvin, the judge requested Calvin to place the ring on the third finger of Mary Jane's left hand (where her engagement ring already resided) and say the words, "With this ring, I thee wed" which Calvin happily recited with a big smile on his face. Handing Calvin's ring to Mary Jane, the judge said "Mary Jane, please place this ring on the ring finger of Calvin's left hand and say these words, "With this ring, I thee wed". Mary Jane complied without hesitation. "In accordance with the authority vested in me, I now pronounce you to be Man and Wife, and what God has joined together, let no man put asunder".

"Calvin, you may kiss your bride", smiled the judge. Calvin swept Mary Jane into his arms and soundly kissed her lips amid the cheers and congratulatory remarks of the entire wedding party and the popping of flashbulbs by the photographer. Speaking loudly, Calvin said, "Mary Jane and I invite you all to have lunch with us at the Willard Hotel, and that includes you, Judge Melbourne, if you can fit it into your schedule." "Thank you, Calvin, and since I make my own schedule, I will be pleased to join you all. Let us all adjourn to the Willard Hotel." Calvin and Mary Jane waited by the entry door as the mothers, fathers and guests filed past and personally conveyed their congratulations to the newlyweds, and the photographer finished taking a few final photos. After everyone had left, Calvin grabbed Mary Jane and held her in a long embrace. "Mary Jane, you are so beautiful that it makes my heart skip a beat whenever I look at you", revealed Calvin. "Why, thank you, Calvin, and as some folks say, 'all I want is an unfair advantage.' Come, let's travel over to the Willard." Walking out of city hall, Calvin noticed his father waving vigorously to them, so he and Mary Jane hurried to the Dodge and climbed in. Thank you for waiting for us, Dad and Mom", said Calvin. "It is too far to walk and we knew that you did not have a car", said Mrs. Honeycut. "Well, Mary Jane, how does it feel to be a wife for all of 45 minutes?", asked Mr. Honeycut. "For whatever reason, this day, thus far, seems more like a fairy tale dream than the real world", offered Mary Jane. "Don't you worry, honey, in time it will all sort itself out", observed Mrs. Honeycut. Following that exchange, Calvin's father turned the Dodge into the Willard parking lot where the valets took over. Valets hurried to open all the doors of the Dodge so that the passengers could exit with ease. Entering the restaurant, the Maitre d' led the party to a private dining room where the other guests were already assembled.

1300 Tuesday
17 March 1942
Willard Hotel
Des Moines, Iowa

Taking their places at the head table, Calvin smiled at Mr. and Mrs. Thomas to acknowledge his thanks once again, for without their approval, there might not have even been a wedding. A number of waitresses began circulating among the guests, taking drink orders while the menus were being studied. "Mary Jane, I have to admit that this is much better than Jackson's Drive-in", said Calvin with a smile. "You won't get any argument from me on that observation, Calvin. I just love this place and am so happy that we will be spending the night here", volunteered Mary Jane. Lowell was seated to Calvin's left and in a lull in the conversation, Calvin leaned over and asked, "Lowell, are you and Cathy giving any thought to getting married soon?" "No, we really haven't discussed marriage yet, although it has been going through my mind for some time, especially this afternoon. I guess I am just a bit timid when it comes to such discussions", offered Lowell. "Well, I suspect that if the truth were known, Cathy would be eager to engage you in such a discussion. Don't underestimate Cathy, Lowell, for she is a smart person and knows her own mind, from what I have seen", said Calvin. "No argument there, Calvin. I agree that Cathy is one smart lady. And I do hope that one day we will be married", replied Lowell.

With the drink orders having been delivered, food orders were taken while the party continued to engage in lively conversations. Mary Jane and Cathy carried on their own private conversation, and Calvin happily observed his mother and father speaking with Mary Jane's parents. It was truly a happy occasion, thought Calvin, and again all of it produced by his decision to join the U.S. Navy. How remarkable, he thought, and not for the first time. When the meals had been consumed, a wedding cake was brought in and served with Calvin and Mary Jane feeding each other in the traditional post-nuptial manner with the photographer recording all of the festivities on film.

The wedding cake ritual was followed by a champagne toast. When all of the guests had received their flute of champagne, Calvin stood and the room became quiet. "Ladies and gentlemen, Mary Jane and I wish to thank you all for joining us here today to share this most special day in our lives. At the same time, I wish to acknowledge with a special thank you to those of you who took an active part in our wedding ceremony. You have all done Mary Jane and me a particularly great honor. At this time, it is my pleasure to propose a toast to Mary Jane's parents for their cordial generosity in allowing me to become a member of their family. Without their loving support, this luncheon would not have occurred. "To the Thomas's", said Calvin as he tipped his glass and took a swallow of his champagne. Applause rippled through the party. "In a similar fashion, I wish to toast my parents for their kind willingness over the years to keep me on a straight and narrow path. "To the Honeycuts", said Calvin, taking another drink to more applause. "And I would be remiss if I did not also acknowledge the contribution made by Judge Melbourne. To you, judge, our eternal thanks" and Calvin took another drink to the applause of the entire party for the judge. "And last, but by no means least, I wish to toast my lovely wife, Mary Jane, for her willingness to marry me and share my life's ambitions. A toast to Mary Jane with love", said Calvin as he raised his glass. An extended applause ensued.

"In conclusion, I would like you to know that Mary Jane and I will depart Des Moines at the end of my 10-day leave and move to Nevada where I will attend a U.S. Navy Gunnery School. We shall miss you all and wish you Godspeed in your life's endeavors". Whereupon Calvin took his seat and was given a standing ovation.

With the newlyweds duly initiated into marital bliss, as they were, the guests began to drift away, leaving Calvin and Mary Jane alone with their parents. By then, the time was approaching 1530 and the Honeycuts needed to get back to their farm and take care of their evening chores. "Calvin and Mary Jane, Mother and I need to get back to the farm so we will leave now and look forward to seeing you in the morning", said Mr. Honeycut. "Thank you again for everything, Mom and Dad, and we'll see you tomorrow", said Calvin. "We had best be running along too", said Mr. Thomas. "And I wish to add that Mary Jane's mother and I welcome you with open arms, Calvin, into our family". "Thank you both again for your understanding in my wanting to marry Mary Jane", replied Calvin. The Honeycuts and Thomas's left together, leaving Calvin and Mary Jane alone in the vacant dining room. "Mary Jane, what do you say to our checking in now and going to our room", said Calvin "I'd say let's do it, but where are our bags?", said Mary Jane. "Oh, the bellman placed them in a secure storage room. Come along, let's go retrieve them", said Calvin.

1400 Tuesday
17 March 1942
Willard Hotel
Des Moines, Iowa

Walking to the customer service counter, Calvin registered and received their room keys, at the same time requesting that a bellman bring their bags to Room 653. Taking the lobby elevator, Calvin and Mary Jane were soon on the 6th floor walking in the direction of their room. Although they realized upon entering that their room was not the 'bridal suite', it was certainly adequate for their needs, what with its king-size bed and suite with refrigerator and kitchen cooking facilities. They had previously decided to spend the rest of the week at the Willard, but had not yet done anything about transportation. It was Calvin's opinion that he could use his parents' 1939 Dodge for his and Mary Jane's travel needs until it was time for them to board their train for Nevada. He would confirm that impression tomorrow. Within five minutes, the bellman arrived with their bags and knocked on the door. Calvin went to the door and admitted the bellman who deposited their bags on a sturdy valet table. Calvin tipped the bellman as he departed and hanging a 'do not disturb' sign on the doorknob, Calvin locked the door to their suite again. "Mary Jane, I have been pondering this question all day. Do you have any regrets over the fact that we were able to convince your parents to permit us to marry without revealing the existence of our baby?", queried Calvin. "Oh, no, Calvin, I have no regrets at all. In fact, I am proud of the fact that I am carrying your baby right this minute. That is something that no one can take away from me. And the timing is such that I am certain that no one will ever question the length of my gestation period", exclaimed Mary Jane with a satisfied smile. "I am pleased to learn that, Mary Jane, for I would hold myself to blame if you felt otherwise", admitted Calvin. Calvin arose from the chair where he was sitting and sat down on the bed beside his young wife. It isn't dark outside yet, but do you think that it is too early to consider making love?", asked Calvin with a degree of hesitancy. "No, I don't, and by the way, in my opinion it can never be too early for that. Let me take a shower and then you can do the same."

Twenty minutes later, Mary Jane returned in her bathrobe and then it was Calvin's turn to shower. Again, Calvin marveled to himself over the fact that, here he was, in one of the finest Des Moines hotels, sharing a room with his brand new wife and was about to clean up so that he could enjoy her body even more. What a 'gold mine' his joining the Navy had turned out to be. Just thinking about Mary Jane had given Calvin an unbidden erection which he resisted by running the shower water just as cold as he could tolerate. Stepping out of the shower to towel dry, Calvin turned on the ceiling heat lamp to ward off the effective chill that his body was enduring. Slipping on his bathrobe, Calvin walked into the bedroom where he found Mary Jane laying naked and fully exposed on the bed. "What a beautiful and tantalizing surprise, mind if I join you?", asked Calvin. "If you don't, and right this minute, I'm going to file for divorce", joked Mary Jane. "Let's not get hasty now, I am certain that we can come to a mutually agreeable understanding about this, like the judge said, lets be cooperative as best we can", joked Calvin. "Mary Jane, I became chilled in the shower. Would you mind if we got under the covers for a little warmth?", asked Calvin. (Calvin was ashamed to reveal the real reason for his request.) "No, not at all", and with that Mary Jane rolled over and pulled the bed covers down for Calvin to enter.

Safely inside a comfortably warm cocoon, Calvin relaxed and then reached over and pulled Mary Jane's warm, soft body to himself and kissed her sweet lips. He enjoyed exploring her tongue and he enjoyed her performing the same exploration on himself. Even in the face of his cold shower, Calvin could sense the return of his erection, and Mary Jane sensed it too and tenderly took it in her hand and felt the pulsations of Calvin's racing heart. Calvin was spellbound and merely lay there as Mary Jane gently squeezed and stroked his organ from time to time. "Mary Jane, I can't take much more of that, perhaps you had better stop for awhile so we can employ it in another way", suggested Calvin. Under protest, Mary Jane threw her arms about Calvin and kissed him into submission, at the same time easing herself on top of Calvin, and then taking him inside her body, Slow and easy movements followed as the two lovers made love for the first time in their married life. In due course, Mary Jane and Calvin reached their passionate climax and clung to each other gasping for breath amid the ecstasy of their lovemaking orgasms. "Mary Jane, I have to say that you certainly know how to treat a husband", bragged Calvin. "It seems to me that we make a natural pair when it comes to making love", replied Mary Jane. By that time, Calvin was over his bout with the "chills" and Mary Jane had flung the bedcovers off to cool down from her own energetic exertions, Calvin delighted in the cooling-down period during which he enjoyed kissing Mary Jane's lips and shapely breasts. With a calmness more or less restored to their naked bodies, Calvin inquired, "Mary Jane, are you getting hungry?" "As it turns out, all of this physical exertion has made me very hungry", agreed Mary Jane. "Very well then, here is the room service menu, pick out whatever you desire. and I will do the same", advised Calvin. Mary Jane quickly picked out a grilled cheese sandwich and french fries with a coke to drink. Calvin, however, opted for an open face roast beef sandwich and a glass of milk with apple pie on the side. Having decided on their meals, Calvin went to the telephone and called the order in to room service.

"Mary Jane, I have been meaning to ask you something else and I hope that you will not resent my inquiry. It seems, from hearsay, that so many women dislike having sex, and as a result actively resist their husband's attentions. However, in you, I do not sense any reluctance to engage in sexual activity", questioned Calvin. "Calvin, my love, I just know that I find great pleasure in it, as I know you do, so for our purposes we are a compatible team and should never have any controversy about when or how much sex to have. And, Calvin, I do not resent and will never resent your questioning me on any topic. I want our marriage to be based upon uninhibited trust. And one way of accomplishing that is to never be afraid to ask a question". "Thank you, Mary Jane, you have made me feel so much better about it all. By the way, we need to slip on our bathrobes for the arrival of our food.", said Calvin. "Yes, I think that you are correct. Here, let me quickly make up the bed and when the food arrives we can have it delivered into the kitchen where there is a table and chairs.", said Mary Jane. At that point Calvin opened their room door and retrieved the 'Do Not Disturb' placard.

A short time later, a knock on the door announced the

arrival of room service. Calvin went to the door and opened it. "Room service, sir, and where shall I place the cart?". "If you don't mind, we would like to move it into the kitchen", said Calvin. "That is not a problem, sir", said the bellman as he rolled the cart into the kitchen area of their suite and parked it next to the kitchen table. "Will there be anything else, sir?", asked the bellman. "No, thank you, that is all for the time being" and so saying, Calvin signed for their meal and at the same time handed the bellman a generous tip. "Thank you very much, sir, and have a nice evening." "You're entirely welcome", said Calvin as he closed and locked the door behind the bellman. "Mary Jane, do you realize that this is our second meal together as man and wife?", asked Calvin. "No, I hadn't thought about it, but I dare say that you are correct. Come to the table now and let's eat", said Mary Jane. The food tasted ever so good and the newlyweds enjoyed the food and the loving privacy of each other's company. Calvin finished first and then walked to the bathroom where he brushed his teeth. Upon his return, he stood behind Mary Jane's chair, and leaning over her shoulder, inserted his hands beneath her bathrobe grasping an ample breast in each hand. How smooth and tender they seemed, thought Calvin. As he fondled her breasts, Calvin sensed the miraculous erection of each pink nipple. Mary Jane did not flinch or protest as Calvin pulled her robe aside, kneeled down and took her left breast into his mouth. "Oh, Mary Jane, you possess such a divine pair of delicacies and I love fondling them so much", murmured Calvin. "I'll give you about ten hours to stop that, Calvin, and I want you to know that there are no limits on what you can touch on my body. Just consider it open season on me", joked Mary Jane. "Well, in that case, let's go back to bed where our sex can be simpler and nicer", suggested Calvin. "I'll second that motion, Mr. Honeycut. Let's make it happen now", happily agreed an eager Mary Jane. So without further adieu, Mary

Jane and Calvin moved into their bed to further explore their "wedding night rituals".

Eventually, Mary Jane and Calvin satisfied their pent-up desires and relaxed, happily content as "newlyweds", clinging to each other and calmly enjoying the serene feeling of the heat radiating from their partner's body. Although unintended, peace and tranquility overcame their senses as Calvin and Mary Jane were paid a visit by Morpheus and they fell into a deep, but heavenly sleep, not to awaken again until the bright morning light.

With the sunlight streaming through a curtained window, Mary Jane stirred and left their bed for the bathroom. When Calvin finally awoke, he could hear Mary Jane singing in the shower. He felt the pure luxury of having no commitments to meet and merely lay there thinking about what the day might bring. He felt a magnificent contentment in his heart, but he soon realized that his stomach was growling and he was exceedingly hungry. Making love will do that to a person, he thought. All too soon, Mary Jane glided across the carpeted floor and leaned over to give Calvin a good morning kiss. "Good-morning, my sweetheart husband, and how did you sleep?", asked Mary Jane. "Never better, my sweet wife", admitted Calvin. "However, I am starving; let me shower quickly and then we'll go see about some breakfast", said Calvin. "I am exceedingly hungry, too", admitted Mary Jane.

While Calvin showered, Mary Jane dressed for the day. She was enjoying a private moment with her innermost thoughts about her wedding day when Calvin came into the room dressed to go. "You are a handsome man in your dress blues", observed Mary Jane. "My thanks to you, fair lady. I just remembered that I failed to tell you how much I love you when we awoke", belatedly concluded Calvin. "Thank you for remembering, kind sir, and for your information, I love you more than life itself and especially so for the sake of our baby", smiled Mary Jane.

"Shall we move on down to the restaurant and have breakfast?", asked Calvin. "The sooner the better, as far as I am concerned", replied Mary Jane. Opening their door, Calvin said, "Follow me" as he removed the 'Do Not Disturb' sign, and hung it on the inner doorknob. A few minutes later the newlyweds entered the Willard lobby and went directly to the restaurant where they were seated without delay. Inspecting their menus, Calvin said, "This morning I am going to have two eggs over easy with ham and hash browns, along with toast and jelly, with milk to drink". "You are reading my mind for I want to have the same breakfast", agreed Mary Jane. A waiter took their orders and soon returned to deliver their food. "That was mighty quick service", observed Mary Jane. "Yes, it was, and I really appreciate that fact", said Calvin. At that point, the newlyweds commenced to eat their breakfasts in silence. The other guests in the dining room paid them no mind and that suited Calvin and Mary Jane just fine. With their breakfast finished, Mary Jane asked, "Well, what's first on the order of business for today, my husband?" "First, let's return to the room so I can telephone my parents and find out if we can use the Dodge for the remainder of my leave", said Calvin. "That certainly sounds like first things first", smiled Mary Jane.

Leaving the restaurant, Calvin and Mary Jane went directly to their room where they brushed their teeth as the first order of business. Then, Calvin lifted the telephone receiver and the operator connected him with his parents' telephone number. The telephone rang several times before he heard his mother say, "Hello". "Hello, Mom, and how are you this fine morning", asked Calvin. "Oh, I am fine and so is your father" said Mrs. Honeycut. "Mom, I want to speak with Dad to determine whether or not Mary Jane and I can make use of the Dodge for the remainder of my leave", concluded Calvin. "I'm certain that he will be pleased to lend you the car, but wait a moment and I will get him", replied Calvin's mother. "Hello, Calvin, Mother tells me that you are calling about using the Dodge for a few days?", said Mr. Honeycut. "Yes, that is so, Dad, if you don't mind, I would appreciate using the Dodge very much", confirmed Calvin. "We will be pleased for you to use the car and since we have to be in town in a couple of hours, your Mother and I will stop by the Willard and pick you two up", said Mr. Honeycut. "That will be wonderful, Dad, and Mary Jane and I will be waiting by the front door for your arrival and we thank you for this accommodation", said Calvin. "You're more that welcome, Son. We'll see you soon" and with that Mr. Honeycut hung up his telephone.

"Mary Jane, we have about two hours to kill in which we must pack our clothes, check out of the hotel and be waiting for Mom and Dad in the lobby area", advised Calvin. "So, that means that we will not be staying at the Willard any longer, doesn't it?", asked Mary Jane, somewhat disappointed. "Yes, that is so. Are you terribly disappointed? I just thought that it would be worthwhile for us to save the money by staying in my room at the farm, if you have no objection", replied Calvin. "Oh, Calvin, I admit to a fleeting sadness, but I don't object at all, and, in fact, I feel that your plan is a grand idea and saving money is a mighty good idea anytime", said Mary Jane. "My room is quiet, very private and roomy with its doublebed so my folks will not be disturbed by the noise of our lovemaking", offered Calvin. "Well, Calvin, that's the best news of all", grinned Mary Jane. The newlyweds moved at a leisurely pace as they packed and prepared to check out of the Willard Hotel. Calvin and Mary Jane carried their bags to the elevator where Calvin pushed the button for the lobby. On the way down he took the occasion to help himself to another kiss. Looking out the foyer, Calvin noticed that it was another sparkling day with lots of sunshine. The rain storm of a few days ago would cause the spring flowers to soon show their faces along the Des Moines highways and residential gardens.

1000 Wednesday
18 March 1942
Willard Hotel
Des Moines, Iowa

Arriving at the lobby, Calvin visited the front desk and paid their bill while Mary Jane walked to the front entrance where the valets were busy herding automobiles for a few early lunchtime guests. Five minutes later, Mr. Honeycut was blowing his horn to attract the newlyweds' attention. Calvin said, "There they are, let's hurry over and get in the back seat". "You go first, since you have our bags which you should probably place in the trunk", said Mary Jane. "The trunk it is", acknowledged Calvin. As they approached the Dodge, Mr. Honeycut called to Mary Jane, "How are you today, Mary Jane?". "I'm just fine and happier than any new bride has a right to be", replied a smiling Mary Jane. Having placed their luggage in the trunk, Calvin walked up and opened the rear door of the Dodge for Mary Jane and himself to enter. With everyone seated, Mr. Honeycut drove out of the driveway of the Willard Hotel and made his way to the highway leading to the farm. Before they had traveled a mile or so, Calvin said, "Mom and Dad, with your permission, Mary Jane and I would like to spend the rest of my leave using my old room at the farm. It is comfortable and big enough for the two of us". Calvin's mother looked over at her husband and smiled an 'I- told-you-so' smile. "Calvin, the lady that I married, namely your Mother, is a mind reader, and she already had anticipated your request. Of course, the answser is yes. We are more than pleased to have you. In saying that, we have a selfish motive inasmuch as we will have additional opportunities to see you two that we would not have enjoyed had you stayed at the Willard." "Thank you so much, Mr. and Mrs. Honeycut", said Mary Jane. "Mary Jane, since you have married our son, Marcella and I feel that we should be addressed as Mom and Dad by you", suggested Mr. Honeycut. "I am pleased that you feel that way, Dad, and, incidentally, we promise not to throw any wild parties during our short stay", joked Mary Jane. Their discussion ended as Mr. Honeycut turned into his driveway and stopped at the front door for all to exit the Dodge which was then moved to its stall in the garage after Calvin removed their luggage from the trunk.

1200 Wednesday
18 March 1942
Honeycut Farm
Des Moines, Iowa

"Mary Jane, tomorrow we will make a run over to your house so that you can pick up more of your casual clothes", said Calvin. "That will be nice, Calvin, as I could really use some jeans and other less formal attire to use here at the farm", responded Mary Jane. "Why don't you call your parents now and determine whether one time or another will fit in with their schedule", suggested Calvin. "The telephone is right over there on the wall", added Mrs. Honeycut, with a wink of her eye. Mary Jane walked to the phone and requested the operator to ring her parents' number. Almost immediately, Mrs. Thomas said "Hello". "Hi, Mom, it's Mary Jane, and how are you and Dad feeling today?", inquired Mary Jane. "Oh, we're just fine and are getting ready to go to the movies", said Mrs. Thomas. "Mom, the reason I'm calling is to find out what time I can stop by tomorrow to pick up some of my clothes. You see, Calvin and I decided to move out of the Willard Hotel and use his old room at the Honeycut's farm", revealed Mary Jane. "Well, I give you kids a lot of credit for making a sound decision like that; after all, 'money doesn't grow on trees', as the saying goes", said Mary Jane's mother. "Mr. and Mrs. Honeycut picked us up at the Willard an hour ago or so and we are at the farm now. Will you please tell Dad in case he wants to call?", requested Mary Jane. "Why don't you plan on stopping by around 9:00 a.m.? On second thought, please be here around 8:00 a.m. and have breakfast with us. And, yes, I will give your dad your message. See you in the morning", Mrs. Thomas said as she hung up her receiver. "Calvin, will it be all right if we have breakfast with Mom and Dad Thomas in the morning so I can get the clothes I need?", said Mary Jane. "I don't see why not, and by the way, there is a beautiful day going to waste outside. Why don't we take a walk up to the pond? Mom and Dad, Mary Jane and I will return in an hour or so", said Calvin. "Take your time and enjoy yourselves", smiled Calvin's mother.

Fifteen minutes later, Calvin and Mary Jane were soaking up the sunshine on the shore of the pond. A gentle breeze was blowing carrying with it the scent of spring flowers. Calvin studied his wife for a time and then said, "Mrs. Honeycut, you are one exceedingly beautiful woman. And, I wonder sometimes how it was that you became my very own treasure", said Calvin, filled with extreme happiness as he was. "Calvin, in my opinion our union is something that God ordained and I, for one, do not question it", offered Mary Jane. As she was speaking, Calvin leaned over and kissed his very own bride on her cheek. "Do you know, Mary Jane, that every time I look at you, my heart bursts with pride", said Calvin. "No, Calvin, I did not know that, but I believe that I feel the same effect in my own heart", replied Mary Jane.

By the time Calvin and Mary Jane returned to the house, Mom was preparing dinner. "Mary Jane, would you mind setting the table, please?", asked Mom. "Not at all,

Mom", replied Mary Jane. The family soon gathered around the harvest table to enjoy a fried chicken dinner. After dinner, Calvin's thoughts turned to his rapidly disappearing military leave of ten days. In the beginning, 10 days had seemed generous enough, but here he was with four days having already passed by. But at the same time, he realized that his and Mary Jane's marriage had resulted in the greatest portion of the loss and for that he was not critical. After all, gaining a partner for life was worth any sacrifice, he thought. From his seat at the dinner table, Calvin's dad spoke up and said, "Calvin, how about us 'menfolks' moving into the living room and taking in the evening news on the radio." "I would enjoy that, seeing as to how I have been rather isolated from current events lately", replied Calvin. "I'll stay here and help Mom with the dishes", offered Mary Jane. Whereupon, Calvin and his dad left the kitchen.

Realizing that he would soon be leaving Des Moines for Nevada, Calvin enjoyed the opportunity to spend some quality time with his father. Although he relaxed and absorbed some of the news broadcast, Calvin was more interested in observing his father who was getting on in years. He suffered a brief pang of remorse for his move to join the Navy and leave his father to fend for himself in managing his farm. Perhaps, he thought, it was too selfish of him to have taken that action. Calvin wondered if he should discuss his bothersome feelings with his father, but, in the end, decided to 'let sleeping dogs lie', primarily because any discussion at this point would be purely academic and could not possibly change anything. About the time the news program ended, Mom and Mary Jane came into the living room and sat down. In Mom's case, she took out her knitting project and proceeded to 'work her needles', and to Calvin's very pleasant surprise he noticed that she was making a tiny pair of booties for her forthcoming grandchild. How wonderful, thought Calvin, for her to be thinking that far ahead about their as yet unnamed baby.

As time passed, Calvin and his father engaged in small talk and their discussions dissipated the concerns that Calvin had felt earlier in the evening. Mary Jane busied herself with a copy of the House Beautiful magazine while the menfolk continued to discuss various farming issues. Feeling fatigue envelop her, Mary Jane said, "I think that I feel the need of a little sleep about now" and she stood to go upstairs to Calvin's (now their) room. "Dad and Mom, I feel a little wrung out myself so I think that I will follow Mary Jane's example. Have a good rest of the evening", called Calvin as he stepped onto the stairs to their room. "Sleep tight you two, and by the way, I put fresh sheets on Calvin's bed", volunteered Mom. "Thank you, Mom, for taking such good care of us", replied Mary Jane.

Upon following Mary Jane into their room, Calvin threw his arms about her waist and kissed her lips. "I've been waiting for quite a while to do that", he admitted. "Well, you are more than welcome, my sweet husband", said Mary Jane. "Mary Jane, would you be awfully disappointed if we did not engage in sex tonight?", asked Calvin. "That would suit me just fine", agreed Mary Jane. "For whatever reason, I am unusually tired this evening and perhaps we can make up for lost time on the train to Nevada", speculated Calvin. "Oh, Calvin, your statement conjures up visions of a wonderful new life for us", replied Mary Jane. Over the next thirty minutes the couple relaxed on their bed and engaged in small talk. Once beneath the covers, Calvin pulled Mary Jane close to him and gave her a good-night kiss and then turned out the lights. Calvin's waning thoughts were of their appointment in the morning to have breakfast with Mary Jane's parents. He had made up his mind to thoroughly enjoy the aura of peace that now permeated his thoughts as a result of his marriage.

0630 Thursday
19 March 1942
Honeycut Farm
Des Moines, Iowa

Calvin shut the alarm off and went into the bathroom to shower. After he had dressed, he awakened his wife. "Time to get a wiggle on, Sweetheart, if we are to arrive at your mothers by 0800", said Calvin. "Oh, Calvin, I hate to leave such a wonderful dream. You and I were together in our own home playing with our baby", marveled Mary Jane. Mary Jane dressed and the two of them went down stairs. "Good-morning, Mom", said Mary Jane. "Why, hello, Mary Jane and Calvin. Did you two get rested up a bit?" "Yes indeed we did and I feel like I could lick my weight in wildcats. We're leaving now to be at the Thomas' by 0800. You and Dad have a nice day", concluded Calvin. "Please drive carefully", added Mrs. Honeycut.

0800 Thursday
19 March 1942
Des Moines, Iowa
The Thomas home

Mary Jane rang the doorbell as she unlocked the front door and stepped inside calling out "Good-morning, Mom and Dad". "We're in the kitchen, so come on out", came Mr. Thomas' reply. Calvin and Mary Jane joined her parents in the kitchen where Mrs. Thomas was putting the finishing touches on scrambled eggs, pancakes and sausage. "My, whatever you are cooking certainly smells wonderful", observed Calvin. "Here, pull up a couple of chairs and sit down", said Mr. Thomas. "What will you have to drink, Calvin?", asked Mrs. Thomas. "Well, I am a milk fancier myself, if it's all the same to you. For whatever reason, I have never been able to cultivate a taste for coffee, although I love the fragrance of it when I open a fresh can of coffee for my parents", admitted Calvin. "Then milk it is", said Mrs. Thomas, handing over a tall glass full of ice-cold milk. Mrs. Thomas served her food and then sat down at the kitchen table. "Tell us, what exciting things are you two planning today?", asked Mrs. Thomas. "Well, to tell the truth, we don't have any plans at the moment aside from picking up Mary Jane's clothes. It seems that we make our choices about various activities as we go along. You might say that we are just sort of hanging loose", concluded Calvin. "Our only concern is that we may run out of time before we run out of things to do. "When you get right down to it, ten days is not a very long time and we have already used up four of them", complained Mary Jane. "Well, just look on the bright side, Mary Jane, there are two of you now to do the deciding and enjoying", reminded Mr. Thomas. "Don't make the mistake of taking life too seriously", added Mrs. Thomas.

Having finished her breakfast, Mary Jane said, "If you'll excuse me, I'll go select the clothes that I need to take to the farm". "Do you need any help, dear?", asked Mrs. Thomas. "Yes, if you please, I could use some assistance", replied Mary Jane. The two women left the kitchen and Mr. Thomas said, "Come, Calvin, let's go into the den while the womenfolk take care of Mary Jane's clothing needs." "I'm right with you, Dad", said Calvin as they walked through the house. As on an earlier evening, a nice fire was blazing in the fireplace notwithstanding the fact that winter was over. Mr. Thomas turned on the radio for the morning farm radio broadcast. Although he was retired, in his working life he was a farmer. And 'once in the blood, always in the blood', thought Calvin. Thirty minutes later, Mary Jane entered the den with a large suitcase in hand. "Mom, as we get closer to our day of departure, I will stop by and pack the clothes that I will want you to ship to our new address. It will be a week or so after we leave before I will know what that address will be", said Mary Jane. "We'll be happy to ship them whenever you say, Mary Jane", replied Mrs. Thomas. "Well, I have to do some shopping for our trip so we had best run along. Thank you so much for the delicious breakfast, Mom", concluded Mary Jane. "Yes, indeed, that was an excellent breakfast, Mom, and I thank you for inviting us", said Calvin. "You're welcome any time Calvin and Mary Jane", replied Mrs. Thomas. "Have a great rest of the day", added Mr. Thomas.

Calvin drove Mary Jane to her department store of choice and waited while she obtained several items for their upcoming railroad journey. When she finally returned, Calvin drove back to the farm where he helped Mary Jane place her clothes in his closet for convenient access. Over the following days the newlyweds indulged themselves in movies, dancing, roller- skating and similar pursuits utilizing the remainder of Calvin's Navy leave time. Near the end of Calvin's leave, Mrs. Honeycut invited a large group of Calvin's friends to the farm for a bar-b-cue cookout, including, of course, Mr. and Mrs. Thomas and many of Mary Jane's close friends. The function was well attended and provided the opportunity for farewells that might otherwise have been missed. Lowell and Cathy attended, to the absolute delight of Calvin and Mary Jane. Following this activity, Calvin booked their compartment on the train to Nevada. It would be a first for both Calvin and Mary Jane since neither one had traveled cross country on a train before. The experience promised to be an extremely memorable one.

0800 Thursday
26 March 1942
The Honeycut Farm
Des Moines, Iowa

And then there were none. At last Calvin's leave was over and it was time to depart Des Moines for the Navy Gunnery School in Nevada. The family was up early and bags that had been packed the previous day were loaded into the trunk of the Dodge. Fortunately, there was enough trunk space to avoid the necessity of taking the pickup truck to the railroad station. Mr. Honeycut urged everyone to the Dodge so they would not be late for the noon train. Mary Jane and Calvin, along with Mr. and Mrs. Honeycut, took their seats in the Dodge and Mr. Honeycut slowly drove his car down the driveway. Calvin's eyes lingered on his boyhood home until he could see it no longer as his father turned toward town at the end of the long, tree-lined driveway. Calvin was happy that he had taken time to tell Skippy good-bye as he gave the dog's ears a longer than usual rub. Leaving his home permanently, as he was, left Calvin in a somber melancholy mood. He would miss Skippy and even his Jersey cows, not to mention his own parents.

1130 Thursday
26 March 1942
Railroad Depot
Des Moines, Iowa

Arriving at the train station, Calvin presented his travel voucher to the conductor who accompanied him and Mary Jane to their Pullman car where they were assigned to compartment 'C'. Mr. and Mrs. Honeycut tagged along. Arriving at the long green Pullman coach, the conductor bid them to enter. Calvin held Mary Jane's arm as she approached the small step box placed on the platform opposite the steps leading into the coach. In a similar manner, Mr. Honeycut assisted Calvin's mother in climbing the steps. Inside the coach, the conductor unlocked compartment 'C' and led the way inside where he handed Calvin the compartment keys. Although not mentioned by the conductor, Calvin and Mary Jane were in luck as their compartment was in the exact center of the length of the coach, which the laws of physics further guaranteed the smoothest possible ride. Calvin and Mary Jane were surprised at the compartment's spaciousness as they were joined by Calvin's parents. "My, oh my, what plush surroundings", observed Calvin's mother. "Why, thank you ma'am. Our railroad strives for comfort. This coach is the latest Pullman design and rides on two six-wheel trucks giving it the ultimate level of smooth riding comfort. At the same time, this coach is heavily insulated to make it as soundproof as possible. In addition, the next car to the rear is the dining car and it will be available continuously throughout your children's journey. I have other passengers to board, so I must leave you now, but if you need anything after we leave the station, Mr. and Mrs. Honeycut, please don't hesitate to call on me." "Thank you very much", said Calvin, as he placed his travel voucher in a desk drawer in his compartment. Calvin's parents sat down on a plush couch in Calvin's and Mary Jane's compartment and relaxed since it was still thirty minutes before departure time.

Through the large plate glass picture window, many other passengers could be seen hurrying toward the front of the train. It turned out that the Pullman cars were purposely placed on the rear of the train in the interest of keeping them as far removed as possible from the locomotive and its attendant noise, whistle blowing, and dirty coal cinders and smoke, etc. Eventually, the engineer caused his whistle to emit a long mournful sound to notify any visiting passengers of the train's imminent departure. With that, Calvin hugged his mother and father, as did Mary Jane. "Take care of yourself and Mary Jane", said his father. "Never fear, I will concentrate on that endeavor and will send you a letter along the way", promised Calvin. As Mr. Honeycut walked down the coach steps, Mrs. Honeycut lingered beside Calvin and hugged him tightly, gaining one last kiss. Just after Mrs. Honeycut had reached the depot platform, with her husband's assistance, the engineer whistled two quick melodious tones and the train began to glide out of the station. Calvin and Mary Jane stood at the 'dutch door' vestibule waving to the Honeycuts. All too soon Calvin's parents faded from view and the newlyweds reluctantly returned to their compartment.

"Mary Jane, shall we go have our lunch now?", asked Calvin. "Yes, Calvin, I am so hungry", agreed Mary Jane. "Then come with me and take my hand so I can help steady you against the rocking movement of the train." Holding Mary Jane's hand, Calvin pushed the door of their coach open, crossed its vestibule and then crossed the dining car vestibule, at the same time pushing open the door into the dining car. The fragrances that immediately greeted their nostrils were pleasant and further stimulated their appetites. A dining car steward led them to a table containing a white tablecloth together with a slender vase displaying a single red carnation. "How beautiful", exclaimed Mary Jane. "All the comforts of home and then some, I would say", remarked Calvin. The midday sun shined down on the passing countryside visible on both sides of the dining car. The steward returned with their menus and inquired about their beverage orders. Calvin ordered a coke while Mary Jane ordered sweet iced tea. Studying the menu, Calvin decided to have a sirloin steak with french fries and green beans. For her part, Mary Jane selected prime rib with mild horseradish sauce. The steward appeared and recorded the newlywed's meal orders and retired to the kitchen. Mary Jane was fascinated by the moving panorama of images beyond their windows. When the dining car passed a country road railroad crossing, Mary Jane could faintly hear the musical clang of the crossing guard signal bell and see its prominent flashing red warning lights. The sound reminded Mary Jane of the alarm bell of her grandmother's Westbend alarm clock, lo those many years before in Des Moines when as a young child she visited her grandmother and stayed for seven days. Eventually, the steward brought their meals and they were enjoyed immensely, as was the continuously moving countryside that by now had changed from city dwellings to rural countryside images. There were many farmers' fields and also many red barns in the distance, with herds of cows and steers grazing. Also visible in the distance were several windmills that were whirling rapidly in the strong breeze, pumping water into overflowing cattle watering troughs. Taking their eyes away from the pastoral scene, Calvin and Mary Jane realized that other diners were lining up and that their table was in demand for other hungry passengers. Calling the steward for their check, Calvin paid for their meals and they prepared to leave. Calvin stood first, and then helped Mary Jane to her feet as the dining car swayed slightly as it negotiated a sharp curve in the tracks. Walking toward the head end of the train, they passed out of the dining car, through its vestibule and into their own Pullman car vestibule. Walking halfway through the coach they came to compartment 'C', unlocked the door and entered, locking the door behind them. The sun was still shining as the train passed through the flatlands of western Iowa. Their first stop would be in Omaha, Nebraska, and then only just long enough for a fully-serviced locomotive and tender to be attached to the train. Since it was still early afternoon, Calvin and Mary Jane elected to spend some time reading. In Calvin's case he had several documents relating to antiaircraft guns and Mary Jane had brought along a novel to keep her entertained.

1300 Thursday
26 March 1942
en route to Nevada

The Honeycut compartment was quiet save for the occasional distant sound of the locomotive whistle warning wayward automobile drivers of its approach to country grade crossings. "Mary Jane, do you care to join me for a while and read your novel?", asked Calvin. "Yes, I really haven't gotten into my story very far and this would be a good time to find out what is happening to the characters in the story", remarked Mary Jane. Calvin relaxed on their couch and selected a manual outlining the activities that he would find at the Navy Gunnery School in Holman, Nevada. He was very favorably impressed by the degree of sophistication built into the Navy antiaircraft machine guns that he would learn to operate. He read about the state-of-the-art target pointing directors that were applied to both the 20-mm and 40-mm guns. The 40-mm gun, he noted, was manufactured in either twin-mounts or quad-mounts equipped with four barrels. In any event, the guns represented lethal, antiaircraft weapons of the latest most modern designs.

While Calvin was deeply engrossed in his Navy literature, Mary Jane relaxed on their bed and began reading. At the same time, she found it difficult to exclude the images of the countryside flashing by their picture window. In the end, she elected to pull a curtain over the window to eliminate the distraction. After all, reading was supposed to be fun, but the convoluted story line in her book required her undivided attention to fully understand the plot. Two hours later, Calvin had tired of reading his Navy literature and said, "Mary Jane, why don't we take a break from our reading and check out the club car which I understand is several cars further up front toward the locomotive.", Mary Jane stretched and replied, "That has to be the best idea that

I have heard all afternoon." Rolling up the curtain covering their window, Mary Jane took time to briefly view the countryside through which the train was passing and then went to their bathroom to check her make-up. Returning a few minutes later, Mary Jane announced that, "I am ready whenever you are, my sweet husband". Calvin stood and approached Mary Jane, whereupon he helped himself to a mini kiss, taking care not to destroy her makeup. "Thank you, kind sir", responded Mary Jane to the show of affection. With all in readiness, Calvin and Mary Jane stepped out into the adjacent passageway and turned right toward the head end of the train. It turned out that reaching the club car became a battle of the vestibules for the club car was separated from their Pullman coach by five day coaches. This separation translated into twelve bouncing vestibules that had to be crossed one by one.

Persevering as they did, the couple eventually reached the nice airy coach that served as the club car. It was finely appointed with a long, well-varnished mahogany bar with plenty of stools. Although there were many passengers present, Calvin and Mary Jane quickly found a vacant table and sat down next to a picture window. Almost immediately, a steward approached, "May I take your order, please", offered the steward. "Mary Jane, what is your pleasure this afternoon?" asked Calvin. "Please bring me a strawberry frozen margarita", said Mary Jane. "And I will settle for a sweet Tom Collins, thank you", concluded Calvin. "Thank you, sir, and I shall return momentarily with your drinks", advised the steward. One hour and two drinks each later, Calvin and Mary Jane had finished their second drinks and the club car was becoming inundated by other thirsty passengers. With the noise level in the car beginning to bother Calvin, he said, "Mary Jane, do you wish to have another drink or shall we return to our compartment", asked Calvin. "I am quite satisfied and would just as soon return to our compartment", replied Mary Jane. Leaving the club car behind, Calvin and Mary Jane returned to their Pullman compartment, navigating again the numerous vestibules.

1900 Thursday
26 March 1942
Western Iowa
en route to Nevada

During their absence, the porter had made up the newlyweds' bed, leaving behind fresh towels, extra blankets and a carafe of ice water. "What a nice touch", observed Mary Jane. "Yes, I'm inclined to agree with you; it seems that the railroad company desires to kill us with kindness", joked Calvin. "Honey, it has been a long day and I am inclined to dress in our PJ's and get into bed. What is your pleasure", asked Mary Jane. "I agree with you for it has been a very long, tiring day and I am as tired as you are, and I have to admit that that trip to the club car rather wore me out", complained Calvin. Brushing their teeth and getting into their PJ's took only a few minutes and then the Honeycuts climbed into bed. "Good-night, Sweetheart", Calvin whispered to his bride as he kissed her sweet lips. The familiar side-to-side movement of their coach lulled them to the threshold of sleep. Calvin closed his eyes and, for a time, pictured Skippy rounding up his Jersey cows as he nipped at their heels while herding them to the barn for milking. He recalled discussing Skippy's talent with the young man who took over Calvin's cow milking duties. These thoughts merged into a pleasant dream about life at home with his parents on the Honeycut farm.

0930 Friday
27 March 1942
Eastern Nebraska

With no schedule to keep during the day, Calvin and Mary Jane enjoyed sleeping-in while on their journey. Calvin awoke first, took his shower and dressed in his Navy uniform with the third class gunner's mate petty officer patch on his sleeve. At length, Mary Jane woke up, but seemed in no hurry to leave her bed. "Sweetheart, are you hungry yet?" asked Calvin. "Actually, I am quite hungry, but I dislike leaving the most perfect dream that I have ever had. I recall that the war was over and you and I were playing in our backyard in Des Moines with our baby twins, a boy and a girl. It was a wonderful dream and I hated to see it end", complained Mary Jane. "I can appreciate your desire to extend your dream, but perhaps you could continue it this afternoon when you take your nap", suggested Calvin. Eventually, Mary Jane took her shower and dressed and the couple left their compartment for breakfast in the dining car. Mary Jane took Calvin's arm as they began the familiar trip to the adjacent dining car. Opening the vestibule door and stepping out of their passageway, Calvin led Mary Jane through the Pullman vestibule and on into the dining car vestibule where he pushed on into the dining car itself. From their position at the entry door, Calvin and Mary Jane could see a steward beckoning them to take the table where he was standing. "Good-morning, Mr. and Mrs. Honeycut. May I serve you some coffee this morning?", asked the steward. "No, thank you; it turns out that we are milk lovers, if you don't mind, and you can bring the milk with our meals, please.", said Calvin. "Well, Mary Jane, what looks good to you on the menu this morning", asked Calvin. "I have decided to have hot cakes and sausage and two eggs sunny-side up for, after all, I am eating for myself and our baby", bragged Mary Jane. "I am going to order the same meal", revealed Calvin, as the steward marked his order form and then walked the length of the dining car to deliver it to the cooks in the kitchen.

Through the large plate glass picture windows, Mary Jane noticed that the sun was almost overhead with the time approaching noon, and it had turned a layer of fluffy cumulus clouds to a crimson glow on their fringes. It was a magical moment, she thought. And the best thing of all is the fact that I am carrying Calvin's baby right this moment, and September can't get here too soon to suit me, Mary Jane confided to God and her heart. Their food orders soon arrived and the couple enjoyed savoring their eggs and sausage. Calvin was very pleased to find that his glass of milk was exceedingly cold, just the way he liked it. With their meal consumed, Calvin and Mary Jane returned to their compartment.

2000 Friday
27 March 1942
Eastern Nebraska

As the train crossed the countryside after sunset, houses near the railroad right-of-way were illuminated as dim outlines, and occasionally a commercial building flashed by with a blazing neon sign proclaiming the reason for its existence. It was time for their evening meal and the steward approached to take their orders. Mary Jane ordered a bacon, lettuce and tomato sandwich and a bowl of French Onion soup, while Calvin ordered his favorite, pork chop dinner. Their drinks of coke and sweet iced tea had been delivered earlier. Other diners were present, and Mary Jane caught more than one of them giving the newlyweds their approving glances. Their food arrived at the same time that the train passed by a brightly-lighted baseball park, surrounded by seemingly hundreds of people sitting in tall well-lighted bleachers. Neither she nor Calvin could determine what town it was, but, clearly, the local populace enjoyed the game of baseball. Eating in silence, Mary Jane wondered what her parents were doing at that very moment. It was the first time that she had thought about home since they had left Des Moines. But, she was a big girl now, making her own way in the world, so she put those meaningless idle thoughts out of her mind. Having finished their meals, Calvin paid the steward and he and Mary Jane left to return to their compartment. Passing through the vestibules, the 'clickety-clack' of the coach wheels on the rail joints assaulted their ears causing them to hurry to gain the protection waiting behind the Pullman coach vestibule door. Mary Jane thought that it was always such a relief to walk down the vacant hallway with the muffled sound of the clicking wheels on rail joints reduced almost to the point of inaudibility. At last, Calvin and Mary Jane entered compartment 'C'.

2200 Thursday
26 March 1942
en route to Nevada
Eastern Nebraska

During their dinner time absence, the porter had made up the newlyweds' bed, leaving behind the usual fresh towels, extra blankets and a carafe of ice water. "I cannot get used to all of this fine service", observed Mary Jane. "Yes, I'm inclined to agree with you; it seems that the railroad company truly values the comfort of its passengers", commented Calvin. "Honey, it has been a long day and I am inclined to undress and get into bed. What is your pleasure", asked Mary Jane. "I agree with you; and I also think that it is time for us to exercise the special benefits of being man and wife, if you are in agreement", suggested Calvin. "By all means, I am in perfect agreement", Let me shower and brush my teeth and then you can do the same." Fifteen minutes later a sexy-looking Mary Jane returned from her shower and climbed into bed while Calvin showered. Eventually Calvin returned and joined Mary Jane in their bed. Dimming the compartment lights and at the same time lowering their window curtain, Calvin kissed his wife and fondled her beautiful breasts in preparation for their lovemaking. The newlyweds made love for ever so long, after which they fell to sleep wondering what tomorrow would bring. They were lulled to sleep by the gentle side-to-side swaying movement of their Pullman coach and the subdued "clickety-clack" of the coach wheels and the occasional whistle of the locomotive as it approached grade crossings along the way.

0900 Friday
27 March 1942
en route to Nevada
Grand Island, Nebraska

Calvin and Mary Jane were having breakfast when their train pulled into the Grand Island Railroad Depot. Passengers were lined up on the depot platform waiting to board, and as soon as the train braked to a stop, about 50 passengers left the train, as Grand Island was their destination. There was considerable congestion on the platform until the boarding passengers could work their way up the steps and into their coaches. It seemed that most people were moving forward on the station platform toward the locomotive where the day coaches were located and the fares were less expensive. Although the station stop was long enough to have permitted them to leave the train for a short while, Calvin and Mary Jane elected to remain on board while they finished their breakfast. With a fresh locomotive and tender attached to the head end of the train, thirty minutes later the train pulled out and they said good-bye to Grand Island, Nebraska. Calvin paid for their meals and he and Mary Jane then left the dining car, navigating, as they always did, the gauntlet of the two vestibules separating them from their Pullman compartment. Walking along the unstable passageways of a moving train is always a challenge. Finally reaching the door to their compartment, Calvin and Mary Jane entered and decided to read until lunch time.

1200 Friday
27 March 1942
en route to Nevada

At length Calvin grew tired of reading and said, "Come, Mary Jane, let's go get some lunch". "Is it that time again? It seems that all we have done since leaving Des Moines is eat and make love. Mind you, I am not complaining about the lovemaking part, for I dearly love how you treat me in that department", said an attentive Mary Jane. "Well, I think that part of the problem is our being cooped-up on this train for so long, unable to really move around and get any exercise. The train will lay over in Scottsbluff for several hours, so let's plan on checking out the town and find a good restaurant to enjoy", observed Calvin. "I like your idea, Mr. Honeycut", replied Mary Jane. "In the meantime, let's go get a sandwich", suggested Calvin. Opening the door and taking in the 'Do Not Disturb' sign again, the lovers walked to the dining car. As in times past, there was no waiting line so they were seated immediately. Aside from one other couple, Calvin and Mary Jane had the dining car all to themselves. Mary Jane noticed that the character of the landscape had changed since they had left Iowa. The land through which they were then passing was more mountainous, and she could see stands of evergreen timber growing close to the railroad right-of-way. The steward approached to take their orders, which turned out to be hamburgers and french fries and cokes. "Shades of Jackson's Drive-in", joked Calvin. "Yes, it certainly does remind me of home. Calvin, do you have any idea just how long your Nevada assignment will last?", asked Mary Jane. "To tell you the truth, I haven't been told anything yet, but I would guess that it will not be over six months before I am assigned to a ship. Not to worry, Sweetheart, for I am planning to keep you with me until the very last minute, no matter what", encouraged Calvin. "Well, at least that last part is good news", said Mary Jane, with just a touch of sadness. Their food arrived and Calvin was happy to have an opportunity to change the subject of their conversation. Not surprisingly, the food was excellent and they enjoyed their meal, and even ordered dessert which consisted of hot fudge sundaes. With the steward having been paid, Calvin assisted Mary Jane as she stood, and he held her arm as they left the dining car. They paused in the dining car vestibule long enough to gaze out at the countryside rushing past. It was a beautiful day, with plenty of sunshine and excellent visibility. Moving on to their compartment, they entered and decided to read for a while. Mary Jane's novel was getting interesting and Calvin still had several gunnery documents that he had yet to read. An hour later, the lovers decided to snooze for awhile.

1700 Friday
27 March 1942
en route to Nevada
Scottsbluff, Nebraska

The noisy, somewhat-jolting, stop of their Pullman coach woke both Calvin and Mary Jane. Peering out of the curtained window, Calvin could read the station sign and said, "Well, here we are in Scottsbluff. The weather is nice so I don't think that we will need a jacket. Do you feel like doing some walking, Sweetheart?", asked Calvin. "Yes, indeed I do, it will be nice to walk down a non-moving and stationary sidewalk for a change", joked a smiling Mary Jane. Leaving their compartment, the couple walked to the vestibule and found that the conductor had placed his step box at the bottom of the coach steps. Absent the step box, that last step would be a gigantic and dangerous one, thought Calvin. As they reached the platform, the conductor informed the lovers that the train would depart in five hours. "Please don't be late as we would hate to leave you behind", warned the conductor.

Mary Jane and Calvin left the depot behind, walking slowly along Main Street. The locale surrounding them seemed to be one that was being protected by a Historic District designation. The buildings all seemed to date from the last century, but were fully restored and maintained in like-new condition. The couple passed a few antique shops and decided, on an impulse, to enter one that was posted 'The Second Time Around'. "That's a very clever name for an antique shop", observed Mary Jane. "It really is", agreed Calvin. The interior of the shop was well lighted and a pleasant female proprietor came forward and offered assistance. "May I help you?" "We have a few hours before our train leaves, and we just thought that it would be nice to see a little of Scottsbluff and get a bite to eat", replied Mary Jane.

"Well, then, be my guest and browse to your heart's content, and if I can answer any questions, please call me", offered the proprietor. Calvin and Mary Jane intently scanned the many glass display cases and marveled at the extensive collection of antique and collectible items. Along the way, Mary Jane spotted a small ceramic figurine of a United States Navy sailor. It was about six inches tall and authentically clothed in the standard dress blues uniform, the same as the one Calvin was wearing at that moment.

"Oh, Calvin, would you purchase this for me?", pleaded Mary Jane. The item was unmarked so Calvin sought out the proprietor who told him that the price was 75 cents. "Please wrap it up and we will be on our way", said Calvin. Mary Jane was beaming with boundless joy. "What a wonderful souvenir of our honeymoon", she remarked.

Leaving the antique store, Calvin and Mary Jane continued walking along Main Street and soon came upon a Mexican restaurant. "Do you enjoy Mexican food, Mary Jane?", asked Calvin. "Oh, yes, I love crispy tacos, refried beans and all the rest", said Mary Jane "Let's go in and check it out", suggested Calvin. Inside, 'Jose's Cactus Patch', turned out to be quite a lively place. A waiter seated them in a secluded corner. He then took their drink orders. Calvin ordered a frozen margarita while Mary Jane ordered a frozen strawberry margarita. While studying the menu, they found many of the traditional Mexican dishes including a number of house combinations. Mary Jane ordered four crunchy tacos, refried beans and a chili relleno. Calvin ended up ordering the same. With their drink orders, the waiter delivered a large basket of warm, crisp tortilla chips and plenty of salsa in both hot and mild varieties. The hot salsa was a bit too spicy for Mary Jane's taste, so she settled for the mild variety, which tasted exceedingly good. Within ten minutes their food orders were delivered. By that time they were famished, and began eating their food with gusto. During the meal, loud Mexican music was playing on a jukebox . There was plenty of time in which to return to the train, so it became a leisurely meal. After Calvin paid for their food, he and Mary Jane began walking at a leisurely pace toward the train depot. Even though there was some time remaining before the train departed, they did not want to risk the chance of accidentally becoming stranded in Scottsbluff, Nebraska, with no way to reach Nevada on time. Becoming an AWOL sailor was something to be avoided at all costs.

By the time they arrived back at the train, Friday was ending and it was also becoming dark as the sun had already set. High-intensity lights illuminated the station platform and Calvin assisted Mary Jane in ascending the coach steps. Passing through the vestibule they entered the passageway leading to Pullman compartment 'C'. The coach lights were already turned on and Calvin and Mary Jane passed by other passengers walking to their adjacent compartments. Not long after they entered their compartment, the locomotive whistle was heard blowing its double tone departure warning signal. Mary Jane pulled their window curtain down and then the Honeycuts were in their own private world again. Such a nice way to travel, thought Mary Jane to herself. "Calvin, I want you to know how very much I appreciate your buying me that little memento of Scottsbluff this afternoon. It will forever remind me of this day, and especially of you, Sweetheart, and our Honeymoon Special Train", said Mary Jane. "Mary Jane, I assure you that it was my pleasure to give you something that will make you happy, now and in the future", replied Calvin. "When I return to Des Moines, this antique figurine will occupy a special place adjacent to 'Sir Calvin' in my bedroom", volunteered Mary Jane. "I am sorry that there was not enough time to permit us to explore a larger area of Scottsbluff", said Calvin. "Yes, it would have been nice to have been able to reach the center of town, and perhaps obtain some souvenirs of the state to take home with us" lamented Mary Jane. "I agree with you, but with the train schedule controlling our movements, we just do not have the flexibility to venture too far from the depot. Perhaps after the war is over we can return to Scottsbluff again", replied Calvin.

0900 Saturday
28 March 1942
en route to Nevada
In Colorado

Since the train with Calvin's and Mary Jane's Pullman coach in tow had been traveling throughout night, Calvin and Mary Jane awoke to find themselves several hundred miles closer to Nevada. Awakening to find the usual cyclical swaying movement of the bed in their compartment, Calvin and Mary Jane were hungry and they needed food now. Calvin got up first and bathed and then dressed in his Navy Dress Blues uniform. Mary Jane was proud of him wearing his brand-new uniform adorned with the sparkling third class Gunner's Mate petty officer patch on his sleeve. She entered the compartment following her bath, dressed in a pretty, casual dress and color-coordinated shoes. In Calvin's mind, she was 'pretty as a picture'. "Sweetheart, how did you sleep last night?", asked Calvin. "I slept just fine and am happy to report that I dreamed about our forthcoming baby again", advised Mary Jane. "When we arrive in Nevada, I want you to see a doctor ASAP to make certain that everything is on schedule", said Calvin. "Not to worry, Calvin, for I will do exactly that. Doctor Wilson gave me the name of a primary civilian and alternate Navy doctor at Holman", said Mary Jane.

"It's breakfast time, so let's head for the dining car", suggested Calvin. Taking Mary Jane's hand, Calvin opened the compartment door and they moved into the passageway and turned left toward the dining car and followed another couple heading in the same direction. Passing through the two vestibules, Calvin pushed on into the dining car with Mary Jane in tow. A steward met them and showed them to a vacant table, with menus already in place. "What looks good to you this morning, Sweetheart?", asked Calvin. "The eggs and French toast sound good to me", answered Mary Jane. "They offer a pecan waffle and I think that I will order it and a large milk with an egg sunny side up on the side", replied Calvin. The steward returned and took their orders to the kitchen. In the diner this morning, the railroad provided copies of the newspapers from a major city through which the train had passed during the night. The free newspaper given to Calvin was 'The Daily Sentinel' from Scottsbluff, Nebraska. Thinking that reading the paper at the breakfast table would be discourteous to his wife, Calvin decided to wait and read it in their compartment. Within ten minutes, their food was delivered, and as usual, Mary Jane enjoyed the changing scenes passing by the dining car's large picture windows. It was another beautiful sunny day with no rain in sight. Mary Jane was quiet eating her meal, as was Calvin. But their reticence arose from different reasons. In Calvin's case, he was thinking about his parents and how he had left them to fend for themselves, while Mary Jane was caught up in some remorse for her not having had the intestinal fortitude to tell her mother of the baby that was growing within her womb. With their meals finished, Calvin paid their check, and they left the dining car without revealing the concerns that were bothering them both. Returning to their compartment, Calvin could sense from Mary Jane's demeanor that she was not feeling her usual happy self. "Sweetheart, I sense that you are concerned about something. Is it something that I can help you with?", asked Calvin. "No, not really, Calvin. It is just that I feel uncomfortable because I failed to tell my mother about the baby before we left home", revealed Mary Jane. "I appreciate your concern, but to have told her might have prevented our marriage, and besides, you can call her on the telephone next month and give her the wonderful news", encouraged Calvin. "Yes, I suppose if I think about it, another month's delay will not really make that much difference", said Mary Jane somewhat tentatively.

1400 Saturday
28 March 1942
en route to Nevada
In Colorado

After returning from a visit to the bar car Calvin and Mary Jane felt the need of sexual activity. "Calvin, let's bathe together now, like they do in Japan", said Mary Jane. "Although it will be a new experience for me, I can handle that", replied Calvin. Entering the bathroom, Mary Jane filled the bathtub half full of warm water while at the same time she added some bubble bath oil. Calvin undressed and entered the bathroom to find Mary Jane quite naked. As always, Calvin could not keep his eyes off her perfectly formed breasts. Walking to her side, Calvin placed his arms around Mary Jane's waist and kissed her inviting lips. Mary Jane returned his kiss eagerly, and then pushed him away. With plenty of water in the tub, hiding beneath the fragrant layer of bubbles, Mary Jane said, "Calvin, you get in first and sit down, then I am going to sit in your lap" announced Mary Jane.

"You just lead and I will be more than pleased to follow", replied an intrigued Calvin. Calvin sat down in the warm water and relished the soothing effect of the bath oil on his skin. Kneeling beside the tub, Mary Jane reached through the layer of glistening bubbles and found Calvin's limber manhood. Taking it in her hand, she gently massaged his organ and readily produced his first erection of the day. "How nice that you are so easy to prepare", observed Mary Jane. "Well, as I have told you before, I aim to please", laughed Calvin. Calvin's throbbing organ was erect and wavering to the beat of his heart. At the same time, its circular movement was tracing small, invisible circles just beneath the surface of the layer of bubbles. "Calvin, slide down a bit for I am going to climb in now and sit in your lap, facing you, with my legs extending on each side of your body", advised Mary Jane. True to her word, Mary Jane gracefully stepped over the rim of the tub and gently settled herself into Calvin's lap while, at the same time, guiding Calvin's manhood inside her. The thrill that passed through Calvin's body was unimaginable. 'Needles and pins' didn't begin to describe the essence of the electrifying sensation that Mary Jane's action stirred within Calvin's groin. "Oh, Mary Jane, I did not know how much we were missing", admitted a smiling Calvin. With his organ throbbing inside Mary Jane, Calvin could feel her periodic contractions and knew that she was as sexually stimulated as he was. Bracing her arms on the smooth rim of the tub, Mary Jane began to gently raise and lower her body, to the instant delight of Calvin. "I love what you are doing, Mary Jane, but please be aware that I can't take too much of it without exploding", cautioned Calvin. "But, Calvin, you don't understand; that's the whole idea of my movements", laughed a concentrating Mary Jane. "By the time you are ready to explode I will be there too", she smiled ever so shyly. Calvin's body repeatedly shivered from the tantalizing sensations permeating his body as his drowned manhood slid in and out of Mary Jane's body. With Mary Jane doing all the work, Calvin felt that he was in the lap of luxury and probably was as close to heaven as he might ever get. As Mary Jane continued her gentle movements up and down, Calvin's groin began to send powerful waves of warning to his brain from that most sensitive spot. "Mary Jane, we need to end this now for I cannot tolerate your caress any longer", lamented Calvin. Instead of ending it, Mary Jane moved ever faster and the two of them were soon releasing their pent-up passion in waves of primal ecstasy. Calvin lay back against the side of the tub as Mary Jane relaxed on top of him. "Oh, Calvin, that was the most wonderful climax that I have ever experienced in my entire life", bragged Mary Jane. "I don't disagree and I think that the Japanese have been keeping this technique a secret", joked Calvin. "Well, at least you can't say that we haven't had clean sex today", added Mary Jane with a wry smile. And with that perfect ending, Calvin pulled the plug and allowed the soft water to escape from the tub, at the same time turning on the shower for him and Mary Jane to rinse off. The couple towel dried their bodies and dressed for lunch.

1500 Saturday
28 March 1942
en route to Nevada
In Colorado

Taking in the 'Do Not Disturb' sign and parking it inside the compartment door, Calvin and Mary Jane hurried to the dining car. It turned out that the exertions of their sexual encounter had given them both exceedingly hearty appetites. A steward seated them at their favorite table, and now knowing the menu by heart, Calvin and Mary Jane ordered their meals of sirloin steaks, home fries and carrots. Calvin ordered his favorite beverage, a large glass of ice cold milk, while Mary Jane requested sweet iced tea. The morning hours had seen their train move from Nebraska into Colorado where the terrain became more mountainous with tall snowcapped peaks rising in the distance. Their food orders arrived and Mary Jane and Calvin began eating. Since it was well after lunchtime, they noticed that they essentially had the entire dining car to themselves, what with only one other couple being served. After finishing their meal, the lovers lingered over their dessert of bread pudding a la mode.

Calvin paid the steward for their meals and he and Mary Jane left the dining car for their compartment. Since leaving Des Moines, passing through the vestibules between the dining car and their Pullman berth had become less and less challenging on account of the daily practice they received at each mealtime. Calvin thought that life at sea must be akin to the railroad trip, where standing could be a challenge due to the constant and sometimes rapid movement beneath one's footing on a pitching wet ship's deck. Returning to compartment 'C', Calvin and Mary Jane found their bed already turned down and the usual carafe of ice water in place. Although it was not normal bedtime, the lovers decided to call it a day and turn in. Mary Jane took her shower and put on her PJ's, after which Calvin did the same. When he came out of the bathroom, Mary Jane was fast asleep. Calvin was thankful for that fact for he believed that Mary Jane needed the extra rest against the rigors of railroad travel. Calvin read his gunnery literature for some time and then he turned out the lights and climbed into bed. Lying there on his back he could hear the mournful whine of the locomotive steam whistle calling out in the night to warn wayward motorists at the many grade crossings they were passing. Within a few short minutes, Calvin was dreaming of his life back on the Honeycut farm with his dog, Skippy, and his beloved Jersey cows.

0900 Sunday
29 March 1942
en route to Nevada
Train In Utah

The train came to a noisy, unexpected and unscheduled stop in Salt Lake City and caused Calvin to take notice. He reached over from the bed and raised the curtain a crack. The sunshine illuminated the world outside and Calvin could see what appeared to be a railroad yard containing a large number of passenger coaches parked on yard sidings. The locomotive engineer was blowing signals on his steam whistle, and soon enough the train continued its forward movement. Calvin lowered the curtain over the window again, hoping that Mary Jane had not been awakened. She made no movement in acknowledgment of the stop and he looked at her lovely face as she breathed softly. How sweet and serene was her sleep. His love for Mary Jane was manifest in his heart and Calvin realized that this trip had brought them closer together than ever before, and for that fact he was supremely thankful. Indeed, their time together had allowed them to learn each other's innermost secrets and effectively made them truly man and wife in an absolutely perfect sense. Light penetrated the compartment through a small space at the lower edge of the window curtain. As Calvin watched, he could see the reflected silhouettes of high-rise city office buildings, bridges and other man-made structures. The train passed by city parks, swimming pools, tennis courts and other improvements intended to make city life more appealing than it might otherwise be. As the scenery passed by, Calvin realized that Salt Lake City was significantly different than his hometown of Des Moines, Iowa. In the midst of his musings, Mary Jane awoke in time to enjoy the view of the train passing over the bridge spanning the Great Salt Lake. This event meant that their train was fast approaching their final destination in Nevada. Stretching luxuriously, Mary Jane rolled over and placed her head on Calvin's shoulder as they lay in bed. "Calvin, I had the most wonderful sleep and feel so much more rested than I did yesterday". "Do you think that your contentment has anything to do with our Japanese interlude?", joked Calvin. Smiling knowingly, Mary Jane said "I wouldn't be at all surprised for that event surpassed all of our lovemaking on this entire trip, in my opinion". "You will not get any argument from me on that fine opinion", agreed Calvin.

"We have passed through Salt Lake City, so shall we get dressed and have some breakfast?" asked Calvin. "Yes, it is time, for my stomach is growling its head off", admitted

Mary Jane. With his wife so close, Calvin could not resist the temptation to reach his hand beneath her PJ's and tweak her rosy nipples with his fingers. Encountering no resistance, Calvin grew more adventuresome and moved her top aside exposing her breasts in all their pristine beauty, the sight of which always took Calvin's breath away. Moving Mary Jane's head off his shoulder, Calvin shifted his body to place his mouth on the nipple of her left breast while he gently massaged its mate. Calvin's efforts caused Mary Jane to relax and emit a contented sigh. For his part, Calvin thought that perhaps, after yesterday's most satisfactory coupling, that they should forego any sex this morning. And on that note, they showered, dressed and headed for the dining car. By the time they were seated and had ordered their breakfast, the train was passing over the western edge of the Great Salt Lake. The surface of the lake appeared calm and green against the cloudless blue sky. A few minutes later the steward delivered their food. Looking out through the dining car window, Mary Jane noticed, for the first time, the radical change that had taken place in the countryside that she was viewing. The green mountains had given way to flat, desert terrain. Cactus plants were present by the hundreds and small clefts in the sandy soil were lined with large rocks; the latter objects having been placed by Mother Nature, not by man. Calvin and Mary Jane ate in silence realizing that this was their last day of travel, for the conductor had advised them to expect arrival in Las Vegas later in the day around 1600. Finishing their meal, an anxious Mary Jane said, "Calvin, I want to spend the rest of the day packing my things to calm myself. My stomach is all jumpy inside from the unknown expectation of what our Nevada future will bring". "Please don't be afraid, Mary Jane, for this will be just another day in the rest of our lives. While it no doubt will be a busy one, it will also be a happy one as is every other day that we spend together", consoled Calvin. With their meal finished, Calvin paid the steward, and they returned to their compartment where Calvin extricated their bags from the small closet provided for personal storage and laid them out on their bed. To himself Calvin thought, "Well, I guess that means that there will be no lovemaking today. Worse luck!" But then again, he and Mary Jane may have already had enough lovemaking to last a lifetime, mused Calvin to himself.

Mary Jane set to work placing all of her clothes from the trip into her bag. "Is there anything that I can help you with?", asked Calvin. "No, thank you, there isn't all that much to do, but I just felt this compulsion to be completely ready when the train stops at the depot in Las Vegas. By the way, what happens once we leave the train?", asked Mary Jane. "Well, the first thing we have to do is find the shore patrol office and present my orders, and from there we will just follow their instructions. I am guessing that they will put us up in a hotel in Las Vegas, and later tomorrow, we will be taken to the gunnery base. It should all be rather routine, I think. As soon as possible, I want to get you situated in comfortable surroundings", concluded Calvin. "Calvin, do you think that we will have time to call your parents and mine when we arrive? We need to let them know that we arrived safely", said Mary Jane. "If we have enough time, I am certain that we can call from the shore patrol office", soothed Calvin. In the distance, Calvin and Mary Jane could see the high-rise hotels of Las Vegas, Nevada, and the ever-present casinos. Of course, gambling is what makes Las Vegas 'tick'. There was a knock on the door and upon opening it, Calvin found the porter outside ready to receive their bags. "If you like, I can move your bags to the vestibule at this time", advised the porter. "Yes, that will be fine for we are all packed". As he spoke, Calvin handed over his sea bag as well as Mary Jane's bag. "I will place them alongside the coach steps and you can retrieve them on your way out", said the porter. "Thank you for your prompt assistance as well as your thoughtful care throughout our trip", complimented Calvin. "You're more than welcome, sir", replied the porter as he carried the Honeycut bags away.

1600 Monday
30 March 1942
Railroad Depot
Las Vegas, Nevada

Amid the hubbub in the passageway as the other departing passengers worked their way toward the coach vestibule, Calvin and Mary Jane were patiently following along. In the vestibule, Calvin entered first and then raised his hand to assist Mary Jane down the steep steps for the last time and over the step box sitting on the depot platform. At last, thought Mary Jane, no more wobbling and lurching to keep her feet steady, as was constantly the case on the moving Pullman coach. Calvin found their bags and retrieved them, passing by the porter and handing him a tip to cover all of his services en route. "Thank you very much for the excellent service throughout our trip", complimented Calvin again. "You are more than welcome, sir. It is always our pleasure to serve our passengers however we can, and have a nice stay here in Las Vegas", said the porter. "We plan to try, but could you point us in the direction of the U.S. Navy shore patrol office?", asked Calvin. "Yes, sir. After you enter the main station waiting room, go to the Travelers Aid desk and they can advise you of its location", replied the porter. "Many thanks again, and have a nice day", said Calvin. "You and the missus do the same", concluded the porter. "Come, Mary Jane, let's walk into the main waiting room", said Calvin. Leaving the Pullman coach behind, Mary Jane's mind slipped back to the many delightful days that she and Calvin had spent on their 'Honeymoon Special.'

A never-to-be-forgotten, once-in-a-lifetime experience, she thought to herself. Five minutes later, Calvin pointed to the Travelers Aid desk and walked over to speak with the female attendant. "Good morning, sir, may I be of assistance?", asked the Taveler's Aid representative. "Yes, ma'am, I need to find the local U.S. Navy shore patrol office so I can report in for duty", said Calvin. "Well, sailor, you don't have far to go. The shore patrol has an office adjacent to the waiting room entrance door, and she pointed at the door as she spoke. "You can't miss it", added the helpful lady. "Many thanks for your assistance", acknowledged Calvin. With Mary Jane at his side and clutching his arm, Calvin walked to the entrance door and found the shore patrol office. Stepping inside he presented his orders to the duty petty officer. "Welcome aboard, Mr. Honeycut, we have been expecting you", said the petty officer. "The bus for Holman will be leaving in fifteen minutes so you had better climb aboard. There is a blue Navy bus in the driveway just outside, and you can stow your sea bag and your wife's suitcase in the rear and take any unoccupied seats. When you arrive at Holman, there will be someone to meet you and set up housing arrangements". Calvin flagged down a porter to assist him and Mary Jane with their possessions in boarding the bus. And, so much for the validity of his guess that the Navy would put him and Mary Jane up at a Las Vegas hotel for the night. And, likewise, calling home to his and Mary Jane's parents would have to wait until another time.

1700 Monday
30 March 1942
Departing Railroad Depot
Las Vegas, Nevada

The bus driver climbed into his seat and announced his destination and the fact that the trip would require approximately one hour to reach Holman. Calvin and Mary Jane settled in as the driver pulled out into traffic and left the railroad depot behind. By then it was about 1700 and would be near sundown when they reached the Navy Base at Holman. Mary Jane was intrigued by the dry desert wasteland that the bus was passing through. Cacti of all kinds existed in the sandy soil, and a few small birds could be seen pecking at blossoms sprouting from the limbs of some of the cactus plants. As the bus rolled along, Calvin placed his arm around Mary Jane's shoulders and flashed a comforting smile in her direction, which she returned, dimples and all. Eventually, the bus reached Holman and Calvin presented his orders to the duty chief petty officer. "Welcome aboard, Mr. Honeycut. We have arranged space for you and your wife in the base enlisted men's quarters. Place your possessions in the Jeep over there and gunnery petty officer Miller will assist you in getting settled in", said the chief. "Thank you very much, chief. We are happy to finally be here and away from the pitching coach that we traveled in halfway across the United States", lamented Calvin. "I know what you mean, for I have made a few cross-country trips on the train myself", commiserated the chief. With that, Mary Jane and Calvin walked outside to the Jeep where Miller was already waiting for them, with their bags on board. "Hello, petty officer Miller. My name is Calvin Honeycut and this is my wife, Mary Jane". "I'm pleased to meet you folks, and just call me 'Mike'" said Miller. "Mike it is", replied Calvin.

Mike started the Jeep and drove several blocks to a barracks building where he stopped. "This will be your home for as long as you are here. Building 36A The ship's store is only a block away so you won't have to carry your purchases too far", offered Mike. Mike helped the Honeycuts move in with their possessions and gave them the keys to Apartment 104 which was a compact one bedroom, kitchen and bathroom arrangement. The apartment was tastefully furnished, complete with linens, kitchen utensils and dishes. "There is a self-service laundry next door to the ship's store and it serves as a sort of community meeting place for families of sailors undergoing training on base. In the morning, please muster across the street on the Grinder at 0800 where you will receive your assignment", said Mike. "Many thanks for your assistance, Mike, and I'll be certain to be at muster on time", replied Calvin. Mike left the apartment and Calvin heard the Jeep's engine start and the transmission whine as Mike returned to his post at the Gunnery Base gate area. "Mary Jane, why don't you take a nap and rest for awhile. I'm going to walk over to the ship's store and find out where the mess hall is. Mike forgot to give us that little detail", said Calvin. "I think I will do exactly that, Calvin, for I am tired, what with all our traveling today", replied an exhausted Mary Jane. The bed in their apartment was not made up so Calvin took the time to assist Mary Jane in applying the sheets and bedspread before leaving for the ship's store. At the same time he and Mary Jane unpacked her bag and placed her things in the drawers of the chest of drawers with which the apartment was furnished. Following completion of that task Calvin left for the ships' store.

1800 Monday
30 March 1942
Navy Gunnery School Base
Holman, Nevada

Five minutes after leaving Mary Jane, Calvin walked into the ship's store where he found about a dozen sailors milling around. Approaching a petty officer operating one of the check-out cash registers Calvin said, "Excuse me, but could you tell me where the mess hall is located? Mike forgot to tell me and I forgot to ask". "Easy question. See that building across the street", as the petty officer pointed in the direction of north. "That is the one and only mess hall on this base" replied the sailor. "Many thanks. I appreciate your assistance", replied Calvin. Having learned all that he needed to know at that moment, Calvin returned to his apartment where he quietly let himself in. Mary Jane was sleeping soundly so Calvin obtained his Navy gunnery literature and sat down at the kitchen table to study his documents once again. Fifteen minutes later, Calvin heard Mary Jane stir as she sat up in bed. "How was your nap, Sweetheart?", asked Calvin. "Very refreshing, I should say, but I find myself still dreaming about our baby", smiled Mary Jane. "Well, I'd say that that dream just goes with the territory, wouldn't you?", asked Calvin. "I guess you're correct on that point", admitted Mary Jane. Noticing her sweet dimpled smile, Calvin left the kitchen table and walked to their bed where he swept Mary Jane into his arms and kissed her while he held her tightly. "I certainly do love you so very much, Mary Jane, and am deliriously happy over the fact that you are my very own wife", boasted Calvin. "Thank you very much, kind sir, and I feel the same way about you", replied Mary Jane somewhat sleepily. "I learned where the mess hall is so why don't we go check out their menu for the day?", asked Calvin. "I'm for that, my last meal from the train has all but faded away by this time", admitted Mary Jane. Assisting Mary Jane to her feet, the couple left their apartment and walked in the direction of the mess hall. Entering the mess hall, Calvin and Mary Jane were greeted by the sounds of metal trays banging together as hungry sailors carelessly laid their metal food trays on the stainless steel runners next to the serving positions. The meal was served cafeteria style with various entrees and side dishes being available. Calvin followed Mary Jane and watched in surprise as she was challenged by the first server. "I can't serve you, ma'am because you don't have a badge", said the server. Moving closer, Calvin said, "We just arrived on base about an hour ago and won't be processed until tomorrow, and here are my orders." "Thank you very much, sir, and you both may proceed through the line", replied the server.

Mary Jane selected the meat loaf plate, green beans and hot rolls and a piece of apple pie, while Calvin decided on macaroni and cheese along with mashed potatoes and gravy, plus banana cream pie and, of course, a large glass of ice-cold milk. Mary Jane opted for her usual sweet iced tea. Mary Jane and Calvin selected an empty table among a dozen or so tables and sat down. As they sat there consuming their meals, another sailor and his wife stopped by with their meals and asked to join them. Of course, the Honeycuts readily agreed. "My name is Maxwell Smith, but everyone calls me Max, and this is my wife, Jo Anne" offered Max. "Hello, you two; my name is Calvin Honeycut and this is my wife, Mary Jane. Have you been at Holman for very long?", asked Calvin. "We arrived about a week ago and expect to leave for a duty assignment in about two months", replied Max. "Well, we just arrived today and haven't been processed yet so I don't have any view as to when we will be leaving for a duty assignment", replied Calvin. "Well, from what I have seen and heard, the average stay is about two months between arrival and departure to an active duty assignment", reported Max. "No doubt I will find out all about it in the morning", observed Calvin.

"Are you folks assigned to housing on the base?", asked Calvin. "Yes, it turns out that we are in Building 36A, Apartment 106", said Max. "What a coincidence, we are in the same building but in Apartment 104", smiled Mary Jane. "So that makes us neighbors", agreed Jo Anne. Thirty minutes later, the Smiths and Honeycuts were still talking about the mundane topics of where they came from, where they went to school, who their parents are and how they happened to end up in the Navy. Eventually the conversation waned and the two couples deposited their trays and utensils on the dishwashing conveyor and left the mess hall to return to their apartments. "Well, Max and Jo Anne, it is certainly a pleasure to have made your acquaintance, and no doubt we will get to see a lot more of you as the days pass by", said Calvin. "Same here, Calvin and Mary Jane, no doubt we will get to see you tomorrow", replied Jo Anne. "Have a good evening and welcome to Holman" said Max. "You folks have a good evening too", added Mary Jane.

Back in their apartment, Calvin and Mary Jane decided that it was too late to call their parents so they postponed their telephone calls to the next day. Calling this late, with the time differential involved, would run the risk of waking their parents, so the postponement seemed the reasonable thing to do. Both Calvin and Mary Jane were tired from their long train journey and mutually agreed that, notwithstanding its desirable attraction, lovemaking should also be deferred until another time. With that decision having been made, Calvin and Mary Jane showered, dressed in their PJ's, and climbed into their bed which, to their delight, was quite comfortably soft. Calvin gave Mary Jane a "good-night kiss" and closed his eyes.

Early to bed and early to rise seemed to be the Navy way of conducting business at each base where Calvin had been assigned.

0700 Tuesday
31 March 1942
Navy Gunnery School Base
Holman, Nevada

Calvin was up early and dressed in his white utility uniform allowing Mary Jane to sleep-in. Once dressed, he left their apartment and walked the block to the mess hall for breakfast, choosing scrambled eggs, bacon, and biscuits for his meal. Leaving the mess hall, Calvin walked to the

Grinder, checking to see that he had his orders with him. Other sailors were already forming up in lines and, in the absence of any other instructions, he fell into line too. Within ten minutes a chief gunner's mate appeared and said "ATTENNNTION! Recruits. All recruits who arrived yesterday fall into a line on my left behind Yeoman Driscol, and those of you who already have your assignments are dismissed.", drawled the chief. All but Calvin and six other recruits departed the Grinder heading for a bus parked nearby.

Calvin fell into line behind the yeoman and waited his turn. When his turn came, Calvin offered his orders, which were promptly accepted and logged into the Holman Gunnery Base records. "Calvin, you are assigned as a member of Company 42-136 which is slated to graduate on 31 May 1942, at which time you will be assigned to a permanent shipboard duty position. In the meantime, muster with your company each day and check the bulletin board in your classroom beside the ship's store for your curriculum, classroom study schedule and gunnery range schedules. Here is a copy of your weekly schedules, but be certain to check the classroom schedules regularly because unannounced changes can occur. Your textbooks will be issued in each study class and remain your property upon graduation. Your company has just formed up and I suggest that you hurry over to the study hall where you will find your instructor and the other members of your company. Should you have any questions later, please come to see me in the executive officer's office. But for now, hurry over to your classroom".

Calvin found his classroom next door to the ship's store as the yeoman had told him. The building contained four classrooms and Calvin entered the only one containing students. The gunnery petty officer noticed Calvin enter and asked his name. "Gunner's Mate third class Calvin Honeycut, sir", responded Calvin. "Yes, you are in the right place for I have your name on my roster; come to my desk and receive your textbook", said the petty officer. Calvin walked to the petty officer's desk and received his text book. Calvin's class was comprised of about 30 students, all of whom had received their books. "Men, this class is a familiarization class covering the Navy's 20-mm automatic antiaircraft guns. Your first order of business is to study your basic gun manual with the objective of memorizing the purpose and function of each and every physical part of the gun. Once you have accomplished that task, you will visit the gunnery range and receive further instruction on the disassembly, reassembly, cleaning, lubrication and firing of the weapon. In addition, you will learn the different types of shells that the gun is capable of firing", related the petty officer.

"I am releasing you now to go to your barracks or other location in which you feel comfortable and study your textbook. Immediately following muster in the morning, I will give you all a test to ascertain just how much information you have managed to retain during your study efforts. Company ATTENNNTION! -- Dismissed!". Amid the scraping of chair legs on the wood floor, Calvin stood and looked around. He was disappointed not to see a single familiar face. Picking up his book, Calvin walked to the door and turned in the direction of his apartment. He had already decided that his apartment would be the ideal place to study his gun manual in peace and quiet.

Tapping gently on the door, Calvin unlocked it and entered to find Mary Jane sitting at the kitchen table. "Hello, Mary Jane, did you have a restful sleep?", asked Calvin. "Yes, Calvin, I slept most of the morning and feel so rested at the moment. Thank you for letting me sleep in!", said Mary Jane. "Have you had anything to eat today?", asked Calvin. "No, I wasn't hungry until now", said Mary Jane. "Well, I know that the mess hall is closed so let's walk over to the ship's store and get you a sandwich or something else to eat", offered Calvin. "That sounds inviting and perhaps at the same time we can call our parents on the telephone?", queried Mary Jane. "Okay, let's leave now for I have to hurry back and study for a test that our instructor will give the class in the morning", said Calvin. Ten minutes later, Calvin and Mary Jane were shopping at the ship's store where Mary Jane selected a ham and cheese sandwich, corn chips and a coke to take to their room. Adjacent to the store was a communications office where they could make their telephone calls home. Calvin gave the numbers to the attendant and then he and Mary Jane moved outside to the booth area to receive their callbacks. Within ten minutes, their telephone rang and they both entered the booth and Calvin lifted the receiver. "Hello", said Calvin. "Hello" came the reply from his mother. "How are you, Mom?" "Oh, your Dad and I are just fine and are so happy to hear from you", replied Mrs. Honeycut. "Just a second, I want to put Mary Jane on the line", said Calvin. Handing the receiver to Mary Jane, Calvin said "It's Mom." "Hello, Mom", said Mary Jane. "It's so nice to hear your voice, Mary Jane, and how was your train trip?", asked Mrs. Honeycut. "It was wonderful and we got to see lots of these United States along the way. We are in Nevada now and Calvin has just started his gunnery school", revealed Mary Jane. "Mary Jane, just a second while I put Dad on the phone", said Mrs. Honeycut. "Hello, Mary Jane. I understand that you had a nice cross-country trip on the train", said Mr. Honeycut. "Yes, Dad, it was a wonderful trip and we ate a lot of nice food along the way", replied Mary Jane. "Just a second, Dad, while I put Calvin back on the telephone". Handing the receiver to Calvin, Mary Jane said, "It's your Dad." "Hello, Dad, it's so nice to hear your voice again", said Calvin. "Same here, Son". "We got in too late yesterday to call you so we are playing catch-up a bit", said Calvin. "No problem, Calvin, we knew that you would call us when you could", acknowledged Mr. Honeycut. "I had my first class this morning and I am learning all about antiaircraft guns and have my first test in the morning with lots of studying between now and then.", said Calvin. "Well, Son, I know that you will do well with that 'bear trap' memory of yours", complimented Mr. Honeycut. "I guess that is about all for this time, Dad. You and Mom take care of each other and good-bye until next time", said Calvin "Good-bye, Son, and we love you and Mary Jane", concluded Mr. Honeycut.

Calvin leaned toward Mary Jane and said, "Dad wants you to know that they love you very much". "How nice of him to say so", said Mary Jane. The telephone in the booth soon rang again and Mary Jane was the first to answer. "Hi, Dad, and how are things in Des Moines", asked Mary Jane. "Why, Mary Jane, it is a special treat to hear your voice again. Is Calvin all right?" "Oh, yes, he is just fine and I'll put him on the line in just a minute. Is Mom around? I'd like to hear her voice too", said Mary Jane. "Yes, she is right here beside me, just a minute and I'll put her on", said Mr. Thomas. "Hello, Mary Jane", greeted a happy Mrs. Thomas. "Hi, Mom, I can't tell you how nice it is to hear your voice again after all this time", replied Mary Jane. "Mary Jane, we miss you so much", lamented Mrs. Thomas. "Calvin and I miss you all too, Mom. Just a second while I put Calvin on the telephone", said Mary Jane, handing the receiver to Calvin. "Hello, Mom, and are you feeling all right?" asked Calvin. "Yes, I am feeling fine and so is Dad; here, let me put him on the line." "Hello, Calvin, and are you taking good care of that daughter of mine?", asked Mr. Thomas. "Yes, indeed, I am, and you can count on me continuing to do the same thing", bragged Calvin. "Mary Jane and I arrived here in Nevada yesterday, but it was too late to call you folks without waking you up so we just waited until today", offered Calvin. "Well, thank you for your consideration, Calvin."

"Here, Mary Jane, tell your folks good-bye", said Calvin as he handed over the receiver. "Hi Dad, it's me again on the line to say good-bye. Can I tell Mom goodbye?" "Here she is" said Mr. Thomas. "Hi, Mary Jane, and thank you so much for keeping in touch", said Mrs. Thomas. "We'll call again real soon; good-bye until then and we love you both", said Mary Jane as she hung up the receiver. "How wonderful it was to hear their voices again, Calvin." "Yes, indeed, there's nothing so good as these modern-day conveniences", said Calvin. On their way out of the building, Calvin paid for their long distance telephone call charges.

"Now, let's go back to the apartment so I can study and you can have something to eat", said Calvin. The lovers entered their apartment and Mary Jane went to the kitchen to eat her sandwich while Calvin took a comfortable overstuffed chair and opened his gunnery text book. The inch-thick book was complete with many exploded diagrams and color photographs that identified the various components of the 20-mm gun as well as its 20-mm shell magazine. The text included all of the pertinent technical descriptions as well as many assembly drawings. As he read, Calvin underlined important statements and also made notes in the notebook that he had purchased at the ship's store the previous day. Calvin spent the afternoon studying, stopping only when it came time to visit the mess hall for their evening meal. While he studied, Mary Jane took cat naps on their bed. When he finished his study period, Calvin gently woke Mary Jane. "Sweetheart, it is time for supper", said Calvin. "Oh, Calvin, I was having such a wonderful dream. The war was over and we were living in our own little white house with a white picket fence, and the babies were already one year old. It was a lovely dream", murmured Mary Jane. "I'm sorry to have to spoil your nocturnal interlude, Honey, but my stomach is complaining", replied Calvin. "That's all right, I can sleep later and another dream will appear. It happens all the time I am happy to report", said a smiling Mary Jane.

Calvin and Mary Jane walked hand-in-hand down the street to the mess hall. They entered, picked up their trays, and followed the chow line already assembled. Mary Jane selected fried chicken and mashed potatoes, and rice pudding for dessert, while Calvin decided on a hamburger and french fries along with a dinner salad. Leaving the serving line, they noticed the Smiths alone at a table and walked in their direction. "Hello, Max and Jo Anne; mind if we join you folks?", asked Calvin. "Not at all. Pull up a chair and sit down", encouraged Jo Anne. "Well, Calvin, did you get checked in and join a new company?", asked Max. "Indeed I did, and was advised that I would graduate with Company 42-136 on 31 May 1942", replied Calvin. "Interestingly enough, that is only two weeks after I graduate", said Max. "Well, at least we will have a few weeks in which to get to know each other better", said a smiling Jo Anne. "I am looking forward to that opportunity", chimed in Mary Jane. "I'm sorry that I have to eat and run, but I am facing a test in the morning and I have to scoot back to our room and finish my studying", apologized Calvin. "Mary Jane, why don't you hang loose and return later at your own convenience. I'm afraid I won't be much company this evening", said Calvin. "I'll be along later, Calvin, after the Smiths leave", said Mary Jane.

Calvin left the mess hall and hurried to his apartment where he reviewed the material he had covered before dinner. An hour later, Mary Jane returned and got into her PJ's, and with a magazine that she had bought on the train, she climbed into bed. The room was quiet save for the rustle of pages as Calvin continued his studies. At 2100 Calvin called it a day, dressed in his PJ's, climbed into bed and snuggled up against the warm body of his sleeping wife. He felt comfortable with the technical material that he had covered and felt that he would do well on the forthcoming examination the next morning. If he had any apprehension at all, it was in the area of identifying all of the mechanical components of the 20-mm gun. The gun was comprised of so many individual components that it was difficult to keep them straight.

0700 Wednesday
1 April 1942
Navy Gunnery School Base
Holman, Nevada

As with the previous day, Calvin got up, showered, dressed and let Mary Jane sleep-in. Leaving with his text book he went to the mess hall and ate his breakfast. Returning to his apartment, he brushed his teeth and then left to muster on the Grinder. Company 42-136 was called to attention and roll call taken by the platoon leader petty officer. Immediately following roll call, the company was excused to report to their classroom. The same petty officer as yesterday was sitting at the head of the class and had written his name on the blackboard, 2nd Class Gunner's Mate Howard Briggs. "Good-morning Mr. Briggs", said Calvin. "Good-morning, Calvin, and how did you get along with your study of the 20-mm gun since yesterday's class?" "Well, I have to admit that I don't know it all yet, but I have a good appreciation for what the gun is capable of, as well as what it takes to operate it", replied Calvin. "Fair enough, Calvin. By the time you leave Holman, you will be an expert on that gun as well as the companion 40-mm gun", said Mr. Briggs. By then, the other members of the company had straggled in and taken their seats.

"Men, as I stated yesterday, I have a test for you to take this morning. It is mostly a true/false test but there are six essay type questions at the end. You should be able to finish the test before lunchtime. Take your time and go over your answers carefully. When you have finished, bring your papers to me and I will correct and grade them. This is a closed book test and we will take a 15-minute break at 1000". And with that, Mr. Briggs handed out his test sheets of which there were seven pages per set. Calvin sat back and leafed through the seven pages while glancing at the essay questions. It had been his experience in high school that essay questions were the most labor-intensive part of any examination that he had ever taken. And, he saw nothing in the test sheets to make him change this impression. Calvin commenced his work on page one and found that he knew the answer to every question on the page. Turning to page two, he filled in all of the answers without any hesitation. When he turned to page three, he began to wonder if there was something that he had missed for the questions seemed to him to be so elementary as to be unchallenging. Nevertheless, he continued apace and carefully studied each question to make certain that there was not a trick question lurking on the page. By 0945 Calvin had filled in more than half of the true/false questions. At that point, he decided to concentrate on the essay questions of which there were six in all. Thinking back to his study of the preceding evening, Calvin recalled the details that he needed with which to answer the first essay question. While concentrating on his answer, petty officer Briggs called the class to a halt for its break period. "All right, gentlemen, it is time for a break. Plan on being back here in fifteen minutes".

Calvin decided to step across the street to the ship's store and purchase a 'coke', and then he returned to his desk and sat down to sip on the cold liquid. While he waited for the examination period to begin again, Calvin conjured up visions of his 20-mm gun textbook and essentially performed a thorough review during his break period. At 1000, Mr. Briggs called the class to order and the test period began again. Calvin elected to finish the true/false questions first and then concentrate on the remaining essay questions. By 1100 he had finished answering all of the questions and then began his review to make certain that he had not left anything unanswered. It was during this time that he harked back to that day when he had assisted Lowell with his math deficiency, there at the kitchen table of the Honeycut home in Des Moines, Iowa. How very long ago that session seemed to him now. Satisfied that he had answered all of the questions, Calvin carried his test pages to Mr. Briggs and handed them in. "Thank you, Calvin. Please have a seat while I grade your work", said Mr. Briggs.

As he sat at his desk, Calvin thought about the fact that he was having to neglect his wife in deference to his training assignment, but at the same time, he decided that there was little that he could do to change the situation except, perhaps, to be a bit more solicitous and attentive to her at the end of each day.

"Calvin, you may come up and receive your grade. I will retain your test papers on file." Mr. Briggs handed Calvin a small slip of paper on which he had written the grade of A+ and appended the comment "excellent work". "Thank you, Mr. Briggs", said Calvin. "You may leave here now, but plan on returning at 1300 for some additional instruction on topics not included in your text", said Mr. Briggs "Thank you, Mr. Briggs. I'll be here with bells on", replied Calvin.

Leaving the classroom, Calvin hurried to his apartment where he found Mary Jane snoozing. As he closed the door, Mary Jane sat up in bed and he went to her side and held her tightly as he kissed her sweet lips. "Hi, Honey, are you feeling all right?", asked Calvin. "Oh, yes, Sweetheart, I feel fine and I spent some time with Jo Anne after having breakfast. She is such a nice person", replied Mary Jane. "Honey, I am so happy that you have someone with whom you can spend these otherwise lonely hours when I am busy learning", said Calvin. "Thank you for thinking of my welfare, Darling.

It isn't every man who would concern himself with such things", observed Mary Jane. "Listen, I have to be back in class at 1300; would you care to have lunch now or do you want to wait until later?", asked Calvin. "Now would be fine, since I didn't have too much to eat for breakfast", replied Mary Jane.

Leaving their apartment, Calvin and Mary Jane walked down the asphalt road to the mess hall. Calvin appreciated the compact nature of the Gunnery Base as opposed to the extremely large and widespread nature of the Great Lakes Naval Boot Camp. "By the way, I obtained an A+ on my first examination this morning", remarked Calvin. "Well, congratulations are in order then", said Mary Jane. "I am certain that that is just the first test of many", said Calvin. "Well, if I know you, you will ace them all", bragged Mary Jane. The chow line moved quickly and Mary Jane selected the special of the day, honey-baked ham and sweet potatoes with mixed vegetables and dinner roll. Calvin was tempted, but settled for the chicken and dumplings, a favorite of his from his childhood days on the farm. Food in hand, Mary Jane and Calvin moved to an empty table and enjoyed being alone for a change. "Sweetheart, I haven't had time lately to tell you how much I love you and I apologize for that circumstance", said Calvin. "Honey, don't concern yourself with that. I know that you are thinking about me and our babies and that is all that counts", replied Mary Jane appreciatively. "Speaking of the babies, have you obtained an appointment with the doctor in Las Vegas yet?", asked Calvin. "As it turns out, I spoke with his nurse this morning and have an appointment tomorrow afternoon, and I can take the Navy bus to Las Vegas and be back by the time you are finished for the day", said Mary Jane.

"Mary Jane, my time is running out so I must leave you now, I don't want to be late for class.", said Calvin. "You run along, Honey, I'm going to have a piece of pie and perhaps Jo

Anne will come along and we can talk some more", replied Mary Jane. "See you at 1700 then" Calvin called over his shoulder as he left the mess hall.

1300 Wednesday
1 April 1942
Gunnery School Navy Base
Holman, Nevada

Calvin took his seat as Mr. Briggs was speaking with several recruits at the front of the classroom. They were gathered around a device that appeared to be a cross between a special type of camera and a submarine periscope. "Gentlemen, this afternoon I am going to be discussing the features of the mark 33A 20-mm gun director, a sample of which you see before you. Please take notes because there is no literature available yet on this brand-new product development", cautioned Mr. Briggs. The clicking sound of opening 3-ring notebooks could be heard throughout the classroom. "And I am certain you can all appreciate at this moment the indisputable fact that for a gun to be effective it must be accurately pointed in the direction of the target. And, in the case of moving targets, it is also necessary to lead the target's movement such that when the projectile reaches the target it can effectively penetrate it and destroy it. In the past, pointing the 20-mm gun at moving targets has been facilitated by the use of what are known as tracer shells. Such shells leave the muzzle of a 20-mm gun and provide an illuminated visible reference of the projectile's trajectory or actual path to the target. In so doing, the gunner can determine the direction as well as the extent of any correction that might be required to reliably and repeatedly hit the intended target. In actual practice, the Navy has decided to make use of both elements to achieve maximum accuracy and the highest number of target hits. This new director makes use of electronic elements that allow the gunner to follow a target in his target window and be assured that the proper amount of lead and elevation are automatically provided to match the distance that the projectile must travel to effectively meet and destroy the moving target. Thus, the director and the backup tracer shells give the gunner the maximum support to achieve his objective of bringing down an attacking airplane. And, I might add, this same director is also being applied to the more powerful 40-mm guns now entering the fleet. In the case of the 40-mm guns, however, the directors are usually remotely mounted in either twin or quadruple gun configurations. One of the interesting aspects of the application of this new director to the 40-mm guns is that the director need not be attached to the gun itself as it is in its 20-mm application. Instead, it is mounted in close proximity to and slightly above and to the rear of the 40-mm guns in what is known as a director tub where the operator is situated with an unobstructed view of the target range available to the 40-mm guns. In convoy operations, provision is made in the form of an interlock to prevent a 40-mm gun from accidentally firing into an adjacent ship in the convoy", concluded Mr. Briggs. "Tomorrow, this company will travel to the gunnery ranges where you will each have the opportunity to fire live ammunition at moving targets that are towed by aircraft to provide a realistic and practical environment for training purposes. In these demonstrations, both directorized and non-director equipped 20-mm guns will be employed. This approach is necessary because the directors are only just now entering the fleet and it is likely that you will find the 20-mm post assigned to you will not be director equipped as yet. Are there any questions?", asked Mr. Briggs. No hands were raised. "In that case be ready to travel following roll call in the morning and have a good rest of the afternoon", concluded Mr. Briggs.

Leaving class with his textbook, Calvin returned to his

apartment hoping to find Mary Jane there. Lightly knocking on the door, Calvin entered to find Mary Jane taking a nap. With dinnertime yet three hours away, Calvin removed his clothes and slid in beside Mary Jane. Calvin listened to Mary Jane's calm and relaxed breathing and moved close enough to bring their bodies into contact. He decided not to wake her, but to just doze himself until she awakened on her own accord. Calvin lapsed into a dreamy sleep and was transported back to the Pullman coach in which they had spent so many wonderful days. As his dream was taking shape, Mary Jane awoke and was startled to find Calvin next to her. "Oh, Calvin, what a nice surprise to find you here", said Mary Jane. "Our class was dismissed early so here I am", smiled Calvin. In response, Mary Jane flung her arms about Calvin and drew him close while at the same time finding his lips with hers and letting him know that she was ready for some serious lovemaking. Being caught somewhat off-guard, Calvin quickly recovered and moved to eliminate Mary Jane's PJ's to clear the field for action, so to speak. With her breasts exposed, Calvin captured the left one in his mouth and proceeded to exercise its sensitive nipple and sensed the immediate erection of the pink trophy. Treating it, oh so gently, Calvin captured her other breast in his right hand and gently massaged its tender curves. In time, he moved his mouth to the opposite breast and continued to enjoy the taste of her nipple and sense its vibrant erection.

Rolling her body to face him, Calvin kissed Mary Jane and explored her tongue while he continued his exploration of her plump breasts. Now breathing hard, Calvin flung the covers off the bed and he could not suppress his gasp at the pleasurable sensation flooding his groin area. He and Mary Jane were locked in an exciting embrace and made love for the next hour. The couple was a contrast of blonde pubic hair versus red pubic hair as they satisfied each other's need for sexual release. As Mary Jane achieved her own passion amid a tiny squeal, Calvin did not remove his organ, but merely lay down beside his wife and allowed his limp organ to remain captured within Mary Jane's warm body.

"What a wonderful way to end an afternoon siesta", commented Mary Jane. "You've certainly got that right, Sweetheart", replied Calvin. When their body heat had returned to normal, Calvin and Mary Jane showered together. While they were drying themselves, Calvin said, "You know, Mary Jane, you have to be the most beautiful lady in the world and I am so happy that you are all mine". "Well, Calvin, if you're happy, then so am I". Following this exchange, the couple dressed for their evening meal. The sun was setting in the cloudless Nevada sky as Calvin and Mary Jane walked to the mess hall to enjoy their last meal of the day.

0700 Thursday
2 April 1942
Gunnery School Navy Base
Holman, Nevada

Leaving Mary Jane undisturbed to sleep-in, Calvin hurried through his breakfast and then headed for the Grinder and morning roll call. His platoon leader ordered the company to board the blue Navy bus which would take them to the firing ranges an hour distant into the forbidding arid desert. The ranges were totally isolated from public access and were rigidly controlled to assure the safety of all persons authorized to use the facility. And so it was that the bus arrived at the ranges about 0900. The company was initially taken to a training auditorium for a briefing on the day's planned events. The first speaker was the range safety officer, a lieutenant (jg) who explained the required procedures that would minimize the likelihood of any injuries occurring while the recruits completed their practice sessions using live ammunition. Following the range safety officer, a Chief Gunner's Mate took the podium, and using the static 20-mm gun mounted on the stage, demonstrated the proper loading, tracking and gun firing procedures. Using what he termed a dry firing exercise, no live shells were actually discharged during the demonstration. The Chief dwelt at length on the use of the safing control on the 20-mm gun to prevent it from being fired unintentionally. Calvin carefully followed the demonstration seeking to learn as much as he possibly could about the 20-mm weapon.

With the preliminaries complete, the company was divided into two-man teams for purposes of the day's firing exercises. Calvin was paired with another recruit by the name of Jimmy Miller who hailed from Ontario, California. Leaving the instructional building, the recruits were marched a quarter mile east to a series of about forty 20-mm guns mounted on permanent concrete foundations in a straight line that extended for several hundred feet. The barrels of the guns were oriented facing the south and had command of unoccupied, cactus-covered, desert land. It had been explained that a small single-engine airplane would appear towing a cloth target at which the novice gunners would shoot. The airplane was a single-engine Cessna with a military designation of L-19. The target was towed by a light rope that positioned it about 300 feet behind the airplane, hopefully keeping the pilot out of harm's way.

An experienced second class Gunner's Mate petty officer was assigned to each team of recruits, and Calvin volunteered to assist the instructor in mounting the 20-mm magazine containing the live 20-mm ammunition. In preparing to fire, the instructor Gunner's Mate cautioned the recruits to always place cotton wadding in their ear canals to safeguard their ear drums from the intense noise of the exploding shells. The Gunner's Mate also mentioned that the 20-mm magazine was filled with a mixture of standard and tracer shells. He demonstrated the manner in which the gun was cocked, made ready to fire, and placed in the 'safe mode'. Calvin and Jimmy were assigned to the first gun in the line-up and were ready for action when their instructor Gunner's Mate warned of the impending arrival of the towed target. It had been determined by a coin toss that Calvin would get to fire first. As the plane approached, Calvin moved the 'safety' lever to the 'off' position and he could see that the target would pass a few hundred feet south of their position, so he rotated the barrel of the gun to the right at about a forty-five degree angle to the horizon, intending to follow the target as it passed overhead. Calvin had the target in sight when the Gunner's Mate gave the command to "fire when ready". Calvin pulled the trigger and the 20-mm projectiles noisily leaped from his weapon, and he was able to direct his fire to lead the target by noting the paths followed by the tracer projectiles. Calvin observed that he was able to fire only a few shells due to the effective range to the target changing and moving out of range all too quickly. Subsequent guns also fired at the target and the company spotter recorded two hits for Calvin.

Ten minutes later, Jimmy got his turn on the second pass of the target and also scored two hits on the moving target. An hour later, Calvin and Jimmy were moved to a different 20-mm gun that was equipped with the newly-developed target director appliance. Taking his position behind the gun, Calvin was quite intrigued by the seemingly delayed response of the target objective to the moving target visible in the viewing port as it moved within the director. It seemed to him that the delayed reaction of the target objective was something akin to a person swimming in a huge bucket of oil, trying to outrun a shark. When it came time to shoot, Jimmy took his turn first while Calvin paid close attention. With the 'safety' off and the target approaching, Jimmy raised the gun barrel and prepared to fire. At the Gunner's Mate's command he fired and easily nailed the target, and one could see several tracer shells penetrate the target. "Good shooting, Jimmy", said Calvin. "With this new director, hitting a target is a piece of cake", bragged Jimmy. In a few minutes, the plane returned and Calvin took his turn to shoot. Lining up the director on the target, Calvin delayed a few seconds to get a feel for the lead/lag function of the director, and then he pulled the trigger and happily watched the tracers drill the target several times. It was a satisfying feeling knowing that, as inexperienced as he was, he could still hit a moving target so easily. Both Calvin and Jimmy received high marks for their performances that afternoon. It turned out that the company, as a whole, scored extremely well in the overall firing exercises that day. With the firing exercises completed, the company returned to the bus and relaxed on the hour-long return trip to their base.

In the following weeks, Jimmy and Calvin completed approximately fifty-five firing exercises at the firing ranges. These exercises included both 20-mm and 40-mm guns of non-directorized and directorized configurations. Calvin demonstrated an above-average aptitude for gunnery proficiency, and was commended by his instructors for his high marks scholastically and his demonstrated accuracy in shooting the guns on the gunnery ranges. At graduation time Calvin was awarded a commendation by the base commander and advanced to the rating of gunner's mate first class with the attendant increase in pay from gunner's mate third class to that of a first class petty officer. Calvin's meritorious advancement could be attributed mostly to his essentially photographic memory.

In contrast to the graduation ceremonies of the Great Lakes Naval Boot Camp, no parents or other visitors were permitted to visit the Gunnery base. In fact, there was no formal recognition of the graduation event at all. The recruits were merely provided with orders for their next duty assignment and, in Calvin's case, he was assigned to travel by the most direct route to catch the U.S.S. Zeilin where he would join the other gunner's mates in the crew somewhere in the South Pacific.

When he received his orders, Calvin visited the executive officer's office and spoke with yeoman Driscol regarding how he was supposed to reach the U.S.S. Zeilin. The yeoman advised him that he would receive a travel voucher for him and his wife that would get them to San Diego, where he would go on board a new destroyer that was leaving for the South Pacific and would deliver him to the U.S.S. Zeilin. Unfortunately, Calvin would have to make his own arrangements for his wife's travel to return to Des Moines, Iowa. Due to Mary Jane's sensitivity on the subject of her leaving Calvin in San Diego, Calvin elected to forego any discussion of their movements beyond the Holman Gunnery Base. There would be time enough for that once they arrived in San Diego where he would explain everything to her. Of course, Calvin realized that mere words were not gong to pacify Mary Jane as their time of parting came closer and closer. Calvin looked forward to that day with great foreboding and much dread. His route of travel would take Calvin to the South Pacific waters via San Diego and then Pearl Harbor, and ultimately to Wellington, New Zealand.

1000 Sunday
31 May 1942
Gunnery School Navy Base
Holman, Nevada

Travel orders in hand, Calvin and Mary Jane left Holman on the same bus on which they had arrived two months earlier. They would reach Las Vegas in an hour and then board a Pullman coach on the Santa Fe Railroad destined to arrive in San Diego two days later. Their Pullman coach would be switched off the Las Vegas train in Los Angeles and attached to another train that would take it to San Diego, where Calvin and Mary Jane would collect their sea bag/luggage and then find the U.S.S. Kingfisher that would take Calvin to the South Pacific. Although Mary Jane tolerated the relocation, she was increasingly depressed by the realization that Calvin would soon be leaving her.

1000 Tuesday
2 June 1942
Santa Fe Railroad Depot
San Diego, California

Calvin carried his sea bag and Mary Jane's suitcase to the coach vestibule where he handed them off to a depot porter for delivery to the taxi stand in front of the depot. Calvin and Mary Jane followed along as the porter led the way. At the taxi stand, Calvin spoke with the driver indicating that he and Mary Jane needed to be taken to the Destroyer U.S.S. Kingfisher that was tied up at the Navy pier on Harbor Island. With the door held open by the driver, Mary Jane and Calvin climbed into the rear seat and relaxed. Fifteen minutes later, the taxi pulled to a stop next to the pier beyond which the Kingfisher was tied up. The driver unloaded the couple's possessions, and after receiving payment, drove away. Orders in hand, Calvin approached the officer of the deck and requested permission to come aboard. Stepping onto the quarterdeck, Calvin turned toward the colors and saluted smartly, while Mary Jane waited impatiently on the dock. Saluting the lieutenant jg, Calvin said, "Good morning, sir". "Good morning, sailor, and what may I do for you today?", the lieutenant (jg) replied. Handing over his orders, Calvin said "Well, sir, according to my orders I am to accompany this ship on your journey to the South Pacific where I will transfer to the U.S.S. Zeilin APA-3, an Attack Troop Transport. However, I must admit at this point that I do not know where that transfer will take place". "Your orders are properly executed, so I suggest that you take them to our executive officer's office on the next level below, and that ladder over there will take you there", the lieutenant (jg) said, gesturing toward the nearest ladder. Calvin saluted again while thanking the lieutenant for his assistance, and headed for the ladder and climbed down to the next deck. The executive officer's office door was well marked and open, so Calvin walked in and spoke to the yeoman petty officer sitting just inside the door. Offering his orders, Calvin said, "Excuse me, but the officer of the deck sent me here; can you assist me? And, by the way, my name is Calvin Honeycut". The yeoman looked up and took Calvin's orders and examined them. "My name is Harry Bartlett, and I assume that you are an in-transit crew member of another ship. We have several of you aboard at this time", offered Harry. "Yes, it would seem that way", replied Calvin. "Well, you are one of many that will be making this trip. The ship departs day after tomorrow so you need to finish any business that you have ashore right away." "Thank you for the warning for I need to get my wife on a bus to Des Moines, Iowa, before the ship leaves. Will I need a pass to reboard the ship if I leave at this time?", asked Calvin. "Yes, here is a temporary badge that will allow you to come and go while the ship is tied up at the dock." "Thank you very much", said Calvin, taking the pass and placing it in his jumper pocket. "May I leave now and see to my wife's needs?", asked Calvin. "By all means, do so, but be aware that the ship departs promptly at 1300 day after tomorrow." "I am leaving to get my wife into a hotel room where we will remain tonight and I will see her off on a Greyhound bus in the morning", offered Calvin. Bidding Harry good-bye, Calvin, went back up to the quarterdeck, and saluting the colors, returned to Mary Jane waiting impatiently on the dock.

"Oh, Calvin, I was fearful that you were not coming back", lamented Mary Jane. "There is no problem, I just had to get my paperwork completed and receive a pass so that I can return to the ship tomorrow. Come, let's get a taxi and go check into a hotel in San Diego. The yeoman recommended the Drake Hotel on Union Street", advised Calvin. Snagging a taxi that had just been vacated by another sailor, Calvin said to the driver, "We need to get to the Drake Hotel on Union Street, please." "No problem, we'll be there in ten minutes", said the driver. Arriving at the Drake Hotel, Calvin paid the taxi driver and allowed the hotel valet to move Mary Jane's luggage into the hotel. Walking to the registration desk, Calvin said, "We require a room for one night, please. The yeoman on the U.S.S. Kingfisher recommended your hotel." "Thank you, sir, and we happen to have a nice oceanfront room for $15.00 on the third floor. Will that be satisfactory?", asked the clerk. "That will be fine, and here is a $15 deposit. "Thank you, sir, and here is your receipt and two room keys", replied the clerk, at the same time ringing for a bellman to handle the luggage and move it to their room on the third floor.

"Sir, I need to arrange for a bus ticket for my wife to return to Des Moines, Iowa. Is there a bus terminal nearby that I could visit?", asked Calvin. "As it turns out, we have a Greyhound office in this building. Just follow those stairs over there to the lower level and you will find an attendant who will be most happy to assist you and your wife", replied the clerk. "Come, Mary Jane, let's get this detail out of the way now", said Calvin. Taking her hand, Calvin led Mary Jane down the curving marble stairsteps to where the Greyhound sign was suspended above several desks on the lower floor, behind which ticket agents sat. "May I assist you, sir?" asked a pleasant blonde-headed lady. "Yes, if you please, I desire to purchase a one-way ticket leaving tomorrow from San Diego to Des Moines, Iowa, for my wife", requested Calvin. "The schedules show that there are many choices available. What time does your wife wish to leave?", asked the lady. Mary Jane spoke up saying, "I'd like to leave around 10 a.m., if possible". "It so happens that there is space for you on our 10 a.m. bus #465 and it will arrive in Des Moines two days later. The fare is $21 and I will require it to be paid now so that I can issue your ticket", concluded the Greyhound agent. Calvin handed over the money and Mary Jane's ticket was provided forthwith. "Please arrange to be in front of the hotel by 9:30 a.m. tomorrow so the bus can be loaded and depart on time", requested the lady. "Thank you very much for your assistance", said Mary Jane. "You're quite welcome", replied the Greyhound agent. "Come, Mary Jane, let's go up to our room and check it out", said Calvin.

The elevators were just around the corner from the Greyhound office so they did not have to retrace their path back up the stairwell to the lobby floor. Pushing the call button, Calvin waited with his wife until the door opened and they both stepped inside where he pushed the button for the third floor. In no time at all, the floor signal emitted a loud 'ding' and the elevator doors opened on the third floor. Calvin found their room two doors to the right of the elevator, where he inserted his key and he and Mary Jane entered to find their luggage neatly arranged on a small rack in the corner of the room. Walking to the window, Calvin marveled at the wonderful view of the ocean and the fact that he could plainly see the U.S.S. Kingfisher tied up to its dock along with many other U.S. Navy ships. "Come here, Mary Jane, and enjoy this lovely view", requested Calvin. Mary Jane joined Calvin, but he could sense that she was extremely depressed over the fact that they would be parting and going their separate ways in the morning. "Mary Jane, I know that you are disappointed that our time together is coming to an end, but from the beginning we have both known that we were living on borrowed time. We have had three wonderful months together; months that, in the beginning, neither of us thought would ever happen. We have been blessed to have this time together, and twice blessed by the fact that you are carrying our baby", consoled Calvin. "I know that what you say is absolutely true, but it is difficult for me to think about leaving you tomorrow and your leaving the next day for the South Pacific", lamented Mary Jane with tears in her eyes as well as tears streaming down both cheeks.

"Well, Mary Jane, let us place all this talk about leaving behind us for the moment, and go out and have ourselves an excellent dinner and then come back to our room and have the most romantic evening of our lives. Would that suit you, Sweetheart?", tempted Calvin. "Oh, yes, Calvin, that all sounds too wonderful for words", replied Mary Jane, making a supreme effort to stop crying. The hotel offered the famous Harvey House Restaurant so Calvin and Mary Jane elected to eat there. Arriving at the dinner hour of 1700, the Maitre d' seated Calvin and Mary Jane in a private corner away from other guests. Since it was a celebration of sorts, both lovers ordered margaritas to start the evening. Mary Jane savored the sweet flavor of the tequila and decided that she would limit herself to one drink so as to avoid any adverse impact on their after-dinner appointment. Calvin and Mary Jane both ordered steaks and a baked potato as well as a dinner salad for their meals. Eating at a leisurely pace, Calvin enjoyed observing his beautiful wife, and she gave him a dimpled smile from time to time. Like Mary Jane, Calvin limited his alcoholic intake to the one margarita for the same reason as his spouse. He absolutely did not want his sexual performance to be impaired for any reason on this 'night of nights'.

With their meal finished, Calvin paid their check and

escorted Mary Jane to the bank of elevators in the lobby where one stood open. Stepping inside, Calvin pushed the button for the third floor, and before he had time to steal a kiss, the door opened on their floor and other guests were waiting to enter. Stepping off the elevator, Calvin led Mary Jane to the right, and two doors later opened their room door and locked the door after they had entered. "Sweetheart, do you want to shower first or shall I?" asked Calvin. "Please go first and then I will take my turn", replied Mary Jane, now more able to control her composure. While Calvin was in the shower, Mary Jane stood at the open window marveling at the beautiful view of the Pacific Ocean across the bay surrounding San Diego. The Navy ships and their colored lights added to the beauty of the scene, as did the flashing lights of the airplanes coming and going to and from Lindbergh Field. Wordlessly, Calvin appeared in his bathrobe and, reluctantly, Mary Jane left the window scene and went to the bathroom to take her shower. While Mary Jane showered, Calvin carefully turned down the bed covers and smoothed the sheets ever so carefully. At the same time, he turned off the room lights leaving only the ambient light that filtered in from the setting sun and the San Diego Bay environment. The net effect of his endeavor was to produce a room illuminated by a soft warm glow approaching a peach color. The temperature of the room was perfect, and with the window now closed, it was also an exceedingly quiet, private, and secluded place for a rendezvous between a man and his wife. Calvin thought to himself that the room qualified as paradise!

With all in readiness, Mary Jane entered the room in all her glorious and naked beauty, voluptuous oval breasts and all. Calvin allowed his robe to fall to the floor and walked to where Mary Jane stood and took her in his arms, kissing her sweet lips, while searching her tongue and inviting her to do the same. As he stood holding his wife tightly in his arms,

Calvin gently urged Mary Jane toward their bed and then laid her on her back with her head in the center on a large, soft pillow, after which he lifted her legs and straightened them on the bed. For an unusually long moment, Calvin merely stood immobile enjoying and absorbing the heavenly vision of Mary Jane's body and breathtaking beauty, as if to commit the vision to a permanent and unfading image in the recesses of his brain. Calvin moved to lay next to Mary Jane, and kissed her body.

Taking her left breast into his mouth, he gently ran his tongue over her sensitive pink nipple and observed its familiar response to his manipulation. It was the same response that he had noticed in countless times past, beginning in her bedroom in Des Moines before he left for boot camp and then again on their wedding night at the Willard Hotel as well as on board the 'honeymoon' train's Pullman coach during their trip to Holman, Nevada. At the same time, he caressed her right breast with his right hand and continued to stroke her lithe body from breasts to legs as though laying on a film of body oil. His movements elicited shivers of joy and pleasure from Mary Jane. Thus it was that for the next several hours, did Calvin and Mary Jane satisfy each other's needs as they made love time after time. At length, the lovers lay in each other's arms and enjoyed the steady rhythm of their heartbeats as their passions cooled down and their sexual senses returned to normal. "What a way to end the day", was Mary Jane's spontaneous remark. Spent as they were, the lovers fell into a deep sleep, not to wake until the morning hours.

Having left a wake-up call for 0800, Calvin hurried to the telephone when it rang the first time. "Good-morning", said Calvin to the faceless voice on the other end of the line. "Thank you for the wake-up call", said Calvin as he hung up the receiver. Next, Calvin woke Mary Jane and led her to the shower where, in the interest of saving time, he joined her. With bus departure time approaching, the showers were all business except for Calvin's quickly stolen kiss planted on Mary Jane's left breast. Soon they were leaving their room to have breakfast at the restaurant off the hotel lobby. On his way past the registration desk, Calvin paid their bill and requested that a bellman bring their luggage to the lobby. While they ate their bacon and eggs, Calvin ordered a take-out roast beef sandwich and sweet iced tea beverage for Mary Jane to enjoy on the first leg of her bus trip, and when these items were delivered, he gave his wife enough spending money to last until she arrived in Des Moines, and then some. Calvin paid for their breakfast meals and he and Mary Jane made their way to the front of the hotel where they would await the arrival of the Greyhound bus.

0930 Wednesday
3 June 1942
Drake Hotel
San Diego

Departure time was approaching all too quickly. As Calvin and Mary Jane waited on the sidewalk, the hotel bellman delivered the bags of another female guest with space reserved on the Des Moines bus. In her deep depression, Mary Jane did not feel disposed to greet her fellow passenger at that moment.

0935 Wednesday
3 June 1942
Drake Hotel
San Diego, California

Following breakfast, Calvin and Mary Jane moved her luggage to the bus pickup zone at curbside in front of the Drake Hotel. It was quite early and they were essentially all alone on the sidewalk. Mary Jane clung to Calvin's waist as tears of sadness glistened in the corners of her blue eyes. It would be an extremely lonely trip returning to Des Moines, Iowa, all alone. "Mary Jane, I will write you often and send along my new address so you can write to me and let me know how your's and the baby's health is progressing", remarked Calvin. "Oh, that reminds me, Calvin, I never thought to tell you that the Las Vegas civilian doctor told me that everything was perfectly normal when he examined me last week before we left the Holman Navy Base for San Diego", reported Mary Jane. "I am so happy to learn that good news, Sweetheart. I am just so sorry that I will not be able to share the birth of our baby with you", complained Calvin. Before I forget, Mary Jane, I have arranged for an allotment to be sent to you by the Navy, so that you will receive monthly checks to pay for your living expenses" advised Calvin.

At that point the Greyhound bus pulled up to the curb with air brakes hissing and the driver stepped off the bus and quickly opened the doors to the cavernous baggage compartment. Calvin handed over Mary Jane's suitcase and moved his own sea bag to the front of the hotel so that it would not accidentally find its way into the luggage compartment and end up in Des Moines or some other point east of San Diego. In a loud voice, the driver called out, "All aboard", as Calvin swept Mary Jane into his arms for the last time and kissed her sweet lips. "I love you, Mary Jane, and will write you often to tell you of that fact", comforted Calvin. "Oh, Calvin, I can't bear to leave you like this", cried a distraught Mary Jane. Calvin kissed his index finger and placed it against her lips and squeezed her tightly one last time, and then she stepped into the bus. Calvin paced alongside the bus, staying opposite Mary Jane as she made her way down the narrow aisle. Eventually, she took a seat next to the window where he stood, and smiled her dimpled smile for him alone. Amid the hiss of air signaling release of the air brakes, the driver gunned his diesel engine and pulled away from the hotel curb. Calvin waved to Mary Jane until the bus rounded a corner and he could no longer see her. Calvin then hoisted his sea bag onto his shoulder and walked to the hotel taxi stand where he found transportation back to the U.S.S. Kingfisher.

0950 Wednesday
3 June 1942
Navy Pier
San Diego, California

Arriving at the dock, Calvin paid the taxi driver and walked up the gangplank, saluted the colors, and checked in with the officer of the deck, displaying his temporary pass. The officer of the deck cleared Calvin aboard and sent him to the executive officer's office for assignment of an in-transit berth by yeoman Bartlett. "Good-morning, Harry, and how are you doing this morning?", asked Calvin. "Hi, Calvin, did you get your wife off to Des Moines on time?", asked Harry. "As a matter of fact, the bus left right on time and I understand that her trip home will take two days. Harry, I came to see you because I need a place to call home while we are underway". "Yes, you do, Calvin, and I thought that it would be a good idea for you to muster with the other gunner's mates on the Kingfisher, so I am placing you in their compartment. Give me a couple of minutes to call someone to come up and show you the way to their compartment", concluded Harry. "Many thanks, Harry, but take your time, I've got all day", said Calvin. Five minutes later, Gunner's Mate Joseph Faulkner appeared and led Calvin to the division compartment near the stern of the ship. Joe placed Calvin's sea bag on an unoccupied top bunk and announced, "Well, Calvin, this is your 'home away from home' for the next week, so get comfortable; and over there, as he pointed to the starboard bulkhead, is a locker that you can use to house the items that you need on a daily basis such as your shaving gear, writing tablet, etc", concluded Joe. "Many thanks, Joe. I appreciate your hospitality." As Calvin settled in for his trip to the South Pacific, he had no doubt that he would be expected to stand gunnery watches like the rest the gunner's mates. In the rush of activities associated with settling into the Kingfisher routine, Calvin momentarily forgot about the fact that his wife had left for home.

1245 Wednesday
3 June 1942
Navy Pier
San Diego, California

Just before the U.S.S. Kingfisher set sail, Calvin hurried to write Mary Jane a short note so that he could get it posted before the ship left the dock and it would be waiting for her when she returned to Des Moines at the end of her trip on the Greyhound bus.

Calvin Honeycut
Gunner's Mate 1st Class
U.S.S. Kingfisher FPO 2695
San Francisco, California

My Darling Mary Jane:

The U.S.S. Kingfisher is about to cast off for its journey to Pearl Harbor, and before that occurs I wanted to send along a few lines to give you the address that will suffice to get your letters delivered to me when we reach port again.

I miss you so much already and want you to remember that I love you with all my heart and always will. Take care of yourself so that our child will be born healthy and strong.

When you arrive home, perhaps it would be an opportune time for you to confide in our parents, the fact that they are prospective grandparents.

I will leave that up to your discretion, but I think that it is time to let them know.

Till next time, I am, your loving husband.

CALVIN

Calvin quickly placed his letter into an envelope, wrote "Free" on the corner where a stamp would normally go (a wartime courtesy given to service personnel in WWII by the U.S. Post Office Department). He then hurried up on deck and down the gangplank to the U.S. Post Office box mounted on a concrete post beside the dock, where he dropped it in the slot and then quickly returned to the ship. The time was approaching 1300 which was the revised target departure time for the voyage to Pearl Harbor. Next came a call over the PA system urging all deck hands to man their departure stations. Calvin observed from a secluded, out-of-the-way location near the wheel house, as the bow, stern and spring lines were singled-up and then pulled in and the 'rat guards' were removed, and the lines were then finally stored in a deck locker. Amid a double blast on the ship's horn, the U.S.S. Kingfisher moved slowly away from the dock into mid-channel where it turned toward the south to exit San Diego Bay and then turn west toward Hawaii. With the ship rounding the tip of Point Loma, Calvin caught his final view of San Diego harbor. The U.S.S. Kingfisher was soon up to its cruise speed of 25 knots and Calvin could feel the vibrations set up by the engine and propellers through his feet.

On his way to the Gunner's Mate compartment, Joe intercepted him and delivered a message to visit the Chief Gunner's Mate's office. Approaching the office, Calvin was somewhat apprehensive, not knowing exactly what was to come. Knocking on the door jamb, the Chief said, "come in", and Calvin walked in to find the Chief seated behind a small desk. "Have a seat, Calvin. I had you stop by so that I could give you a copy of the duty schedule for our voyage to Hawaii", and with that the Chief handed over a printed page listing all of the Gunner's Mates' names and their daily duty and General Quarters locations and times. As Calvin studied the document, the Chief asked, "Do you have any questions?" "Yes, I do", replied Calvin. "Ask away", said the Chief. "Although I suspect that it shows up in my records, I thought that you should know that I am not qualified for the operation of the larger guns on this ship. In Gunnery School I was only taught to fire the 20-mm and 40-mm antiaircraft guns", revealed Calvin. "Not to worry, Calvin, we will teach you how to handle the five-inch guns that are in our main battery", said the Chief. "There will be gunnery practice en route and I will see to it that you are assigned to one of our top gunners, and in no time at all you will become an expert", encouraged the Chief. "Thank you, Chief. I am always anxious to expand my knowledge reservoir", replied Calvin. "Good for you, Calvin; it is always a pleasure to meet someone who is not afraid to learn something new. You will note that I have you assigned to the forward five-inch gun, and Joe Faulkner will teach you all you need to know about its operation when we undertake gunnery practice in a couple of days", concluded the Chief. "That is all that

I have for this time. Thank you for stopping by, Calvin". "It was my pleasure", and with that Calvin returned to his compartment to write a more lengthy letter to Mary Jane, for posting in Pearl Harbor.

Notwithstanding the Chief's announced intention, gunnery practice sessions were canceled on the voyage to Pearl Harbor, so Calvin missed out on his five-inch gun training indoctrination.

1200 Monday
8 June 1942
Pearl Harbor, Hawaii

Five days out of San Diego, the U.S.S. Kingfisher pulled into Pearl Harbor and Calvin was appalled to see the extent of the damage still visible from the Japanese attack, yet to be cleaned up in the harbor. The U.S.S. Kingfisher was scheduled to remain at Pearl Harbor for five days and then depart for Midway Island. However, the route of travel of the ship would not connect with the U.S.S. Zeilin so, in consultation with Navy transportation specialists, Calvin was instructed to move his possessions into the Navy in-transit facility barracks and await further orders. The result of that move was that Calvin became a lost soul, with no one particularly looking out for his interests. He enjoyed going on liberty every day, and covered the island of Oahu daily, essentially as a tourist. The months of July, August, and September came and went, and still Calvin languished in his Navy in-transit barracks. Enjoying the limbo in which he found himself, Calvin sent a telegram to Mary Jane advising her of his temporary mailing address as well as the fact that he was in a never-never land far removed from the fighting going on in other parts of the South Pacific. He also requested that she notify his parents of his new address.

On the 20th of September 1942, Calvin received a

telegram from Mary Jane that was to bring a supreme joy to his being.

WESTERN UNION TELEGRAM:

20 SEPTEMBER 1942

TO: GUNNERSMATE 1st CLASS
CALVIN HONEYCUT
C/O NAVY IN-TRANSIT BARRACKS
HONOLULU, HAWAII
FPO 6630

FROM: MRS. CALVIN HONEYCUT

SUBJECT: YOU ARE A FATHER!

MY DARLING CALVIN:

TODAY AT APPROXIMATELY 0600 HOURS, I GAVE BIRTH TO TWINS;ABOYANDAGIRL.STOPASWE AGREED, THEY WERE NAMED AMY LOUISE AND ALBERT LEROY STOP MOTHER AND CHILDREN ARE IN PERFECT HEALTH STOP MORE DETAILS TO FOLLOW IN A LETTER. STOP GRANDPARENTS OVERJOYED STOP I LOVE YOU, MY HUSBAND

MARY JANE HONEYCUT

END OF MESSAGE.

Calvin slumped in a chair and tried to comprehend Mary Jane's message and his misfortune in not being able to be with her when his children were born. But he consoled himself with the fact that the kids were born healthy and that they and Mary Jane were receiving good care. Calvin immediately sat down to write Mary Jane a letter.

1400 Sunday
20 September 1942
Navy In-Transit Barracks
Oahu, Hawaii

Gunnermate 1st Class Calvin Honeycut
C/O Navy In-transit Barracks
Honolulu, Hawaii
FPO 6630

My Darling Mary Jane:

Your telegram of this date just reached me and I am happy beyond any description that I can place on this page. Thank you, Darling, for being my partner in life and thanks to Sir Winston too!!!!!!

How I wish that I could be there to hold and kiss you and the children. Please perform that little task for me, if you would. When you can fit it into your schedule, please send me a photograph of MY VERY OWN FAMILY! I will look forward to seeing it sometime in the future. I am certain that Amy is as beautiful as her mother and Albert has to be as handsome as I am. Hee Hee.

Honestly, Darling, the mere thought of our marriage and the few days that we enjoyed together in Nevada and San Diego fills me with such a love for you that cannot be expressed in mere words on a *sheet of paper. Please take care of yourself and the children, and I hope to see you one day soon when you least expect me.*

YOUR LOVING HUSBAND
CALVIN

Having finished his letter, Calvin addressed the envelope, marked the corner "Free" and ran to the nearest U.S. Post Office mailbox and dropped his letter in the Main Land slot.

1000 Wednesday
30 September 1942
Des Moines, Iowa

Mary Jane had just finished feeding her children when the front doorbell rang. Hurrying to the door, she met her mother who was already halfway there. Opening the door, Mrs. Thomas saw their mailman with an envelope in his hand. As she opened the storm door, the mailman said, "I noticed the Navy postmark and thought that you would want to see this right away." "Oh, thank you, Mr. Smith. The letter is from my son-in-law and my daughter has been anxiously awaiting its arrival. Thank you so much for your courtesy", said Mrs. Thomas. Taking the letter, she handed it to Mary Jane who had come up behind her and heard the last part of the conversation. "Oh, Mother, it's a letter from Calvin", she exclaimed with glee. "Yes, like Mr. Smith, I surmised as much, what with the U.S. Navy postmark and all", replied Mrs. Thomas. Quickly opening the letter, Mary Jane read it and then handed it to her mother. "Oh, Mother, just look at this", she said. "Now that is what I call a precious letter", agreed Mrs. Thomas. "I want to share this with Calvin's family too", exclaimed Mary Jane. "That would be a nice gesture and I am certain that they would be over-joyed to have you do that", replied Mrs. Thomas. Reaching for the telephone, Mary Jane requested the Honeycut number from the operator. "Hello" came a voice from the other end after but a single ring of the bell. "Hello, Mom, do you have a minute?", said Mary Jane. "Of course, Mary Jane, I will always have time for you", she said. "I just received a letter from Calvin and I wanted to share it with you and Dad", replied Mary Jane.

After she had finished reading the letter, Mrs. Honeycut said, "Such a wonderful letter, Mary Jane. Thank you for your willingness to share it with us." "I know that Calvin would not mind", replied Mary Jane. "Although I do not have a way of copying the letter, I will make a handwritten copy for you and dad and send it to you in the mail", said Mary Jane. "Thank you, Mary Jane, that is so considerate of you to do that for us. I know that Dad will appreciate seeing Calvin's words", said Mrs. Honeycut. "When you have the opportunity, please stop by and visit your grandchildren, Mom", said Mary Jane. "Is one time better than another, Mary Jane?", asked Mrs. Honeycut. "No, any time will be fine, and bring Dad too", replied Mary Jane. "We have to be in town this afternoon so we will plan on stopping by at that time", said Mrs. Honeycut. "That will be fine and I look forward to seeing you then. Bye till later". "Good-bye Mary Jane", and Mrs. Honeycut hung up her telephone as did Mary Jane.

0800 Friday
1 October 1943
Navy In-Transit Barracks
Honolulu, Hawaii

Having spent essentially 17 months (from June 1942 to October 1943) awaiting transfer to the U.S.S. Zeilin,

Calvin questioned whether or not the Navy really needed him after all. Since he had exhausted his chain of command options in seeking remedial action within the in-transit barracks, Calvin decided to seek a higher authority. In so doing, he realized that he might jeopardize his career, but to do nothing also seemed equally unacceptable. Thus it was that he boarded a Navy bus at the barracks that would take him to the Pearl Harbor Base Personnel Office. Entering the white brick building, Calvin went to the window marked "Information" where a young female yeoman was standing. "May I help you, sir", she asked. "Yes, if you please. My name is Calvin Honeycut, Gunner's Mate 1st Class", whereupon Calvin handed the yeoman the orders he had brought with him from San Diego. "I came to Hawaii on the U.S.S. Kingfisher, but was off-loaded because that ship could not take me to the U.S.S. Zeilin where I am assigned. And I have been stuck here ever since, waiting for something to happen. Can you help me get to my ship?" lamented Calvin. "Wait here, Calvin, while I check with the lieutenant", replied the yeoman. Returning a few minutes later, the yeoman said, "Calvin, please walk down that hallway over there to Lieutenant Jorgenson's office. His name is on the wall beside his door, and he is expecting you." "Thank you very much", replied Calvin. Walking down the hallway, Calvin passed four offices before coming to Lt. Jorgenson's office where he knocked on the open door. "Come in", greeted him immediately. Stepping inside, Calvin stood at attention in the presence of the lieutenant. "At ease, sailor", said the lieutenant. "I understand from yeoman Butterworth that you are a man without a ship", said the lieutenant. "Yes, sir, that certainly is my problem and waiting any longer for something to happen on its own does not seem to be the answer to my problem", again lamented Calvin. "Well, Calvin, we come across these missing person situations once in a great while, but yours seems to be exceedingly unusual if for no other reason than the length of time you have been here in Hawaii and no one has seen fit to send you on your way. Interestingly enough, we have no record of your arrival here, nor do we have any follow-up inquiry from the U.S.S. Zeilin regarding your whereabouts. Those facts notwithstanding, I will fix the problem by setting you up to take a military air transport service (MATS) flight to catch up with your long-lost U.S.S. Zeilin", offered Lieutenant Jorgenson. "When can you leave?", the lieutenant asked. "I can go pack now and be ready in the morning", replied Calvin. "Very well. Here are your orders and I have included the necessary voucher to allow you to board the plane at Hickam Field. You can take the Navy bus from the in-transit barracks to the field. The plane leaves at 0800 so give yourself some extra time and don't be late. You will be flown to Espiritu Santo where the Zeilin is presently located. I want to apologize to you for whatever happened to delay you here in Hawaii so long", said the lieutenant. "Thank you so much for straightening it all out", replied a relieved Calvin. Catching the same Navy bus back to the in-transit barracks, Calvin busied himself the rest of the day packing his sea bag with all of his personal possessions. Once he was packed, Calvin visited the mailroom and filled out the necessary form to assure that his mail would be forwarded to the U.S.S. Zeilin. With nothing else to do, Calvin rode the Navy bus to Hickam Field to scope out the place for tomorrow's big day. He identified the terminal building where MATS flights originated, and then returned to the barracks to write Mary Jane a letter.

Gunner's Mate 1st Class Calvin Honeycut
C/o Navy In-transit Barracks
Honolulu, Hawaii
FPO 6630 Forward To U.S.S. Zeilin,
At Espiritu Santo

Dear Mary Jane, Amy and Albert:

I hope that this letter finds everyone in good health and enjoying life. Today, I finally succeeded in speaking with a Navy lieutenant who arranged for me to leave Hawaii and finally catch up with my ship the U.S.S. Zeilin. I fly tomorrow to Espiritu Santo in the New Hebrides Islands where the ship is presently located. Somehow, my orders were lost and I have essentially been on an extended vacation here for the past 14 or so months. I have enjoyed seeing all of Oahu, but am ready to move on with my life. There are no guns to shoot around here. Hee Hee. I trust that your mom and dad are fine as well as my own. I have not heard from them in a while. Well, I guess that is all for this time. I will write again when I arrive on board the U.S.S. Zeilin. Till then, you know that I LOVE you all!

All my love from your husband and father.

Calvin

Calvin placed his letter in an envelope wrote "FREE" on the corner where the stamp would normally go and walked to the mail room where he dropped it into the U.S. Main Land slot.

0630 Saturday
2 October 1943
In-Transit Barracks
Honolulu, Hawaii

Calvin arose at 0630, showered and dressed for his trip to the New Hebrides Islands. Carrying his sea bag, he walked to the front of the barracks and sat down on a bench at the bus stop. He had hardly had time to sit when the bus arrived. Walking to the bus, he carried his sea bag and climbed aboard. Twenty minutes later he was leaving the bus at Hickam Field. Entering the MATS gate area he walked to the petty officer who seemed to be managing the passenger boarding process and handed over his travel voucher. Returning his orders, the petty officer said "Please have a seat and we will be calling for boarding in about fifteen minutes". From a developing habit, Calvin took a seat next to the access gate to the plane which he could see outside the large window. It was a Douglas C-47 and he was familiar with the plane, having ridden in its civilian counterpart known as a Douglas DC-3 traveling to and from his Navy boot camp assignment. At 0745 the boarding call was made and Calvin joined the other passengers walking through the door carrying his sea bag which he deposited on the baggage cart at the bottom of the steps leading into the plane. Walking inside, Calvin took a seat in front of the wing adjacent to a window. He selected a seat on the side that he knew would be away from the sun while the plane was airborne. He knew that the view would be better looking away from the sun rather than into it.

Promptly at 0800 the pilot started the engines and was soon taxiing to the main runway. "Ladies and gentlemen, please secure your safety belts in preparation for our departure", warned the pilot. A female Navy petty officer walked the aisle checking for compliance with the pilot's order. The roar of the two engines assaulted his ears during takeoff and caused Calvin to wish that he had some cotton wadding as he used on the 20-mm gun firing range at Hollman, Nevada. Calvin was relieved when the noise level decreased significantly once the plane reached its cruising altitude and the pilot retarded the throttles to cruise power. The flight was about 2,700 miles and would be completed in about nine hours.

1645 Saturday
2 October 1943
Espiritu Santo Airport

Landing at Espiritu Santo, Calvin was in awe at the primitive facilities that passed for an airport. However, this was wartime and an out-of-the-way location at that. Leaving the plane, Calvin collected his sea bag and sought directions to the shore where he would find the U.S.S. Zeilin. A Navy jeep was nearby and a friendly chief petty officer offered Calvin a ride. "Where are you headed, sailor?", asked the chief. "Well, my name is Calvin Honeycut and I am about 14 months late in reaching the U.S.S. Zeilin on account of a foul-up at Pearl Harbor", complained Calvin. "My name is Chief Willouby, so take a seat and I will have you at the U.S.S. Zeilin's dock in no time at all. As it turns out, I am part of the crew of the U.S.S. Zeilin myself, but I am on detached duty helping out at the airport for a few days", said the chief. Throwing his sea bag in the back and climbing in, Calvin relaxed as the chief drove off toward the north where the anchorages were located. Fifteen minutes later, Calvin got his first glimpse of the long-lost U.S.S. Zeilin anchored about a mile off shore. The chief pulled to a stop on a block-long dock and parked. "This is as far as I go. A launch will be here shortly and it will take you out to the ship", said the chief. "Thank you very much for the lift, Chief Willouby. I really appreciate your assistance", replied Calvin, as he retrieved his sea bag and placed it on the dock.

Within ten minutes, the launch tied up to the dock and Calvin climbed aboard with his sea bag at the urging of the coxswain. Several sailors departed the launch and the chief took two of them back toward the airport. After waiting fifteen minutes, the coxswain fired up his Cummins diesel engine and backed away from the dock to return to the U.S.S. Zeilin. Calvin relaxed on the launch and enjoyed the short Higgins boat ride out to his ship. Climbing the gangway to the quarterdeck, Calvin carried his sea bag, and after saluting the colors, presented his orders to the officer of the deck. "Welcome aboard, Calvin" offered Lt. (jg) Thompson, officer of the deck, and that is when Calvin and Melvin Eugene Hacker met each other for the very first time. It was sheer happenstance that I was passing the quarterdeck as Calvin came aboard ship. I was off duty, at the time, and had just come from the mess hall and was returning to the '7th' Division compartment. "Melvin, would you mind showing Calvin to the executive officer's office?", asked Mr. Thompson. "It will be my pleasure, Lieutenant.", I replied. "Calvin, let me give you a hand with your gear and then follow me.", I said. Pointing to my right, I said, "We need to take that ladder to the deck below and the office you seek is right at the bottom." Five minutes later we were standing in front of the executive officer's office and Calvin entered to hand over his orders to Yeoman Shropshire, as I said, "See you later, Calvin." "Many thanks, Melvin, and I will look you up once I get situated in the gunner's mate quarters.", replied Calvin. "Good enough, but bear in mind that I go on watch at 2000 and will be on duty until 2400" ,said Melvin. "On that basis, I think that I will just plan on seeing you at breakfast in the morning", said Calvin. "I'll be there about 0700", I replied. "See you then", said Calvin, as I climbed the ladder back up to the quarterdeck.

Example of a DC-3

Melvin Eugene Hacker with his arm around his sister Ida Mae who is sitting on the hood of Mel's 1936 Ford sedan. Sister Marilee Van is standing next to the front fender. Mel is wearing the insignia of a RADARman Second Class. This photo dates from 1944 when Melvin was home on leave from the U.S.S. Zeilin (APA-3).

Seaman First Class Melvin Eugene Hacker while he was assigned to the U.S.S. Zeilin attack troop transport (APA-3). Campaign ribbon earned during the invasion of Kiska, Alaska. Circa 1943.

This photo dates from 1944 when Melvin and Calvin Honeycut were on liberty in Pearl Harbor, Hawaii where the photo was made.

Melvin Eugene Hacker taken by street photographer while on liberty in Manila, P.I. Uniform is rumpled due to rain storm that blew in.

Melvin Eugene in the uniform of a Second Class RADARman from the U.S.S. Zeilin. Circa 1944.

CHAPTER THREE

KAMIKAZE THE DESPERATE TIME

0900 Friday
31 December 1943
Sokubei Yamagucci Home
Tokyo, Japan

Seventeen-year-old Yaeko Yamagucci was born to Sokubei and Shuko Yamagucci on 25 March 1926. Coming as he had from a merchant family, Yaeko was schooled by his parents in the rituals of Japanese commerce. He spent his formative years in the Japanese public school system, in and around the city of Tokyo. When war with the United States became a reality on 7 December 1941, Yaeko consulted with his father and mother on how he could best serve his emperor. By that time, he had not entered any of the Japanese military services because he was underage. The result of that meeting was Yaeko's decision to pursue a long-standing interest that he had developed in flying. As a youngster, Yaeko had joined various flying clubs, where he had learned the principles of aircraft operation as well as the scientific principles of flight itself. Indeed, one of the clubs that he joined flew gliders. It turned out that Yaeko was an extraordinarily apt student, and soon became proficient enough to not only fly solo from a field near his home, but he also became a certified flight instructor for gliders and was licensed by the Japanese government.

Barely three weeks following Japan's sneak attack on Pearl Harbor found young Yaeko accompanying his father to the headquarters of the Japanese Naval Air Force recruiting office in Tokyo. There, enlistment papers were duly signed and witnessed. Yaeko was required to complete a battery of aptitude tests, which he passed with above-average test scores. These tests became the basis for the selection of his first duty assignment which was to a Naval Aircraft Training Academy based at Kobe, Japan, on the shores of the Harima Sea. Arriving at the Japanese seaplane base, Yaeko was immediately assigned to a primary flight training regimen, along with approximately 50 other new pilot recruits. Yaeko's initial training included classes to study the Mitsubishi A6M2 Zero Model Carrier-based single engine airplane. Its 950 horsepower 14-cylinder engine earned it a sterling reputation among U.S. pilots of WWII. It was capable of outperforming many of the American fighter planes in the early part of the war in the Pacific The ultimate objective of the Japanese training program was to qualify the young pilots to operate their aircraft from aircraft carriers upon graduation. Japan needed an inordinately large number of pilots to man the flight decks of aircraft carriers then engaged in supporting Japan's expansionist endeavors in the South Pacific and other regions including Alaska, such as the Aleutian Islands.

Thus it was that Yaeko was assigned to a barracks on the seaplane base and commenced his primary training. Upon arriving the first day, all recruits were issued their uniforms, shoes, parachutes, and other items of clothing and equipment designed especially for pilot needs. At the same time, Yaeko was issued training texts associated with the airplanes that he would eventually learn to fly. Included in the materials that he received were flight schedules and a training syllabus for his ground school classes. Although the pilots would not be required to maintain their training aircraft engines or air frames, they nevertheless were expected to be able to suggest corrective measures, based upon their observations of any abnormal aircraft performance condition.

For the first three weeks at the training academy, Yaeko did not get close to an airplane. Instead, he and the other recruits were exposed to endless hours of lectures by instructor pilots in the flight performance parameters of their aircraft in general, as well as to the operational characteristics of the specific airplanes that they would eventually encounter when they moved from textbook classes to actual flight operations. Not all of the recruits were as dedicated as Yaeko, and there was an undercurrent of complaining among many recruits because of the long study days that were enforced. Of course, the intent of the government's accelerated training program was to produce as many competent pilots as possible in the shortest amount of time possible consistent with turning out 'safe' pilots. After all, airplanes did not grow on trees and marginal pilots tended to crash their planes at a rather high rate. Not only would the government lose the cost of the very valuable aircraft itself, but in many cases the pilot would be killed, thereby losing the government's investment that had been sunk into his training. Nevertheless, the long hours prevailed and, in the main, resulted in yielding highly qualified pilots. Yaeko applied himself diligently and took copious notes on topics and tips that had not been reduced to writing and published in Japanese pilot training manuals. This was particularly important when the topic of aerial combat techniques was presented by veteran Japanese pilots just back from the warfronts in the South Pacific and elsewhere. Once the novice pilots had absorbed the fundamentals of flight, including takeoff and landing procedures, normal stall modes, accelerated stall modes, never-exceed airframe speeds, control limitations and all of the other parameters, including weather prediction, it was time to think about actually climbing into an airplane and leaving 'mother earth'. At the end of 30 days of intense instruction, Yaeko was assigned to his first (and only) flying instructor, Major Aritomo Sako, a 30-year veteran of military flying, now occupying a training command assignment on account of a minor service connected physical disability.

0700 Monday
31 January 1944
Japanese Navy Base
Kobe, Japan

Having observed his assigned flying schedule on the barracks bulletin board the previous day, Yaeko was waiting for his instructor at the primary training field designated for fledgling pilots. Yaeko was filled with pleasant anticipation over his finally being able to fly, even if it was with a training instructor. And, how different powered flight would be, contrasted to his earlier days of flying gliders. Yaeko was standing in the ready room waiting when Major Sako walked in. Yaeko saluted smartly and accompanied his tall instructor outside to their Zero model training plane. "Yaeko, if you do not learn anything else from me, I want you to concentrate on the steps that I take to assure that our airplane is ready to fly today. Too many novice pilots make dangerous and careless assumptions about an airplane's flying condition and those assumptions often end up killing the unwary pilot. To begin with, we will perform a 'walk around' to visually verify that all is in readiness for us to start the engine and take off. First of all, please climb into the cockpit and remove the "control lock fixture", requested Major Sako. (A control lock is standard equipment on every airplane, notwithstanding who the manufacturer is, and is provided to minimize the possibility of damage to control surfaces and control cables when gusty wind conditions prevail while the aircraft is tied down, by immobilizing the rudder, elevator, and ailerons.) "Yes, sir, it will just take me a moment", replied Yaeko. Opening a small aluminum door in the side of the plane, Major Sako said, "Please place the control lock in here so that we will have it available when we land later on". Yaeko complied without comment. "In performing a 'walk around' one of the most important aspects is consistency; that is, always perform the 'walk around' exactly the same way every time. In that way, you will not omit an important inspection that could bring you and the plane down out of the sky needlessly", warned the major.

"The inspections begin at the tail assembly where we gently move the elevator throughout its full up-and-down limits to verify that there is no impediment to its travel. As you know, it is the elevator that determines the horizontal attitude of the plane. While moving the elevator, inspect the hinge points for missing hardware such as cotter pins, lock nuts, spacer washers, etc. and be attentive to any resistance, hesitancy or binding in the movement of the elevator. Following the elevator inspection, move the rudder full left and right while also checking for any missing or loose attach hardware at the hinge points. At the same time look for any deformation in the control surfaces. If any bent surfaces are noted, these need to be reported, and the airplane grounded pending its repair. If there is any resistance observed in either the rudder or elevator controls, do not fly the plane, but refer your observation to the airframe mechanic for inspection of control cables, pulleys or other elements of the control system. Continuing from the tail assembly, we next look at the static port on the port (left) side of the fuselage to verify that it is unobstructed. Sometimes, maintenance crews will place transparent tape over that port to exclude water while washing the plane. With that port blocked, your altitude, rate of climb and other atmospheric pressure-sensitive instruments will not provide correct indications. And in making this inspection, place your fingertip on the port to physically verify that there is no transparent tape covering the orifice. Being on the port side, we next inspect the aileron for both movement and damage and, as before, we look for any missing attach hardware. Moving to the leading edge of the wing, we inspect the pitot tube for any possible obstruction. If the pitot tube is obstructed, your air speed indicator cannot reveal your actual flying speed and this deficiency can be very disastrous. Bear in mind that small insects have been known to build mud nests in the pitot tube orifice so look carefully into the opening every time you fly.

"Following the pitot tube, make a visual observation of the fuel level. A pilot can never have too much fuel. If the tank is not full, summon the line boy and have the tank 'topped off'. Next we check the quality of the fuel by capturing a small sample in the transparent fuel test tube. There are three inspection points on this plane. One beneath each wing tank and one beneath the engine compartment near the carburetor. All three points must be checked for the presence of water. Water will not mix with aviation fuel and appears in the test tube as individual droplets of a colorless liquid. If water is found, continue taking samples until the fuel is clear and no water is forthcoming. If the tank was not full and the line boy adds fuel, you must recheck the quality of the fuel in each tank again to verify that no water was introduced during the refueling process. It is extremely important that you realize that only a very small amount of water can disable an engine and cause it to shut down. Next we check the stall-warning blade that protrudes slightly ahead of the wing leading edge on the port side. Gently move the blade and release it to return to its normal position. It shall not be restricted in movement nor shall it bind or 'hang-up' in an abnormal position. While walking around the wing, look for any bent areas on the tip and leading edges that might interrupt normal air flow. And speaking of normal air flow, one must be doubly alert to surface contamination during winter months. A thin layer of frost can interrupt normal air flow to such an extent that the plane can stall and crash on takeoff. Always have your wing and tail surfaces de-iced in winter conditions.

"Moving to the engine compartment, we first check the oil level. If it does not reach the 'full' mark on the dipstick, have the line boy add oil. Pay attention to the quality and quantity of the oil supply for it is the lifeblood of your engine. All of our airplane engines utilize a viscosity rating of 50W. Close and secure the oil inspection port and then check the propeller for nicks or other damage. Nicks of up to one-sixteenth inch depth are allowed, but if the propeller is bent or otherwise damaged, do not start the engine or fly the plane; instead call a mechanic. Moving to the starboard (right) side of the airplane, check the wing tank for fuel level, leading edge and tip for dents or other damage. While under the wing, inspect the tires and landing gear for damage and adequate tire tread. As on the port side, do not forget to check the starboard static port for any tape obstruction. Remember to check the aileron for movement and any deformation that would be cause for grounding the plane. In the 'walk-around', verify that the radio antennas are in place and undamaged. In this verification, include both the communications antenna and the radio navigation antenna. As a reminder, the Zero is considered a complex airplane because it is equipped with retractable landing gear and a variable pitch propeller" concluded the major.

0900 Monday
31 January 1944
Japanese Navy Base
Kobe, Japan

With the 'walk around' complete, student and instructor climb into the Zero and prepare to launch. Wearing their parachutes, Yaeko and the major have good visibility through the Zero's glass canopy. Using his engine start check list, Yaeko soon has the engine idling and warming up. By means of the local intercom channel, the major directed Yeako to taxi to the main runway where they waited for takeoff clearance from the local tower. While waiting, Yaeko performed his engine run-up, magneto checks and propeller cycling exercise as well as verifying that adequate oil pressure was present. At length, they receive a green light from the tower and Yaeko smoothly applies power as he rides the right rudder pedal with his foot to offset the engine torque that attempts to push the Zero off the runway centerline to the left. The aircraft quickly reaches flying speed, and Yaeko notices that the tail of the aircraft is already flying as he gently pulls back on the elevator control stick and the airplane leaves the runway. Yaeko mused that his glider training was standing him in good stead from the point of view of making control inputs of a smooth and gentle nature. Once in the air, Yaeko reduced his engine 'RPMs' to cruise climb power and retracts his landing gear and wing flaps. He also adjusts the variable pitch propeller to the proper setting. Flying above the nearby cities, Yaeko experiences a mind wrenching feeling of pleasant exhilaration and happily wishes that his flight would never end. Major Sako interrupted Yaeko's reverie with instructions to turn to various headings while climbing and descending. At the end of an hour of intensive maneuvers, the major instructed Yaeko to return to base without specifying a heading to follow. Yaeko was concerned at first for he had not really paid attention to the direction that they had traveled from their home field. Of course, he was further confused as a result of all of the many turns and altitude changes that Major Sako had given him during the hour. Pulling out his local area aeronautical chart, Yaeko soon oriented himself by referring to his compass and comparing the chart to prominent landmarks visible beneath his Zero. Following a clearing turn to check for the presence of other aircraft, Yaeko turned south toward the training field on a heading of 185 degrees. As he flew the Zero closer to the field, he could soon see the tower, and at that point he contacted the controller by radio for landing instructions. The tower operator cleared Yaeko to land on the same runway from which he had departed about an hour earlier. On the intercom link, Yaeko asked, "Major, is it your intention that I land the plane today?" "Yes, it is. Just come in over the threshold at 90 knots and flare as you have learned from your text and the simulator. However, be certain to perform your landing check list to make absolutely certain that nothing is omitted, and your landing will be a successful one", advised the major. Yaeko went through the checklist noting most importantly the 'gear down' check and 'flap' settings. With no crosswind to speak of, Yaeko slightly reduced his engine 'RPMs' and set up his descent of 500 feet per minute toward the threshold. He brought the Zero in over the runway numbers in a gentle descent and essentially greased the plane onto the runway, noting with extreme satisfaction the gentle 'chirp' of the tires as they kissed the runway. Evenly applying the individual wheel brakes, Yaeko brought the plane to an exit taxiway, and then parked the plane in the same place that he had vacated earlier that morning.

"Yaeko, that was an excellent flight altogether, and the landing was especially good. I am very favorably impressed with your abilities as a pilot with no more experience than you have had", complimented the major. "Thank you very much, honorable major. It all felt very familiar for some reason. Will we be flying again tomorrow?", asked Yaeko. "Yes, indeed, we will. In fact, we will be flying every day for the next week, so that we can quickly work into instrument flight conditions, as well as emergency descent maneuvers. You still have a lot to learn before I turn you loose on the fleet." The major's remarks were music to

Yaeko's ears. "And once you have mastered the Zero, you will graduate to the Hayate Ki-84 Hurricane, and then the twin engine 'Betty' Bomber", concluded the major. "Yaeko, I also want to commend you for your ability to maintain your 'situational awareness' while flying. That attribute is extremely important for a pilot to cultivate. Many students are unable, for whatever reason, to develop that ability. When I directed you to return to base, I intentionally did not give you a heading so that I could ascertain whether or not you could determine where you were and then turn to a heading that would bring you home. You did exactly the right thing by pulling out your aeronautical chart to determine your present position and then select a course on which to return to base. A most favorable performance, Yaeko-san", said the major. "I am honored. Flying was a very harmonious experience", replied Yaeko. At that point the major made the appropriate entries in Yaeko's pilot logbook and then returned to his quarters. Yaeko lingered by the Zero for a few extra moments while basking in the warmth of the knowledge that he had successfully completed his first fledging flight, albeit one with an instructor aboard. Prior to leaving the plane, Yaeko installed the control lock and wheel chocks.

During the next several weeks, Yaeko's time was divided between flying and classroom instruction. His flying time was devoted to flight maneuvers of ever-increasing complexity. These included power-on and power-off stall recoveries, spin entry and recovery, minimum speed at which controllability can be maintained, as well as dead-stick landings in the face of an engine that has failed, were practiced repeatedly. This latter maneuver taught Yaeko to nail the specific airspeed for the Zero that will produce the greatest forward movement of the aircraft for the least amount of altitude loss. (Every airplane has its own specific airspeed number for this condition, and it is always published in the Pilot's Operating

Handbook for the airplane of interest). In his quest for pilot certification, Yaeko occasionally compared notes with some of his novice pilot friends and found that none of them had a better instructor than Major Sako. Some students complained bitterly about the treatment that they were accorded at the hands of some of the all-too-often arrogant, high-time instructors who seemed bent upon intentionally disqualifying their novice student pilots. Yaeko offered those friends his sympathy, but, of course, there was nothing that he could do to aid them, other than to encourage them to persevere and hope for success in the end.

0900 Saturday
26 February 1944
Japanese Navy Base
Kobe, Japan

With no training flights scheduled for the weekend, Yaeko requested weekend leave and his request was approved by Major Sako. With his liberty pass in hand, Yaeko traveled by electric train to Tokyo for a visit with his parents and family as a whole. It would be his first trip home since enlisting. Although he had written home to tell his family of his progress in becoming a pilot, he had not called them on the telephone. In return, he had received two letters from his mother in that period.

Knocking on the front door of their unpretentious home, Yaeko entered, called out to his parents and was immediately greeted by his mother in her silk kimono and obi. Clasping her arms about her son, Mrs. Yamagucci spoke softly into his ear. "I am most happy to see you, honorable son. Father will return home soon and will be equally happy to greet you", confided Mrs. Yamagucci. "Mother, how nice to hold you in my arms once again", replied Yaeko. "Tell me, how long can you remain with us?", asked Mrs. Yamagucci.

"Unfortunately, not too long for I have to be back on base first thing Monday morning", said Yaeko. "Such a short visit, but we know that this is your karma. I will prepare your favorite foods and we will enjoy the aura of peace in each other's company", said Mrs. Yamagucci. By then, she and her son had moved into the kitchen where dinner was being prepared. Based upon a main course of shrimp and lobster, Mrs. Yamagucci had prepared side dishes of cabbage and noodles along with vegetable soup and hot baked rolls. The fragrance in the kitchen was overwhelming to Yaeko, who had not tasted a home-cooked meal since leaving for his solitary military life.

Yaeko's father returned home and entered noisily, not realizing that his oldest son had come for a visit. "Yaeko, what a wonderful surprise to see you here again. And will you be with us for very long?", asked the father, parroting his wife's greeting.. "I'm sorry to report that I must be back at my Kobe base on Monday morning. That means that I must take the late train from Tokyo on Sunday evening to avoid being AWOL", lamented Yaeko. "I have one full day to enjoy mother's home cooking, and what a treat it will be to absent myself from the mercy of the military chefs", joked Yaeko. Interrupting at this point, mother Yamagucci encouraged her husband, Yaeko and the rest of the family to move into the dining room where the traditional, almost floor-level tables and tatami pads were to be occupied by the family. At that time, Yaeko greeted his two sisters and younger brother who had been outside playing games with the neighborhood children. It was a festive occasion, and Yaeko's mother had ignited several incense sticks and the fragrance brought back fond memories to Yaeko, and it was a struggle for him to retain his composure and will away the tears of happiness that gathered behind his eyelids.

Mrs. Yamagucci served their food and then joined the family as Yaeko's father offered a short prayer for the health of his family, the nation and that of the emperor. Small portions of warm sake were served following the meal, and Yaeko particularly enjoyed this treat, for the drinking of alcoholic beverages by pilots-in-training was absolutely forbidden and strictly enforced on base. Yaeko had observed more than one of his friends who disobeyed this requirement and were promptly and unceremoniously discharged from the military flying service. With the meal consumed, Yaeko and his father moved to the living room to occupy comfortable chairs while they discussed the progress of the war with the United States. The other children went outside again to continue their games as mother cleared away the soiled dishes and, in general, cleaned up her kitchen. Yaeko and his father enjoyed each other's company until eleven p.m. when it was time to retire for the day. Yaeko's room had been taken over by his younger brother following his departure to the military, so his mother made him a pallet on the living room floor for his short stay. As she left the living room his mother bid Yaeko "good-night" and at the same time turned out the lights except for a dim 'nightlight'. After brushing his teeth, Yaeko lifted the blanket of his pallet and laid his tired body down. It had been a long day and he was happy to be at home, perhaps for the last time before he was shipped out to some unknown military duty assignment. As he drifted off to sleep, he was vaguely aware of the tantalizing aroma of his mother's incense still lingering in the calm air. "Oh, to be home", he thought to himself, "brings such happiness", and Yaeko fell asleep with visions of his precious Zero airplane dancing in his dreams. Although Yaeko's flying schedule resulted in a somewhat hectic existence, he did not object to that fact for he reasoned that the more he flew, the better pilot he would eventually become. Resting at home, as he was, gave him an excellent opportunity to contemplate any problem areas that were confronting him at the academy.

1000 Sunday
27 February 1944
Yamagucci Home
Tokyo, Japan

Yaeko enjoyed the luxury of sleeping-in after his first night at home. When he finally awoke, he could hear his mother and father conversing quietly in the kitchen, where the family normally took their meals. Rolling out of bed, Yaeko went to the bathroom to brush his teeth and get dressed. Leaving the bathroom, Yaeko passed his younger brother waiting in the hallway who he acknowledged by playfully ruffling his dark hair as he passed by. Yaeko straightened up his pallet and then went to the kitchen to greet his parents. "Good-morning, honorable mother and father. Thank you for allowing me to sleep-in this morning", said a grateful Yaeko. "It seemed the least that we could do knowing that your military life is accompanied by very early arising each day", replied his mother. "Yes, indeed, I know about such things, having been a soldier myself. It seems to me that military men always operate in a sleep deprivation mode and rarely get the opportunity to catch up", concluded Yaeko's father. "This is most true", replied Yaeko. "However, now that I am part-way through my pilot training, I am finding that I do not have to spend quite so much time studying my text books in the evening as was the case when I first entered basic training. It is still a hectic life in some ways, but I am accustomed to it and can accept the sacrifices involved", concluded Yaeko.

"Sit down, Son, and let me serve you some breakfast", said mother Yamagucci. "Thank you, Mother, I could certainly enjoy something to eat about now", replied Yaeko. "We are having rice cake, cold noodles, and your favorite tea", replied Mrs. Yamagucci. Yaeko's father was quiet during the exchange, but then spoke up, "What are your plans for today, Yaeko?", asked his father. "Actually, I do not have any plans. I did not want to be constrained to anything special, I merely wanted to have time to spend with you, my parents", concluded Yaeko. "Well, in that case may I make a suggestion?", asked Mr. Yamagucci. "Yes, most honorable father", replied Yaeko. "When you were younger, we used to walk down by the sea on weekends and watch the boats in the bay, as well as the sea gulls wheeling overhead in the blue sky. It was my thought that we might be able to relive old times", said Yaeko's father. "I think that that is a wonderful idea, and we can leave as soon as I finish my meal. Thank you for thinking of such a memorable activity", said Yaeko.

The Yamagucci's lived only four blocks from Tokyo Bay and son, mother and father were soon walking down a sidewalk leading to the bay. Although it was a cool end-of-the-winter day, the sun shone brightly from a cloudless blue sky and the pleasant fragrance of hibiscus blossoms filled the air. The trio walked along at a leisurely pace basking in the warmth of each other's company. Yaeko spoke of some of his flying experiences, while his father recounted some of his recent business dealings which, coincidentally, were most positive as well as profitable. It seems that Mr. Yamagucci's fledgling company had recently secured a government contract to furnish uniforms for a branch of the military, and the contract meant that the family's earlier struggle to launch their business was at an end. Yaeko congratulated his father and mother on their good fortune. About that time, the family reached the shore of the bay and walked along it for a short distance, at which time Yaeko stopped, knelt down, and removed his shoes to walk barefoot in the cool damp sand. The parents elected to leave their shoes on as they continued their walk. The tide was in, and fifty yards from shore rode a number of colorful fishing boats at anchor. Presently, Yaeko and his parents came upon a local bay-shore fish market laid out on beached skiffs lining the shore of the bay. The local fishermen displayed their early morning catch on crushed ice within glass gayly painted display cases. The prices were reasonable, and Yaeko asked his mother if she would agree to cooking some fish if he made a purchase. "By all means, Yaeko, it would be my pleasure", replied his mother. Yaeko selected several halibut and yellowtail fish and the fisherman carefully cut them up and wrapped them in seaweed, ice, and newspapers to maintain their freshness until the family returned home.

After leaving the fish market, the trio continued their walk and soon came to a pier extending out into the bay. They elected to walk out onto the pier, and the gulls that Yaeko's father had recalled in their earlier conversation were squawking overhead and competing for food being tossed to them by children running along the pier. At the end of the pier, which was perhaps 1,000 feet in length, they came upon a vendor who was selling sushi. Yaeko purchased a portion for each of them and they sat down and relaxed on a concrete bench at the edge of the pier. Several men were fishing nearby and the family watched as several catches of sea bass were pulled onto the pier as they continued to enjoy their snack. The day was passing by all too quickly, and with Yaeko's train time approaching in early evening, it was decided that they had best return home and see to the cooking of their fish dinner.

Thirty minutes later, Mrs. Yamagucci was in her kitchen with a pan of cornmeal, breading their fish dinner and preparing her oven to bake them a golden brown. The fisherman had already skinned the fish and cut it into manageable slices making them ready for cooking. While the meal was cooking, Yaeko went into the neighborhood and found his siblings to ask them to return home for an early dinner. In this task he met no resistance, as his sisters and brother were hungry from their afternoon of play. Returning home, the children helped place napkins and dishes in the dining room and the two girls busied themselves at making a large pot of rice.

When the fish pieces were cooked, the family gathered in the dining room and became silent as Mr. Yamagucci offered a prayer of thanks for their food, and again blessed his family, nation and the emperor. There was little conversation during the meal and that suited Yaeko, as he disliked the prospect of leaving his family again after such an extremely short visit. After he had eaten his meal, Yaeko said his good-byes to his brother and sisters and his parents. Hugging his father, Yaeko said, "Thank you so much for such a wonderful day. Our trip to the bay brought back so many fond memories". "You are most welcome, honorable son. Your mother and I experienced the same joy at recalling the times long since past", replied Mr. Yamagucci. Hugging his mother, Yaeko said, "Mother, I want to thank you for the fine meals that you prepared while I was here, and the pleasant hospitality as well". "It was my pleasure, Son, and I hope that you can come again very soon", replied Mrs. Yamagucci.

With his train departure time approaching, Yaeko left his home at a brisk walk for the few blocks to the railroad depot and purchased his ticket. By that time, the sun had set and the darkness of night was already upon the station platform. The train arrived amid the sound of screeching brakes and Yaeko entered a nearly empty coach. There was no waiting time as the train moved out of the station almost as soon as Yaeko sat down in his seat. Although the coach was well lighted, Yaeko had brought nothing to read so he merely observed the passing images through his window. The tracks passed through what could only be termed the 'seedy' part of Tokyo itself. Tenement slum dwellings were crammed together with commercial structures and the few lights that existed gave a gloomy aura to the track-side melange. The gloom was enhanced by the thin fog that was drifting in from Tokyo Bay. An hour later, the train stopped and Yaeko walked onto the platform at Kobe. It was a ten-minute walk to the naval base. Upon arrival, Yaeko presented his identification badge and was admitted by the posted navy security guard. By then, the base was quiet as one would expect on a Sunday night with all flight operations having been terminated over the weekend. Yaeko returned to his barracks and slipped into his nightclothes and went to bed. For a time, he tossed and turned, reliving his brief visit with his family. Eventually, he fell asleep dreaming of his walk along the beach beside Tokyo Bay with the seagulls flying in circles and squawking loudly overhead.

0700 Monday
28 February 1944
Japanese Navy Base
Kobe, Japan

Following breakfast, Yaeko went directly to the flight line and performed a 'walk around' of the Zero that had been assigned to him for use that day. Based upon his accumulated flight hours, Yaeko had previously been certified for solo flight, so Major Sako would not fly with him today. Nevertheless, Major Sako had signed off in Yaeko's flight log that he was qualified to make the solo flight. With the major's certification, Yaeko was authorized to make has first long distance, solo cross-country flight. This flight would take him about 300 miles north of Kobe and test his ability to navigate, using only checkpoints on the earth's surface. On the return leg, he would be permitted to use his radio navigational aids, but not on the outbound leg. It was what pilots call a 'CAVU' day (clear and visibility unlimited). Absolutely blue skies and calm winds; the best of all pilot worlds. Yaeko's destination was a small navy auxiliary field located at Shizuoka on the shores of Suruga Bay. Checking his charts one last time following his 'walk-around' inspections, Yaeko climbed aboard and, as was his habit, moved his controls throughout the extreme ranges of their movements. He observed that the ailerons moved in the correct directions as did the elevator and rudder. Major Sako had repeatedly impressed upon Yaeko the importance of performing this check because airframe mechanics had been known to accidentally miss rig control wires during maintenance tasks, causing needless and, at times, deadly crashes.

Yaeko started his engine, checking immediately that there was adequate oil pressure, and then allowed the engine to warm up. When he was satisfied that all was in order, he called the control tower and requested taxi instructions. The tower cleared him directly to the end of the main runway 36. Arriving at the runway, Yaeko locked his brakes and performed his usual engine run-up to check his magnetos and variable pitch propeller. All indications were normal, so he returned the engine to idle. Rolling in the proper amount of takeoff elevator trim and wing flap deflection, Yaeko called the tower and was immediately given takeoff clearance. Applying right rudder to keep the Zero lined up with the runway centerline, in the face of the extremely high engine torque, Yaeko's plane quickly reached flying speed and he eased back on his control stick and observed the Zero leave the runway. With no other planes in sight, and a positive rate of climb having been achieved at 100 feet elevation, Yaeko retracted his flaps and landing gear and set his cruise climb power and assumed the direct heading of 060 degrees toward his destination. From his cruise flight altitude, Yaeko called the tower and requested that his flight plan be opened. Having spent so many flight hours in the Zero, Yaeko was perfectly at ease during his solo flight. The air was smooth and the drone of the strong engine gave him a feeling of power that he had never noticed before.

Approximately one and one-half hours into his flight,

Yaeko had verified his passage over Osaka, Mtsusaka and Toyohashi checkpoints. Twenty minutes from his destination, Yaeko called the local tower at Shizuoka for landing instructions. He was advised that there was no traffic in the pattern and he was to use the main north south runway 18. Descending gradually with his flaps extended, Yaeko lined up on his downwind leg of 360 degrees, and was at pattern altitude when he passed the field and turned left on his 270-degree base leg at the desired 90 knots of airspeed. With his gear extended, and his pre-landing check list complete, Yaeko noted that the windsock was pointing directly down the runway toward him, so there was no crosswind correction required. Pulling the throttle back, the Zero gently floated down to a perfect touchdown, after which Yaeko departed on a taxiway toward a main hanger where he could obtain fuel for his now near-empty tanks. As he braked to a stop next to another Zero, Yaeko shut down his engine, again performing the required shutdown check list (pilots live by check lists). A line boy appeared and inquired, "Will you be needing any fuel?" "Yes, I would appreciate your topping off both right and left tanks, please. Also, please provide me with an invoice that I may submit to Kobe so that you can be compensated for this fuel load", requested Yaeko. "That is no problem, for it is our standard practice where the military is concerned", replied the line boy. "There is something else that I need. My flight today is a long, cross-country training mission, and I would appreciate having you sign my pilot log as proof that I actually arrived at Shizuoka", requested Yaeko. "Most certainly, I will gladly sign it now", replied the line boy. Yaeko climbed down from the cockpit and opened his pilot logbook on the edge of the wing for the line boy to sign. Next, Yaeko walked into the Base Ops office to purchase a soft drink and stretch his legs in the process. Sitting confined in the cockpit of the Zero for more than an hour tended to cramp his legs.

After consuming his soft drink, Yaeko went to the pilot's ready room and called for a weather briefing, during which time he closed his flight plan from Kobe. Thankfully, the clear skies that he had passed through on his way to Shizuoka would remain for his return trip to Kobe. Following the briefing, Yaeko filed his flight plan and then returned to his aircraft for yet another 'walk around'. Although the routine was time-consuming, and seemed to Yaeko, at times, to be of questionable value, he faithfully performed the required inspections. Better 'safe than sorry' was his motto. Even though he had requested that his fuel tanks be topped off, Yaeko dutifully opened the fuel tank caps and inspected both left and right tanks to verify that the fuel was actually in place, which it was.

Following this inspection, the fuel quality inspections were completed, but no water was detected. Removing the wheel chocks and pulling on his parachute harness, Yaeko climbed into the cockpit. After attaching his safety belts and radio headset, Yaeko ran down the pre-start checklist and then, with his feet on the brake pedals, started his engine. Oil pressure came up instantly, as was expected, and he relaxed while the engine warmed up a bit. He had been on the field long enough for the engine to completely cool down. Although he was not as yet what one would call a journeyman pilot, Yaeko had learned that a warm engine was less likely to stumble or balk with the application of full power on takeoff if the cylinders had had a chance to reach a reasonable level of heat.

Yaeko called the tower for takeoff instructions and was directed to use the same runway on which he had landed. Rolling onto the run-up pad, Yaeko locked his brakes and performed the run-up magneto checks as well as propeller cycling and RPM verification checks. At the same time, he moved his control stick throughout its ranges of movement and observed that the ailerons and elevator still moved in the correct directions, and that the rudder responded correctly to his left and right pedal pressures, as it should. Pulling the throttle to idle, he called the tower for takeoff permission, which was given immediately. While speaking to the control tower operator, Yaeko requested that his flight plan for the return trip to Kobe be opened. The tower operator reported that his plan was open. Checking that his flaps were in the correct position, and the elevator trim was properly set, Yaeko slowly pushed his throttle forward and waited for the Zero to reach flying speed, at which time he gently pulled back his control stick and the Zero became airborne again. Passing through 100 feet, Yaeko retracted his landing gear and flaps as he set up cruise climb power. With no other traffic in sight, Yaeko climbed to 5,000 feet for his return trip and reduced his RPM's to cruise power level. Upon reaching cruising altitude he also tuned in the navigation radio to the Kobe frequency, at the same time taking up a heading of 240 degrees. Of course, Yaeko realized that he was much too far from the Kobe transmitter to expect to receive its rather weak direction finding signal from his present position, so he merely headed in the general direction of Kobe, looking again for the ground checkpoints that he had used on the outbound leg of his solo flight. Somewhat over an hour later, Yaeko noticed his direction finding needle 'come alive'. As soon as he observed a solid lock-on, he made the minor course correction required to fly directly to his home field. Twenty miles from his destination, Yaeko called the tower operator for landing instructions. The tower operator advised Yaeko to descend to pattern altitude and call again when five miles out. Pulling his throttle back slightly, Yaeko put in a notch of flaps when his speed had bled off to the safe flap-operating speed. By the time he reached the five-mile checkpoint, Yaeko was at pattern altitude when he checked in again. The main runway 36 was clear of traffic by that time and the operator cleared him for a straight-in approach to landing. Cranking in landing flaps and extending his landing gear, Yaeko finished his pre-landing check list as he lined up on final for a straight-in approach to runway 36. Ever more comfortable with the flying characteristics of the Zero, Yaeko enjoyed hearing the 'chirp' of the tires as they smoothly contacted the runway and told him that his plane had quit flying. Another flawless landing, he thought to himself. Rolling out to a taxiway, Yaeko called the tower and requested that his flight plan be closed, as he flipped the switch to retract his extended flaps. Yaeko parked his plane in its usual place and inserted the control lock just before he climbed down from the cockpit. Throwing his leg over the edge of the cockpit, Yaeko found that his legs were more than a little stiff from the long duration of the outbound and return flights. Walking into the base ops building, Yaeko delivered his fuel invoice to the airman in charge and then sought out Major Sako. Finding him in his office, Yaeko proudly displayed his log entry for his long cross-country flight. "Good work, Yaeko. You are making excellent progress", he added. "Thank you, honorable major. I very much value your opinion. It seems that the more I fly, the easier it gets, but I suppose that is the natural way of things", observed Yaeko. "There is no doubt about it, that 'practice does, indeed, make perfect', Yaeko", replied Major Sako.

3 March to 31 March 1944
Japanese Navy Base
Kobe, Japan

For the remaining four weeks of March 1944, Major Sako kept Yaeko busy increasing and refining his knowledge of flying procedures. A significant and most important accomplishment during this period was Yaeko's qualification as an instrument-rated pilot. Over 100 hours were spent in the air as well as practicing on a simulator teaching Yaeko to fly using only the flight instruments visible on the plane's instrument panel. In the beginning, Yaeko was apprehensive when all he could see was fog when he looked out of the cockpit canopy while inside a cloud. But, as time went by and he became more adept at reading and interpreting the instruments for airplane speed and attiude, as well as listening to his engine RPM's as they rose and fell, he was able to relax and beneficially apply himself to the tasks at hand. After he had accumulated about 125 hours under the hood (flying in clear weather but with blinders in place that prevented him from seeing outside the cockpit) Major Sako took Yaeko up for his instrument check ride. Upon landing at the conclusion of his evaluation, the major signed Yaeko off as a certified instrument pilot in his pilot logbook. "Yaeko, you have fulfilled all of the requirements of the academy for single engine aircraft with the exception of undertaking landings on aircraft carriers at sea. Acquiring this important knowledge will be your next assignment. Please accompany me to my office and I will provide you with a copy of the pilot operating handbook for the Nakajima Ki-84 Hayate (Hurricane). This aircraft has come to be known as the 'Frank' for American identification purposes", concluded Major Sako as he and Yaeko walked through the door to the major's office. "Yaeko, take this manual and study it this evening, and tomorrow I will fly with you to Yokosuka where there is a suitable training facility for practicing carrier landings. Please note that this aircraft is a single seat interceptor and fighter bomber and is equipped with a 1,900 horsepower fuel-injected radial engine comprised of two rows of nine cylinders for a total of 18 cylinders. The fundamentals that you have learned while flying the Zero apply equally well to the 'Hayate' so you should not experience any difficulty in transitioning to this more sophisticated as well as more powerful airplane", concluded the major. "Honorable major, I will be prepared for tomorrow's flight and am looking forward to it with pleasant anticipation", replied Yaeko as he saluted smartly and returned to his barracks to begin studying his new aircraft manual.

0700 Monday
10 April 1944
Japanese Navy Base
Kobe, Japan

Walking into the Base Ops office early Monday morning, Yaeko checked the duty schedule to ascertain which airplane had been assigned to him for his flight to Yokosuka. Memorizing the tail number, he signed the aircraft control log and then headed for the flight line. Among a series of nine Zero aircraft on the flight line, Yaeko located his 'Hayate', and after removing the control lock, commenced his 'walk-around' inspection. The 'Hayate' was offered in two configurations, and he noted that his assigned aircraft was the 'Ki-1-a' model and was equipped with armament of two 20-mm Ho-5 cannon in the wings, each with 150 rounds; two 12.7mm type 103 machine guns in the upper fuselage each with 350 rounds and two racks beneath the outer wing panels for bombs or fuel tanks of up to 550 pounds. Fully loaded, the plane had a maximum speed of 388 miles per hour and could achieve an initial climb rate of 3,600 feet per minute. The specimen that Yaeko was inspecting was a training version that was equipped with two pilot seats, one for the student pilot and one for the instructor who had access to dual controls. The 'Hayate' was also manufactured in "Ki-1-b and "Ki-1-c models that were equipped with larger caliber guns.

Yaeko verified that the control surfaces and propeller were undamaged and that the rudder, elevator and ailerons were free and unimpeded in their movements, and that all attach hardware was properly in place. Since this was an orientation flight, Yaeko verified that there was no ammunition on board. Yaeko found the fuel tanks to be full and fuel samples to be free of water contamination. As Yaeko completed his 'walk-around', Major Sako appeared with his parachute already in place. "Good morning, honorable major, and how are you this morning?", asked Yaeko. "Well, Yaeko, I am feeling fine and what say we fire this 'Hayate' up and go for a ride", joked the major. "It will be my distinct pleasure to do just that", replied Yaeko. Snapping his parachute straps in place, Yaeko removed the wheel chocks and climbed into the front cockpit as the major mounted the rear cockpit and slid his canopy closed. Yaeko pulled on his radio headset, while closing and locking his canopy at the same time. As Yaeko was preparing to run through his engine start check list, Major Sako came on the intercom line. "Yaeko, I just want to comment on the fact, in case you missed it in your reading last evening, that this airplane is somewhat more demanding than the Zero that you are used to flying. For one thing, the 'Hayate' engine has about twice the horsepower compared to the Zero so you have to be prepared for things to happen much more quickly. I believe that it would be best if we limit our travel today to a 100-mile radius from Kobe and cancel our plan to fly to Yokosuka", concluded the major. "Yes, honorable major, I was quite impressed by the specifications of the 'Hayate' and wish to have you guide me through an indoctrination flight in this aircraft. If you are ready, I will take off now", stated Yaeko. "Yes, I am ready and once we are at a safe distance from this airport I will suggest several maneuvers for you to practice", offered the major. Yaeko then ran through his engine start check list and soon had the Nakajima Homare Ha-45 model #11 18-cylinder engine idling smoothly. He then called the local control tower for a weather briefing and runway assignment. The weather briefing concluded with "Hayate' 84-Zulu cleared to runway 36 and remain on this frequency until otherwise advised".

By that time, the engine temperature and oil pressure was normal and Yaeko applied enough throttle to cause the plane to roll onto the taxiway as he turned toward runway 36. Reaching the run-up pad, Yaeko locked his brakes and exercised the engine magnetos and propeller prior to setting his elevator trim and takeoff flaps. Pushing the mixture control to 'full rich', Yaeko called the tower and announced his readiness to depart. "Hayate 84-Zulu cleared to depart and fly runway heading", replied the tower operator. With all in readiness, Yaeko gradually advanced his throttle and he was greatly surprised by the rapidity with which the plane responded to the applied power from its 1,900 horsepower engine. Flying speed was gained quickly, and riding the right rudder pedal to keep the plane on the runway centerline, Yaeko eased back on his control stick and the 'Hayate' immediately became airborne. On the way up to 100 feet, Yaeko retracted his flaps and landing gear and set in cruise-climb power. The Kobe tower called and advised, "Hayate 84-Zulu, resume own navigation and frequency change approved." With no need to converse with other aircraft, Yaeko dialed in the Kobe airport common channel radio frequency which he would monitor throughout his familiarization flight.

While on a heading of 360 degrees and climbing through 10,000 feet, Major Sako broke the silence on the intercom channel by asking, "Yaeko, do you know what a chandelle maneuver is." "Yes, sir, I am familiar with the maneuver in theory, but have never performed one", replied Yaeko. "Well, then, let's see if you can take your theory and put it into practice. In a dogfight, the chandelle is a very valuable tool to allow you to reverse course in an expeditious as well as safe manner", counseled the major. Remembering the profile of the chandelle from his textbooks, Yaeko made a clearing turn to check for any conflicting traffic nearby, and finding none, lowered the 'Hayate's nose slightly and applied additional throttle. The speed of the airplane quickly increased as he hauled back on the control stick and pointed the nose straight up. When Yaeko felt the plane slow down in its climb, he pulled the control stick further back and as the plane began to turn over on its back, he put in full left aileron and brought the plane upright to a horizontal attitude and found himself flying in the opposite direction from the beginning of the maneuver. "Yaeko, your execution of the chandelle leaves nothing to be desired. It was a textbook execution", complimented the major. For the next hour, Yaeko executed more than a dozen chandelles as well as many other 'dogfighting' maneuvers that the major described and Yaeko rendered in the air.

At the end of three hours of flying the major requested that Yaeko return to base. Dialing in the Kobe radio direction finding frequency, Yaeko found the heading to be 185 degrees and he promptly turned to that heading. Five miles from the field, Yaeko called the tower and was cleared to land on runway 36. From his present heading, he overflew the field on a heading of 180, and a mile past the runway turned on his base leg of 090 degrees and then left to 360 degrees for his final approach. Lined up on final, Yaeko performed his pre-landing checklist, bringing in his flaps, extending his landing gear, and setting up a 500 feet per minute descent. Since the 'Hayate' was a much heavier plane than the 'Zero', Yaeko elected to come in over the numbers at 100 mph and arrest his descent just before the landing gear touched down. Yaeko observed a satisfying 'chirp' as the 'Hayate' smoothly met the runway after which he parked the plane in the location from which he had departed several hours earlier. Shutting the engine down, again by the checklist, Yaeko heard Major Sako on the intercom complimenting him on the quality of the flight. "Yaeko, I am exceedingly pleased that you take your flying so seriously. Your perusal last evening of the pilot's operating handbook for the 'Hayate' showed in everything that you did this afternoon, and I am proud to have been an observer on this flight. I did not observe any action on your part that was dangerous or in any way abnormal", concluded the major. "Thank you, honorable major, I am pleased to learn of your observations", said Yaeko. Returning to the major's office Yaeko handed over his pilot logbook for it to be endorsed for the day's 'Hayate' familiarization flight. Although Yaeko found the 'Hayate" to be a much more responsive aircraft than the Zero by virtue of its much more powerful engine and its harmonious control system, the added power did not cause him to feel intimidated in any way. Indeed, he looked forward to his next flight in the airplane with pleasant anticipation. Regardless of the compliments delivered by Major Sako, Yaeko resolved to spend additional time studying the Hayate pilot operating handbook, particularly where emergency procedures were concerned.

1 April to 7 April 1944
Japanese Navy Base
Kobe, Japan

During the first week of April 1944, Major Sako put Yaeko through increasingly complex maneuvers in the 'Hayate' fighter/bomber. His intent was to prepare Yaeko for certification as an aircraft carrier fighter pilot. Yaeko completed several hundred landings on an aircraft carrier that was, fortuitously, on maneuvers in the vicinity of the Yokosuka Naval Base following repairs of wartime damage. The result of this intensive period of training was the certification of Yaeko as a qualified carrier pilot. With his certification as a carrier pilot came a promotion for Yaeko from cadet to ensign, and happily an increase in pay. Yaeko called his parents immediately to inform them of his advancement and they congratulated him on his good fortune and noteworthy progress in his flying career. At the same time, he invited them to attend the award ceremony slated for one week hence.

1600 Sunday
9 April 1944
Hero's Shrine
Japanese Naval Aircraft Training Base
Kobe, Japan

Cadets, officers and their families filled the seats of Hero's Shrine located on the Kobe Training Academy Base. The occasion was the acknowledgment of promotions to new military ranks that were achieved by active students-in-training. Vice-admiral Matome Ugaki, in all his sparkling military finery, was seated in a prominent location on the stage. At 1605, the Kobe Base Commander moved to the podium, which was flanked by many flags of the Rising Sun. Following the commander's welcoming remarks, the admiral took his place at the podium to add his own welcome to those in attendance. "Ladies and gentlemen, officers and students, parents and instructors. I come here today to bring the best wishes of our Emperor for your valiant efforts in preparing yourself to protect your homeland. The enemy that we are fighting is strong and resourceful, but we must be even stronger and more resourceful. I have witnessed your combined efforts here at your academy and am satisfied that Japan is second to none in the field of aircraft development and utilization. You novice pilots are being provided with the finest and most advanced aircraft in the world today, and I am certain, will give an excellent accounting of yourselves once you reach the front-lines of our conflict with the United States. I conclude my brief remarks by extending my congratulations to each of you pilots for your demonstrated skills and well-earned ratings that will now be bestowed upon you. You will leave Kobe with the knowledge and abilities required to vanquish your foe on the field of battle. I thank you for your kind attention".

The assembled audience came to their feet and acknowledged the admiral's comments by energetic applause. As the applause waned, the Kobe Base Commander took the podium and announced, "Will the members of the awards committee please take your places." Following this announcement, staff instructor pilots walked onto the stage, as award recipients lined up alongside the stage. There were 200 pilots-in-training on the base and all of those students in Yaeko's class had been in training long enough to be promoted to the rank of sho-i (Naval rank of Ensign). Yaeko stood in line and waited patiently for his turn to receive his wings. Thirty minutes later, Yaeko heard his name called by Major Sako and he climbed a two-step riser to the stage. Whereupon, the major began to read a citation that he had prepared. "Ladies and Gentlemen, this pilot is Yaeko Yamagucci of Tokyo, Japan. It has been my extreme pleasure to have had Yaeko assigned to me as his instructor. Within the first week of our association, I observed that Yaeko was a natural born flyer. That is, he demonstrated an intuitive knowledge and ability to absorb the techniques of the many flying procedures and effectively demonstrated them in the air. In my view, Yaeko is quite gifted as a pilot and it is my distinct pleasure to present him with this certificate and gold wings which are emblematic of the pilot position of sho-i in the Japanese Naval Service. Yaeko, please accept this emblem as a token of the esteem in which you are held at this base." "Thank you, major, I will certainly do my utmost to live up to the noteworthy confidence that you have expressed in me here today. If I may, at this time I would like to also express my appreciation to my mother and father for their unfailing support of my flying endeavors over the years." As Yaeko was the last pilot to be so recognized, the Base Commander again took the podium to invite the assembled audience to the base mess hall for an evening meal. "Ladies and Gentlemen, if you will, please follow the pilot corps as they leave the hall, they will lead you to the mess hall where a meal awaits you. Thank you very much for taking the time to attend this celebration." Yaeko shook hands with the major after the major had pinned Yaeko's wings in place. "Major, will you be going to the mess hall?", asked Yaeko. "Absolutely, Yaeko". "The reason that I inquired is that I would like to introduce you to my mother and father." "It will be my very great pleasure to meet them", said the major. Over the next fifteen minutes, Yaeko and the major walked to the mess hall where they eventually found Yaeko's parents. "Mother and father, I am pleased to introduce you to Major Arimoto Sako, my pilot instructor. Major, this is my father, Shuko Yamagucci, and my mother Sokubei", said Yaeko. "It is a great pleasure and honor to make your acquaintance, Mr. and Mrs. Yamagucci. Yaeko has told me a great deal about you in our off hours of flying", revealed the major. "Likewise, major, Yaeko from the beginning has sung your praises as the 'best instructor on the base", said Yaeko's father with a cordial smile. With the introductions complete, the foursome moved to the serving line and enjoyed each others' company as they ate their food. Later in the evening, Yaeko went to bed with a warm glow about him for the fact that he had finally made officer rank in the Japanese Navy.

0700 Monday
10 April 1944
Japanese Navy Base
Kobe, Japan

Following his breakfast, Yaeko headed for Major Sako's office where he found the major waiting. Today, Yaeko was to receive his indoctrination flight in the twin-engine 'G4M Ishiki Rikukoh Bomber'. This bomber was commonly known in the U.S. and Allied circles as the 'Betty Bomber'. As Yaeko entered the major's office, he called out "Good-morning, major". "Good-morning, Yaeko, and let us go out to the flight line and I will take you up on a familiarization flight in one of our new twin engine 'Betty Bombers'. In addition to piloting the plane, you will eventually be instructed in how to manage your flight crew on bombing missions as well as protecting against enemy fighter aircraft attacks", said the major.

Leaving the major's office, Yaeko lengthened his stride in an attempt to keep up with his tall instructor. On the flight line, the Mitsubishi 'Betty Bomber' was an imposing, even intimidating, war machine. Built around a long cylindrical fuselage, it was supported by an even longer tapered wing that included two 1,800 horsepower radial Mitsubishi engines mounted near the fuselage, with space for the landing gear to retract into the engine nacelles. The major and Yaeko spent fifteen minutes completing the 'walk-around' inspections. Then, the major disappeared into a belly access hatch, and Yaeko followed along behind. Inside, the major took the left command pilot seat and motioned Yaeko into the copilot position. Pulling out a checklist from a side pocket of the cockpit, Major Sako began the pre-engine-start regimen. Yaeko followed along as best he could, realizing that he had a lot more to learn than he had ever bargained for. With the engines primed, the major closed the start switch and the engines sprang to life. Following a couple of throat clearing 'pops,' the engines settled into their loping rumble with propeller and engine vibrations being passed along into the air frame. Major Sako handled the radio requirements and was given taxi instructions to reach the main runway. Yaeko was favorably impressed by the high vantage point of the pilots' seats and the excellent visibility through the windshield.

Major Sako maneuvered the heavy bomber to the main runway where he parked on the run-up pad to check the performance of each engine. "Yaeko, the engine check procedures are the same as for a single engine airplane. The only difference being that there are two of them to contend with.", advised the major. With the brakes locked, the major ran each engine up and checked magnetos, oil pressure and propeller cycling. Satisfied that everything was within limits, he pulled the throttles back. "This is a very heavy airplane, Yaeko, so it is vitally important that you set the elevator trim before you attempt to take off. Not attending to this little detail may mean that you do not take off at all, but end up nosed into an airport fence at the far end of some runway", warned Major Sako. "I will plan on paying particular attention to that aspect of the airplane in the future", promised Yaeko. With all in readiness, after being cleared for take off, Major Sako smoothly advanced the two throttles and the bomber lumbered down the runway. With the normal flap and trim settings, the bomber essentially flew itself off the runway at about 100 miles per hour. The earth fell away as the major gently pulled the yoke toward himself. "Yaeko, one thing that you should know up front, is that this airplane can become a beast very quickly if you lose an engine on takeoff. There is a specific procedure that absolutely must be followed for you to have any hope at all of avoiding a crash and killing yourself and perhaps your crew. I won't go into the details on this flight, but will expect you to commit those procedures to memory from the Pilot Operating Handbook that I will give you when we return to base. Now, take the control yoke and let's see what you can do with this bomber", said Major Sako. Yaeko was taken by surprise for he had no expectation that he would be allowed to fly the plane on his very first flight in it.

Gingerly touching the yoke with his sweaty hands, Yaeko could feel the throbbing engines and checked out the present compass heading and altitude, and attempted to hold the plane in the same orbit that the major had established. Amazingly enough, the bomber was not as ponderous on the controls as he had anticipated. "May I change altitude and direction? I would like to get a feeling for the plane in different attitudes?", asked Yaeko. "Be my guest, take the plane anyplace you care to go", replied the major.

Yaeko had decided that the best way to handle the multi-engine plane was to make any control inputs as gentle and gradual as possible. After all, it was not a fighter aircraft and was not expected to be very agile. Looking in all directions for conflicting traffic and seeing none, Yaeko turned left and added enough rudder to keep the turn coordinated to prevent skidding. At the same time, he pulled the yoke back enough to produce a gentle climb. However, he did not change the throttle settings. Leveling off 1,000 feet higher, Yaeko initiated a right turn and was beginning to sense a feeling of the control forces at play in the simple maneuvers. Next, Yaeko turned left and began a gentle descent and he could hear the engines speed up slightly with the reduction of loads on their propeller blades. Yaeko and the major flew for perhaps two hours, and then the major took control of the plane to return to the Kobe airfield. Yaeko read off the pre-landing checklist for the major, and assisted in configuring the plane for landing. Yaeko added flaps as required and extended the landing gear as the major directed. The major lined up with the main runway following instructions from the tower. and arrived over the numbers about 15 feet above the runway. The height gradually bled off about a third of the way down the runway, leaving plenty of distance for normal braking. Using both foot brakes and differential engine power, the major turned the bomber toward the flight line and parked in the space they had vacated two hours or so earlier. Going through the engine shutdown checklist, the bomber's engines were soon quiet. "Well, what do you think?", asked the major with a smile on his face. "I have to admit that walking up to the plane, I found it to be quite intimidating, but once we were in the air it seemed to me like just more of the same as far as controlling the plane's attitude is concerned", replied Yaeko. "You are not far off in your observation. I believe that the main thing is, like everything before this, you just need to get in a great deal of practice and the more flying hours you get in, the better your proficiency will become. Follow me, and let me get you a copy of the handbook that you need to study", said the major. With that, the major climbed out of his cockpit seat and Yaeko installed the control lock and then followed along, exiting the hatch and checking to make certain that wheel chocks were in place so that the bomber would not accidentally roll into a hazardous position.

In his office, Major Sako endorsed Yaeko's pilot logbook for his first multi-engine flight and then handed over a thick technical manual on the Mitsubishi airplane. Yaeko could see that his work was, indeed, cut out for him. "We will go up first thing in the morning", was the major's parting remark. "I will be there waiting for you, sir", replied Yaeko.

3 April thru 30 April 1944
Japanese Navy Base
Kobe, Japan

Throughout the remainder of the month of April, Yaeko was confronted with an intensive training period that would teach him how to safely pilot the 'Betty Bomber'. Normal and emergency procedures were practiced unceasingly, as were aircraft munitions loading procedures, and accurately completing bombing missions. Of all the procedures, however, single engine operation gave Yaeko the most difficulty. Nevertheless, this fact was not unusual because it was a common weakness among all multi-engine pilots. Single engine procedures were of such a demanding nature that they had to be drilled into pilots' heads and repeated over and over again, so that pilots could maintain currency as well as proficiency in executing the correct moves at the correct instant without thinking about them. These emergency maneuvers had to become as automatic as breathing. By the end of April Yaeko was certified in the 'Betty Bomber' and his logbook was signed off by Major Sako.

In a meeting in the major's office on 1 May 1944, Yaeko was advised of his next duty assignment. "Yaeko, it has been my great pleasure to have had you as a student. You will do well in the fleet regardless of whatever your duty assignment might be. In the meantime you are being sent to the Philippines to fly in support of our troops in various engagements around the greater Manila locale. You will make the trip to Manila in a military transport and be assigned a 'Betty Bomber' upon your arrival at the local airfield there. Your transportation will depart in two hours, so I suggest that you hurry to your barracks and pack your belongings and bring them to the boarding area", ordered Major Sako. "Honorable Major Sako, I want to thank you for your patience in making me the pilot that I am today. I will try to remember all of the pointers that you have given me and strive to become a credit to your staff and this training command", offered Yaeko. "Yaeko, you have been one of the most conscientious and dedicated students to pass through this training command and I am certain that you will be a credit to the empire wherever you go", complimented Major Sako. Before you leave, however, I have been authorized to promote you to the rank of tai-i (first lieutenant) and here is the patch for your uniform. Perhaps a seamstress in Manila can place it and others like it on your uniforms", said the major. "My thanks to you, Honorable Major, for without your support during my stay at the academy, I do not believe that I could have attained the promotion that you have given me", said Yaeko. " Not at all, Yaeko. Promotions such as yours are never given; they have to be earned and there is no question in my mind that yours was earned by due diligence from the very beginning of your training", concluded Major Sako.

0800 Monday
1 May 1944
Japanese Navy Base
Kobe, Japan

An hour later, Yaeko walked into the Kobe terminal boarding area carrying his bag and offered his orders and travel voucher to the officer-in-charge. "Have a seat, Yaeko, the plane will board in about ten minutes", said the officer, returning Yaeko's orders as well as the stub from his travel voucher. Yaeko walked through the waiting room and stood next to the boarding door so that he could be first in line and have an opportunity to pick the best seat on the plane. Through the glass door Yaeko could see the twin-engine transport which he identified as a Kawasaki Ki.-57 that the Americans called 'Topsy'. The plane was equipped with two

Mitsubishi Ha 102 engines of 1,050 horsepower each and had a cruise speed of 290 miles per hour and a range of 4,800 miles. No sooner than he had taken his place by the ramp access door than the boarding officer announced that all Manila passengers could proceed to the plane parked on the ramp. Yaeko led the group with his bag in hand which he dropped on a small baggage wagon at the side of the plane. Walking up the boarding steps and entering the fuselage, Yaeko took a window seat on the port (left) side, forward of the wing. While settling into his seat, Yaeko felt the engines start on the twin engine transport and the pilot began his announcement, "Good-morning, gentlemen, and welcome aboard. This flight to Manila will take approximately ten hours and we will make one refueling stop at Okinawa which is approximately 850 miles distant. Fasten your safety belts and we will be on our way immediately." Yaeko had brought his 'Betty Bomber' Pilot's Manual to study on the trip. With the engines revving up, the plane moved to the main Kobe runway that Yaeko would be leaving for the last time. How familiar it all seemed even though he was a passenger and not the pilot. As the plane reached its cruising altitude, Yaeko decided to snooze for the first part of his trip.

1100 Monday
1 May 1944
Japanese Airfield
Okinawa

Three hours later, the transport plane landed at Okinawa for refueling. The passengers were allowed to deplane. Yaeko's first thought was of food since nothing was served on the plane during the first leg of his journey. The small terminal building offered a limited selection of food items, so Yaeko selected two soft drinks and two portions of his favorite noodles from the old noodle man to see him through to Manila. Forty-five minutes later the reboarding call was announced and Yaeko took his same seat placing his food items on the seat beside him, which had remained empty throughout the first leg of the trip. The pilot wasted no time in getting airborne, and Okinawa quickly disappeared behind the plane as it flew south over the open waters of the blue Pacific Ocean. Opening his 'Betty Bomber' Pilot's Operating Handbook, Yaeko decided to review the single engine emergency operation procedures. Although he was certified as a command pilot in the aircraft there was always room for improvement. Sitting in the transport plane cabin, Yaeko recalled the many pleasant hours that he had spent learning to fly from Major Sako. It was with a sense of regret that he was leaving behind a friend for life in the form of his instructor; Major Sako.

1400 Monday
1 May 1944
Japanese Airfield
Manila, Philippines

Three hours from Okinawa, the pilot deftly set the transport plane down on the runway of the main Japanese airfield at Manila, P.I. Yaeko retrieved his bag from the baggage cart next to the airplane and asked a nearby guard for directions to the base commander's office. The guard pointed to the north side of the field where all military operations were controlled. Entering beneath the sign identifying the base commander's office, Yaeko encountered the field administrative officer and handed over his orders. "Welcome aboard, Yaeko, we have been expecting you and I look forward to observing the results of your flying prowess. Please accompany seaman Omura and he will take you to the pilot barracks where you will find sleeping quarters", advised the officer. "Thank you, sir. The idea of sleep is most pleasant, for it has already been an extremely long day for me", replied Yaeko. "Please plan on mustering at 0800 in the morning and ask Omura to show you the location of the mess hall along the way", concluded the officer. "Thank you very much, sir, and I shall look forward to seeing you tomorrow", replied an extremely tired Yaeko.

On their way to the pilots' barracks, Omura pointed to the mess hall which happened to be adjacent to them at the time and only one building removed from his barracks. The pilots' barracks turned out to be a rather crude building, made of plywood walls and rough timber interior. Of course, this was to be expected being more or less on the front lines of the war zone. Nevertheless, Yaeko found the bunk bed to be very soft and quite comfortable, and he appreciated the fact that the barracks contained the traditional communal bathing area, with a small cleaning area and its great tub of hot water in which to rinse. Donning his nightclothes, Yaeko collapsed into his bunk and was soon fast asleep. Sleep became impossible past 0600 as the sound of reconnaissance aircraft engines warming up began to rend the humid air. Yaeko rolled out, grabbed a towel and his toothbrush and headed for the bathhouse. Feeling very refreshed by his bath, Yaeko dressed and decided that it was time for breakfast and walked to the mess hall. Standing in line, Yaeko looked around to see if he might find a familiar face. He was greatly disappointed not to find a single familiar face among a crowd of about 75 fliers and aircraft mechanics. Yaeko ate his cold rice balls and fish and drank his delicious hot tea. With his meal finished, Yaeko noticed that it would soon be time to muster at quarters and walked in that direction.

0800 Tuesday
2 May 1944
Japanese Airfield
Manila, Philippines

At 0800, the base commander and his staff came to the muster area and roll call was taken. There were no absentees, and the Manila staff was all accounted for. Following muster, Lieutenant Toshi Datsu took charge of Yaeko and advised him of his flying position within the overall squadron formation. Datsu took Yaeko to the flight line and there assigned a 'Betty Bomber' to his personal command along with a four-man flight crew. Although Major Sako had mentioned that a flight crew would be involved, he had never stated its size. The pilot's operating handbook had been no help in this regard, because the staffing of the bomber was left up to the discretion of either the pilot or base commanding officer.

Toshi Datsu introduced the flight crew to Yaeko and also took Yaeko to the operations tent where mission assignments were originated on a day-to-day basis. For the past few weeks, the squadron had been bombing American installations on New Guinea as well as U.S. Navy ships supporting the U.S. amphibious landings taking place there. The intent of the bombings was to disrupt the American invasion and its supply lines to the greatest extent possible. While in the operations' tent, Yaeko was provided with charts and squadron configuration data for the upcoming raid, scheduled to commence that afternoon at 1300.

Yaeko took his crew aside and discussed the scope of the planned raid. His crew consisted of:

Masaru Ibuka - copilot
KanjiIshiwara - bombardier
Yataro Iwasaki - tail gunner
Takashi Masuda - nose gunner

With his crew in tow, Yaeko walked to the flight line where his 'Betty Bomber' (Japanese Name Ishiki Rikukoh) was tied down. The 'Betty Bomber' was manufactured by the Mitsubishi Aircraft Company of Japan with a designation of G4M1 Type 1 and was equipped with two 1,800 horsepower Mitsubishi MK4P Kasei Radial engines. It could be flown by a seven-man crew or fewer if need be. With an empty weight of 8.5 tons, the 'Betty Bomber' could carry 2,200 pounds of bombs or two 1,700 pound torpedos over a range of 2,250 miles at a speed of 195 miles per hour. The maximum speed of the plane at 14,000 feet was 250 miles per hour.

Protective armament for the 'Betty Bomber' was comprised of four 7.7mm machine guns; one in the nose, one on top and two firing from beam positions. And last but not least, the bomber armament included a 20-mm cannon that fired from the tail position.

Yaeko spoke with his crew chief to verify that the plane had been fueled and serviced, and bombs and machine gun ammunition placed aboard for the raid. While speaking with the crew chief, Yaeko assigned the copilot to perform the 'walk around' inspection at precisely 1230, and untie the plane at the same time in advance of the assigned takeoff time. Referring to his charts, Yaeko noticed that all of the needed information regarding radio frequencies and password authentication designator codes were listed on the charts. With the mission readiness confirmed, Yaeko dismissed his crew to be reassembled in the bomber at 1245.

Yaeko was in an apprehensive mood, and went to his plane at 1230 and climbed into the pilot's cockpit. Shortly thereafter Masaru arrived and performed his 'walk around' inspection, untied the airplane and then took his copilot seat, at the same time removing the control lock. "Masaru, have you been on many raids over New Guinea?", asked Yaeko. "No, honorable Yaeko, like you, I am new to this base and this is my first raid", replied the copilot. "Well, then, that means we will have the opportunity to learn together. At 1255, I plan to start the engines to give them a chance to warm up a bit", said Yaeko. "Yes, honorable Yaeko, the warmer the better. I have been a witness to the problems encountered in trying to take off in a plane with cold engines. It was a near-death experience for me as the plane almost crashed", lamented Masaru. About that time, the bombardier and the two gunners climbed aboard. When 1255 appeared on his watch, Yaeko loudly shouted "Clear" out of his open cockpit window, and completing the start checklist, started his engines. The very familiar rumble of the Mitsubishi Radial engines came to his ears and hands through the control yoke vibrations. Yaeko listened to his radio for takeoff instructions and soon heard his aircraft number called to taxi into position and hold. Yaeko acknowledged the call and applied just enough throttle to cause the 'Betty' to begin rolling toward the end of the somewhat primitive, unpaved dirt runway. Reaching the end of the runway, Yaeko locked the brakes, set his elevator trim, and performed his engine run-up routine and propeller cycling exercise for both engines. He then moved his control yoke through its extreme positions and observed that all control surfaces moved in the proper directions. All instruments were 'in the green' so Yaeko announced his readiness to depart. "Cleared to depart", came back immediately through his radio headset earphones. The winds were calm so the 'Betty' used about 75% of the runway to become airborne. Lifting off the runway, Yaeko turned to the assigned course-line and set cruise climb power while requestimg the copilot to retract the landing gear and flaps and set the proper propeller angles.

At 1,000 feet, Yaeko entered a racetrack pattern waiting for the other members of his flight to join up on him. It required four turns around the pattern before the three remaining 'Betty Bombers' of his flight were in position.

"Angels flight of four, check in, please", said Yaeko over his radio. Calling in sequence, the other three members of the flight confirmed that they were in position and listening on the channel. Yaeko dialed in a course of 140 degrees on his directional gyro for the 1,550 mile flight which came to 6.2 flight hours to reach the target area, cruising at 250 mph.

Flying in a loose diamond formation, the four 'Betty Bombers' maintained radio silence. Speaking over the local intercom channel, Yaeko requested the nose and tail gunners to arm their machine guns with ammunition and test fire them. A little over six hours later, approaching the target, Yaeko increased his altitude to 8,000 feet and summoned his chicks to follow him in trail. Yaeko's tail gunner confirmed that the flight members were in trail at 1,000 foot intervals as specified in mission plans. "Leader to chicks, follow me", said Yaeko. Passing over the target, the bombardier released his bombs in sequence over the American beachhead. There was no return fire, and two of the following 'Betty Bombers' turned, as planned, to bomb several ships that were anchored in the small harbor. The bombs falling on shore breached an American ammunition dump and caused many secondary explosions. The bombs that fell from the planes in trail hit a destroyer in Wasior Bay, as well as an LST, and also caused several secondary explosions. Leaving the target area, Yaeko could see the destroyer listing badly to port with fires visible above and below deck, and he was satisfied that the mission had accomplished its purpose. At the end of his uneventful return trip of six hours on a course of 320 degrees, Yaeko was cleared to land at Manila. With the aid of his copilot performing the pre-landing check, Yaeko lined up for the main runway and retarded his throttles and descended to the runway. The copilot extended the flaps and landing gear on the way down. The 'Betty' came to the far end of the runway where Yaeko elected to remain, with engines idling, pending arrival of the other three planes of his flight. Ten minutes later, with the other planes on the ground, Yaeko taxied back to his parking place and shut his engines down. Leaving the plane, he went directly to the intelligence tent to report the outcome of his mission, and walking away, observed that his crew chief had chocked the Betty's wheels and refueling was in progress.

June through December 1944
Japanese Airfield
Manila, Philippines

Over the next seven months, Yaeko and his crew flew countless missions to New Guinea, Leyte and other Philippine targets and was fortunate in never receiving enemy fire, save for a brief encounter with a U.S. Navy F-4U Chance Vought Corsair fighter plane. That enemy plane was scared off by the nose gunner's brief machine gun burst. By late 1944, the Japanese fortunes of war were in decline on all fronts. The United States military manufacturing machine output far outstripped the equivalent Japanese capability. Japan was severely hampered by the loss of access to needed strategic raw materials, which resulted in limited output of even the most fundamental military products, such as replacement airplanes and ammunition. In the face of these hard times, the Japanese war planners attempted to devise alternate strategies to continue the prosecution of their war effort. One such plan was conceived by a Navy vice-admiral, who proposed the formation of a series of squadrons comprised of airplanes that would be loaded with high-powered explosives and then crashed into United States warships with the hope that the ships would be sunk. The initial strikes were carried out on Wednesday, 25 October 1944, employing volunteer pilots. These raids by 25 planes were so successful that Vice-Admiral Onishi Takijiro quickly recruited additional squadrons, and the Japanese Army Air Force followed suit and formed its own squadrons. The units so formed were designated 'The Divine Wind Special Attack Corps'.

The Japanese military ethic specifically prohibited military personnel from surrendering in battle. The 'Divine Wind' endeavor, even though it was based upon a volunteer rationale, resulted in the Japanese government effectively sanctifying Kamikaze pilot suicides in pursuit of a plan to save a desperate homeland. Notwithstanding the success of the initial raid, the overall impact of the Kamikaze squadrons upon the outcome of the war was essentially negligible. During the war, over 1,200 pilots gave their lives and also destroyed approximately 1,200 Japanese aircraft in the process. With the defeat of Japan on 15 August 1945, Admiral Onishi Takijiro committed hara-kiri. History does not reveal the number of American deaths suffered at the hands of the Divine Wind Corps.

Thus it was that Yaeko became a member of a group of pilots assembled from his squadron on a cold December day in 1945. The local Manila commander had been tasked to provide at least six volunteer pilots to join a Kamikaze Corps squadron. They would take part in an attack that was designed to blunt the invasion of the Philippines through the Lingayen Gulf north of Manila. The highly-placed Japanese officers painted a glorious picture of the honor that such participation would bring to the family of everyone who elected to participate, as well as the individual and magnificent personal glory that would be bestowed upon the pilot himself. Although Yaeko had been aware of the Kamikaze Corps for some time, he had never personally considered the prospect of giving his life for the emperor in such a manner. Nevertheless, in the heat of the moment, he finally relented and elected to participate and become one of the six volunteers from his squadron.

Following the squadron meeting, Yaeko went to his room and wrote a letter to his parents. He planned to request that his copilot arrange for its delivery to his parents some time following his mission.

Letter to Be Delivered to Sokubei Yamagucci:

Friday, 12 December 1945
Manila, Philippine, Islands

Dear Honorable Father and Mother:

I find myself in the midst of a dilemma, from which I am unable to extricate myself. With the intention of bringing good fortune to my country, its emperor and my honorable family, I volunteered to join the "Divine Wind" Corps. to help beat back the enemies of Japan.

Tomorrow, I will do my small part for our war effort and in so doing will give my life for that cause. I ask you to pray for my soul and know that my thoughts are of you, my father and mother, as well as my brother and sisters.

Although I participate in this undertaking of my own freewill, I regret that we will not meet again until we see each other in heaven.

Your loving son,
Yaeko

Having written his farewell letter, Yaeko sealed it in an envelope and sought out his copilot who he found in the mess hall. "Hello, Masaru, may I have a minute of your time?", asked Yaeko. "By all means, Yaeko, have a seat; what can I do for you?" "Well, Masaru, it turns out that I have volunteered to join the Divine Wind Corps and I have written a letter to my parents and was hoping that you might be willing to see that it is delivered to them", replied Yaeko. "Yes, by all means, I will be pleased to take care of that matter for you, and I will deliver it in person as soon as I return to Tokyo. Of course, I have been aware of the solicitation of volunteer pilots for the corps but, thus far, I have not been able to convince myself that I should participate in that endeavor. Nevertheless, I admire you for your decision and I will tell your parents of the many hours that we have flown together and of our wonderful personal friendship", concluded Masaru. "You have my eternal thanks and I have very much enjoyed our flying relationship and have recommended you as my replacement to command my 'Betty Bomber', said Yaeko with a wry smile. "I believe that the lieutenant was favorably disposed to my suggestion and I expect that he will be in touch with you soon. You certainly have enough flying time in the Bomber to qualify for command", concluded Yaeko. "Thank you very much, Yaeko, for your confidence in my flying abilities", offered Masaru. "Masaru, it has more to do than having confidence in your flying abilities. In my opinion, you have always displayed a dedicated effort in performing your tasks from a position of great knowledge, and I have never found you to be wanting in any aspect of our flying profession. I am certain that you will do well in a command position", concluded Yaeko. "Thank you again, Yaeko, and have no fear, your letter will be faithfully delivered", said Masaru.

0700 Saturday
13 December 1945
Japanese Lingayen
Philippine Air Field

The previous day, Yaeko's commander had assigned him a single engine Nakajima Ki-84 'Hayate' fighter/bomber in which to fly his Kamikaze mission. His aircraft was known as the 'Frank' by the Americans. He observed that it was the same version of the plane in which he had qualified shortly before leaving the Kobe Flight Training Academy; the only difference was that the plane lacked the second instructor pilot cockpit. When he arrived at the field for his pre-flight 'walk around' inspection, Yaeko observed that the plane had been fitted with a single 500-pound bomb. In addition, his crew chief pointed out the addition of a quantity of light-weight incendiary bomblets placed in a nose compartment. Yaeko ascertained that the weight and placement of the additional incendiaries, together with the 500-pound bomb itself, did not shift the weight and balance parameters of his 'Hayate' beyond safe flying limits. Around 0730, the morning reconnaissance flight returned with the latest intelligence on the position of the American Invasion Fleet which, at that time, was withdrawing in the vicinity of Manila Bay. Making a final check with the local commander, Yaeko received his orders and said his good-byes to his crew who, of course, would not be flying with him today. Performing his final 'walk around' inspection, Yaeko wondered whether or not he should reconsider his decision to volunteer for Kamikaze duty and certain death, but, at the same time, he belatedly realized that it was much too late for second thoughts. Not only would he lose face, with dire consequences if he changed his mind now, but such an action would surely adversely impact the lives of his family as well. In the end, he untied his plane, removed the wheel chocks and control lock and climbed into his cockpit. Snapping his safety belts in place, Yaeko adjusted his helmet and clamped his German radio headphones over his ears. It was a familiar feeling having his ears pushed against his skull by the pressure of the earphones headband. Running through the pre-start check list, Yaeko set his flaps and takeoff trim and then started his engine to warm it up. With his engine performing normally, Yaeko called for takeoff clearance which was given immediately, together with solemn best wishes for a successful flight, even though it was destined to be his last and one from which he would not return.

Although the 'Hayate' had a reasonable payload weight capability, the powerful engine and strong wing quickly lifted the fighter/bomber off the runway and Yaeko climbed alone to a cruise altitude of 2,000 feet. Although there were five other Kamikaze planes assigned from his squadron to support today's mission, none were required to be associated with Yaeko. It was a day of broken clouds, and Yaeko thought of his mother, father and siblings as he turned his aircraft to a direct course toward the American convoy. As he turned the coming events over in his mind it was his hope that his parents would understand his reasons for attempting to aid his homeland in the manner that he had chosen. Within thirty minutes, Yaeko could see that other Japanese Kamikaze aircraft were in the vicinity attacking the convoy where columns of black smoke were issuing from several large troop transport ships and an aircraft carrier. For the first time, he could see that antiaircraft shells were bursting at his altitude. As he approached the convoy, Yaeko reasoned that it would be best to spend the least amount of time possible in range of the American guns. For this reason, Yaeko climbed to 6,000 feet and had a wonderful view of the convoy through the broken clouds passing beneath his wing. Of the 20-odd troop transport ships in the flotilla, Yaeko noticed the lead ship in the center column extended out front of the other transports. Yaeko surmised that that ship must be the command ship. Indeed, Yaeko was correct for that ship was the U.S.S. Zeilin, the flagship carrying the commodore and his battle staff.

Slowly pitching the plane over into a shallow dive, Yaeko saw his airspeed quickly approach the red-line limit which, if exceeded, might tear off his wing. Pulling back his throttle to reduce his engine rpm's, yet maintain the top of the red-line arc, Yaeko pointed the nose of his bomber at the center of the U.S.S. Zeilin; it was then approximately 0815. As he descended, Yaeko noticed that a layer of clouds obscured some of the ships in the convoy thus protecting him from their gunners. At the same time, Yaeko became aware of the presence of two U.S. Navy F6F Hellcat fighter planes that were firing on him from his six o' clock position.

Simultaneously, Yaeko observed antiaircraft shells bursting near his plane, but he ignored them as he took evasive action to escape the Hellcats that were closing rapidly. Yaeko sought the safety of a nearby cloud bank as he temporarily turned away from the U.S.S. Zeilin. Hidden in the cloud, Yaeko flew on instruments for two minutes and then performed a chandelle maneuver to reverse his course. With that maneuver occurring in a cloud, Yaeko escaped the Hellcats as he again flew in the direction of the convoy while still hidden in the cloud bank. Less than a minute later, the 'Frank' exited the cloud and Yaeko again lined up his aircraft targeting the U.S.S. Zeilin. As he flew closer, he could see the trajectories of tracer shells coming to meet him and soon he could hear the shells penetrating his airplane and rattling noisily around between the aluminum skins of his wing. As he descended through a height of about 100 feet above the transport, Yaeko's windshield suddenly disintegrated amid an ear-splitting explosion caused by a direct hit from a 20-mm tracer shell. Seconds later, he felt blood trickling down his cheek from a forehead cut by flying glass. With the windshield having disappeared, there was now a ferocious wind assaulting Yaeko's body. The screaming noise of the wind entering the cockpit was almost unbearable. The 20-mm tracers continued to reach him and he saw the projectiles stitch a line of holes along the leading edge of his port wing, at which time he threw caution to the wind and shoved the 'Frank's' throttle wide open and roared out of the smoky sky. Yaeko believed that he was close enough to the transport, at that moment, that he need not worry any longer about losing a wing, for the momentum and stable trajectory of his aircraft would surely carry his 'Hayate' unerringly to the 20-mm gun position that he had selected as his primary target. In an ever-steepening dive, 25 feet above the transport, a 20-mm shell found Yaeko at his cockpit controls mortally wounding him. With both hands now frozen to his control column in a death spasm, Yaeko's dying thoughts were of a fleeting memory of his life in Tokyo as a child of five holding tightly to his father's hand as they walked along the shore of Tokyo Bay. As the 'Frank' continued on its death dive toward the U.S.S. Zeilin, the right wing collided with the port boom of the #6 cargo hatch and caused the plane to turn slightly to the left on its collision course. Colliding with the immovable object at 0821, the plane drove into the port-side House Top 20-mm gun position crushing the three Navy gunners amid the deformation of the plane's aluminum wings and spilling aviation fuel from its ruptured wing tanks. At the same time, the force of the concussion blew several sailors overboard to uncertain ends. One of the crewmen was later picked up by the U.S.S. Saufley following behind the U.S.S. Zeilin. As it turned out, the 500-pound bomb failed to detonate, but several of the incendiary bomblets ignited, but failed to cause significant damage. These happenstances were a blessing for the U.S.S. Zeilin as the damage, if the bomb explosion had taken place as planned, may have sent the transport to the bottom of the sea. The U.S.S. Zeilin damage control crew arrived at the crash site quickly, but were unable to immediately quench the gasoline-fed flames emanating from the ruptured wing tanks. Essentially, all they could do was monitor the fire and prevent it from spreading. As a result, Yaeko's body was incinerated in his distorted cockpit and ultimately became unrecognizable from the rubble of other burned debris of his 'Frank'. Navy hospital corpsmen quickly arrived to give first aid to several injured crewmen near the crash site.

The following day, 14 January 1945, a temporary boom was rigged by the deck crew with which to hoist the engine, wing, fuselage and other major pieces of the plane clear of the boat deck and drop the debris over the side to a watery grave. Thus, the death of Yaeko Yamagucci became just another footnote in a WWII battle that raged for 45 months from 7 December 1941 until Japan's surrender aboard the Battleship U.S.S. Missouri on Sunday, 2 September 1945.

Example of the Ki-84 "Frank"

Above: Examples of the G4M “Betty Bomber”

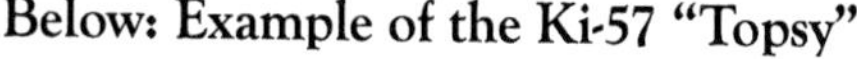

Below: Example of the Ki-57 “Topsy”

Above: Examples of the A-6M "Zero"

Below: Example of the U.S. Navy F6F "Hellcat"

CHAPTER FOUR

SAIPAN AND PHILIPPINE BATTLES

0900 Monday
22 November 1943
U.S.S. Zeilin en route to Espiritu Santo
New Hebrides, Islands

Having transferred all of the wounded Marines from the Tarawa invasion to a waiting hospital ship, the U.S.S. Zeilin set a southeasterly course for the island of Espiritu Santo some 1,100 nautical miles distant. At a cruise speed of 17 knots, the trip will take about two and one-half days. With no troops on board, the ship's company returned to their normal duty schedule. Daily muster at quarters resumed and duty hours changed from the four hours on, four hours off, regimen that is enforced in the invasion combat mode, to normal duty times of eight hours duration. A side benefit of there being no troops on board is the fact that food quality for the crew improves in a very material way. Gone are the days of the 'shit on a shingle' sandwich meals (that is, toasted bread covered with ground-up Spam mixed with cheddar cheese). Although nourishing, a steady diet of this concoction becomes objectionable after but a few days on an invasion site.

The U.S.S. Zeilin is not accompanied by any other troop transports from the Tarawa invasion. However, the ship is accompanied by a lone destroyer screening vessel. The U.S.S. Zeilin is not equipped with SONAR (an electronic submarine finding system) and the essential purpose of the destroyer is to protect the U.S.S. Zeilin from Japanese submarines that roam the areas surrounding the Marshall, Gilbert and Solomon Island chains. Shortly before our departure from Tarawa, a Navy PBY amphibian aircraft arrived and brought with it an unexpected shipment of mail from the States. Deliveries were made to all ships in the convoy. These deliveries were indeed a surprise since, typically, mail does not reach the U.S.S. Zeilin unless it is tied up in a major port for several days. Nevertheless, the crew was appreciative of the Navy's efforts to bring some cheer from home. In my case, I received not only a number of letters from my family and sweetheart, Lucille, but I also received a specially packed box of cookies, salted peanuts, candy and other "goodies" from my mother. To maintain freshness throughout an indeterminate delivery interval, she had sealed all of the items inside small 'Mason Jars' equipped with rubber gaskets. Thus, on that day, Melvin E. Hacker received a reasonable collection of mail and food stuffs straight from home. Mom's letters included several photographs of herself, Daddy and brother Marvin and sister Ida Mae. She even included photographs of my oldest sister, Marilee, who had just been married in June to her high school sweetheart, Eugene Van. Born in 1941, my sister Ida Mae was two years old her last birthday and brother Marvin was five years old, and there were photos of each in the collection that Mom sent.

Mail call came around 1000 and I had the noon to 2000 watch, so I quickly scanned the various letters and then put them in my locker to be answered at a later time. I had just enough time to have my midday meal before going on watch, so I headed for the mess hall and joined several crew members waiting in line. (Standing in that chowline that day, I promised myself that I would NEVER again participate in the practice, once I returned to civilian life after the war). At 1130, the mess hall doors opened and the line quickly moved inside to the fragrance of fried chicken, mashed potatoes, gravy and apple pie topped with cheddar cheese. Never having developed a taste for coffee, I chose water as my beverage. In fact, I attempted throughout my two-plus years 'hitch' in the Navy, to learn to like the flavor of coffee, but I never achieved that objective. Even though a 'joe pot' ran 24 hours a day in the RADAR shack, and provided ready access to coffee, I never acquired a taste for the liquid. Interestingly enough, the same was true of beer. Liberty parties among the various Atolls always included an allotment of six bottles of beer for each sailor. Since I did not care for the taste of the brew, I traded my beer for coke, and there was never a dearth of sailors interested in trading coke for my beer allotment. None of the RADAR gang was present for the meal, so I ate with gunner's mate friend Calvin Honeycut. Finishing my meal in about 15 minutes, I returned to my compartment, brushed my teeth, and then set out for the RADAR shack located immediately behind the U.S.S. Zeilin's wheelhouse and navigation bridge.

1100 Monday
22 November 1943
U.S.S. Zeilin en route
to Espiritu Santo

Entering the dimly-lighted RADAR shack, I joined Doug Jones, Alvin Carruthers, and Marshall Herron, who will operate the RADAR systems with me for the next eight hours. To relieve eyestrain, each operator is periodically relieved from his RADAR position. I assumed the operating position on the Surface Search RADAR while Alvin relieved Manuel Ortega on the Air Search RADAR. The relieved crew dutifully identified all active targets which, at that time, were comprised of only several long distance land-mass targets, which had previously been reported to the officer of the deck. Because the RADAR set receivers are prone to drift slightly in frequency over time, the first task upon relieving a watch is to tune the receiver of each RADAR system so that it exactly matches the frequency of the transmitter. Absent completion of this task, one runs the danger of having the captain (or perhaps the officer of the deck) lean over your shoulder in the darkened RADAR operating room to inquire about the distance and bearing to a target visible from the bridge, but not yet reported by the RADAR operators. This condition is known as the 'nth degree of embarrassment' for a RADAR operator. (I speak from personal experience on that mind-numbing event for it has happened to me). To circumvent this problem, I religiously tune the receiver of whatever RADAR I am operating every 30 minutes while I am on watch. Tuning the RADAR is a simple task anyway, amounting to nothing more than turning a small black knob akin to the station selection knob on a civilian radio receiver until the 'A' scope (distance measuring CRT) image is at its peak sensitivity. What could be simpler or easier? In later years, some smart electronic engineer designed a circuit that automatically and continuously tunes the receiver to the proper transmitter frequency, but manual tuning continued to prevail throughout WWII.

Our watch was uneventful, and at 2000 our relief crew arrived and the rest of us bailed out to 'hit the hay'. The '7th' (Electronics) division was quiet and dim with only the red 'night vision bulbs' illuminating the compartment. When I climbed down the ladder and found my bunk, only the rumble of the massive twin propellers beneath our compartment broke the stillness. I learned early in my Navy career to select the top bunk of whatever row appealed to me the most. On the one hand you are assured that no one will walk on your clean mattress cover and, also, one needs to pick a bunk in close proximity to an air supply duct. In the tropic zone, where the U.S.S. Zeilin spent most of its wartime duty, heat builds up below decks. Selecting a bunk adjacent to an air-supply duct permits one to guide his own democracy; that is to say, one can open a small metal flap on the duct and receive a plentiful supply of cooling air upon demand. This supply would not be refrigerated air for there was no air conditioning equipment on board the U.S.S. Zeilin.

1400 Wednesday
24 November 1943
U.S.S. Zeilin en route
to Espiritu Santo

Espiritu Santo is on the horizon as we muster at quarters. Having had the 2000 to 0400 duty last night, I will not have any further RADAR duty on this cruise for we will be dropping anchor within the hour. Notwithstanding the zig-zag path that the U.S.S. Zeilin and its escort followed in reaching Espiritu Santo, no Japanese planes or submarines were encountered. During muster of division personnel, Lieutenant Thompson revealed that the U.S.S. Zeilin was scheduled to board U.S. Army personnel for training and eventual delivery to the invasion beaches on the island of Saipan. It is my impression that America is going after Japan in a very big way, knocking off island after island and forcing the enemy to give up their ill-gotten material resource gains. By 0900 we are at anchor in the main harbor and a Navy tanker has pulled alongside to transfer fuel into the depleted U.S.S. Zeilin fuel tanks.

Traditionally, the RADAR gang has been 'fair game' for working parties, as well as standing radio watches, because its personnel do not normally stand RADAR watches while in port. Espiritu Santo was not to be an exception. The ship's intercom system was soon piping all RADARmen to the port quarterdeck to join a provisioning working party. I did not usually object to such duty, as invariably a box of apples or other edible foodstuffs would get broken open (however accidentally) and we would help ourselves while continuing to work. Two hours later the working party was secured and I went up on deck to absorb some sunshine. Passing the quarterdeck I ran across Calvin Honeycut and we stopped to chat for awhile. He told me about his being stranded in Pearl Harbor for some 14 months, and the fact that he was married and had brand-new twin children who were born on September 20th. Of course, I congratulated him on his good fortune and told him about my sweetheart, Lucille. In passing, I mentioned that the U.S.S. Zeilin was part of the convoy being assembled to carry out an invasion of the island of Saipan. Calvin had come aboard during an earlier U.S.S. Zeilin visit to Espiritu Santo. Since that time he had become a valuable member of the "Z"s gunner's mate team and is scheduled to be trained in the operation of the main, three-inch batteries of the U.S.S. Zeilin's antiaircraft guns.

0800 Friday
26 November 1943
U.S.S. Zeilin at Espiritu Santo Anchorage

There were to be no working parties this morning, so after muster I grabbed my writing materials and headed for my favorite spot to be alone with my thoughts of home, and write some letters. There was an emergency liferaft positioned on the starboard side of the fantail, just forward of the twin 40-mm antiaircraft guns and their director tub. The raft was large enough to accommodate about 30 men and was equipped with emergency rations, oars, fishhooks, a sail and kegs of fresh water. Mounted on a slanted track, one man could release the restraining clamps and allow the raft to self-launch over the side of the ship if there was an emergency condition. There were more than a dozen of these rafts around the perimeter of the U.S.S. Zeilin. Of course, in a real emergency, the U.S.S. Zeilin could also fall back on the thirty or more Higgins landing craft on board to allow the crew to survive a sinking. However, the landing craft do not normally carry emergency rations or water. Nevertheless, the Higgins boats would be better than nothing in the event the U.S.S. Zeilin ever went down.

It was a sunny, blue-sky day with not a cloud in the sky, and as I prepared to get my thoughts in order, I noticed Calvin down below and called out to him. He looked up and I motioned for him to climb up and join me. In a couple of minutes, Calvin was pulling himself into the raft and settled into the nylon netting that served as the floor of the raft. "How are you doing, Calvin?", I asked. "Everything is just fine and I want to thank you again for being my fairy godfather the other day when I arrived", said Calvin. "I assure you that it was my pleasure. Have they set you up with a watch schedule yet?", I asked. "No, the Chief told me that it would take a few days for him to determine how he would rearrange his schedule to work me into the mix", replied Calvin. "I know the Chief and from what I have seen he is a good man", I offered. "When I met him he seemed to me to be a no-nonsense, straight shooter and I believe strongly in first impressions", said Calvin. "Calvin, I should mention that these rafts are not off-limits to the crew. There are many scattered around and I come here when I want to be alone with my thoughts and write letters home. You are perfectly welcome to join me any time I am here or come here even if I am not here", I said. "That is mighty kind of you, Melvin. I guess we both have the same needs in that regard. I need to write a letter to my wife and let her know what has happened to me since I left San Diego some months ago. We are newlyweds and I had to send her home alone to Des Moines, Iowa, on a bus the day I boarded a destroyer to travel to the U.S.S. Zeilin", revealed Calvin. "I know about those sad departure times. I am not married, but Lucille and

I are planning to marry as soon as the war is over, so I keep sending letters her way and she writes me most every day as well", I said. "Here Calvin, this is an extra tablet, take it and this pen and write your wife a few lines. We are scheduled to leave Espiritu Santo in a few days, but any mail that gets ashore before we depart will be on its way to its destination", I concluded. "Many thanks, Melvin, and I will take you up on your kind offer", said Calvin. Calvin took the tablet and began to write. "By the way, Calvin, what is your wife's name", I asked. "I should have told you already. Her name is Mary Jane and she is a very beautiful blonde-headed lady, biased though I may be", bragged Calvin. "Well, congratulations, Calvin, and by the way, in my opinion, married men have a natural right to be biased where their wives and children are concerned", I said with a smile. "Thanks for understanding, Melvin", replied Calvin.

We both lapsed into silence at that point and I began writing a reply to Lucille's most recent letters, and was intent on getting my letters to her and my mom on shore before the U.S.S. Zeilin pulled up its anchor and sailed away in two days. Calvin and I spent a couple of hours concentrating on our writing, and continued until word was passed that the mess hall was open for the evening meal. By then we were both hungry and climbed down from the raft and walked toward the bow of the ship and the mess hall.

Carrying our writing materials, Calvin and I ate our meals together. I enjoyed his company and learned something more of his background on his father's farm in Des Moines, Iowa. During our conversations, I shared information about my own background and the fact that I left high school early, as he had done, to avoid being drafted into the Army. So we had more than just a little in common. With nothing to do after we ate, we decided to return to the raft and enjoy the approaching evening and share additional facts about our lives, family and friends. When we reached the raft, I could see Calvin eyeing the 40-mm guns and their director tub. "I am itching to get my hands on those guns along the way", said Calvin. "Well, they usually have target practice in-transit and I am certain that you will get your chance", I replied. "While I was in school I was given the opportunity to fire the same type of gun quite frequently", said Calvin. "From what I have seen, the Chief Gunner's Mate rotates his men so that everyone gets to fire both the 20-mm and the 40-mm guns, and even the three-inch guns on the bow and stern", I said. "I have never fired a three-inch gun before, but expect that someone could teach me how", observed Calvin. "No doubt someone will teach you during our cruise to Saipan", I replied.

"Calvin, did it take much persuasion to convince your parents to sign for you to join the Navy before you were 18?", I asked. "No, not really. Lowell, a good friend of mine, and I left school and visited the recruiting office one day not long after the Japanese raid on Pearl Harbor. That same evening, I discussed my desire to join the Navy with my parents and they seemed perfectly amenable to the idea. The next day we visited the same Navy recruiting office and I signed up with their support and signatures on the early enlistment applications", said Calvin. "They knew that I could not avoid the draft, and that by enlisting I could control my own destiny and take that decision away from some faceless draft board clerk. I am sorry to report that my good friend Lowell's parents refused to sign for him", lamented Calvin.

"Yes, I know what you mean. My folks disliked the prospect of my having to go, but they agreed that an Army life was not to be desired", I said. While we spoke, the sun set over the palm tree covered island and clearance lights began to appear on ships anchored around the harbor. When darkness finally set in and we could no longer see to write on our paper, we said good evening and climbed down to go our separate ways. "I guess I will hit the shower and then call it a day", I said. "Sounds like a winner to me, Melvin. Thank you for sharing your afternoon with me", said Calvin. "We'll do it again real soon", I replied as I stepped down the ladder into the '7th' division quarters, and grabbing a towel and soap, I headed for the shower. With no troops on board, the U.S.S. Zeilin's evaporators could keep up with demand and the crew could enjoy freshwater showers. Showering with saltwater, even with the special saltwater soap, never left me feeling clean.

0700 Friday
8 October 1943
U.S.S. Zeilin departs Espiritu Santo Anchorage

With approximately 1,200 troops and their equipment having been loaded during our stay at Espiritu Santo, the U.S.S. Zeilin departs to undertake training exercises on the island of Efate in the New Hebrides Islands chain. After leaving Espiritu Santo, the U.S.S. Zeilin forms up with the rest of the convoy totaling 21 troop transports and a protective screen of aircraft carriers, battleships, cruisers, submarines, destroyers and tankers. The distance to the training site is approximately 110 nautical miles or about six cruising hours at the U.S.S. Zeilin's usual 17-knot speed. Arriving at dusk, the transports anchor in accordance with the plan already developed for the strike against Saipan beachheads interspersed with the screen vessels. As was typical for amphibious invasions, the U.S.S. Zeilin was placed 3,000 yards offshore while the companion troop transports took anchorages also specified in the Saipan invasion plan, nearby. Arriving late in the day as we had, no training exercises were launched this day.

0500 Saturday
9 October 1943
U.S.S. Zeilin at anchor off Efate Island

At 0500, troops were awakened and moved to the mess halls for breakfast. Having finished breakfast, the troops were then moved to their debarkation stations while the Navy crews launched all Higgins boats and brought them in sequence to the cargo nets down which the soldiers and Marines would climb and enter their assigned boats. Once loaded, the boats moved to a nearby staging area to join up with other boats prior to being released for their run to the designated mock invasion beaches. By 0600 all boats were loaded and released to make their runs to their assigned beaches. Following close behind, the tank lighters made their runs to off-load their cargos of tanks and heavy vehicles as well as artillery guns that would support the troops on shore. In the simulated maneuvers, no guns were fired by the support ships of the line. During this activity, all of the RADARmen were on duty providing progress reports to the officer of the deck along with the commodore and Captain Fitzpatrick. Reports from the beachmaster were positive, and by 1100 the exercises were terminated and judged to be a complete success. Over the next three hours, the process was reversed as the troops and their equipment were returned to their points of origin and loaded aboard the respective transport ships.

1400 Monday
8 November 1943
U.S.S. Zeilin departs Efate Island

At the end of almost a month of daily training exercises, and with the troops on board and all support tanks, heavy guns and trucks secured in their cargo holds, the U.S.S.

Zeilin raised its anchor and slowly got underway for the return trip to Espiritu Santo. The RADAR gang was busy during the initial movement, advising the officer of the deck of marginal clearances among some of the other transport ships that, for whatever reason, did not achieve the proper separation and were therefore 'off station'. Such anomalies were immediately resolved through the use of radio communications directives to the offending ships. By sundown, all ships were on station, including all screen vessels, and the convoy was making good its usual 17-knot zig-zag speed. Although I was on watch for the entire day, a relief crew showed up at 1600 and I went below to get something to eat. By sheer happenstance, I met Calvin Honeycut in the mess hall and we ate together. "How was your day, Calvin?", I asked. "It was a rather lackluster day, I'm afraid", replied Calvin. "Okay, and why was that?", I inquired. "Well, I guess it is just a case of me having an itchy trigger finger and knowing that I would not get a chance to fire my 20-mm gun.", replied a disappointed Calvin. "Well, not to worry, when the real thing comes along next June I suspect that your trigger finger will be mighty busy", I replied. "Do you really think so, Melvin?", asked Calvin. "Yes, I do. The Japanese are not going to give up without a fight. I don't know how many airplanes they have on Saipan, but there are over 23,000 Japanese soldiers there, so the American soldiers and Marines being carried in this convoy will have their work cut out for them", I speculated. After our meal, Calvin and I went to our life raft hideaway for a few hours of friendly discussion.

0100 Monday
29 November 1943
U.S.S. Zeilin at Espiritu Santo Anchorage

The convoy covered the 110 nautical miles in about the same time as on the outbound run. My watch assignment was from midnight to 0800 and the return trip was uneventful. No Japanese conflicts were encountered nor was there anything other than landmass targets apparent on the Surface Search RADAR. Of course, I was busy advising the officer of the deck with information on the position of all transports and screen vessels throughout the voyage. Upon arrival at Espiritu Santo, the troop transports and screen vessels anchored in their assigned locations. With the RADAR no longer required by the officer of the deck, I shut down both the surface and air-search machines. At that time, I made entries in the running time logs for both RADAR systems. This information serves as a basis for completing maintenance routines on operating elements, such as the cooling fan filter replacements as well as vacuum tube replacements. The administration of these tasks fell under the jurisdiction of our RADAR officer, Lieutenant (jg) Warren R. Davenport, together with Kenneth Fonticello, the RADAR gang's first-class electronic technician. Maintenance programs are detailed in the Navy service manuals for each RADAR and are all based upon a schedule that is determined by the number of hours of operation of a given RADAR system. These planned preventive maintenance routines assure that trouble-related 'downtimes' at sea are minimized to the greatest extent possible.

December 1943 to June 1944

Throughout this seven-month period, the convoy made monthly training voyages to Efate Island to hone the capabilities of the invasion force as a whole. During the period of 11 June 1944 to 14 June 1944, a U.S. carrier task force standing off Saipan conducted bombing runs along the two-mile length of the proposed invasion beaches. Although the Japanese sent up their aircraft in opposition to the U.S. airplanes, they were quickly neutralized by the new F6F Hellcats flying from the carrier group. The island of Saipan is 17 miles long and nine miles wide, and the highest point on the island is at an elevation of 1,554 feet. Since its capture by the Japanese, the island has served as the headquarters of the Japanese Central Pacific Fleet. Saipan is located approximately 1,500 miles south of Tokyo and 150 miles north, northeast of Guam. Considering the length of time that the Japanese have controlled the island, there is little doubt that it is heavily fortified.

0900 Sunday
11 June 1944
U.S.S. Zeilin en route to Saipan

The voyage from Espiritu Santo to Saipan will take slightly more than five days and is scheduled such that the convoy will arrive on 14 June at the end of the bombing operation undertaken by a U.S. Navy carrier task force. Making good its usual 17 knots, the convoy maintained a northwesterly course and followed the standard war zone zig-zag course changes to safeguard against Japanese submarine attacks. At 0930, there was a call to general quarters when a destroyer SONAR contact with an unidentified submarine was reported. A total of four destroyers was dispatched to prosecute the attack on the target and a wide-ranging pattern of depth charges was laid down. The destroyers were successful in sinking the submarine, which was confirmed by the recovery of debris that identified it as of Japanese origin. Japanese naval charts and life jackets were among the items found among the recovered flotsam. Although the area was swept for several hours after the convoy passed by, there were no survivors to be found, so the destroyers returned to their assigned screen positions around the convoy.

At 1330, the U.S.S. Zeilin RADAR gang identified an unfriendly aircraft target and the convoy was again called to General Quarters. The aircraft was visually identified as a Japanese reconnaissance plane, but it turned away from the invasion task force and no shots were fired. Thirty minutes later, the commodore passed the word to secure from General Quarters. As the General Quarters condition was canceled, I headed for the mess hall for lunch. Walking through the chow-line, I met Calvin and we enjoyed a meal of sugar-cured ham, sweet potatoes and green beans together. Neither of us felt the need to discuss the day's activities aboard the U.S.S. Zeilin.

0900 Monday
12 June 1944
U.S.S. Zeilin en route to Saipan

Following muster at quarters, I met Calvin at our favorite life raft hideaway. "Well, Calvin, at least you got to see a Japanese airplane for real yesterday, even though it was too far away to take a shot", I lamented. "Yes, for certain it proves that we are actually in a war zone. No doubt things will get hotter the closer we get to Saipan", Calvin observed. "And that submarine exercise yesterday also confirms that we are passing through hazardous waters", I concluded. "I have to agree with you on that point since we are only two days out now. It would not surprise me to find the Japs haunting us tomorrow or the next day for they obviously know that we are coming to get them", I speculated. "Melvin, does the fact that we are in an exposed area cause you any particular concern?", asked Calvin. "No, I am no more concerned now than I have ever been. I expect that it has to do with my reliance on the protection that the convoy has in its screening vessels", I replied. "I don't know, it seems that the closer we get, the scarier it all becomes", observed Calvin. "If I could change anything, I think that it would be to the correspondence censorship requirements, for I would enjoy telling my parents where I am and exactly what it is like to be in an active war zone", I said. "I don't disagree with you, Melvin, for I have felt for a long time that I would like to tell Mom and Dad about my travels in the South Pacific, but I expect it will be quite a while before that is possible", said Calvin. "Perhaps there will come a time when you can get a leave to go home and tell them in person", I suggested. "I would classify that possibility as an extremely remote one, realizing that I only just recently came aboard the U.S.S. Zeilin", complained Calvin.

0800 Tuesday
13 June 1944
U.S.S. Zeilin en route to Saipan

The "7th" Division officer had just finished taking roll call when the warning call to general quarters stations sounded. Climbing the single ladder up to the RADAR shack took only a brief minute and then I was entering the perpetually darkened space where the only illumination was the glow of the CRT's (Cathode Ray Tubes) of the surface and Air Search RADAR display units and the equally dim projector on the DRT (Dead Reckoning Tracer). Lieutenant (jg) Warren Davenport was on duty and I said to him, "Sir, what threat caused the GQ to be initiated?" Pointing to the air search display, he said "Check those clumps of bogeys 60 miles out. There is no IFF identification so I am certain that they are Japanese planes. Their airspeed is 250 miles per hour and they are on a direct course to attack the convoy. Orders have already been passed along to the screen to increase their speed in order to intercept the enemy planes as far ahead of the convoy as possible, and the aircraft carriers of the screen are launching their Hellcats as we speak", he concluded. At that point, RADARman 2nd class Felix Gonzalez called the lieutenant over to his display unit. "Lieutenant, it is clear now that those three target clumps consist of at least 50 aircraft each, so there are over 150 aircraft heading this way", said Felix. Alex Miller was manning the sound-powered phones tied into the ship-wide damage control network (DCN), and the lieutenant directed Alex to advise the bridge of the latest assessment of the incoming Japanese threat. Immediately thereafter, a ship-wide announcement was made to direct the attention of all gunners to the range and bearing of the incoming planes as well. The announcement also noted the fact that all gunners were released to "fire at will" when the enemy targets came within range of their guns, with an additional warning that there will be American planes launching in the area and to avoid firing on them.

Several minutes before the Jap planes came within range of the U.S.S. Zeilin's guns, long-range five-inch antiaircraft guns of the destroyers and cruisers in the advanced screen commenced firing. Lookouts stationed on the bow reported over the DCN seeing two planes plummet flaming from the sky and splash into the sea. As the screening vessels continued to fire, additional reports of flaming, out-of-control planes were passed over the network, and Alex gave a running account of what he heard for the benefit of the visually 'blind' members of the duty RADAR crew. At the same time, Lieutenant Davenport relayed the latest RADAR data to the bridge via Alex's telephone station.

Only a few minutes after the guns of the screen vessels commenced firing, the Jap planes came into range of the U.S.S. Zeilin gunners, and the 20-mm and 40-mm guns commenced firing. The noise and commotion became such a din that one needed ear protection to save his eardrums. According to the bow lookouts, the Jap planes were in trail and not taking any evasive action. Additional planes were shot down, and at that point it appeared that at least 25 planes had been destroyed. Bombs were being dropped, but thus far all bombs had dropped into the sea and exploded harmlessly. The attacking planes passed over the convoy and then, about a mile behind the convoy, made a wide sweeping turn taking up a course that would bring them down the center of the convoy for the second time. The ships trailing far behind the U.S.S. Zeilin had the first opportunity to intercept the Jap planes on their second pass. The stern lookout reported that the lead plane was shot out of the sky before reaching the convoy, as was the plane in the number two position. A lookout reported that the second plane came down in a flat spin and rotated about six times before plunging into the sea where it broke apart. There were no parachutes seen leaving the planes. With an unknown number of attackers remaining, the gunners on the three transports at the trailing end of the convoy, plus the rear screen vessels, maintained a continuous barrage and picked off the attackers one by one. The upshot of the defensive firepower of the Navy ships was such that none of the attackers reached the convoy for their second pass. All were shot down and splashed into the sea well to the rear of the last ship in the convoy. This fact was a disappointment to the U.S.S. Zeilin gunners for they were denied the pleasure of shooting down any planes after the initial pass over the convoy. Neverthelesss, the captain passed the word, 'A hearty well-done' congratulatory salutation to all of the gunners on the U.S.S. Zeilin. And, indeed, the commodore in command of the convoy passed a 'well-done' encoded radio message to all of his ships for their success in destroying the enemy threat and allowing the convoy to escape unharmed.

Following the raid, the screen vessels returned to their normal stations around the convoy as the aircraft carriers recovered their F6F Hellcats and serviced them for further duty along the way. At this time, the convoy resumed the zig-zag course changes.

With no other threats visible on the RADAR systems, the ships of the convoy secured from their general quarters status. Since I did not have the watch for another five hours, I left the RADAR shack and went to the liferaft where I expected to find Calvin appearing before long. It was actually about half an hour before Calvin arrived. I could tell that he was quite excited as he slung his leg over the side of the raft and relaxed in his usual place. "Tell me about it, Calvin, since we are blind as a bat inside the RADAR shack and can see nothing happening topside. What really happened?", I asked. (Calvin was one man of a three-man gunnery team on a 20-mm cannon on the portside upper boat deck). "Melvin, you wouldn't have believed it. It was like the sky was raining out-of-control airplanes dropping in flames into the ocean. I could see this destroyer far off our starboard bow blasting away about two miles ahead of the U.S.S. Zeilin and that is when the planes began to blow up. A few actually disintegrated into small pieces that just seemed to slowly float down through the air. I think that the gunners who shot the Japanese planes that reacted in that manner must have hit a bomb in its bay that literally blew the planes apart in the sky. It looked to me as though about half of the Jap planes were destroyed on their first pass over the convoy, and I believe that our gun accounted for at least two of the 'Betty Bombers'. I could clearly see our tracers penetrate the two planes that we had in our sights and they, like many others, literally blew apart in the air falling into the sea like so much popcorn. And, I did not see a single parachute deploy from any Jap airplane. The 40-mm crew on the U.S.S. Zeilin fantail accounted for two more 'Bettys', but their hits merely caused the planes to catch fire and spin out of control into the sea amid huge geysers of saltwater. It really seemed to me to be sort of like a 'turkey shoot' back on the farm. Had the Jap planes flown at a higher altitude, I think that they might have caused much more damage. Certainly their bombing efforts were totally ineffective", Calvin added. "Well, congratulations on a job well done, Calvin. You and your team have now had your 'baptism under fire' and given a good account of yourselves", I said as a compliment. "Thank you, Melvin. I appreciate your confidence in us. I knew that you would want to know all about the engagement, but I was delayed getting here because we had to dismantle our gun and clean and lubricate it and load up some more 20-mm magazines in case the gun is needed again today. "With the extent of the damage inflicted upon the Japanese Air Force this morning, I doubt that they will be in any hurry to mix it up with our convoy any time soon", I said.

Once I had learned all about the battle, Calvin and I decided to head for the mess hall and have our lunch. Today, the cooks were serving Sloppy Joes with mashed potatoes and gravy, along with vanilla pudding dessert. The meal was very tasty, I thought. I was scheduled to have the 1600 to midnight duty, so I left Calvin to take a shower and get ready for watch. Walking into the RADAR shack at 1600, things were quite calm compared to the hectic confusion that I found there during the morning's Japanese air attack. The convoy was still about 250 nautical miles from Saipan so special care was taken by the RADAR operators to seek out possible threats of whatever kind that might be lurking in the area. Submarines represented probably the most serious exposure to the convoy, hence our complete dependence upon the SONAR men aboard the destroyers of the screen. As it turned out, the watch was uneventful, and about the time we were to be relieved by the morning watch, the island of Saipan was just beginning to weakly appear, almost ghostlike, on the air search RADAR, dead ahead at 225 miles. It was not a solid image, but clearly the 1,554-foot mount Tagpochau peak on Saipan was reflecting enough radar energy to register on our CRT. The timing was superb and the Thursday invasion was exactly on schedule. Knowing that it would be a busy day tomorrow, I hurried to my compartment to get some shuteye and dream a while of Lucille. Letter writing to my sweetheart would have to wait until the invasion was over.

0800 Tuesday
13 June 1944
U.S.S. Zeilin
en route to Saipan

It turned out that the convoy was slightly ahead of schedule when the ship's navigator took his celestial fix Tuesday morning, so the commodore issued orders for a slight reduction in speed to bring the convoy to its launch point early on the morning of 15 June 1944. The carrier task force charged with bombing the designated beaches would finish its 'softening-up' operation at sundown today, 13 June 1944. Recognizing that the slowly moving transports and screen vessels would make very inviting targets, lookout posts were doubled throughout the convoy and RADAR watches on each ship were placed on continuous duty. At 1300, general quarters was set, and I hurried to the RADAR shack along with all of the other off-duty RADARmen. Lieutenant Davenport was on duty and quickly advised us of an unidentified target approaching from Saipan at 250 miles per hour at a distance of 75 miles. As before, the forward screen vessels increased their speed to engage the incoming targets at the greatest distance possible ahead of the convoy well before the intruders could reach the troop transports.

At 1310, operator Doug Jones advised the lieutenant that the target had resolved itself into a flight of 50 aircraft, and this information was immediately passed on to the captain by Manuel Ortega who was manning the damage control telephone. A short time later, we heard the sound of the five-inch antiaircraft guns of the lead destroyers laying down a deadly hail of shells. The lead bomber of the Jap flight exploded in flight and tumbled into the sea, according to a bow lookout report coming over the DCN. (Damage Control Network) Next, larger caliber guns of the cruiser screen added to the din reaching our ears. By then, six of the attacking 'Betty Bombers' had been confirmed shot down and reported by the U.S.S. Zeilin lookouts; then we began to hear loud explosions near our ship. The lookouts reported bombs falling and the captains of each ship were already in the midst of making emergency evasive turns. About that time, gunners on the U.S.S. Zeilin opened fire and the noise level reached an almost unbearable intensity. From within the RADAR shack, we could hear the 20-mm guns spraying the sky, as well as the more throaty roar of the U.S.S. Zeilin's foreward and after 40-mm cannons tracking the Japanese planes. As was the case during the earlier raid, the Jap bombers continued past the convoy, in trail, and reversed their course about one mile beyond the convoy to again overfly it. However, their ranks had been thinned to only six surviving 'Betty Bombers'. The screen vessels and rearmost transports redoubled their efforts, but their gunners missed the lead bomber as it quickly turned to port to avoid the convoy shell fire. In so doing, it loosed a bomb that struck the bow of the rearmost transport on the port side of the U.S.S. Zeilin. The blast disabled the 40-mm gun mounted on the bow and a small fire ensued. As the bomber continued on its path, a Navy shell found its mark and the bomber fell into the sea disintegrating into tiny pieces of aluminum as it fell. The two halves of its wing tumbled in opposite directions and the fuselage fell like an arrow and disappeared with a splash into its watery grave. Although the remaining three bombers dropped bombs along the way, they all exploded harmlessly in the sea. In contrast to the earlier convoy bombing incident, the remaining 'Betty Bombers' that survived the gauntlet of fire from their first pass over the convoy, regrouped at the rear of the convoy and held their course over its center, giving U.S.S. Zeilin gunners a second opportunity to avenge the damage inflicted upon the convoy. One by one, U.S.S. Zeilin gunners shot the remaining 'Betty Bombers' out of the sky. Two of the bombers were hit in their bomb bays and disintegrated in the air, while the last one had its left wing shot away and entered a death spiral and splashed into the sea. In no case were there any parachutes observed deploying during this second air raid.

Following the raid, the troop transport U.S.S. Eureka reported to the commodore, that although the bomb damage did not seriously impair operation of the ship apart from losing the firepower of the destroyed 40-mm gun, three gunners mates and one lookout were killed in the engagement. The commodore immediately sent a message of condolence to the shipmates of the dead sailors and, of course, would later author letters of condolence to the families of the deceased crewmen.

With the attack ended, the convoy reformed and continued toward its Saipan destination. With the distance to Saipan constantly decreasing, the convoy remained at general quarters for the remainder of the day. The RADAR gang rotated its relief to permit operators to obtain their meals and a minimal amount of sleep on a four-hours-on, four-hours-off duty cycle. With the limitations imposed by our respective duties, I would not see Calvin again until after the U.S.S. Zeilin departed from the Saipan invasion. My time would be spent operating the U.S.S. Zeilin RADAR systems while Calvin would be busy manning whatever guns were assigned to him.

0400 Friday
16 June 1944
U.S.S. Zeilin anchored at Saipan

The convoy arrived under cover of darkness and deployed along the four-mile invasion beachfront according to the invasion plan. The fully-loaded transports were anchored in a line 3,000 yards offshore interspersed with the screen vessels for protection from any surviving Japanese aircraft. The troops were fed and moved to their debarcation stations in preparation for off-loading. The convoy carried members of the V Amphibious Corps 2nd and 4th Marine Divisions, as well as the Army 27th Division. At 0430 the Higgins landing craft boats were lowered into the water and pulled alongside their respective transports to receive their passengers. Once loaded, the boats moved to their assigned staging areas in preparation for their run to the designated beachheads. At 0600 the boats were released for their journey to the beaches where they would encounter fierce Japanese resistance. Prior to their landing, heavy guns of the cruisers and destroyers raked the beaches to, as much as possible, destabilize the Japanese defenders.

Once on the beach, however, the U.S. troops came under heavy artillery and mortar fire, but by noon the Marines had secured two shallow beachheads, each two miles long. With the beachheads secured, crewmen of the U.S.S. Zeilin and the other transports expedited unloading operations of tanks, trucks and related equipment needed to support the attack in progress. Loads of ammunition and flamethrowers, were prominent among the early loads of provisions needed by the invasion force. Saipan would prove to be yet another of the bitter WWII Pacific island battles. The entrenched

Japanese could not be simply bombed into submission on account of their having dug deeply into the rocky terrain and buried their defenses such that only direct frontal assaults, supported by artillery, flamethrowers and bazookas, could eradicate the enemy forces. Fighting continued until 7 July 1944, a period of three weeks, when the island was finally declared secure. In the process, American losses were placed at 16,000 men while the Japanese lost 23,811 killed and 1,810 captured. Of the 430 battle-ready airplanes available to Japan on Saipan at the beginning of the invasion, the Americans destroyed 405. The loss of Saipan caused such a furor in the Japanese Parliament, that Prime Minister Tojo was ousted and extensive realignments in the army and navy command structures were made.

Having unloaded all troops and equipment, the U.S.S. Zeilin accepted a full load of wounded Marines and soldiers, and delivered them to a waiting hospital ship for further treatment and rehabilitation. From Saipan, the U.S.S. Zeilin was sent back to Guadalcanal to prepare for the invasion of the Philippines in late 1944 and early 1945.

During the months from July 1944 through December 1945, a mighty American armada was assembled in the South Pacific for the purpose of pushing the Japanese out of the Philippine Islands. The spearhead for this strategic move came on 23 October 1944, through 26 October 1944, with the invasion of the island of Leyte and its ultimate capture. It was on the island of Leyte that General Douglas MacArthur was able to fulfill his promise to return to the Philippines following his abandonment of Bataan earlier in WWII.

0400 Friday
15 December 1944
U.S.S. Zeilin anchored at Tacloban,
Island of Leyte, Philippine Islands

The U.S.S. Zeilin arrived at Tacloban along with 19 other troop transports for the purpose of boarding units of the Sixth Army that had successfully captured the island of Leyte from the Japanese in October 1944. These soldiers were selected for the invasion of Lingayen Gulf on the northern island of Luzon, with the objective of eliminating Japanese control of the city of Manila. Troops and their equipment were loaded on the transports, and several weeks of amphibious training followed. The fact that the military units of interest were already battle-hardened veterans of earlier amphibious invasions, significantly reduced the time needed for training purposes. During this period, Calvin Honeycut and I spent many hours in our life raft hideaway when our Navy duty assignments did not otherwise require our services. Because the ship had spent a number of weeks moored at Tacloban, mail was routinely received and letters to loved ones and family were sent to the United States. As the training cruises were completed, it was clear to Calvin and me that our departure for the Lingayen Gulf invasion would soon be upon us. Calvin shared his letters from Mary Jane with the comforting news about his growing children. In reciprocal conversations, I described the plans that Lucille had made for our wedding at the end of the war.

0900 Sunday
17 December 1944
Convoy departs Tacloban

With all of the training cruises having been completed, the convoy departed Tacloban heading north to turn east at Biliran Island and thence through the Samar Sea. There, after the convoy turned west across the Visayan Sea via Jingtotolo Channel, and then around the island of Mindoro through the Mindoro Strait; then due north along the west coast of the island of Luzon toward Lingayen Gulf. The total distance to be traveled was approximately 650 nautical miles. Although there were pockets of bypassed Japanese army elements near where the convoy passed, there was no apparent enemy interference with the convoy. In the confines of the east-west passage where there was a natural location for a Japanese surprise surface attack, none was forthcoming.

1200 Thursday
11 January 1945
Lingayen Gulf, Philippine Islands

The U.S.S. Zeilin and its retinue arrive and commence unloading operations that will ultimately lead to the elimination of Japanese control of Manila. Surprisingly, the landings were unopposed and the next day, its unloading operations having been completed, the U.S.S. Zeilin departed together with the balance of the convoy.

0800 Saturday
13 January 1945
Convoy off Manila Bay,
Philippine Islands

When the convoy arrived 50 miles offshore from the mouth of Manila Bay, well out of sight as well as out of range of Japanese shore-based artillery, unidentified RADAR targets were detected arriving from the north, at the approximate distance of the Lingayen Gulf, Japanese Airfield. General quarters condition was set in the convoy and the screen vessels deployed to meet any southbound threats. Planes from the U. S. aircraft carriers of the task force were sent into battle against an enemy of unknown strength. The initial RADAR targets eventually resolved into a Japanese flight of over 100 'Betty Bombers'. The Navy fliers quickly shot down 25 bombers, but a number of bombers were able to elude both the antiaircraft shells of the screen and the fury of the U.S. Navy fighter planes. U.S.S. Zeilin gunners were on the job and succeeded in knocking down six 'Betty Bombers', but one of the planes that was not knocked down turned out to be a single engine Kamikaze fighter/bomber known to Americans as a Japanese 'Frank' aircraft. Amid the din of the battle noise, the Kamikaze turned toward the U.S.S. Zeilin since it was the most prominent lead transport of the convoy. It was a day of broken clouds laying several thousand feet above the convoy, and from his position at the trigger of his 20-mm antiaircraft gun located on the upper boat deck, port side, Calvin Honeycut looked up and noticed the Japanese plane fly out of a cloud bank and rotate slightly as it was lining up for its approach to the U.S.S. Zeilin. Calvin observed that his tracer shells were penetrating the wings and cockpit of the bomber, and it seemed to him, at that instant, as though he could reach out and almost touch the pilot. The Japanese pilot was clearly visible wearing his dark green uniform, helmet, goggles and radio headphones. Still the plane continued on a collision course directly toward Calvin's exposed position. All too soon, Calvin realized that the silver-colored airplane, displaying the prominent red 'Meat Ball' insignia of the Japanese Naval Air Force, would smash into his position, but he continued firing hoping against hope that he could shoot off a wing or otherwise disable and divert the aircraft. As the plane's angle of attack shifted, Calvin compensated to bring his tracer shells unfailingly into his target. Although Calvin's aim was good, the "Frank" survived the bullets sent forth by Calvin's best effort. In an ever-steepening dive, the Kamikaze fighter/bomber smashed into the 20-mm gun position instantly killing Calvin, whose last conscious thought was of his children and wife Mary Jane who he would never see again in this lifetime. At the same time, Calvin's two gunner's mate partners also died instantly as they were smashed by the engine and wings of the plane and covered by the inferno of burning aviation gasoline. The shock of the crashing airplane was felt throughout the U.S.S. Zeilin, and the damage control crew arrived on the scene immediately, but could do nothing for the U.S.S. Zeilin 20-mm gun crew-members who were already dead.

The remainder of the Japanese bombers were destroyed by the F6F Hellcats from the carriers steaming nearby before they could harm any other troop transports or screen vessels. Standing in the RADAR shack, I monitored the progress of the attack, and happened to be looking into the navigator's chart room from our access hatch when I observed my 3rd class quartermaster friend dive for the deck. Realizing that he could see a threat that I could not, I dropped down to the deck as well. At that moment, I felt the U.S.S. Zeilin shudder from an unknown, but very powerful explosion. Within a minute, the DCN was reporting on the crash of the bomber into the upper port side boat deck. Clarifiying details came soon enough, and I learned that my good friend, and confidant, Calvin Honeycut, had been killed in the crash and subsequent fire. Following the initial shock, my first thoughts were of the impact that Calvin's death would have on his young family who would now have to be informed by the Navy of the calamity. With the attack over, the convoy continued on its course to Manus in the Admiralty Islands.

1200 Sunday
14 January 1945
U.S.S. Zeilin at sea

With the ship returning empty from the Lingayen Gulf invasion, Captain Fitzpatrick scheduled a burial-at-sea ceremony for the victims of the Kamikaze attack. A suitable pulpit had been erected on the port quarterdeck for the chaplain, along with supports for the canvas entombed, flag-draped bodies. Off-duty members of the crew had gathered nearby as high overhead a flock of white-winged seagulls circled lazily and looked down upon a solemn, bareheaded group of sailors standing in silence near the railing of the port quarterdeck. A choppy sea prevailed and the deck rolled uneasily underfoot, accompanied by the constant rumble of the two massive propellers rotating somewhere in the depths below. It was a moment of silent prayer, and with bowed heads mindful members of the somber group could discern the rustle of the American flag flying from a mast high overhead and the noise of small waves splashing against the ship's hull. At length, the chaplain cleared his throat and began his recitation of the ritual for burial-at-sea. Caps in hand, officers and members of the ship's company of the U.S.S. Zeilin gazed pensively at the chaplain and, intermittently, heads could be seen to turn and briefly contemplate the flag-draped bodies resting on a slightly raised platform at the deck's edge. The fact that I was standing among the group of mourners seemed no more real to me at that instant than had the events of the previous day wherein Calvin Honeycut had been killed. It seemed impossible for me to accept the fact that Calvin, my best friend, was no longer breathing, but lay lifeless beneath one of the American flags. An endless turmoil confused my thoughts, and only now and then did the sobering words of the chaplain filter through and register comprehendingly upon my brain. It was as though my mind was beset by some driving force which, given enough time, could devise an altogether magical formula and thereby create a means of turning back the hands of time; an act which would mercifully restore the breath of life to my departed friend, and simultaneously decree a different course for history to preserve his life for its natural duration. But, alas, such thoughts only made my melancholy grief more profound.

The firing of a rifle honor guard 21-gun salute to our departed comrades brought my senses back to reality, at least temporarily. Coincident with each volley, clouds of blue smoke erupted from the firing chambers of each rifle, and the acrid odor of burning cordite powder penetrated the nostrils of all, save the lifeless, flag-draped bodies nearby. At the conclusion of the honor guard presentment, the chaplain ascended a single-step riser and turned to face the mourners. His face was drawn and his usual cordial smile was replaced by a sober and meditative reflection; tears twinkled hesitatingly in the corners of his eyes. A brisk wind was blustering over the quarterdeck and whirled the chaplain's robes into balloon-shaped spasms, but in the solemnity of the moment, the occurrence went unnoticed. From his vantage point, the chaplain continued his intercession with God for the souls of our departed shipmates, but his words had become less and less distinct; the high wind and the seas and the sounds of the gulls screeching loudly overhead reduced the chaplain's voice to virtual inaudibility. And once again, my mind retreated to a more comfortable refuge in the past.

My thoughts of Calvin turned inward, and I sought solace in the past where on an early afternoon on a warm March day in 1944, the waters of the South China Sea were placid and sparklingly blue beneath a brilliant tropical sun. Frothy-white wakes trailed out behind the large convoy of ships struggling through the water with their cargoes of men and materiel of war. There were twenty-one amphibious troop carriers and a smaller number of escort vessels in the convoy. From time to time during that day, the course of the convoy had been altered, but such changes as had been made never caused the forward progress to greatly deviate from the present west-northwest direction. On board their respective ships, the Navy personnel performed their designated tasks while several thousand soldiers and marine commandos relaxed or otherwise prepared for their imminent rendezvous with an unknown destiny.

At 13:00, my duty section was relieved and I prepared to leave the darkened RADAR room. I exchanged information with my relief crew relative to the course and speed of the convoy, and indicated the presence of two identified targets appearing on the northerly edge of the surface search RADAR; no targets were then in evidence on the long-range air search RADAR. At the conclusion of this brief formality, I removed my lifebelt and helmet from the storage compartment adjacent to one of the high-powered RADAR transmitters and went out on deck.

Outside the hatch, which opened onto a short catwalk leading to the navigation bridge, I stood momentarily holding the railing while my eyes grew accustomed to the intense tropical sun. The overpowering effect of the sunlight rapidly diminished, and with my vision restored, I turned away from the bridge and made my way aft toward the stern gun deck. The ship barely rose and fell on the calm sea, and the ease of traversing the several ladders, catwalks and boat decks impressed me as being in marked contrast to the treacherousness of the same route when traversed under rainy, storm conditions. Within a few short minutes, I was climbing the last ladder to my objective. Perched some 25 feet above and well forward of the fantail deck, the aft gun deck represented one of the primary batteries of the ship's defensive armament. Situated on each side of the gun deck, well below the firing elevation of the 40-mm gun barrels, were two large emergency life rafts. Equipped with necessary emergency supplies under a canvas-lined exterior, the rafts were fastened at a 15-degree angle for ease of launching.

It had long been the custom during some of those endless hours at sea, when neither of us had duty, for Calvin Honeycut and me to visit the raft area and while away the hours in pleasant conversation. The position of the rafts offered a commanding view of the surrounding ocean and included a secondary attribute, that of reasonably easy access to our respective general quarters stations. As is perhaps true of many of the military professions, a sailor's life tends to become a boring monotony after but a few weeks at sea. Little news of the outside world is available and, of course, no mail is available to tell of loved ones at home. Thus, Calvin and I happily seized upon the companionship of our mutual interests to project ourselves away from the realities of a wartime environment.

When I climbed over the edge of the raft and leaned back in the warmth of the sun, only the three men of the duty gunwatch acknowledged my arrival. The steel-helmeted gunner's mates leaned forward in their seats on either side of the gun mount, and on a raised platform to the rear, the director-pointer operator, binoculars in hand, concentrated on some unseen object on the distant horizon. The conversation of the gun crew was barely intelligible and I easily excluded this distraction by contemplating the few white clouds which had drifted into view. As I lay there, I felt the vibratory pulsations of the twin-propulsion screws as of a thousand tiny fingers running up and down my spine. With my eyes closed, I basked in the sun's rays and imagined myself enjoying a warm Sunday outing at Laguna Beach back home in sunny Southern California.

Within ten minutes, my solitary reverie was interrupted by a flashback of Calvin Honeycut's shouted greeting from the deck below. By the time I had raised myself to one elbow and pushed my helmet above the level of my eyes, Calvin had gained the gun deck and was peering over the side of the raft, helmet in hand. A red-haired, freckled-face youth of nineteen, Calvin wore a perennial pixy smile and enjoyed his fellowman, and by his consistent good nature was one of the most popular crewmen aboard ship. And with his fine personality there was, in addition, a considerable number of complementary talents. He played several musical instruments, was a polished orator, displayed an exceedingly precise technical ability at his appointed Naval trade, gunner's mate first class, and could also count an accomplished literary ability, among several other noteworthy attributes. Calvin stepped lightly over the raft's edge, dropped his helmet at his side and leaned back and took a long deep breath of air. "I smell land in the air, Melvin, and not too far away either", remarked Calvin as he loosened his lifebelt and slipped down to a more comfortable position. "Your nose is correct as usual, Calvin. I noticed the same character about the air as soon as I stepped out of the RADAR shack on deck after watch. We're still several hundred miles from the nearest land, however, and probably won't see Luzon until early tomorrow morning", I concluded. "Well, in any event, it is a reassuring feeling just to know that it's out there even though the Japanese do occupy the island for the time being", and with that remark, Calvin closed his eyes and grew silent.

In days gone by, Calvin and I had discussed countless subjects that had taken our fancy including such topics as politics, the fortunes of war, life at home and that happiest of all prospects, what we hoped to become once the war had been won. You will observe from the foregoing that neither of us had the slightest doubt as to the ultimate outcome of the war with Japan; that the United States would emerge as the undisputed victor was a foregone conclusion.

Since Calvin preferred the silence of his own thoughts, I

let my own musings have free rein. For one reason or another, I recalled Calvin's vivid descriptions of his boyhood days at home in a small Iowa farming community. So intense was my recollection of the scenes that he had described, that I could literally feel the finely-powdered sand pushing its way up between my barefoot toes as I mentally followed Calvin down the trail to his favorite fishing hole. Astride an old oak log, far out from the edge of the stream, I could visualize Calvin pulling in a large catfish and throwing it into a disheveled looking creel, and the fragrance of new-mown hay wafted over the rushing water.

A sudden uneasiness caused me to stir, and I had just lifted my arm and noted that my watch indicated 0800 when the general quarters alarm commenced its ominous clanging warning. In a simultaneous movement, Calvin and I bounded over the side of the raft, crossed the gun deck and, three steps at a time, reached the deck below.

"See you later for chow, Melvin", called Calvin as he darted toward his station at a 20-mm cannon located on the portside of the upper boat deck. "Don't wait for me if I'm not there", I replied and continued on a run toward the RADAR shack. The GQ alarm broke into my flashback reverie.

Inside the RADAR shack, the duty crew was busily engaged in plotting the courses and speed of a large group of unidentified aircraft. The convoy screen had already deployed for action, and aircraft of the three aircraft carriers assigned to the convoy were just getting into the air. When not on duty during the signaling of a general quarters alarm, my assignment called for manning a set of sound-powered phones connected to the ship's Damage Control Network (DCN). As a general rule, the traffic on the net was virtually non-existent following the perfunctory reports of stations in readiness for action; this occasion was no different since within two minutes all stations reported a state of readiness, and my headphones became silent.

Seated in the dimly-lighted room near the hatch leading to the bridge, I could see my third-class quartermaster friend, binoculars in hand, scanning the northern horizon. Behind him, the helmsman stood ready to respond to the wheel commands of the captain, and within the RADAR shack the suspense mounted as the unidentified aircraft were determined to be committed to a course of interception with the convoy. I stayed busy making reports on the status of the potential threat, which was estimated to consist of over 100 Japanese planes, via the local intercom channel to the captain on the bridge.

The luminescent hands on the clock above the plotting table indicated 0810 and the target had closed in range to twenty-five miles. With no identification as friendly aircraft, it was clearly evident that the planes were Japanese fighters and bombers, and hardly had this thought occurred to me than the first thunderous reports of the five-inch guns of the lead destroyers reached my ears. As if on signal, the captain barked an order and the helmsman leaned into the wheel; the heavily laden transport heeled sharply to port under the strain of an evasive turn. The twenty transport vessels representing the balance of the convoy initiated a similar turn, and over the damage control net, the bow lookout excitedly passed word of two falling fireballs and of the geysers erupting on the horizon as the enemy planes crashed into the sea. We were to learn later that the first enemy losses were two twin-engine Japanese 'Betty Bombers'.

The larger guns of the cruisers stationed on the inner screen soon projected themselves upon the confusion of the moment. The chief quartermaster continued looking intently toward the direction of the coming threat and relayed the captain's periodic commands to the attentive helmsman. The compass barely became stabilized on a given heading when a command to change to yet another heading was given. Friendly aircraft had engaged the enemy at a distance from the convoy, but the superior numbers of the enemy made it impossible for our planes to effectively thwart the Japanese attack. And thus it came to pass that within a few brief minutes following the first defensive blast from our lead destroyers and the second commotion from the guns of the secondary cruiser screen, our own ship's guns went into action. The twin 40-mm guns in the bow were the first to speak and these were quickly joined by the multitude of tracer firing 20-mm cannons, and finally the sounds of all of the other ships' guns were overpowered by the stern three-inch rifle; altogether it became one continuous, shuddering, deafening roar accompanied by the lurching of the ship from side to side, as the captain continued his efforts to evade the falling bombs.

A series of continuous eye-witness reports of the events occurring topside was now being carried by the damage control network. To those of us, like myself, who had little or no view of the happenings topside, the reports helped allay a sense of apprehension. Airplanes were diving, firing, exploding, falling, and the sky was described as being alive with an infinite number of enemy aircraft; those crewmen on deck reported a sensation akin to some biological process in that for every enemy plane destroyed, two additional enemy planes seemed to appear, as if by magic, to take the place of their fallen comrades. As the battle raged, several ships were hit by Japanese Kamikaze planes and long columns of black smoke trailed from the convoy. The action had been continuous for thirty minutes, and at last the tempo seemed to diminish. The evasive maneuvers continued unabated, but a definite reduction in the intensity of the firepower, both from our own ship's guns as well as those of the screening vessels, was observed.

At length my leg developed a cramp and I stood, headphones on my head, to relieve the throbbing pain. As I flexed my leg at the knee, I chanced to glance through the hatch facing the wheelhouse. A third class quartermaster friend of mine was turning to walk toward the starboard wing of the bridge when I heard him shout some unintelligible warning and drop from sight as he dove for the deck. The only other person in view on the bridge was the helmsman and he also dropped to a prone position on the deck. Sensing an imminent doom, I scrambled for the RADAR room deck and crouched in a corner, while at the same time calling out to the duty radar operators to do likewise. Over the damage control phones I heard a scream of panic coincident with the sound of a violent explosion and felt a thunderous upheaval somewhere on the ship; the bulkheads and deck of the RADAR shack quaked frighteningly. The uncontrolled gyrations had partially subsided when the report came over the damage control network, "Fire, fire on the upper boatdeck. All damge-control fire personnel bear a hand and man your fire stations", concluded the announcement.

Only after the fire was being brought under control did it become clear that our ship had been hit, not by a falling bomb, but by a Japanese fighter/bomber, a Kamikaze suicide pilot had crashed his aircraft on the upper port side boat deck. The plane struck the port side and disintegrated into a flaming mass of volatile magnesium and burning gasoline. I did not immediately associate the significance of the area of damage with my friend Calvin or, for that matter, any of the ship's company; only after hearing requests for medical aid for the crew of the 20-mm gun emplacement in that area did I realize that, indeed, some of our men had been injured. Greater and greater detail came over the DCN and I was shocked into disbelief when word of the death of Calvin and two others was passed to the captain via the damage control network.

The damage to the ship was not extensive and the fire was quickly brought under control. By the time the fire was extinguished, the remaining enemy planes had departed and the order to "Secure from general quarters", was passed. I removed my headphones and made my way toward the bridge deck. As I stepped outside, three blanket-covered stretchers were being carried forward to sickbay and the impact of the scene brought tears to my eyes and those of the other crewmen standing nearby.

And with the tears streaming down my cheeks, I blinked away an unrecognizable and blurred image, and in its place came the crisp, reverent features of the chaplain. "Unto Almighty God we commend the souls of these, our departed brothers, and commit their bodies to the deep --- in the sure and certain hope of the resurrection of life and of life everlasting --- Amen."

The honor guard slowly lifted the funeral platforms and the three American flags stirred restlessly, as the canvas entombed bodies splashed into the white-capped waters of the South China Sea. The sound of this event was muffled by the wind whistling through the ship's rigging, and the thought occurred to me then that, but for the Grace of God, go I there!

Unidentified black and white photograph of burial at sea detail aboard the U.S.S. Zeilin—January 1945

National Archives Photo #80-G-58481.
Kwajalein Operation, January - February 1944
Men climbing down nets from a transport into landing craft to be transferred to LST's, here they will man amphibious tanks for the invasion of Kwajalein Atoll 31 January 1944.

National Archives Photo #80-G-47548
Kiska Operation
August 1943
Troops march up the beach at Adak during pre-invasion loading for the Kiska Operation 13 August 1943. Note their M-1 rifles and packs. LCM behind them is from U.S.S. Zeilin (APA-3). U.S.S. Pennsylvania (BB-38) is in the right distance.

National Archives
Photo #NH-89369
Okinawa Operation
1945
Marines climb down a debarkation ladder from a Coast Guard manned assault transport to board an LCVP to take part in the initial attack on Okinawa 1 April 1945.

National Archives
Photo #80-G-213104
Marshall Islands
Operation January through February 1944.
Marines climb down a transport's cargo net to board landing craft for the invasion of Marshall Islands Objective. Note combat gear and M-1 "Garand" rifles one with a sheathed bayonet.

This image of the aftermath of the kamikaze crash into the U.S.S. Zeilin shows crewmen inspecting the damage to be cleaned up. The PA3 with symbolic arrow is attached to the gunwale of the Captains gig which was utterly destroyed. The 18 cylinder airplane engine penetrated the upper boat deck on the house top and ultimately lodged itself in a Higgins boat hanging in one of the Wellin boat davits.

U.S.S. Zeilin: damage in officer's quarters caused by crash of Japanese kamikaze bomber into ship on Saturday 13 January 1945.

National Archives Photo N-18849F Meritorious Award Ceremony U.S.S. Zeilin January 1945 (APA-3) Silver star awarded to Robert H. Vinson mm2/c Award presented by Captain John Benedict McGovern. Silver Star presented for meritorious action associated with the Japanese kamikaze attack on 13 January, 1945.

EPILOGUE

RETURNING TO CIVILIAN LIFE

0900 20 February 1945
Ulithi Atoll
Caroline Islands

With my 10-day delay en route transfer orders in hand, I left the U.S.S. Zeilin for the States intending to enjoy nine months of electronic maintenance training at the Navy Base Electronic School located on Treasure Island in San Francisco Bay; this event was due to the courtesy of Lieutenant (jg) Warren Davenport, the U.S.S. Zeilin's Radar officer. At the time, the U.S.S. Zeilin was preparing to board troops for the invasion of Iwo Jima. Returning on an Army troop transport to the States, I reached San Pedro, California, and from there covered the 60 miles to my home by hitchhiking. Once I arrived home, I concentrated on enjoying my ten-day leave with my new sweetheart and parents in Ontario, California. About that time, my former sweetheart Lucille had married another sailor and unceremoniously cut me loose. Checking in at Treasure Island in San Fransisco Bay on 5 March 1945, I was chagrined to learn the following day that my name was included on a Navy draft out of Portland, Oregon where I would become a RADARman 2/C on the U.S.S. Warren (APA-53). In those days, the Navy managed its business using hundreds of IBM punched card-sorting machines, and to this day I blame a faulty punched-card for snagging my name and cheating me out of my chance to receive a good indoctrination in electronic equipment repair. At the time, I had visions of opening a radio repair shop after the war was over. Unfortunately, I was unable to interest anyone in authority in investigating the reason for the change in my orders. As a result of that assignment, I spent the remainder of WWII traveling to most of the remaining invasions of Japanese-held territories in the South Pacific.

1000 Monday
4 February 1946
Depart San Diego, California
on WWI Destroyer

By early 1946, I had accumulated enough points (calculated by adding your age and years of Navy service) to qualify for discharge from the Navy, and left the U.S.S. Warren and returned to San Diego where, on a nice sunny day, I joined about 200 other 'Ruptured Duck' candidates (slang term applied to the symbol of an eagle with widespread wings appearing on the honorable discharge emblem of the U.S. Armed Forces) aboard a WWI destroyer which transported us to the Navy Base at San Pedro, California, where we were all separated from the Navy. It was a fitting end, I thought, to a Navy career that continued for two years, ten months and six days.

Upon leaving the Navy, I obtained employment at the General Electric Small Appliance Division in Ontario, California, where I worked for a year and one-half. In those postwar days, GE was the principal employer in the small town of Ontario. My father and brother were employed there, as were my prospective mother-in-law and her two sons. I had met Shirley Maxine Chapman late in the war after Lucille had decided to marry another Navy man. Deciding to forego the expense of a church wedding, Shirley and I eloped on 9 November 1946, to Yuma, Arizona, where we were married by a Justice of the Peace. We accomplished, at that time, the event that friend Calvin Honeycut and sweetheart Mary

Jane had contemplated, but never achieved, a few years earlier.

It came to pass, that a decision was made by the Ontario GE management team in late 1946 to transfer all of the extraneous consumer products such as sandwich toasters, waffle irons, heating pads and portable bathroom heaters to GE's Bridgeport, Connecticut, Division, leaving the Ontario factory as the sole location where GE-manufactured electric irons would be produced. There were three types of irons in production in those days, regular household irons, steamirons used by tailors and small travel irons. By October of 1947, I had advanced to the highest paid hourly rate position in the factory, which was buffing on final assembly on the swing shift. (This shift extended from 4:00 p.m. to midnight) I elected to work that shift because of the 10% bonus that GE paid for night work.

The buffing craft involves the use of 2" wide 12"-diameter cotton cloth wheels, on which a fine abrasive compound is applied to remove lime and other foreign matter from the chrome-plated irons just before they were packed for shipment. The cloth wheels spin at a high rate of speed on a large, waist-high double-ended electric motor such that two men attend to the irons as they pass by on a conveyor belt partially submerged in a water-filled cooling tank. Prior to reaching the cooling tank, the assembled irons were circulating on a conveyor system near the ceiling of the factory with electricity applied to each iron and upon descending, the irons were given a final temperature test just before entering the cooling tank. One night, in early August 1947, my coworker and friend, Shorty Rose, accidentally let the cord of the iron that he was buffing become entangled by the shaft of the buffing machine. The iron was jerked from his hands flung around the shaft, breaking the integral electric cord connection within the iron handle which, at that instant, converted the iron into a projectile. At the end of its short 24" flight, the point of the iron ended up piercing Shorty's left shoe and nearly severed his big toe.

Naturally, that incident brought the hazardous nature of my position forcefully to my attention, and I immediately contemplated changing jobs. Inasmuch as my days were free, the following day I visited the telephone company offices in Pomona, California, and applied for a position. There was nothing open at the time, but I was encouraged by Mr. Sheppard, the plant superintendent, to check in with the company periodically. I began making weekly follow-up visits to the telephone company and got to know the superintendent's secretary quite well. Three weeks into October I drove the six miles to Pomona to check once again for an open position. Following our usual greeting, the secretary mentioned that a new plant superintendent had arrived and would I be interested in meeting him? Of course I said "Yes". The secretary showed me in to Mr. Clay Mosely's office where we were introduced. At the conclusion of our informal greeting, Clay leaned back in his swivel chair with a smile on his face and said, "I understand that you want to go to work for the telephone company." I was somewhat taken aback by the statement realizing that Mr. Mosely already knew that I desired a position. After only a moment's hesitation, I decided to take a positive approach and said, "Yes, Mr. Mosely I am very interested in working for your company, and Mr. Sheppard promised me a job". Mr. Sheppard was Clay's predecessor in his position as plant superintendent and kept encouraging me to not give up for eventually a position would open up for me; he had just never told me when that would occur. At that point, Clay stood up and offered his hand again and with a grin on his face replied, "Oh, is that so? Well, Mel, you come and see me at 8:00 a.m. tomorrow morning". "Thank you, Mr. Mosely, and you can count on me being here on time", I replied as I left his office walking on air. And, at 8:00 a.m.the next morning I became a telephone man for what was then the Associated Telephone Company. The Associated Company had recently bought out the Pomona Home Telephone Company.

8:00 a.m. Tuesday
October 27, 1947
280 South Mountain View Avenue
Pomona, California

Thus it was that I left GE and took a position with the Associated Telephone Company in Pomona, California, as a telephone installer. This event occurred one month from the day that our first daughter, Susan Marie was born on 27 August 1947. Dial telephones had finally come to the Ontario/Pomona area and the precise title of my position was 'dial changer'. Regardless of that fact, I never changed the first dial. Instead, after spending an hour filling out all of the usual paperwork associated with new hires, I was placed with a journeyman installer by the name of Charlie Banks to 'learn the ropes'. In those post-WWII days, the telephone company did not operate any type of training schools. That would change in later years when training schools were established for all craft construction and installation positions. There was a pent-up demand for telephone service in those days, and the telephone company was busy installing many new central switching offices in the towns surrounding Ontario and Pomona because all of the existing central offices were completely filled with existing WWII customers and there was no room for growth.

8:00 a.m. Tuesday
December 27, 1947
280 South Mountain View Avenue
Pomona, California

Eight weeks later, following my indoctrination by Charlie Banks, I was assigned to my own installer truck (It was a 1939 Chevrolet Custom Chassis on which was mounted the traditional steel box enclosure containing ladders and all of the wire, insulators, protectors, terminal blocks and related hardware necessary to install telephones.) See Photo on Page 515.

While under Charlie's wing, I learned how to climb up telephone poles and climb down again without killing myself. This knowledge was obtained on a Black Diamond pole behind Charlie's home where we stopped to eat our lunch each day. Starting up my truck that first day, I drove happily from the pole yard with eight telephones to install my very first day alone. At that time, I naively assumed that I had finally arrived at the pinnacle of my civilian career. It had not dawned on me yet that there was still plenty of room for professional growth. For here I was, essentially my own boss, with no one looking over my shoulder, driving around any one of several towns in Pomona Valley, in my own service truck and meeting lots of nice people and getting paid for it all. Even in the face of Shorty Rose's admonition that by leaving GE I was making the biggest mistake of my life, and some day I would be back on GE's doorstep begging for a job; as it turned out, that day never came. Speaking of pay reminds me that my early years of telephone work caused considerable stress and friction at home. This circumstance arose from the fact that I left a job paying $2.10 per hour on the swing shift at GE and took a position that paid only 90 cents per hour with the telephone company. Therefore, our income was essentially reduced by 57% when I signed on with the telephone company. At the time of my employment, I also applied for 'on the job' subsistence pay under the Government's GI Bill. A month later, in January of 1948, I began receiving $45 per month from the government as an 'on-the-job training allowance.' This added income served to reduce some of the stress encountered on the home front, but there were still several lean years ahead for the Mel Hacker family income to catch-up with our actual needs.

8:00 a.m. Tuesday
October 30, 1949
280 South Mountain View Avenue
Pomona, California

Two years later, in 1949, I transferred into the Telephone Repair Department where I spent three years working to correct residential telephone trouble conditions. It turned out that the telephone company could not obtain enough new wire to replace deteriorated residential lines during WWII, so for three years repairs were implemented by merely patching broken wires and taping up the splices. Naturally, rainstorms typically brought many, many trouble complaints. In 1949 many old lines were of open wire construction not yet replaced by copper cable. When a repairman was sent on residential services that were fed by such a facility, it was mandatory that the repairman, whoever he was, climb the pole as gingerly as possible so as not to cause the rusty iron wire to fall. I quickly learned to climb those old poles by throwing my lineman's belt around the pole and adjusting it to the proper size set my climber's spur into the pole and then hitch my belt up with each step I took until I could reach and repair the defective wire, hoping all the while that the vibrations from my climbing would not cause a line wire to fall. Three years as a repairman was enough and then I applied for a position in the PBX Department. Moving into the PBX Department was a dream come true since I no longer had to climb telephone poles or work outside during rainstorms. In my new department, I learned to install teletype machines as well as small PBX switchboards and pushbutton telephone systems for lawyers, doctors and other professional clients. Throughout this period I received pay increases every six months, and by the time that our second daughter, Christine Yvonne, was born on 15 November 1949 our financial position had improved significantly.

5:00 p.m. Tuesday
4 June 1953
280 South Mountain View Avenue
Pomona, California

When I arrived at the pole-yard at the end of my work day, Everett Wood, the PBX foreman, called me aside and explained that I was being assigned to a special job located at the Ontario Airport Control Tower. He further advised me that I should drive my company truck home that evening and report directly to the airport the next day and meet Clay Mosely and Bill McNee at the control tower at 9:00 a.m.

During the six years that had passed since Clay had hired me, he had been promoted to a high-level position in the General Office Plant Department in Santa Monica. Of course, I enjoyed meeting Clay again and meeting Bill McNee for the first time. When we met at the customer location the next day we found that all of the required cable, relay apparatus, terminal blocks and related hardware had been delivered by the Pomna Supply Department. Bill, Clay and I spent an hour or so reviewing the circuit and mechanical drawings and deciding where the telephone cables would be installed. With those decisions having been made, I busied myself pulling the 25-pair copper-wire cables in place and terminating them at the proper locations. Cabling the system would occupy me for the next four days.

The control tower project involved the installation of a newly developed key telephone system (Type 109A, as I recall) for the Ontario Airport Control Tower. The Ontario airport had entered a period of rapid growth and had simply outgrown its existing communications system which was unable to support the increased commercial traffic landing at Ontario. The Type 109A Key telephone system included a number of features that had the promise of simplifying controller communications with aircraft either in flight or on the ground.

9:00 a.m. Wednesday
June 8, 1953
Ontario Airport

Bill and Clay drove from Santa Monica each day, and I drove from home in Ontario to the airport. Driving from home eliminated the 12-mile drive to the Pomona Pole Yard each day. Of course, I thought nothing of this chance assignment at the time, since I was mostly performing 'gruntwork' pulling in multi-conductor copper-wire cables and fanning the wires out on terminal strips at various control positions in the airport tower, as well as wiring the relay equipment remotely located in a room at the base of the control tower. The work was interesting and I enjoyed learning how to read and interpret the associated wiring diagrams as well as performing system tests to verify proper operation at the end of the installation phase. With the airport job completed, I returned to Pomona full-time and began completing installation orders for key telephone systems for attorneys and doctors' offices (These systems employed multi-pushbutton telephone sets to permit accessing any of several business telephone lines.)

5:00 p.m. Monday
December 14, 1953
280 South Mountain View Avenue
Pomona, California

At quitting time on a busy Monday, I received a long distance telephone call from Bill McNee during which he offered me an engineering management position in the Customer Equipment Engineering Department in the company's headquarters location in Santa Monica, California. At the time, Bill was the manager of a group of engineers who developed standards for telephone equipment intended for residential and business applications. With only a high school diploma, that I would not actually receive until 1948, I did not feel qualified for the position, and I explained my concern to Bill. Nevertheless, Bill convinced me that he was not searching for a design engineer, but merely wanted to hire someone who was very experienced in applying business communication systems in the field. By that time, of course, I had at least seven years of that kind of field experience under my belt.

When I returned home that evening, I explained the events of the day to Shirley and we took the time to visit her mother and my parents to consult with them about the opportunity. It was our hope that they would tell us whether or not to accept the new position. In the end, their views were that Shirley and I were free, white and 21, and could therefore make up our own minds, which we did and I accepted the position. By then our third child, Royce Eugene, had been born on 3 October 1953; and in January of 1954, we moved to El Segundo, California, into a new house that had just been completed. The high price of real estate in Santa Monica prevented us from locating our home there. With three children to raise, we needed more bedrooms than we could afford in the price ranges quoted by Santa Monica real estate agents. However, we found homes in El Segundo to be in a range that we could afford and the ten-mile drive to the office in Santa Monica did not seem too intimidating to me. It turned out that several other telephone engineers were located in El Segundo so our comfort level with the city was quite high. Also, the city was the home base for the local Standard Oil Refinery and this fact assured us that property taxes were reasonable and would remain so.

8:00 a.m. Monday
January 12, 1954
805 McCarthy Court
El Segundo, California
Moving to El Segundo

So it was that Shirley and I selected a new two bedroom and den home in El Segundo only ten miles from my Santa Monica office. In later years, I was to marvel at the fact that each of our moves within the telephone company was accompanied by the purchase of a home that cost about twice as much as the one we left behind. When Shirley and I were first married, we made up our minds that we would not rent our home. Rent receipts do not buy a person anything, so we elected to purchase our own home. Of course, at the time of our marriage we did not have a meaningful bank account. However, Shirley's mother was willing to lend us $600 for the down payment on a small one-bedroom cottage in Ontario. The owner of the cottage was willing to carry the note for the difference between the down payment and the sales price of $4,500. It was arranged that we would make our monthly payments directly to the local Bank of America branch in Ontario. Following the birth of our daughters we attempted to borrow money from a bank with which to expand our small one-bedroom cottage. Because it was less than 900 square feet in size, the bank declined to grant a loan. In 1952, we found a new home in a developing Ontario subdivision that we purchased on a GI Bill loan for $7,500 with no money down; just move in and commence paying $52 per month on the GI loan. When we purchased this new home, we decided to rent our first home rather than sell it. When we moved to Santa Monica we moved into a new two-bedroom and den, bath and one-half home in El Segundo and paid $15,850. This move became possible through a loan from the Telephone Company Credit Union. Just prior to our transfer to NYC, Shirley and I had purchased a four-bedroom two-bath home on the west side of El Segundo for $30,000. Our home in Stamford, Connecticut was a four-bedroom 2 & 1/2-bath home with full basement for which we paid $47,500. Admittedly, with each move the size and quality of our homes increased along with the prices.

8:00 a.m. Tuesday
January 2, 1962
Palm Avenue home
El Segundo, California

Accepting the general office position carried with it the necessity of driving the ten-mile distance from El Segundo to Santa Monica, Monday through Friday. The drive was enjoyable enough along the shore of the Pacific Ocean where the weather typically was clear and cool. In the early days, the drive crossed several hundred acres of farmland that was worked by Japanese farmers raising celery and other produce and sold the produce in stands along the nearby Pacific Coast highway. In later years the County of Los Angeles acquired the farmland and it was replaced by a man-made marina that still exists today named Marina Del Rey.

At the time that I joined Bill McNee's Customer Equipment Engineering group, I became aware of the fact that I was competing with other engineers who were much more technically qualified than I was. There were many degreed engineers in the group as well as one Ph.D. Under a company program that paid for tuition and book expenses, I signed up for night school classes at the Los Angeles Trade Technical College. During the ten years following our move to El Segundo, I attended night school continuously and performed several different jobs in the Customer Equipment Engineering Department, and eventually was promoted to work directly for Mr. C. M. Davis, then the Chief Engineer of the company. Dave seemed to like my style of writing and put me to work taking care of personnel matters for his 300-man Engineering Department, as well as writing Telephone Equipment Specifications from time to time. My work for Mr. Davis eventually led to my being offered an engineering managerial position in the New York City Headquarters Office of what, by that time, had become the General Telephone System, the largest independent telephone company in the nation with operations in 31 states. I accepted the position and after arriving at my new position in New York City, I signed up to continue my night school educational program at the Bridgeport Engineering Institute in Stamford, Connecticut. My studies included English composition, algebra, electrical circuit theory as well as advanced mathematics and physics. I earned enough credits to receive the AA degree in Electrical Engineering, but missed out on the EE degree on account of a full-time travel schedule that was assigned to me in 1969 making it impossible for me to attend night school classes. About this time, GTE Engineering Department Management began placing emphasis on the need for personnel who were rated as Professional Engineers. Thus, I studied the required material and applied to the State of Connecticut for a Professional Engineering License. I successfully passed the oral and written examinations and was granted my

Professional Engineering License in 1975.

I moved my family to Stamford, Connecticut, in June of 1962, from which I commuted on the New Haven Railroad to my New York City office for the next 11 years. In 1972, GTE , as it was then known, moved out of NYC to Stamford, Connecticut, where a new headquarters building had been under construction since early 1970. That relocation was a wonderful gift for most of the personnel in the headquarter's office of the company. In my case, we saved the $43.10 per month train ticket expense as well as the New York State and New York City income taxes. I calculated at the time that our family saved about $2,400 per year with nothing else changing except my job location. On top of that, I gained two hours per day additional time with my family by eliminating the commuting time to and from NYC. (And how does one place an economic value on quality time with one's family?) Another fringe benefit came from having a parking space assigned to me beneath the GTE building thereby eliminating the accumulation of snow and ice in the wintertime. It was the best of all worlds!

10:00 a.m. Monday
June 18, 1978
Stamford Connecticut

In 1978, a major realignment of GTE Engineering personnel resulted in the division of our staff of approximately 600 employees into regions that would see employees ending up being transferred to either Irving, Texas, Los Gatos, California, or Indianapolis, Indiana. Since I had transferred to the Headquarters Office from the California company, I considered it likely that I would be returned to that company at either Santa Monica or Los Gatos. About this same time, I was offered a management position with the Northern Telecom Company (a major telephone equipment manufacturing company) and I elected to take early retirement from GTE and accepted the position which was located in Nashville, Tennessee. By then our two girls had already married and Royce had graduated from college and decided to settle down in California. So, Shirley and I moved to Nashville where I spent the balance of my working life, retiring in 1993 at a time when a downsizing program resulted in the elimination of my engineering position. By that time, I had been working in the telephone industry for fifty years. As it turned out, I lost Shirley to pancreatic cancer in July of 1989.

From my earliest childhood days, I have always been interested in airplanes, and flying in general. This interest was fueled, in part, by a daily 1935 children's' radio program that was sponsored by the Richfield Oil company. The story line of the 15-minute nightly program revolved around Speed Robertson, the captain of a DC-3 transport plane, and his copilot Jimmy Allen and their never-ending flying adventures. The intent of the program was for children to encourage their parents to purchase Richfield gasoline and thereby be entitled to receive coupons that could be mailed in with 25 cents to obtain copies of flying lessons. I still have four of those ancient lessons, and the principles explained in those well-illustrated, long-ago lessons are as meaningful and accurate today as they were 72 years ago in 1935.

6:00 p.m. Friday
July 17, 1978
Washington, D.C.
Crown Book Store

In 1978, my engineering duties at Northern Telecom involved arranging to have all of NTI's telephone products registered with the FCC under their Part 68 Rules for customer-owned telephone equipment. In July of that year,

I happened to be in Washington, D.C. to attend a telephone industry meeting involving the implementation of technical changes in Part 68 Rules. With nothing to do one evening, I visited the nearby Crown Book Store to acquire something to read for entertainment and while away the evening hours. Upon entering the store, I was confronted by an eight-foot long table piled two feet high with a miscellaneous assortment of close-out books on sale for 99 cents each. I searched through many volumes and finally selected a book titled "How to Buy a Used Airplane". I began reading that same evening and on the return flight to Nashville, I finished reading the book from cover to cover, and became so fired up with a desire to fly an airplane that I signed up with the local Beechcraft Dealership Aero Club, and the very next day I took my first flying lesson. This was in August of 1983, and by December I had earned my private pilot's license.

Over the 4th of July holiday in 1984, I flew with a novice pilot friend of mine to Cleveland, Ohio, where we attended an auction that included many old, vintage magneto telephone sets. At that time in my career, I was an avid collector of old telephone sets. We left Nashville on a hot, muggy July day with plenty of haze. Nevertheless, the flying conditions were perfectly safe for flying under VFR rules (visual flight rules). The auction took place on Sunday, in a gallery that had no windows on the outside world from the bidding floor. You can imagine my consternation when the end of the auction came and I and my friend went outside to find that a severe rainstorm had blown in, so we went back to our motel room and enjoyed an evening meal. The storm was still present when we awoke on Monday morning. At that point, I made a long distance telephone call to my supervisor in Nashville and explained why I could not be at work that day. Although the worst of the storm had passed by, as Monday evening came it was still too cloudy to permit flying under VFR rules. It wasn't until Tuesday morning that we could finally return to Nashville. As a result of that experience, I resolved to continue my flight training and obtain an Instrument Flight Rating. I began training upon my return to Nashville and a year later, after some 200 flight hours of training, I took my instrument check flight and could thereafter file instrument flight plans for trips under marginal weather conditions. At that point, the utility of my airplane really came into its own. By that time, I had purchased a one-third interest in a Beechcraft Model A-36 Bonanza six-place single engine airplane and very much enjoyed flying that 160 mile per hour time machine. It was not unusual to see 200 miles per hour on our GPS receiver with a nice tailwind. The three-family partnership purchased the plane new and even today it is considered by most private pilots to be the Cadillac of the single engine aircraft fleet.

So it was that it only took me 72 years to realize my boyhood dream of 1935, when my brother and I attempted to build our own airplane. By that time, Harold had also obtained his pilot's license. I enjoyed flying until 1997 when a heart condition caused the FAA to deny my application for a medical certificate. By the time I lost my medical certificate, I had accumulated over 1,100 flying hours. It is still possible for me to fly today, but only with a certified flight instructor to act as pilot in command.

After Shirley's death, I struggled to keep as busy as possible on the job. In this connection, it was necessary for me to visit the second floor of our headquarters building from time to time to have my FCC Telephone registration filings FAXed to the FCC in Washington, D.C. Along the way, the FAX lady in the Office Services group accidentally broke her ankle and a 'Kelly Girl' was brought in to temporarily handle her workload. During that period, I was introduced to Ms. Charo Carrero Skaggs (the Kelly Girl) on Valentine's day of 1990, and after many dates and determining that we were quite compatible, we were married on October 6, 1990.

We flew all of our extended family members to Nashville for the big day. Charo has a son and daughter living in Nashville and an older daughter living in Georgia, My three children are scattered around the country with Suzy in Penfield, New York, Chrissy then in Kensington, Connecticut, and Royce and his wife in Alta Loma, California. Royce is a Central Office technician with the Verizon Telephone Company, and works for the company in Ontario, California; only six miles from his home. Being released involuntarily at the time of my retirement due to NORTEL's downsizing program was a concern to me, but in later years, I came to realize that the company actually did me a favor. I say this because I was able to spend full-time with my new wife a full two years before it would have otherwise been possible.

During March of 2005, Charo arranged a celebration for my 80th birthday. There were 93 friends and family members attending, including my two brothers and two sisters. Also attending were all of my children, and one grandson and two granddaughters. The second grandson, Matthew Salzman, is in the Navy and was away at sea.

During August of 2005, Charo and I were able to attend the annual reunion of former crew members of the U.S.S. Zeilin. (APA-3). Although such reunions had been held for the past eighteen years, for some inexplicable reason I was unaware of their existence. Most recently, Charo and I were favored by a visit from Marshall Herron and his wife, Tiny, who passed through Nashville on their way to a winter vacation in Arizona. Marshall and I had not seen each other since 1962 when I stopped by his home on my way east through Sewickly, Pennsylvania, to my new job with the General Telephone Company in New York City. During their brief visit, Marshall and I enjoyed catching up on events in our lives over the past 43 years. During our conversation, Marshall mentioned that we two are the only surviving members of the 25-man U.S.S. Zeilin RADAR gang of WWII.

In May of 2006, a reunion of the former crew members of the U.S.S. Warren, the second Troop Transport that I served on in WWII (APA-53), was held in Atlantic City, New Jersey, and Charo and I attended. This reunion was essentially anticlimatic inasmuch as I did not know or remember any of the 27 individuals who attended the function and there were no other RADARmen present.

Neither while I was still serving on the U.S.S. Zeilin nor after entering civilian life did I ever learn any information about Calvin Honeycut's family. Nevertheless, I conclude this story with a prayer for Calvin, Mary Jane and the other Zeilin crew members who did not survive the war. God grant that they may rest in peace!

Melvin E. Hacker
Nashville, Tennessee
March 2006

Newly married Eugene Van and Marilee Ruth Van. Circa June 1943.

Shirley Maxine Chapman following her afternoon classes at Chaffey Union High School in Ontario, California. Circa 1945.

Marvin Dean Hacker and sister Ida Mae Hacker on the occasion of Ida Mae's third birthday. The automobile is Melvin's $10.00 1928 Chevrolet rumble seat coupe. Location is the back yard of 459 West Elm Street, Ontario, California. Circa January 1943.

Newly married Shirley Maxine Hacker and Melvin Eugene Hacker. Circa September 1946.

Melvin Eugene holding his daughter Christine Yvonne Hacker and his daughter Susan Marie Hacker sitting on her tricycle. The vehicle is Mel's 1937 Chevrolet telephone service truck. This photograph dates from 1950.

Melvin Eugene Hacker and his family at that time. Left to right are Melvin Hacker, Susan Marie Hacker, Christine Yvonne Hacker and Shirley Maxine Hacker. Circa 1950.

General Electric appliance factory building on Main Street Ontario, California. Circa 1946.

The landmark Ford Lunch Restaurant which was razed following the end of WWII.

The Percy Hacker home place located at 459 West Elm Street, Ontario, California photo taken in December 2006. At that time, the home was 65 years old and is owned today by Mr. Jerry Van, Percy Hacker's grandson.

The Ontario, California Union Pacific Railroad Depot which was razed by the railroad company in recent years.

APPENDIX #1

1. ** KAMIKAZE ATTACK AFTER ACTION REPORT PREPARED BY CAPTAIN THOMAS B. FITZPATRICK OF THE U.S.S. ZEILIN (APA-3).

THIS REPORT WAS SUBMITTED ON 31 JANUARY 1945, 18 DAYS FOLLOWING THE ATTACK. THE TRANSCRIPT OF THE CAPTAIN'S REPORT FOLLOWS:

Action Report
Submitted 31 January 1945
For event on 13 January 1945
APA3/A16-3/A9/A12/s

Serial 06

C-O-N-F-I-D-E-N-T-I-A-L

From: The Commanding Officer.
To : The Commander in Chief, U.S. Fleet.
Via : (1) Commander Transport Division 23 (Temp.) - Commodore H.W. Graff
(2) Commander Amphibious Group THREE - R. Adm. R. L. Conolly.
(3) Commander Amphibious Force, Seventh Fleet - (V. Adm. D. E. Barbey)
(4) Commander Seventh Fleet - (V. Adm. T. G. Kinkaid).
(5) Commander Amphibious Forces, U.S. Pacific Fleet - (V. Admiral R.K.)
(6) Commander in Chief, U. S. Pacific Fleet - (Admiral C. W. Nimitz). Turner.

Subject: Action report- U,S.S. Zeilin (APA-3), 13 January 1945.
References: (a) U.S. Navy Regulations, 1920, Art. 712(2), 712(3), 874(6).
(b) Report of A.A. Action (COMINCHF-01 AA-1, Feb. 1944 (Rev)
(c) Photographs of Battle Damage to U.S.S. Zeilin (APA-3).
NOTE: All of the photographs of the U.S.S. Zeilin's battle damage were not available to the author.

1. In compliance with references the following summaries are submitted.

PART 1. Brief Summary.

A Japanese single engine plane, either a "Frank" or a "Grace" was sighted coming out of low hanging clouds on the Port Quarter of this ship, at a range of about one thousand yards. The plane came out of the clouds banking to the left and then straightened out, heading for the ship in a 40 degree dive. When first sighted, it bore 060 Degrees true (230 degrees relative). On sighting the plane, fire was opened with the after 40mm battery and the Port Battery of automatic weapons. The plane came through the fire and as it approached close to the ship it appeared to bank slightly to the left. The right wing of the plane struck the port kingpost and boom serving number six hatch, swung inboard under the radio antenna and crashed on the starboard side of the house top, frames 32 to 37. From the time of sighting the plane, when it came out of the clouds, until it crashed on deck was about ten seconds.

PART II - Preliminaries.

(a) The Zeilin, with Commodore Transport Division 23 (Temp) (Commodore H.W. Graf) embarked, was in company with Commander Task Group 77.14.6 (Commander Amphibious Group THREE - R. Adm R.L. Conolly) in the Appalachian and Commander Task Unit 79 (Commander Third Amphibious Force - V. Adm T.S. Wilkinson) in the Mount Olympus. The transports were disposed as shown in enclosure (A). (Enclosure not available to the author.)

(b) The disposition had left Lingayen Gulf, Luzon, on the afternoon of 12 January 1945 and was bound for Leyte. The disposition was in latitude 15 degrees - 23' N and Longitude 119 degrees - 10' E.

(c) A single radical (sic) { No doubt the Captain intended to say "Radial"} engine, eighteen cylinder Japanese plane, with twin banks of nine cylinders each, with the windmill propellers, either a "Frank" or "Grace", was the only plane encountered.

PART III Chronological account of the action.

Ship was on base course 169 degrees True, speed 13.5 knots, Zig Zagging according to Plan SIX. The ships course at 0821 was 189 degrees True.

0815 Flash Red. Ship went to General Quarters. Set Condition I and Material Condition Affirm. All guns were loaded, magazines fitted to automatic weapons and placed on safe.

0818 Warning Snapper.

0820 AA Tracer fire observed on port bow. Gun fire was either from the Appalachian, the screen or both. No enemy planes were observed from the bridge of this ship. After the action, the after battery reported sighting a plane intermittently through the clouds, on the port beam, but stated that its identity was not determined.

0821 Plane sighted bearing 060 degrees True, banking to the left coming out of the clouds, distance about 1,000 yards. It straightened out in a 40 degree dive, heading towards the ship. After 40-mm and port automatic weapons opened fire. Right wing of plane struck port boom of #6 hatch, which swung the plane inboard under radio antennas, crashing on housetop. No violent explosion was felt but flames enveloped starboard after part of housetop. Damage control parties were called away and stretcher bearers sent to take away wounded.

0825 Report received that engineering spaces were free of damage.

0830 Fire was extinguished.

The weather was clear with surface visibility at 5 to 7 miles. Clouds were low with a ceiling of from 5,000 to 9,000 feet. It was generally cloudy with wind recorded as coming from 140 degrees True and clouds moving from that direction. Off the port side of the ship the clouds were low hanging about 5,000 feet and dark grey in color.

PART IV Ordnance.

(a) The performance of ordnance material and equipment was satisfactory. There were 10 rounds of 40-mm, 235 rounds of 20-mm and 75 rounds of 50 caliber ammunition expended. Fire discipline was excellent. Hits were observed, both 40-mm and 20-mm, but the speed with which the target approached the ship along with its short run and rapid change of bearing prevented getting off a full magazine from each of the 20-mm guns.

(b) The enemy plane was equipped with 3/4" incendiary missiles of gas pipe construction. These missiles were about three inches in length and filled with incendiary material, presumably thermite.

(c) If the plane carried a bomb it was of small size. No heavy explosion was felt when the plane crashed, however small incendiary missiles were spread about the ship as much as one hundred feet away from the crash. Over a hundred of these incendiaries were picked up, showing no evidence of burning. No great difficulty was experienced in extinguishing the incendiaries, using water and CO_2.

PART V Damage.

Between frames 32 to 37 the housetop deck was blown out and torn, and deck framing was buckled. The outboard structural bulkhead was blasted out between frames 32 to 37. All the area on the bridge deck comprising several officers rooms and Major General Quarters were demolished, with furniture, fittings and plumbing destroyed. Many joiner bulkheads in the starboard passageway of the officer country was destroyed; furniture in the rooms was ripped from deck fittings, ventilation ducts and plumbing was generally torn loose and broken. Several officers rooms on the port side had the joiner bulkheads smashed between frames 32 to 37. The Chief Petty officers bunk room immediately below was demolished. Ventilation ducts in various parts of the ship were blown out. One ventilator blower damaged and one destroyed. Welin Davit No.7 tracks bent. Port boom serving No. 6 hatch requires testing and possible renewal. The Engineroom air trunk casing was damaged and the door ripped off the Engineroom escape. Minor leaks in after settler tanks developed as a result of explosion. On the main deck beneath Chief Petty Officer Quarters the passageway bulkhead is buckled and fidley trunk is sprung. Considerable wiring, both power and lighting cables are burned and ripped loose from the bulkheads in the wake of the explosion. One radio motor generator damaged.

PART VI Special Comments.

(a) The ship was fully alerted. An unidentified plane was known to be in the vicinity and from the direction of the tracer fire the plane was believed to be on the port side.

(b) During the action which lasted about ten seconds, seven of the eight port 20-mm guns fired, two of the five port 50 caliber guns fired (the remainder could not bear), and one 40-mm fired.

(c) The plane was clearly hit by both 40 and 20 millimeter shells. After its first bank to the left and after straightening out on its dive, it appeared as if the plane would strike amidship. When but a short distance from the ship the plane appeared to draw aft. It was at this point hits were observed. The plane appeared to again bank slightly to the left and then the right wing of the plane struck the boom of No. 6 hatch. The left wing of the plane evidentally swung down carrying away the 20-mm pipe bearing guard rail, flattening the port armored shield, on no. 12 20mm gun, and then crashed.

(d) The plane was demolished. The engine passed through the housetop deck and out through the outboard bulkhead and came to rest in one of the landing boats. Debris from the wrecked plane and from the ship was piled out in the bank of Welin Davit boats. Ammunition parties and members of the gun crews adjacent to the crash were believed to be blown overboard. One man was recovered by the U.S.S. Saufley in the screen.

PART VII Personnel performance.

(a) The officers and crew performed their duties in a most creditable manner. Particular mention may be made of Lieutenant Jack R. Powell, Lieutenant Robert J. Kiechlin, Ensign Geroge R. Sass, Chief Carpenter William J. Schranz, Chief Machinist Glenn R. Bowman, Sr., and repair parties for prompt, efficient and fearless performance of duty in subduing the fire. Lieutenant Theodore Harder, Tom "G" Turrieta, Y3c, Robert W. Kay, Y2c, and Robert H. Vinson, MM3c, for preventing extension of the fire by extinguishing many incendiary missiles scattered about the bridge deck before arrival of damage control parties; of Lieutenant (jg) John F. O'Brien and Chief Boatswain's Mate Alfred F. Jacobi for prompt exercise of initiative by opening firing immediately on sighting the enemy; of Jackie Van Cleve GM3c, who busied himself disposing of ammunition which was close to the fire and in danger of exploding; of Robert L. Stewart, CM3c, and John E. McCullum, CM1c, and others in rescuing two officers and enlisted men who were injured and unable to help themselves; and to Lieutenant Commander Morris (Illegible copy) and the officers and enlisted men of the medical department for prompt medical aid and treatment to those who were burned and injured; said prompt treatment resulted in many of the injured being returned to duty within a very short time and unquestionably saved lives of those more seriously burned and injured.

(b) Casualties were as follows.

Killed ---------------------- 5 enlisted men
Missing -------------------- 3 enlisted Men
Died of Wounds ---------- 2 Enlisted men
Injured -------------------- 4 Officers 26 Enlisted Men
Injured Returned to Duty -- 2 Officers 19 Enlisted Men
Injured Hospitalized ------ 2 Officers, 7 Enlisted Men

/Signature/ Thomas B. Fitzpatrick
Captain, U.S.S. ZEILIN (APA-3)

End of Action Report By Captain Fitzpatrick

The information for the foregoing report was provided by Mr. Thomas A. Hoffman and is a verbatim copy of the Captain's Report. It should be noted that Mr. Hoffman is president of the U.S.S. Zeilin Association and continues to serve his shipmates by coordinating the Annual U.S.S. Zeilin reunions.

National Archives Photo #NH-78156
U.S.S. Zeilin in San Francisco Bay, California circa late 1945.

APPENDIX #2
GERMAN RADIO HEADSET RECEIVER UNIT

The morning following the crash of the Kamikaze plane on the upper boat deck of the U.S.S. Zeilin, I visited the site and examined the still smouldering debris. Hidden beneath a bent and partially melted aluminum propeller blade, I found the remains of a Radio Headset Receiver Unit that had been singed by the fire. Interestingly enough, as well as surprising to me, was the fact that the receiver unit contained the markings of a German manufacturer. Included below are photographs of the diaphragm driver coils side of the receiver and also a view of the manufacturer's imprinted characters on what appears to be aluminum material of the opposite side. The receiver cap was missing, and I assumed at the time, that it had been consumed by the post-crash fire as had the headband that would have held the receiver to the pilot's ears. No evidence of the second receiver that would normally have been equipped on the headset was found.

The imprinted characters are: (NIHON MUSEN) (Telefunken Type) (2,000 Ohm)

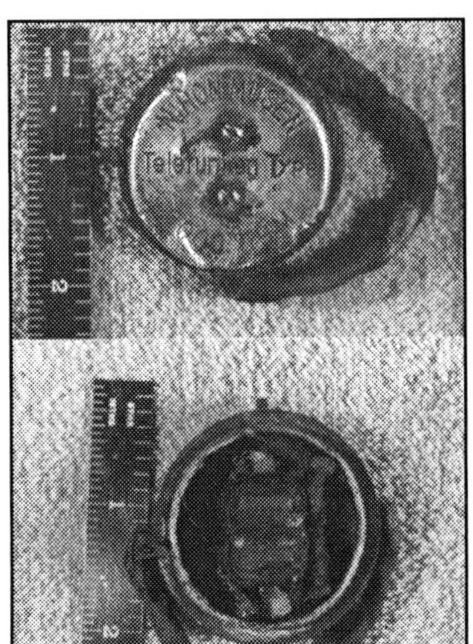

Aluminum Housing and Driver Coils

Radio receiver unit that was salvaged from the Japanese kamikaze bomber that struck the U.S.S. Zeilin in January of 1945 off Manila, P.I. The second receiver unit of the pair was not located and was presumed to have been destroyed in the fire caused by the crash of the airplane.

APPENDIX #3

TRANSPORT DIVISION 23 (COMPOSITION)

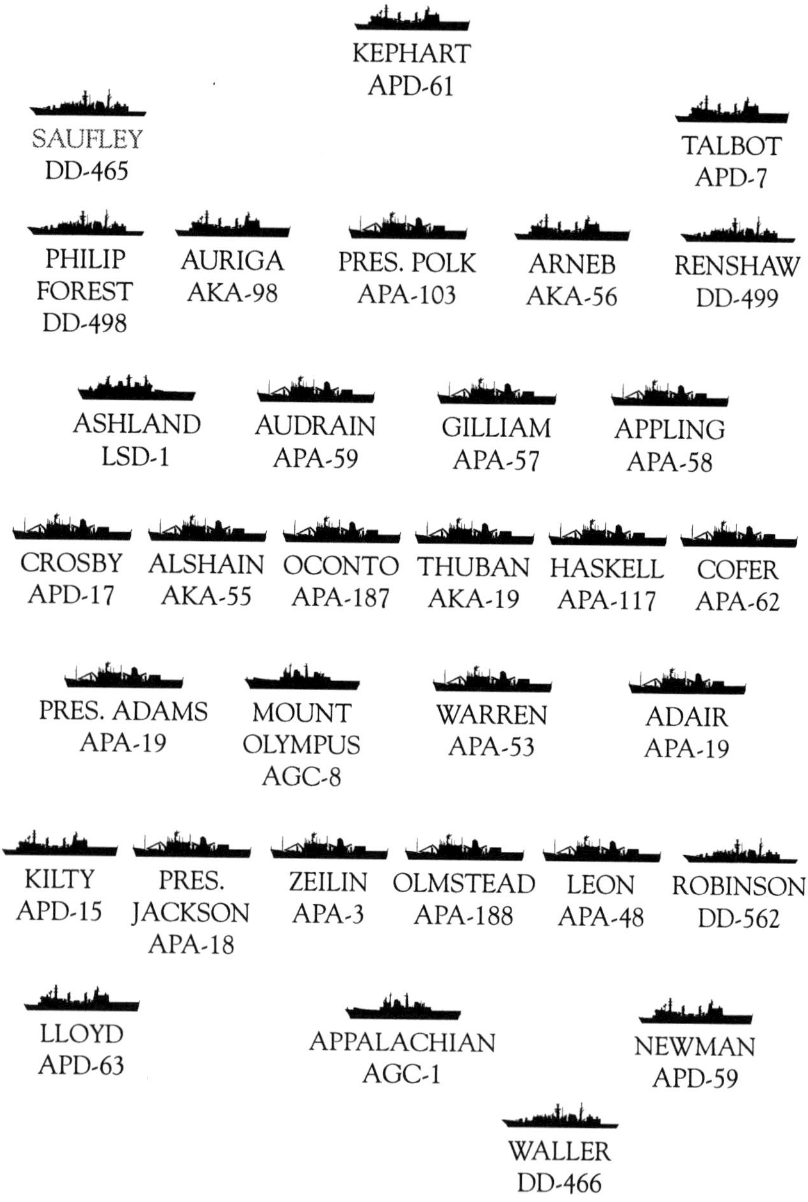

KEPHART
APD-61

SAUFLEY
DD-465

TALBOT
APD-7

PHILIP FOREST
DD-498

AURIGA
AKA-98

PRES. POLK
APA-103

ARNEB
AKA-56

RENSHAW
DD-499

ASHLAND
LSD-1

AUDRAIN
APA-59

GILLIAM
APA-57

APPLING
APA-58

CROSBY
APD-17

ALSHAIN
AKA-55

OCONTO
APA-187

THUBAN
AKA-19

HASKELL
APA-117

COFER
APA-62

PRES. ADAMS
APA-19

MOUNT OLYMPUS
AGC-8

WARREN
APA-53

ADAIR
APA-19

KILTY
APD-15

PRES. JACKSON
APA-18

ZEILIN
APA-3

OLMSTEAD
APA-188

LEON
APA-48

ROBINSON
DD-562

LLOYD
APD-63

APPALACHIAN
AGC-1

NEWMAN
APD-59

WALLER
DD-466

Convoy configuration details for Kamikaze crash provided courtesy of U.S.S. Zeilin shipmate Mr. Richard L. Nihlean of Bartlett, IL.

APPENDIX #4-A

U.S.S. Zeilin sailing schedule. Original data provided by Mr. Luther Mathis

DATE	ACTION	PORT
11 January 1942	Departed	Bremerton, Washington
15 January 1942	Arrived	Tacoma, Washington
25 January 1942	Departed	Tacoma, Washington
29 January 1942	Arrived	San Pedro, California
30 January 1942	Departed	San Pedro, California
31 January 1942	Arrived	San Diego, California
2 March 1942	Departed	San Diego, California
3 March 1942	Arrived	San Pedro, California
5 March 1942	Departed	San Pedro, California
6 March 1942	Arrived	San Diego, California
16 March 1942	Departed	San Diego, California
21 March 1942	Arrived	Tacoma, Washington
24 March 1942	Departed	Tacoma, Washington
28 March 1942	Arrived	San Pedro, California
29 March 1942	Departed	San Pedro, California
30 March 1942	Arrived	San Diego, California
13 April 1942	Departed	San Diego, California
29 April 1942	Arrived	Pago Pago, Samoa
29 May 1942	Departed	Pago Pago, Samoa
31 May 1942	Arrived	Wallis Island
1 June 1942	Departed	Wallis Island
1 June 1942	Arrived	Apia, Samoa
1 June 1942	Departed	Apia, Samoa
16 June 1942	Arrived	San Pedro, California
17 June 1942	Departed	San Pedro, California
18 June 1942	Arrived	San Diego, California
8 July 1942	Departed	San Diego, California
17 July 1942	Arrived	Pearl Harbor, Hawaii

21 July 1942	Departed	Pearl Harbor, Hawaii
1 August 1942	Arrived	Suva, Fiji Islands
1 August 1942	Departed	Suva, Fiji Islands
7 August 1942	Arrived	Tulagi, Solomon Islands
7 August 1942	Departed	Tulagi, Solomon Islands
8 August 1942	Arrived	Suva, Fiji Islands
9 August 1942	Departed	Suva, Fiji Islands
14 August 1942	Arrived	Noumea, New Caledonia
24 August 1942	Departed	Noumea, New Caledonia
28 August 1942	Arrived	Espiritu Santo, New Hebrides
4 September 1942	Departed	Espiritu Santo, New Hebrides
12 September 1942	Arrived	Wellington, New Zealand

APPENDIX #4-B

DATE	ACTION	PORT
23 September 1942	Departed	Wellington, New Zealand
24 September 1942	Arrived	Norfolk Island
24 September 1942	Departed	Norfolk Island
28 September 1942	Arrived	Noumea, New Caledonia
9 October 1942	Departed	Noumea, New Caledonia
13 October 1942	Arrived	Guadalcanal, Solomon Islands
13 October 1942	Departed	Guadalcanal, Solomon Islands
3 November 1942	Arrived	Espirtu Santo, New Hebrides
9 November 1942	Departed	Espirtu Santo, New Hebrides
11 November 1942	Departed	Guadalcanal, Solomon Islands
14 November 1942	Arrived	Espirtu Santo, New Hebrides
1 December 1942	Departed	Espirtu Santo, New Hebrides
4 December 1942	Arrived	Pago Pago, Samoa
4 December 1942	Departed	Pago Pago, Samoa
23 December 1942	Arrived	San Pedro, California
2 March 1943	Departed	San Pedro, California
3 March 1943	Arrived	San Diego, California
7 March 1943	Departed	San Diego, California
10 March 1943	Arrived	San Francisco, California
13 March 1943	Departed	San Francisco, California
16 March 1943	Arrived	San Diego, California
19 March 1943	Departed	San Diego, California
30 March 1943	Arrived	San Diego, California
16 April 1943	Departed	San Diego, California

19 April 1943	Arrived	San Francisco, California
24 April 1943	Departed	San Francisco, California
1 May 1943	Arrived	Cold Bay, Alaska
4 May 1943	Departed	Cold Bay, Alaska
11 May 1943	Arrived	Attu, Aleutian Islands
17 May 1943	Departed	Attu, Aleutian Islands
19 May 1943	Arrived	Adak, Aleutian Islands
22 May 1943	Departed	Adak, Aleutian Islands
31 May 1943	Arrived	San Diego, California
17 June 1943	Departed	San Diego, California
18 June 1943	Arrived	San Pedro, California
19 June 1943	Departed	San Pedro, California
20 June 1943	Arrived	San Diego, California
2 July 1943	Departed	San Diego, California
4 July 1943	Arrived	San Francisco, California
9 July 1943	Departed	San Francisco, California
11 July 1943	Arrived	San Diego, California
19 July 1943	Departed	San Diego, California
23 July 1943	Arrived	San Francisco, California
29 July 1943	Departed	San Francisco, California

APPENDIX #4-C

DATE	ACTION	PORT
6 August 1943	Arrived	Adak, Aleutian, Islands
10 August 1943	Departed	Adak, Aleutian, Islands
21 August 1943	Departed	Kiska, Aleutian, Islands
21 August 1943	Arrived	Adak, Aleutian, Islands
24 August 1943	Departed	Adak, Aleutian, Islands
3 September 1943	Arrived	San Diego, California
12 September 1943	Departed	San Diego, California
19 September 1943	Arrived	Pearl Harbor, Hawaii
20 September 1943	Departed	Pearl Harbor, Hawaii
21 September 1943	Arrived	Honolulu, Hawaii
24 September 1943	Departed	Honolulu, Hawaii
6 October 1943	Arrived	Espiritu Santo, New Hebrides
8 October 1943	Departed	Espiritu Santo, New Hebrides
8 October 1943	Arrived	Efate, New Hebrides
8 October 1943	Departed	Efate, New Hebrides
13 October 1943	Arrived	Wellington, New Zealand
19 October 1943	Departed	Wellington, New Zealand
19 October 1943	Arrived	Hawkes Bay, New Zealand
20 October 1943	Departed	Hawkes Bay, New Zealand
21 October 1943	Arrived	Wellington, New Zealand
1 November 1943	Departed	Wellington, New Zealand
8 November 1943	Arrived	Efate, New Hebrides
8 November 1943	Departed	Efate, New Hebrides
10 November 1943	Arrived	Havana Harbor, New Hebrides
13 November 1943	Departed	Havana Harbor, New Hebrides

20 November 1943	Arrived	Tarawa, Gilbert Islands
25 November 1943	Departed	Tarawa, Gilbert Islands
25 November 1943	Arrived	Appemama, Gilbert Islands
26 November 1943	Departed	Appemama, Gilbert Islands
26 November 1943	Arrived	Tarawa, Gilbert Islands
29 November 1943	Departed	Tarawa, Gilbert Islands
7 December 1943	Arrived	Pearl Harbor, Hawaii
17 December 1943	Departed	Pearl Harbor, Hawaii
18 December 1943	Arrived	Maui, Hawaii
21 December 1943	Departed	Maui, Hawaii
22 December 1943	Arrived	Pearl Harbor, Hawaii
11 January 1944	Departed	Pearl Harbor, Hawaii
13 January 1944	Arrived	Maui, Hawaii
14 January 1944	Departed	Maui, Hawaii
16 January 1944	Arrived	Pearl Harbor, Hawaii
23 January 1944	Departed	Pearl Harbor, Hawaii
1 February 1944	Arrived	Kwajalein, Marshall Islands
4 February 1944	Departed	Kwajalein, Marshall Islands
9 February 1944	Arrived	Funi Futi, Ellice Islands

APPENDIX #4-D

DATE	ACTION	PORT
21 February 1944	Departed	Funi Futi, Ellice Islands
21 February 1944	Arrived	Tulagi, Solomon Islands
24 February 1944	Departed	Tulagi, Solomon Islands
24 February 1944	Arrived	Purvis Bay, Florida Islands
4 March 1944	Departed	Purvis Bay, Florida Islands
4 March 1944	Arrived	Guadalcanal, Solomon Islands
14 March 1944	Departed	Guadalcanal, Solomon Islands
18 March 1944	Arrived	Tulagi, Solomon Islands
23 March 1944	Departed	Tulagi, Solomon Islands
27 March 1944	Arrived	Bougainville, Solomon Islands
27 March 1944	Departed	Bougainville, Solomon Islands
31 March 1944	Arrived	Milne Bay, New Guinea
5 April 1944	Departed	Milne Bay, New Guinea
6 April 1944	Arrived	Cape Sudest, New Guinea
15 April 1944	Departed	Cape Sudest, New Guinea
17 April 1944	Arrived	Goodenough Island, New Guinea
19 April 1944	Departed	Goodenough Island, New Guinea
24 April 1944	Arrived	Hollandia, Dutch New Guinea
24 April 1944	Departed	Hollandia, Dutch New Guinea
26 April 1944	Arrived	Buna, New Guinea
26 April 1944	Departed	Buna, New Guinea
27 April 1944	Arrived	Finchaven, New Guinea
29 April 1944	Departed	Finchaven, New Guinea

30 April 1944	Arrived	Saidor, New Guinea
1 May 1944	Departed	Saidor, New Guinea
3 May 1944	Arrived	Aitape, New Guinea
4 May 1944	Departed	Aitape, New Guinea
6 May 1944	Arrived	Ora Bay, Sudest, New Guinea
7 May 1944	Departed	Ora Bay, Sudest, New Guinea
11 May 1944	Arrived	Guadalcanal, Solomon Islands
19 May 1944	Departed	Guadalcanal, Solomon Islands
20 May 1944	Arrived	Tulagi, Solomon Islands
21 May 1944	Departed	Tulagi, Solomon Islands
22 May 1944	Arrived	Guadalcanal, Solomon Islands
31 May 1944	Departed	Guadalcanal, Solomon Islands
1 June 1944	Arrived	Purvis Bay, Solomon Islands
2 June 1944	Departed	Purvis Bay, Solomon Islands
3 June 1944	Arrived	Guadalcanal, Solomon Islands
4 June 1944	Departed	Guadalcanal, Solomon Islands
9 June 1944	Arrived	Kwajalein, Solomon Islands
12 June 1944	Departed	Kwajalein, Solomon Islands
16 June 1944	Arrived	Saipan, Marianna Islands
1 July 1944	Departed	Saipan, Marianna Islands
3 July 1944	Arrived	Eniwetock, Marshall Islands
17 July 1944	Departed	Eniwetock, Marshall Islands

APPENDIX #4-E

DATE	ACTION	PORT
21 July 1944	Arrived	Guam, Marianna Islands
26 July 1944	Departed	Guam, Marianna Islands
30 July 1944	Arrived	Eniwetok, Marshall Islands
31 July 1944	Departed	Eniwetok, Marshall Islands
7 August 1944	Arrived	Pearl Harbor, Hawaii
10 August 1944	Departed	Pearl Harbor, Hawaii
18 August 1944	Arrived	San Francisco, California
20 October 1944	Departed	San Francisco, California
7 November 1944	Arrived	Finchaven, New Guinea
7 November 1944	Departed	Finchaven, New Guinea
9 November 1944	Arrived	Cape Oro, New Guinea
10 November 1944	Departed	Cape Oro, New Guinea
12 November 1944	Arrived	Hollandia, New Guinea
18 November 1944	Departed	Hollandia, New Guinea
23 November 1944	Arrived	Noumea, New Caledonia
17 December 1944	Departed	Noumea, New Caledonia
21 December 1944	Arrived	Guadalcanal, Solomon Islands
24 December 1944	Departed	Guadalcanal, Solomon Islands
29 December 1944	Arrived	Manus, Admiralty Islands
2 January 1945	Departed	Manus, Admiralty Islands
11 January 1945	Arrived	Lingayen Gulf, Philippine Islands
12 January 1945	Departed	Lingayen Gulf, Philippine Islands
19 January 1945	Arrived	Manus, Admiralty Islands
24 January 1945	Departed	Manus, Admiralty Islands
27 January 1945	Arrived	Maffin Bay, New Guinea
2 February 1945	Departed	Maffin Bay, New Guinea
6 February 1945	Arrived	Leyte, Philippine Islands

7 February 1945	Departed	Leyte, Philippine Islands
10 February 1945	Arrived	Lingayen Gulf, Philippine Islands
10 February 1945	Departed	Lingayen Gulf, Philippine Islands
18 February 1945	Arrived	Ulithi, Caroline Islands
5 March 1945	Departed	Ulithi, Caroline Islands
9 March 1945	Arrived	Iwo Jima, Volcano Islands
27 March 1945	Departed	Iwo Jima, Volcano Islands
2 April 1945	Arrived	Eniwetok, Marshall Islands
4 April 1945	Departed	Eniwetok, Marshall Islands
12 April 1945	Arrived	Hilo, Hawaii
14 April 1945	Departed	Hilo, Hawaii
15 April 1945	Arrived	Pearl Harbor, Hawaii
16 April 1945	Departed	Pearl Harbor, Hawaii
23 April 1945	Arrived	San Francisco, California
29 June 1945	Departed	San Francisco, California
1 July 1945	Arrived	San Diego, California
8 July 1945	Departed	San Diego, California
12 July 1945	Arrived	Seattle, Washington

APPENDIX #4-F

DATE	ACTION	PORT
23 July 1945	Departed	Seattle, Washington
5 August 1945	Arrived	Eniwetok, Marshall Islands
7 August 1945	Departed	Eniwetok, Marshall Islands
11 August 1945	Arrived	Ulithi, Caroline Islands
18 August 1945	Departed	Ulithi, Caroline Islands
22 August 1945	Arrived	Naha, Okinawa
26 August 1945	Departed	Naha, Okinawa
26 August 1945	Arrived	Buckner Bay, Okinawa
26 August 1945	Departed	Buckner Bay, Okinawa
1 September 1945	Arrived	San Pedro Bay, P.I. (Leyte)
4 September 1945	Departed	San Pedro Bay, P.I. (Leyte)
4 September 1945	Arrived	Guinian, P. I. (Samar)
4 September 1945	Departed	Guinian, P. I. (Samar)
5 September 1945	Arrived	Iloilo, P. I. (Panay)
15 September 1945	Departed	Iloilo, P. I. (Panay)
22 September 1945	Arrived	Jensen, Korea
26 September 1945	Departed	Jensen, Korea
30 September 1945	Arrived	Guinian, P. I. (Samar)
2 October 1945	Departed	Guinian, P. I. (Samar)
2 October 1945	Arrived	Tacloban, P. I. (Leyte)
5 October 1945	Departed	Tacloban, P. I. (Leyte)
7 October 1945	Arrived	San Fernando Bay, P. I. (Luzon)
11 October 1945	Departed	San Fernando Bay, P. I. (Luzon)
16 October 1945	Arrived	Jensen, Korea
20 October 1945	Departed	Jensen, Korea
27 October 1945	Arrived	Ulithi, Caroline Islands
29 October 1945	Departed	Ulithi, Caroline Islands
30 October 1945	Arrived	Guam, Marianna Islands
1 November 1945	Departed	Guam, Marianna Islands

14 November 1945	Arrived	San Francisco, California
30 November 1945	Departed	San Francisco, California
2 December 1945	Arrived	Seattle, Washington
3 December 1945	Departed	Seattle, Washington
3 December 1945	Arrived	Portland, Oregon
5 December 1945	Departed	Portland, Oregon
8 December 1945	Arrived	San Francisco, California
9 December 1945	Departed	San Francisco, California
10 December 1945	Arrived	San Pedro, California
10 December 1945	Departed	San Pedro, California
11 December 1945	Arrived	San Diego, California
11 December 1945	Departed	San Diego, California
12 December 1945	Arrived	San Pedro, California
12 December 1945	Departed	San Pedro, California
14 December 1945	Arrived	San Francisco, California
16 December 1945	Departed	San Francisco, California

APPENDIX #4-G

DATE	ACTION	PORT
18 December 1945	Arrived	Tacoma, Washington
18 December 1945	Departed	Tacoma, Washington
18 December 1945	Arrived	Bremerton,Washington
21 December 1945	Departed	Bremerton,Washington
22 December 1945	Arrived	Seattle, Washington
24 December 1945	Departed	Seattle, Washington
27 December 1945	Arrived	Portland, Oregon
27 December 1945	Departed	Portland, Oregon
28 December 1945	Arrived	San Francisco, California
1 January 1946	Departed	San Francisco, California
5 January 1946	Arrived	Seattle, Washington
9 January 1946	Departed	Seattle, Washington
26 January 1946	Arrived	Everett, Washington
26 January 1946	Departed	Everett, Washington
27 January 1946	Arrived	Seattle, Washington
29 January 1946	Departed	Seattle, Washington
29 January 1946	Arrived	San Francisco, California
1 February 1946	Departed	San Francisco, California
4 February 1946	Arrived	San Pedro, California
4 February 1946	Departed	San Pedro, California
14 February 1946	Arrived	Panama Canal
15 February 1946	Departed	Panama Canal
21 February 1946	Arrived	Hampton Roads, VA (Norfolk)
19 April 1946	Decommissioned	
4 May 1946	Transferred To Marine Comm.	
4 May 1948	Delivered to Shipbreakers, Inc., Where She Was Scrapped	

U.S.S. ZEILIN HISTORY

This record of the U.S.S. Zeilin's Ports of Call is incomplete for the reason that it does not include the details of her service as a Passenger Cruise Liner under the names of S.S. Silver Star, and later the S.S. President Jackson, or her journey from the builder's ways to her initial commercial service. As far as I could determine, no records of these periods of service presently exist. Throughout WWII the brass plate engraved with the legend "S.S. President Jackson", mounted beside the ladder leading to the Zeilin Engine Room, was kept highly polished by the Engine Room Crew.

One of the major changes that was implemented during the conversion of the S.S. President Jackson for the U.S. Navy, first as the (AP-9 and later designated as the APA-3), the U.S.S. Zeilin Attack Troop Transport, was removal of the peace-time swimming pool to provide space for the Troop Officers' mess hall. Of course many Wellin boat davits were added to raise and lower a large number of Higgins landing craft that were required to move fighting men and their equipment from the U.S.S. Zeilin to various invasion beaches where they would assault Japanese forces on enemy-held islands. The scope of the U.S.S. Zeilin's missions extended from the Aleutian Islands in Alaska to the Solomon Islands in the South Pacific.

The ship that ultimately became the U.S.S. Zeilin (APA-#3) began life on an unknown date at the Newport News Shipbuilding and Drydock Company at Newport News, Virginia. When completed for its initial civilian passenger liner configuration, it was named "S.S. Silver State" on 16 May 1921, when ownership was assumed by Pacific Steamship Line. The ship passed through a succession of owners including the "Orient Line", and the Dollar Line and finally the American Mail Line, where it was renamed S.S. President Jackson on 23 June 1922.

In 1940, the President Jackson was acquired by the U.S. Navy in July of that year and renamed the U.S.S. Zeilin. At that time the ship was moved to the Todd-Seattle Drydock Company in Seattle, Washington. At the conclusion of the work performed by the Todd Organization, the ship was commissioned the U.S.S. Zeilin (AP-9). On 3 January 1942, with Captain Pat Buchanan USNR in command, the ship was redesignated Amphibious Attack Transport (APA-3) on 26 November 1942. Following its illustrious career during service in WWII in the Pacific theaters of operation the U.S.S. Zeilin was decommissioned on 19 April 1946 at the Norfolk Navy Yard, Portsmouth, Virginia. On 5 June 1946 the name U.S.S. Zeilin was struck from the Naval register. One month later on 3 July 1946 the ship was transferred to the Maritime Administration for disposal. The final disposition of the U.S.S. Zeilin was its sale to the American Shipbreakers Inc. on 4 May 1948. During WWII the U.S.S. Zeilin earned eight battle stars for her timely WWII service to a grateful nation.

National Archives Photo #80-G-379627
U.S.S. Zeilin entering floating drydock (ABSD-6) at Guam for repair of wartime damage on 31 October 1945.
Photo was taken from the drydock showing starboard side of U.S.S. Zeilin and tugs pushing on port bow.

U.S.S. Zeilin Specifications:

Displacement: 13,529t. (lt) 21,900t (fl)
Length: 535'2"
Beam: 72'6"
Draft: 31'3"
Speed: 18 kts.
Complement: 29 Officers, 638 enlisted
Troop Accommodations: 121 Officers 1558 Enlisted
Cargo Capacity 190,000 cu. ft., 2,000t.
Armament: Four 3"/50 gun mounts
One quad 40mm gun mount
One twin 40mm gun mount
Ten 20mm gun mounts.
Propulsion: Eight Yarrow Header-type boilers, two curtis type turbines, twin propellers, designed shaft horsepower 12,000.

Melvin E. Hacker

U.S.S. Zeilin shown at anchor in San Francisco Bay in 1945.

APPENDIX #5A
PHOTO CREDITS

Page Number **Description**

Cover photo U.S.S. Zeilin shown at anchor in San Francisco Bay in 1945. Courtesy of Mr. Richard N. Schell.

3 U.S.S. Zeilin shown at anchor in San Francisco Bay in 1945. Courtesy of Mr. Richard N. Schell.

6 Thomas A. Hoffman, Chief Bos'n Mate. U.S.S. Zeilin who is presently the president of the U.S.S. Zeilin Association. Courtesy of Mr. Thomas A. Hoffman.

6 Martin Luther Mathis, Signalman United States Navy, who died on 21 July 2007. Photo circa 1943. Courtesy of Mr. Martin Luther Mathis.

117 Melvin Eugene Hacker in 1943 during his assignment to the U.S.S. Zeilin (APA-3) as a RADARman. This photo dates from September 1943 following the Kiska, Alaska Invasion. He is wearing his first campaign ribbon. There would be six more to follow during WWII. Courtesy of Mrs. Della L. Hacker.

117 Marshall R. Herron RADARman on the U.S.S. Zeilin (APA-3). Courtesy of Marshall R. Herron.

118 The entire Percy Hacker family as it existed in the year of 1931. Seated on a table is Marilee Ruth Hacker next to her father Percy Eugene Hacker. Standing in front of his father is Harold Ray Hacker, and seated next to him is his mother Della Leonard Hacker and standing next to her is Melvin Eugene Hacker. Courtesy of Mrs. Della L. Hacker.

118 Della L. Hacker on the right and husband Percy Eugene Hacker on the left. Photo taken at William Alexander Hacker's (Percy's father's) residence in home gardens near Corona, California. Date of photo is April, 2nd 1944. Courtesy of Mrs. Della L. Hacker.

118 Left to right in photograph are, Harold Ray Hacker, Marilee Ruth Hacker and Melvin Eugene Hacker; each holding a rabbit from our father's rabbit hutches hidden behind the palm frond wall. Circa 1936. Courtesy of Percy Eugene Hacker.

118 Melvin Eugene Hacker taken at Chaffey Union High School in 1942, his senior class year. Courtesy of Mrs. Della L. Hacker.

119 Seaman First Class Melvin Eugene Hacker while he was assigned to the U.S.S. Zeilin attack troop transport (APA-3). Circa 1944. Courtesy of Mrs. Della L. Hacker.

119 The entire Percy Hacker family as it existed in the year of 1944. The persons standing in the rear are Harold Ray Hacker, Marilee Ruth Hacker and Melvin Eugene Hacker. In the front row left to right are Percy Eugene Hacker, Marvin Dean Hacker, Ida Mae Hacker, and Della Leonard Hacker. Courtesy of Mrs. Della L. Hacker.

119 Melvin Eugene with his arm around his sister Marilee ruth van. This photo dates from 1944 when Melvin was home on leave from the U.S.S. Zeilin (APA-3). Courtesy of Mrs. Della L. Hacker.

153 National Archives Photo #80-G-50921: Attu Invasion, May 1943. Soldiers unload landing craft on the beach at Massacre Bay, Attu on 13 May 1943. LCVPs in foreground are from U.S.S. Zeilin (APA-3) and U.S.S. Heywood (APA-6).

153 National Archives Photo #80-G-50827C: Attu Invasion, May 1943. Soldiers pull an ammunition cart along the beach at Massacre Bay, Attu, 12 May 1943. One of the LCVP's in background is from U.S.S. Zeilin (APA-3).

154 USMC #67706: U.S. Marine Corps; Tarawa Operation November 1943. Marines and sailors study a relief model of Betio Island Tarawa, while en route to the invasion of that place. Circa early - mid November 1943.

154 U.S.S. Zeilin (APA-3) seen in this view with her wartime camouflage paint job.

155 National Archives Photo #80-G-54399: Tarawa Invasion 20 November 1943. Invasion leaders on the bridge of U.S.S. Maryland (BB-46), watching the landings. Taken circa 20 November 1943. In foreground is MGen. Julian C. Smith, USMC. Radm. Harry W. Hill is beyond him, wearing two star helmet.

155 Harold Ray Hacker and Melvin Eugene Hacker (left to right). Melvin at this time was a Third Class RADARman assigned to the U.S.S. Zeilin while Harold was an Apprentice Torpedoman. Courtesy of Mrs. Della L. Hacker.

394 Example of a DC-3. Courtesy of Brian Shera.

394 Melvin Eugene Hacker with his arm around his sister Ida Mae who is sitting on the hood of Mel's 1936 Ford sedan. Sister Marilee Van is standing next to the front fender. Mel is wearing the insignia of a RADARman Second Class. This photo dates from 1944 when Melvin was home on leave from the U.S.S. Zeilin (APA-3). Courtesy of Mrs. Della L. Hacker.

395 Melvin Eugene Hacker taken by street photographer while on liberty in Manila, P.I. Uniform is rumpled due to rain storm that blew in. Courtesy of Mrs. Della L. Hacker.

395 Melvin Eugene in the uniform of a Second Class Radarman from the U.S.S. Zeilin. Circa 1944. Courtesy of Mrs. Della L. Hacker.

395 Seaman First Class Melvin Eugene Hacker while he was assigned to the U.S.S. Zeilin attack troop transport (APA-3). Campaign ribbon earned during the invasion of Kiska, Alaska. Circa 1943. Courtesy of Mrs. Della L. Hacker.

395 This photo dates from 1944 when Melvin and Calvin Honeycut were on liberty in Pearl Harbor, Hawaii where the photo was made. Courtesy of Melvin E. Hacker.

449 Example of the Ki-84 “Frank”. Courtesy of www.ijaafphotos.com.

450 Example of the G4M “Betty Bomber”. Courtesy of www.ijaafphotos.com.

450 Example of the Ki-57 “Topsy”. Courtesy of www.ijaafphotos.com.

451 Example of the A-6M “Zero”. Courtesy of www.ijaafphotos.com.

451 Example of the U.S. Navy F6F “Hellcat”.. Courtesy of www.wikipedia.com.

490 Unidentified black and white photograph of burial at sea detail aboard the U.S.S. Zeilin—January 1945.

491 National Archives Photo #80-G-58481: Kwajalein Operation, January - February 1944. Men climbing down nets from a transport into landing craft to be transferred to LST’s, here they will man amphibious tanks for the invasion of Kwajalein Atoll 31 January 1944.

491 National Archives Photo #80-G-47548: Kiska Operation August 1943. Troops march up the beach at Adak during pre-invasion loading for the Kiska Operation 13 August 1943. Note their M-1 rifles and packs. LCM behind them is from U.S.S. Zeilin (APA-3). U.S.S. Pennsylvania (BB-38) is in the right distance: photographed by Lt. Horace Bristol, USNR.

492 National Archives Photo #80-G-213104: Marshall Islands Operation January through February 1944. Marines climb down a transport's cargo net to board landing craft for the invasion of Marshall Islands Objective. Note combat gear and M-1 "Garand" rifles one with a sheathed bayonet. Photo released by Cincpac, 26 February, 1944.

492 National Archives Photo #NH-89369: Okinawa Operation 1945. Marines climb down a debarkation ladder from a Coast Guard manned assault transport to board an LCVP to take part in the initial attack on Okinawa 1 April 1945. Courtesy of Robert O. Baumrucker 1978.

493 This image of the aftermath of the kamikaze crash into the U.S.S. Zeilin shows crewmen inspecting the damage to be cleaned up. The PA3 with symbolic arrow is attached to the gunwale of the Captains gig which was utterly destroyed. The 18 cylinder airplane engine penetrated the upper boat deck on the house top and ultimately lodged itself in a Higgins boat hanging in one of the Wellin boat davits.

494 National Archives Photo Number N-18849f: Meritorious Award Ceremony U.S.S. Zeilin, January 1945 (APA-3). Silver star awarded to Robert H. Vinson mm2/c. Award presented by Captain John Benedict McGovern. Silver Star presented for meritorious action associated with the Japanese kamikaze attack on 13 January, 1945.

494 U.S.S. Zeilin: damage in officer's quarters caused by crash of Japanese kamikaze bomber into ship on Saturday 13 January 1945. National Archives Photo.

514 Newly married Eugene Van and Marilee Ruth Van. Circa June 1943. Courtesy of Mrs. Della L. Hacker.

514 Marvin Dean Hacker and sister Ida Mae Hacker on the occasion of Ida Mae's third birthday. The automobile is Melvin's $10.00 1928 Chevrolet rumble seat coupe. Location is the back yard of 459 West Elm Street, Ontario, California. Circa January 1943. Courtesy of Mrs. Della L. Hacker.

514 Shirley Maxine Chapman following her afternoon classes at Chaffey Union High School in Ontario, California. Circa 1945. Courtesy of Melvin E. Hacker.

515 Newly married Shirley Maxine Hacker and Melvin Eugene Hacker. Circa September 1946. Courtesy of Mrs. Della L. Hacker.

515 Melvin Eugene Hacker and his family at that time. Left to right are Melvin Hacker, Susan Marie Hacker, Christine Yvonne Hacker and Shirley Maxine Hacker. Circa 1950. Courtesy of Mrs. Della L. Hacker.

515 Melvin Eugene holding his daughter Christine Yvonne Hacker and his daughter Susan Marie Hacker sitting on her tricycle. The vehicle is Mel's 1937 Chevrolet telephone service truck. This photograph dates from 1950. Courtesy of Mrs. Della L. Hacker.

516 General Electric appliance factory building on Main Street Ontario, California. Circa 1946.

516 The land mark Ford Lunch Restaurant which was raised following the end of WWII. Permission to use this photograph was granted by the estate of Mr. Bruce Wilson, deceased proprietor of Wilson's Photo Shop of Ontario, California.

517 The Percy Hacker home place located at 459 West Elm Street, Ontario, California photo taken in December 2006. At that time, the home was 65 years old and is owned today by Mr. Jerry Van, Percy Hacker's grandson. Courtesy of Melvin E. Hacker.

517 The Ontario, California Union Pacific Railroad Depot which was raised by the railroad company in recent years. Permission to use this photograph granted by the estate of Mr. Bruce Wilson, deceased proprietor of Wilson's Photo Shop of Ontario, California.

526 National Archives Photo #NH-78156: U.S.S. Zeilin in San Francisco Bay, California circa late 1945.

527 Aluminum Housing and Driver Coils
Radio receiver unit that was salvaged from the Japanese kamikaze bomber that struck the U.S.S. Zeilin in January of 1945 off Manila, P.I. The second receiver unit of the pair was not located and was presumed to have been destroyed in the fire caused by the crash of the airplane. Courtesy of Melvin Eugene Hacker.

543 National Archives Photo #80-G-379627: U.S.S. Zeilin entering floating drydock (ABSD-6) at Guam for repair of wartime damage on 31 October 1945. Photo was taken from the drydock showing starboard side of U.S.S. Zeilin and tugs pushing on port bow.

545 U.S.S. Zeilin shown at anchor in San Francisco Bay in 1945. Courtesy of Mr. Richard N. Schell.